THE INVENTION
OF COINAGE AND
THE MONETIZATION OF
ANCIENT GREECE

THE INVENTION
OF COINAGE AND
THE MONETIZATION OF
ANCIENT GREECE

David M. Schaps

THE UNIVERSITY OF MICHIGAN PRESS
Ann Arbor

For my wife,
whose price is far above rubies

Copyright © by the University of Michigan 2004
All rights reserved
Published in the United States of America by
The University of Michigan Press
Manufactured in the United States of America
♾ Printed on acid-free paper

2007   2006   2005   4   3   2

A CIP catalog record for this book is available from the British Library.

Library of Congress Cataloging-in-Publication Data

Schaps, David M.
      The invention of coinage and the monetization of Ancient Greece / David M. Schaps.
         p.   cm.
      Includes bibliographical references and index.
      ISBN 0-472-11333-X (cloth : alk. paper)
      1. Coins, Greek.   2. Coinage—Greece—History—To 1500.   I. Title.

CJ335.S3   2003
737.4938—dc22   2003055998

Preface

WHEN MY PREVIOUS BOOK left my hands, somewhat more than twenty years ago, I decided, in my youthful self-confidence, to undertake a project that had defeated two of the great scholars of the economic life of antiquity: an annotated catalog of all the known prices from the ancient Greek world. Gustave Glotz had left behind at his death a manuscript including all the prices known to him—surely a large percentage of all the prices known to anyone at that time. Fritz Heichelheim proposed to publish Glotz's manuscript,[1] but he, too, left this world with the work still uncompleted. I myself have never seen this manuscript (though not for lack of effort),[2] but I undertook to collect all prices that I could and publish them on my own.

It was an unfortunate time for such a decision; after two years of assiduously recording boxes full of index cards, I realized that the work I was doing would become hopelessly out-of-date as advances in computing made the words of Clement of Alexandria and the inscriptions of Acraephia as easily available as the words of Thucydides and the inscriptions of Attica. The

---

1. Heichelheim, 2:171 n. 8.

2. It did not become part of the "Bibliothèque G. Glotz" at the Sorbonne, presumably because it was in Heichelheim's hands when the library was set up. Heichelheim's widow, whom I contacted, thought that it had been returned to the Glotz family. I later learned that Sterling Dow, at approximately the time when I was studying at Harvard, had been in possession of a photocopy of the manuscript, which he lent out to a graduate student and apparently never got back; but I was not that student.

simple collection of information, itself a task for a Glotz or a Heichelheim, was done three times, each time with a vast increase in depth and precision, but each time making the job of evaluating and annotating the material, the task that had defeated both Glotz and Heichelheim, yet more gargantuan. That task still lies before me, and I doubt that I shall complete it in this lifetime.[3]

In the course of this work, however, it became apparent to me that much of the information could not be dealt with intelligently without addressing certain questions of principle. Disagreements between primitivists and modernists; among substantivists, formalists, and Marxists; among historians, economists, philologists, and anthropologists made problematical the interpretation of even the simplest item of economic evidence. Increasingly, I found myself constrained to try to come to an understanding among the various competing models for the ancient economic world. It became, moreover, increasingly clear that the meaning of an exchange in the archaic period was very different from what it became thereafter. Something had happened with the introduction of coinage.

I became convinced that the invention of coinage and its adoption by the Greeks involved an intellectual change of great importance—to put it clearly, if too simply, that the notion of money as we think about it, although it surely had antecedents, was something that had not been thought of before the Greeks adopted coinage. I became convinced, moreover, that this new concept arose at a time when it was particularly appropriate to the Greeks, for whom it offered a way of organizing and of thinking about many crucial matters for which their existing institutions were inadequate. I determined to write a short book about the invention of coinage.

As I came to discuss the effects of that invention, however, I discovered that they were by no means uniform. In some areas of society, the effects of monetization were immediate; in others, much slower. In some, they were complete; in others, much less so. The question of the effects of monetization grew so large that it now occupies more than half of the book to which it was once thought of as a mere concluding chapter.

There will perhaps be those who think that the current book is, as Andy Capp once complained about a shot glass full of six-year-old whisky, a bit small for its age, not to mention its subject. I do not deny that the subject

---

3. It was therefore with no hesitation that I agreed to let William T. Loomis take part of it—the part dealing with salaries in Athens—for his doctoral dissertation, which has since been published, to the great advantage of future researchers. I continue to work on commodity prices, and I hope that that part of the work, at least, will one day be available.

could easily have produced a book ten times the size of the one I have written. The reader should not be misled into thinking that any chapter of this book constitutes a thoroughgoing analysis of the role of money in the particular area discussed—that, for example, chapter 9 is a complete analysis of the role of money in Greek politics. Beside such a project, my original planned list of prices would have shrunk into insignificance. Suffice it to remind the reader that the vastly erudite Böckh, the father of modern scholarship in ancient realia, devoted almost a thousand pages to the economic management of the Athenian state alone and that Kallet-Marx's recent study found quite adequate material for a densely argued book without going beyond the first half of Thucydides.

I have tried throughout only to sketch the ways in which Greek thought and behavior were changed by the introduction of money. Even so, the subject was a large one, requiring me to deal with every age and every aspect of life. It is hardly an exaggeration to say that nearly every paragraph in this book could be expanded into an illuminating article. I have tried to provide in this book a framework in which continued research can take place. By this approach, I hope to have won everybody's thanks: the thanks of the scholars for having offered them fertile fields for further research and the thanks of the less committed for not having inflicted all of that research upon them.

There is an important thread of recent scholarship, of undoubted relevance to my theme, that I have touched lightly, if at all: the explication of themes of exchange in literature,[4] in particular with reference to gender relationships.[5] Exchange relationships, as I shall show and as others have already pointed out,[6] were highly developed among the Greeks before the introduction of coinage and had much to do with the way in which coinage developed in Greece. It follows that not every exchange relationship can be seen, even metaphorically, as a type of monetary relationship and that the extent to which coinage changed the Greeks' way of acting—the subject of the present book—must be investigated independently before we can establish to what extent the observed exchange terminology is a reflection of monetization.

I began work on this book in 1992; at that time, as far as I know, little work had been done on the subject, and my ideas were entirely my own. Under pressure from my university to prove that I was doing something, I have been

---

4. See most notably, Kurke, *Traffic* and *Coins;* von Reden, *Exchange;* Seaford, *Reciprocity;* and Carson.

5. See Rabinowitz; Wohl; and Ormand.

6. See, in particular, von Reden, *Exchange,* part 1; Herman, 73–115.

speaking about the invention of coinage at conferences since 1994. Since then, I have occasionally heard and even read some of my own ideas presented by people who apparently thought they were their own, and perhaps they were (if, after all, my ideas are correct, there is no reason why somebody else should not have realized them as well), although on occasion, it became clear that the people involved had actually heard the ideas from me. Since my hopes for eternal life do not base themselves on this book, I see no need for arguments over precedence. Suffice it to say that I have tried to be exceedingly scrupulous not to peddle anyone else's work or ideas as my own.

For the footnotes, I have preferred a shortened citation form that utilizes short titles where necessary (e.g., "Finley, *Ancient Economy*"), although the author-date form (e.g., "Finley 1985") is today more commonly used in the humanities. Perhaps better scholars than I remember without a moment's reflection the publication date of every book they have ever seen and so know at a glance what book is being referred to by a surname and a year. In case, however, there are those who remember titles better than year of publication, I have given a short title when referring to an author for whom more than one work appears in the bibliography. I apologize, lest anyone suspect me of the opposite, for the fact that, although I have tried to be certain that I am not misrepresenting anyone's opinions, I cannot claim to have read every word of every item mentioned in the bibliography.[7]

Where historical reasons did not dictate otherwise, I have done my best to maintain gender-neutral language. This has introducd a number of stylistic infelicities, but I would rather be awkward than offensive. I think, however, that this problem has not found its ideal solution, and I apologize to the reader for those places where my effort to be courteous has merely made me obscure.

I owe thanks to the Israel Science Foundation founded by the Israel Academy of Sciences and Humanities, who four times gave me research grants; to the American Council of Learned Societies, whose fellowship in 1984–85 got me into the research on prices past the point of no return; to the Center for Hellenic Studies of Harvard University, where I was a Summer Scholar in 1994 and whose directors, Kurt Raaflaub and Deborah Boedeker, along with all of the staff, continued generously to put the scholarly resources of the center at my disposal whenever I was able to use them; to Bar-

---

7. Well after the typescript had left my hands, there appeared an important new book by Georges Le Rider, *La naissance de la monnaie: Pratiques monétaires de l'Orient ancien*. Le Rider's vantage point, as his subtitle shows, is very different from mine; nevertheless, I would surely have made considerable use of his work had it reached me in time.

Ilan University, for internal grants that have continued to help nudge the project along; to the Lechter Institute for Literary Research, by whose grant the book includes illustrations; and to the staffs of the libraries of Bar-Ilan University and Tel-Aviv University, who continue to provide the base for many first-rate research projects. I will add the library of the Institute of Classical Studies at the University of London and the Van Pelt Library at the University of Pennsylvania, whose excellent resources, generously provided, have afforded a more solid foundation for many originally unsupported assertions. Henry Kim of the Ashmolean Museum offered helpful advice about illustrations. At the China Numismatic Museum in Beijing, the hospitality and scholarly generosity of Professors Dai Zhiqiang, Zhou Weirong, and Wang Dan (director, head of the Department of Scientific Research, and curator, respectively) gave me the confidence to write on a subject that is only poorly documented in Western libraries. Although, in the end, I used only one of her illustrations, Cecilia Meir of the Kadman Numismatics Pavilion, Eretz Israel Museum, Tel Aviv, was so generous with her help and her time that I must express my thanks. Professor Miriam Balmuth has offered interest and even a public forum in the spirit of true scholarship, despite the fact that my own opinions differ sharply from those she has expressed (and from which, as the reader can see, I have profited considerably). Similar things may be said of Professor John Kroll. Among various Assyriologists who expressed an interest in my ideas and offered me their own, I am grateful to Professor Aaron Skaist for reading and commenting on a draft of the relevant sections.

Particular thanks go to Dr. Gabriel Danzig, my partner on a two-year project of research into monetization and philosophy. That subject is touched upon only lightly in this book, but our discussions over the course of those two years have contributed greatly to the clarification of my thinking on the main topics involved.

I include thanks to my parents and my wife only because it would be churlish not to do so, not because these words or this book can in any way repay the enormous debt I shall always owe them.

Contents

Figures

Abbreviations

ABBREVIATIONS OF ANCIENT authors and texts follow standard use, similar to that used in LSJ and *OLD*, but occasionally somewhat longer for the sake of easy comprehension. Superscripts indicate the number of edition: for example, *CAH*³ = *Cambridge Ancient History*, third edition.

AJA	*American Journal of Archaeology.*
AO	Robert Develin. *Athenian Officials, 684–321 B.C.* Cambridge: Cambridge University Press, 1989.
APF	John K. Davies. *Athenian Propertied Families, 600–300 B.C.* Oxford: Clarendon Press, 1971.
ARMT	André Parrot, Georges Dossin, et al., eds. *Archives royales de Mari (textes).* Paris: Imprimerie nationale/Éditions Recherche sur les Civilisations, 1950–.
ATL	Benjamin D. Meritt, H. T. Wade-Gery, and Malcolm F. McGregor, eds. *The Athenian Tribute Lists.* Cambridge, Mass: Harvard University Press, 1939–53.
BAR	*British Archaeological Reports.*
BCH	*Bulletin de correspondance hellénique.*
BGU	*Berliner griechische Urkunden (Ägyptische Urkunden aus den Königlichen Museen zu Berlin).* Berlin: Weidmann et al., 1895–.

BMCR   *Bryn Mawr Classical Review.*

CAD   Ignace J. Gelb, Benno Landsberger, and A. Leo Oppen-
            heim, eds. *The Assyrian Dictionary of the Oriental Institute
            of the University of Chicago.* Chicago: Oriental Institute;
            Glückstadt: J. J. Augustin, 1956–.

CAH   *Cambridge Ancient History.*

CP   *Classical Philology.*

CQ   *Classical Quarterly.*

CR   *Classical Review.*

CT   *Cuneiform Texts from Babylonian Tablets in the British Mu-
            seum.* London: Trustees of the British Museum, 1893–.

DK   Hermann Diels and Walther Kranz. *Die Fragmente der
            Vorsokratiker.*⁶ Berlin: Weidmann, 1952.

DMG   Michael Ventris and John Chadwick. *Documents in Myce-
            naean Greek.*² Cambridge: Cambridge University Press,
            1973.

FD   *Fouilles de Delphes.* Paris: de Boccard, 1902–.

FGrH   Felix Jacoby. *Die Fragmente der griechischen Historiker.* Ber-
            lin: Weidmann, 1923–29; Leiden: Brill, 1926–58.

GDI   Hermann Collitz and Friedrich Bechtel. *Sammlung der
            griechischen Dialektinschriften.* Göttingen: Vandenhoeck
            und Ruprecht, 1884–1915. Reprint, Nendeln and Liechten-
            stein: Kraus, 1973–75.

GRBS   *Greek, Roman, and Byzantine Studies.*

HCT   A. W. Gomme et al. *A Historical Commentary on Thucydi-
            des.* Oxford: Oxford University Press, 1945–81.

IC   Margherita Guarducci. *Inscriptiones Creticae.* Rome: Li-
            breria della Stato, 1935–50.

IE   Hermann Wankel et al. *Die Inschriften von Ephesos.* In-
            schriften griechischer Städte aus Kleinasien, vols. 11–17.
            Bonn: Habelt, 1979–84.

IG   Deutsche Akademie der Wissenschaften. *Inscriptiones
            Graecae.* Berlin: de Gruyter and G. Reimer, 1873–. (The
            name of the editing academy has varied with political
            changes.)

Ins. Dél.   F. Durrbach et al., eds., *Inscriptions de Délos.* Paris: Cham-
            pion, 1926–50.

JHS   *Journal of Hellenic Studies.*

KTU   M. Dietrich, O. Loretz, J. Sanmartín, eds. *Die keilalpha-*

	betischen Texte aus Ugarit. Kevelaer: Butzon & Bercker; Neukirchen-Vluyn: Neukirchener Verlag, 1976.
LDÄ	Wolfgang Helck, Eberhard Otto, and Wolfhart Westendorf. *Lexikon der Ägyptologie.* Wiesbaden: Harrassowitz, 1975–86.
LfgrE	Bruno Snell et al. *Lexikon des frühgriechischen Epos.* Göttingen: Vandenhoeck and Ruprecht, 1955–.
LSJ	Henry George Liddell, Robert Scott, and Sir Henry Stuart Jones. *A Greek-English Lexicon.*[9] Oxford: Clarendon Press, 1940. Revised supplement by P. G. W. Glare, 1996.
ML	Russell Meiggs and David M. Lewis. *Greek Historical Inscriptions.* Oxford: Clarendon Press, 1969.
NC	*Numismatic Chronicle.*
OLD	P. G. Glare et al. *Oxford Latin Dictionary.* Oxford: Clarendon Press, 1982.
PCG	R. Kassel and C. Austin. *Poetae Comici Graeci.* Berlin: de Gruyter, 1983–.
PCPS	*Proceedings of the Cambridge Philological Society.*
RE	A. Pauly, G. Wissowa, and W. Kroll. *Real-Encyclopädie der klassischen Altertumswissenschaft.* Stuttgart: Druckenmuller, 1893–.
Reallexikon der Assyriologie	Erich Ebeling, Bruno Meissner, et al., eds. *Reallexikon der Assyriologie und vorderasiatischen archäologie.* Berlin and New York: de Gruyter, 1928–.
SEG	*Supplementum Epigraphicum Graecum.*
TAPA	*Transactions of the American Philological Association.*
UET	*UR Excavations: Texts.* London: Trustees of the British Museum; Philadelphia: University Museum of the University of Pennsylvania, 1928–76.

1   THE REVOLUTIONARY INVENTION

OCCASIONALLY AN INVENTION succeeds so thoroughly that it changes permanently the terms in which its society thinks. It becomes an essential part of the world; life without it is hardly conceivable, and when observing other societies—or indeed, when remembering one's own society before the coming of the invention—one tends to imagine that there must have been something in the society that fulfilled, in a primitive manner, the place of the new invention. Writing was such an invention; not only the nature of communication but also our way of thinking about it has been changed permanently by literacy.[1] Words have lost their wings and can be held for ages; we think we possess knowledge, even if nobody remains on earth who knows it, if only it remains written in a book; the most solemn agreements may not be binding until they have been written down. The clock was another such invention;[2] within a few decades, it had organized society around fixed times of day, known with an accuracy that had once belonged only to the angels. All previous methods of measuring time—the notched taper, the hourglass, the sundial, the water clock (varied instruments serving various purposes)—

---

1. See, inter alia, Havelock; Detienne; Svenbro; Harris, *Ancient Literacy;* Rosalind Thomas; and Small. The recent books on the subject have demonstrated that the "literate revolution" was neither immediate nor absolute—as, indeed, no revolution ever is. Clanchy (7–11) goes still further, questioning whether literacy is a blessing at all.

2. See the perceptive and justly famous article of E. P. Thompson.

were seen as primitive clocks; the new invention had superseded them all, and the difference in their functions became a matter for antiquarians.

Money, particularly coined money, was another invention that irrevocably changed people's way of thought. Here, too, various functions, previously separate, united themselves in a single concept; here, too, the invention has become an essential part of agreements that would once have been binding without it. People may consider themselves happy or miserable in proportion as they possess it, and they may dedicate most of their waking hours—indeed, most of their lives—to its acquisition. Yet money has not always been with us. Adam and Eve were penniless; so, if you prefer them for a pedigree, are the great apes. Money, as ubiquitous as it may seem to us, is not an essential part of the human condition.

Coined money was invented. It was invented in three times and places— Greece or Asia Minor, India, and China[3]—that we can determine with what passes, at this distance, for reasonable exactness. Like other inventions, it developed out of certain predecessors and succeeded because it fulfilled an important need of the society that came to use it. Again like many other inventions, it developed in many extraordinary ways that could not have been foreseen; it had effects in areas of life that would have seemed to be vastly removed from its proper sphere; and it changed the world so profoundly that not only do subsequent generations find it difficult to imagine what the world can have been like without it, but—for that very reason— they can appreciate only with difficulty the effects that it continues to have on them.

The intention of the present study is to trace the invention of coinage and its introduction to ancient Greece, to demonstrate how it differed from its predecessors, and to show how its influence proceeded through the society that adopted it until most areas of that society had been fundamentally altered. This book is a historical one, written in the past tense, discussing things that happened to people long dead. The nature of the subject is such that its study should prove enlightening on many aspects of our contemporary lives, but I have not written it for any polemical purpose. Although I could hardly avoid occasional remarks of contemporary relevance (if only to keep the readers and myself from anachronism), readers are likely to find their own conclusions more interesting than any to which I could try to lead them.

---

3. On India and China, see appendix 2; cf. Schaps, "The Invention of Coinage in Lydia, in India, and in China."

◉ WHAT IS MONEY?

The definition of money has exercised economists for generations, without producing a universally accepted definition. This need not and has not prevented intelligent discussion. Like hard-core pornography, money may be difficult to define, but we know it when we see it.[4]

The question of a proper definition is important and essential for an economist; for a historian dealing with the genesis of an idea, it is not only nonessential but misleading. The purpose of a definition is, as its etymology indicates, to set up boundaries between one concept and another; a proper definition selects one characteristic—not necessarily the most obvious one—and limits the thing being defined to all items having that characteristic. It takes some mathematical sophistication to recognize that a circle—and only a circle—is the locus of all points at a given distance from another point, but this definition makes it possible for mathematicians to speak about a circle in a consistent and productive manner.

For the historian tracing the beginning of an idea, a definition is a hindrance.[5] One person's circle is another person's loop; metaphorical uses ("This is popular in leftist circles"), contextual references ("The Arctic Circle"), and other linguistic phenomena extend a word's meaning yet further. Most problematic is our willingness to apply the term *circle* to any number of more or less round figures, not one of which fits the mathematical definition. Anyone who would discuss the genesis of the concept of a circle (if there ever was such a development) must bring into account many items that people may consider to be more or less circular. A scientist defines a concept in a way that makes it useful for science; that concept, once defined, ceases to mean to the scientist the same thing that it means to the rest of us. Geometry makes great use of circles as it has defined them, even though it is in fact impossible for anything tangible to fit the mathematical definition of a circle, for a circle as defined mathematically has no thickness and no width.

I shall not, then, define money precisely here, though to avoid speaking in

---

4. "Criminal laws in this area are limited to hard-core pornography. I shall not today attempt further to define the kinds of material I understand to be embraced with that shorthand description; and perhaps I could never succeed in intelligibly doing so. But I know it when I see it, and the motion picture involved in this case is not that." Justice Potter Stewart (concurring), *Jacobellis v. Ohio*, 378 U.S. 184, 198 (1964). My thanks to numerous members of the Classics-L list for identifying the source of this often quoted statement.

5. See Dalton, "Primitive Money," 280–81, for an anthropologist's argument against definition.

an utter vacuum, I offer Glyn Davies's "preliminary definition" that "money is anything that is widely used for making payments and accounting for debts and credits."[6] In the contexts I will be considering in this book, money is normally a physical object whose value is widely recognized.[7] One can estimate anything's value in money, and one can buy anything with money. A person who has money is wealthy; a person who does not is poor.[8]

Like any concept, this one becomes fuzzy around the edges. Recent generations have become comfortable with the idea that money need not be a physical object; the government of the United States, for example, may be considered to own more dollars than have ever been minted or even printed. Debts owed to a person may be money, and may even be used to pay others; that is what we do when we write a check. Many items that are used by primitive people may seem to us to be in some sense money, although we cannot ask the people involved what their opinion is without first explaining to them what we mean by money. We are willing to say that time is money or that five cents is not money nowadays. A definition must draw a line that excludes many of these uses and includes others; a historian asks different questions: How did this concept of money arise? Why has it been so powerful and so enduring?

Before approaching these questions, I must deal with another objection: that all concepts are fluid, so that it is tautological to state that earlier peoples did not have our concept of money. To an extent, this is true; not only the ancient Greeks but Europeans and Americans of a very short time ago did not agree to the idea that a note not backed by silver or gold was really money,[9] and I confess myself to having been surprised when I first came to a country where workers are paid with a check stub but no check.[10]

---

6. Glyn Davies, 29. This definition will not suffice for more sophisticated discussions of money in a modern economy; see ibid., 304, 402, 437–38, for successive refinements that have been brought about in monetary theory. Pryor (150–57) offers a lucid discussion of the difficulties of defining money and the distinctions that appear among the various forms of money, which may be included or excluded according to the precise definition.

7. One might perhaps say "universally," for although we all know that there are places where a given coin is not recognized, we consider that insofar as that is true, the item is not completely money, and we may say that a pound "isn't money" in America.

8. See pp. 199–203. *Forbes* magazine testifies to this concept every year by compiling a list of the four hundred richest people in America, defining them by a sum of money said to be the total value of their holdings.

9. Shell, chaps. 1 and 4, with the illustrations at the end of the book.

10. In Israel, the stub, often of folio size, tells us how much has been deposited in our account in the bank; the bank transfers the money on its books from employer to employee, without the latter's receiving any negotiable item.

These developments do indeed point to a modern concept of money that is not the same as the Greeks', and undoubtedly every society has its own way of understanding money. But the underlying concept of money has been extraordinarily stable, so that a modern immediately recognizes a Greek coin as money, although we have more difficulty recognizing a cowrie shell or a three-ton stone as such. Something new happened with the invention of coinage, and it produced a new idea that persists to our day. The questions of its origin and its power are not idle.

THE STATE OF THE PROBLEM

Aristotle did not find it difficult to offer an explanation for the invention of money. He cannot have had any reliable historical information on the subject, but in history, as in science, his uncommon gift of common sense offered a plausible explanation.

> For when, by importing things that they needed and exporting things of which they had too much, people became dependent upon more distant places, the use of money was invented out of necessity. For not all of the things that are required by nature are easy to transport; and so, for use in exchanges, they agreed among themselves to give and take something of a sort that, being itself one of the useful items, was easy to handle for the needs of life, such as iron or silver or anything else like that. At first it was simply defined by size and weight, but finally they also added an impressed stamp, to free them from measuring it, since the stamp was put on as a sign of the amount.[11]

Aristotle's description is of a piece with the best of Greek science—plausible, explaining the unexplained, fitting the well-known facts, and wrong.[12]

The Roman jurist Paulus offered a similar description.

> Buying and selling took their origin in exchange. For once there was no such thing as coin, nor was one thing called a commodity and the other a price, but everybody would exchange what he did not need for what he did, according to the needs of the time and the situation, since it often happens that one person has too little of that of which another has

---

11. Arist. *Pol.* I 9.7–8 (1257a 31–41). All translations from Greek and Latin are my own unless otherwise attributed.

12. See p. 8.

too much. But since it neither always nor easily happened that when you had what I needed, I, in turn, had something that you were willing to accept, a material was chosen to have a fixed value, guaranteed by the state, which could help the difficulties of exchange by equalizing its quantity. That material, struck by the state, shows its use and title not so much by its substance as by its quantity, and no longer are both items called commodities, but rather one of them is called the price.[13]

Paulus is not merely echoing Aristotle. For one thing, Paulus is a jurist: as we shall see in this chapter, the explanations offered by different scholars for the invention of money often reflect differences in the scholars' field of expertise. Paulus is explaining not the origin of money but the origin of the concept of sale, which he identifies as having come about with the invention of coinage.[14] He presumes the invention to have been spurred by local trade, whereas Aristotle thought it came about "by importing things that they needed and exporting things of which they had too much."[15] Most significantly, Paulus attributes the invention of coinage to a state initiative, whereas Aristotle speaks only of something that people "agreed among themselves." The essential idea, however—that money arose from its convenience for trade—remains the same.

In another passage, Aristotle seems to offer a different explanation.

So the builder has to get the shoemaker's product from the shoemaker, and he has to give him some of his own. Now if there is an analogous equality[16] and then each gives what he gets,[17] then what we have spoken of will come about. But if not, the bargain is not equal, nor does it hold, for nothing prevents one person's product from being worth more than the other's; so they have to be equalized . . . So all things that are exchanged have to be somehow comparable. For that purpose, coinage came about, and it becomes a sort of medium, for it measures all things, so that it also measures the excess and the deficit, how many sandals are equal to a house or to food. For the

---

13. *Digest* 18.1.1.

14. As I will show (p. 46), the distinction between purchase and barter is in fact much older.

15. On the question of which phenomenon—local or long-distance trade—is more essential to the origin of money, ancient historians have long tended toward the view of Paulus, while anthropologists have tended to side with Aristotle. The cross-cultural survey of Pryor (149–83) does not bear out a preference for either.

16. That is (in the example quoted), if the two items are of equal value.

17. That is, if each gives the same value as he gets.

number of sandals for a house or for food has to be just like the proportion of the builder to the shoemaker,[18] because if that is not the case, there will be neither exchange nor community.[19]

Here, Aristotle is speaking of the necessity of money to human justice, a necessity that flows from its function as a standard of value by which all things can be measured. This is not presented as a historical fact, but the statement that community is impossible without it surely suffices to excuse those who took it to be such a claim, somewhat at variance with the passage of the *Politics* just quoted.

Between the two of them, the theories that money arose either as a medium of exchange or as a standard of value held the field for over two thousand years and were still the only explanations offered by historians a hundred years ago.[20] John Stuart Mill described the dismal situation in which humankind must have been before the invention of money.

The first and most obvious [inconvenience] would be the want of a common measure for values of different sorts. If a tailor had only coats, and wanted to buy bread or a horse, it would be very troublesome to ascertain how much bread he ought to obtain for a coat, or how many coats he should give for a horse. The calculation must be recommenced on different data, every time he bartered his coat for a different kind of article; and there could be no current price, or regular quotations of value . . . The division of employments could hardly have been carried to any considerable extent. A tailor, who had nothing but coats, might starve before he could find any person having bread to sell who wanted a coat: besides, he would not want as much bread at a time as would be worth a coat, and the coat could not be divided.[21]

To a certain extent,[22] Mill has fallen victim to what I would call the *inventionist fallacy:* the presumption that before one modern contrivance or another was

---

18. On the meaning of this odd statement, see Meikle, 129–46; Danzig.

19. Arist. *Eth. Nic.* V 5.8–10 (1133a 8–24).

20. See, for example, Head (xxxiii) ("This transitional stage in the development of commerce cannot be more accurately described than in the words of Aristotle," whom he proceeds to quote), and Mill, quoted immediately below.

21. Mill, book 3, chap. 7, §1.

22. Mill was by no means naive; he distinguishes different uses of money and understands that one may have preceded the other. He did not, however, have our information about the workings of primitive societies.

invented, the function that it now performs was not performed at all. I have heard people reveal—generally in comments made by the way and without true consideration—that they believe people to have shivered in the cold before electric heaters were invented, to have gone to sleep at dusk before there were electric lightbulbs, and regularly to have relieved themselves in public before the invention of modern sanitary fixtures. It does not take much sophistication to recognize the inaccuracy of these presumptions, and on reflection, nobody would argue that they are correct; but presumptions of this sort often flit around the edges of our theorizing and can cause even historians to speak of the effects of an innovation (technological or other) as if the innovation itself made possible the behavior that it later characterized. In some instances, this was undoubtedly the case: human flight, for example, although possible before the invention of the airplane, was wholly impossible before the invention of the hot-air balloon. Many inventions, however, facilitate what had been difficult, rather than making possible what had been impossible.

Mill was able to explain why gold and silver were the ideal medium of exchange. Unlike shells or stones, they are universally valued. Unlike foods, they are not perishable (others have added that unlike cattle, they need not be fed). Unlike iron, they are easily portable and easily hidden. Unlike jewels, they are easily divided without loss in value. Unlike any animal or vegetable, they exist in the world in amounts not subject to great fluctuations.[23]

Many textbooks, particularly in economics, still offer Mill's arguments, more or less unchanged. "Since the origins of money are seldom discussed in any reputable modern book on economics," writes Frederic Pryor, "most economists draw from the collective unconsciousness of the profession on such matters, that is, the lore that has been passed on in elementary economics courses over the century that is rooted in the Plato-Aristotle-Smith-Jevons tradition."[24] But in fact, quite a bit has changed.

In the twentieth century, anthropology showed us that both commerce and the division of labor can exist, have existed, and do exist without the intervention of money.[25] We have discovered, moreover, that trade is not the only

---

23. Mill, book 3, chap. 7, §2.

24. Pryor, 158 n. 26. For the "Plato-Aristotle-Smith-Jevons tradition," I have contented myself with the quotations from Aristotle and from Paulus. The interested reader can follow up the works mentioned and many others in between to discover how tediously repetitious they can become. I am sure the reader will agree with my choice to economize in citations.

25. On commerce, see Einzig, passim, particularly 338–44; and see pp. 35–42; on the division of labor, it will suffice to look at *DMG*, pp. 133–35.

possible mechanism by which society distributes its material goods to those who need them.[26] The question of why these systems were replaced by the monetary economy in which we live is no longer one that can be answered with a posteriori theorizing. If anything, the contrary is the case: the great importance of money for our market-based economy strongly suggests that this economy itself, at least in major aspects, did not exist before the invention of money and if so it cannot have been the reason for the invention.[27]

Sir William Ridgeway, at the end of the nineteenth century, was perhaps the first to bring comparative anthropology to bear on the subject of the origins of money, but he was interested only in the origins of metrical systems, all of which he considered to be based on the amount of gold that was equivalent in value to a cow.[28] He did not go beyond Aristotle in regard to the question of where the idea had arisen that the value of an ox could or should be measured in gold.

Strikingly original, on the other hand, was the theory of Bernhard Laum, who noticed that in the Homeric poems (which I discuss in chapter 5), the worth of items was expressed in cattle, but cattle were never actually used as a medium of exchange. Other facts as well seemed to indicate that cattle had a particular role in the invention of money: bronze ingots of the Mediterranean Basin seemed to represent the shape of an ox's hide,[29] and the Latin word *pecunia*, "money," was connected to the word *pecus*, "cattle," as the Romans themselves had noticed.[30] Since the idea that one item is the measure of all others is an important step on the way to the idea of money, it followed, according to Laum, that the idea of money did not develop from trade at all. He proposed that the origin of money came from the sacrificial animal's status as a substitute for the sacrificer. When other items came to be accepted in place of cattle, they had to be evaluated in terms of

---

26. See pp. 23–24.

27. "Our whole economic system is based upon the existence of money. It appears to be so eminently useful and necessary in our scheme of things that one cannot even conceive of its absence. But just for this very reason, it is clear that in many respects money must have preceded our institutions. In many important respects economic organisation appears to be the product of money, and it is, therefore, inadmissible to ascribe the origin of money to its special suitability for our existing scheme of things." Helfferich, 3.

28. Ridgeway, particularly 124–54.

29. On these ingots and the current understanding of their shape, see pp. 230–32.

30. Ovid *Fasti* 5.280–81; Pliny *Natural History* 18.11; Plut. *Publicola* 11.6. Modern comparative study has shown, however, that the root involved is one that refers to movable property, so that the connection between cattle and money is indeed a true connection, but in fact it is *pecunia*, not *pecus*, that preserves the original meaning (Benveniste). The point is worth mentioning, since the facile derivation *pecunia a pecore* still finds its way into many discussions of economic history.

cattle: this is the stage we see in Homer. The ox as a symbol, however, was not the last stage in the development of cult: just as the ox could take the place of a person, so cheaper items, such as cakes, could take the place of the ox. When a pure symbol could take the place of an ox, we have reached a stage very close to money, and the earliest forms of money were spits, tripods, and cauldrons—all the appurtenances of the roasting or cooking of an ox. An idea that was religious in origin—Laum entitled his book *Heiliges Geld*—became secularized and only secondarily came to serve the purpose of trade.

By Laum's time, however, Homer had lost his place as one of the two major sources of information about the origins of customs.[31] An evolutionary view of human society brought with it the idea that many societies still existing preserved forms of behavior and organization through which all societies must have passed at some stage. This opinion, which is no longer held in its strict form,[32] meant that many "primitive" societies were still in existence, available for our observation. The description of these societies, both by anthropologists and by colonial administrators, revealed among this or that nation or tribe very many items that served functions that we would consider monetary. The plot was thickening.

Wilhelm Gerloff brought these observations together in a well-documented theory that attributed the origins of money to a social function rather than an economic one. His first observation was that Aristotle's description of the earliest money as "one of the useful items ... easy to handle for the needs of life" was the opposite of the truth. In most societies, objects that serve as money—cowrie shells (figs. 1–2), outsize stones, ritual gongs, knives that cannot cut—are useless for the purposes of day-to-day existence. Precisely because of their uselessness, these items bestow prestige upon their owner. No essential item could do that, for if it is really essential, all people must have it. The items that serve as money are useless but not worthless; on the contrary, since they bestow social position, they are very valuable and therefore appropriate for those special occasions (marriage, hospitality, concluding a treaty) when very valuable items must be offered. This kind of value transfer is the basis for what eventually may develop into true value exchange, where the useless but prestigious items are traded for useful ones—at first, perhaps, for items available only at a great distance,

---

31. The other had always been the Bible, which was now under attack for other reasons as well.

32. Farb, 9–11; Nash, 171–72. In the revised version of his paper for a second edition, Nash eliminated this passage, presumably because he no longer thought the opinion worth refuting.

Fig. 1. Cowrie shells. The most widespread form of primitive money, cowrie shells were hoarded from prehistoric to modern times. (Collection of the Israel Museum, Jerusalem. Exhibit and photo © Israel Museum, Jerusalem.)

Fig. 2. Imitation cowrie shells. Cowrie shells were so popular that they were counterfeited. These Chinese bone imitations are estimated to be four thousand years old. (Collection of the Israel Museum, Jerusalem. Exhibit and photo © Israel Museum, Jerusalem.)

but eventually even for the more ordinary daily needs. Money develops, according to Gerloff, from the universal desire of people for social prestige.[33]

It will be easily seen that Gerloff wrote about a phenomenon very different from the one that Laum discussed. Laum was writing of a development that started in Greece before the Homeric period and culminated in the invention of coinage; Gerloff was speaking in general terms of a phenomenon that he took to be a common one, repeated over and over in human societies. The development outlined by Gerloff led not to the invention of coinage—most of the societies he studied were still far from that stage—but to the designation of one or the other item as something that we could properly call a form of money. These items and the senses in which they might be considered money were obviously much more various than had once been thought. The question of the uses of money, a question that had remained almost static since antiquity,[34] now became a matter of much greater significance.

● THE USES OF MONEY

The chief uses of money have been recognized since antiquity. First, Plato and Aristotle both recognized that it served as a *medium of exchange*,[35] allowing the tailor whose predicament Mill described to buy bread without the inconvenience of barter. The advantages of such a medium are obvious, and once in place, it maintains itself even in the face of adversity. In a sufficiently complex economy, some medium of exchange becomes an absolute necessity.[36] When normal money is unavailable, other items take its place, as do cigarettes in prisons and as did beaver skins in the American Old West.[37] When it is outlawed, it goes underground, creating one of the many varieties of black markets that states attempting to control the economy have not succeeded in eliminating.

Second, money is a *standard of value*, a way of making commensurable things that would not otherwise be so.[38] To take Aristotle's example,[39] how

---

33. Pryor (169 n. 51) did not find empirical confirmation of this connection. I will not pursue the matter, since the subject of this study lies elsewhere.

34. Monroe, 5, 21, 48, 83–84, 161–62.

35. Plato *Rep.* II 371b; Arist. *Pol.* I 9.7–8 (1257a 31–41).

36. See Glyn Davies, 17–22, for an intelligent discussion of the place of barter and its inherent limits in a modern society. Davies's book, combining broad historical knowledge with the understanding of a person who has spent his life in banking, is perceptive, entertaining, and highly recommended.

37. For many more examples, see Einzig, 278–306.

38. Plato *Laws* XI 918b.

39. Arist. *Eth. Nic.* V 5.14–16 (1133b 16–28).

many beds are worth a building? In a sense, this question has no answer: a building is not a comfortable surface on which to sleep, and no number of beds, under normal use, will keep a person from getting wet in the rain. Money gives every item a value and allows us to make some sort of equation between beds and buildings. It is not, perhaps, an exact equation,[40] but it suffices for those situations where values have to be compared.

Third, money is a *way of storing value.* "For future exchange, if one should not need anything now, since there will be a time when he will need it, money is a sort of guarantor for us, for it must be possible for a person who gives it to get something."[41] A farmer who raises lettuce must sell it quickly. He cannot leave it in the ground, and it does not pickle well. Refrigeration, which was not available to the ancients, is in any event a luxury that not everyone can afford. So he sells the lettuce and gets money, which keeps indefinitely.[42] In the case of athletes, who try to subsist for their entire lives by doing things that they can only do when young, or in the case of perform- ers, who may live for years from the proceeds of one night's performance, the ability of money to store value can reach spectacular levels.

Fourth, modern economists recognize money as a *means of payment,* even where no exchange is involved. It is by no means an exchange when the person who has broken another's nose is asked to pay damages; the victim, presumably, would not have "exchanged" a nose for any payment, nor does the assailant get anything tangible in return for the payment. The *wergild,* by which a murderer makes amends to the victim's family, is a very widespread custom, even among peoples who rarely trade; bride-price is usually treated in the same way as *wergild,* even though it may appear to us more like a true exchange.

Other uses of money may be identified,[43] but these four are the ones generally enumerated. The question of which of them is the essential func- tion has long been debated by economists, and various answers have been given. By the middle of the twentieth century, it became possible to phrase the question as an anthropological one, to try to discover what articles perform a monetary function in various societies and the uses to which

---

40. Aristotle himself (*Eth. Nic.* V 5.14 [1133b 18–20]) recognized that the things do not really become commensurable; on the implications of this for his theory of value, see Meikle, 6–27.

41. Arist. *Eth. Nic.* V 5.14 (1133b 14–16).

42. Or so it is often presumed; see p. 207.

43. Einzig (444–54, 458–63) adds the uses of money as liquid reserves, a standard of deferred payments, a means of deferred payments, and primitive foreign exchange. Glyn Davies (27) offers a table of the uses of money, adding to six "specific functions (mostly micro-economics)" four "general functions (mostly macro-economic and abstract)," viz., "liquid asset; framework of the market allocative system (prices); a causative factor in the economy; controller of the economy."

those articles are put. Three scholars approached the problem almost simultaneously and almost independently. Alison Hingston Quiggin and Paul Einzig each published in the same year surveys of what they called "primitive money"; Karl Polanyi, for his part, established an interdisciplinary project that, searching through various societies for alternatives to the market-driven economy of the Western world, changed dramatically the agenda of what is now called economic anthropology.[44] All three made the same observation: whereas "true," modern money serves a number of purposes, the various sorts of "money" used by primitive peoples tend to serve only some of these purposes.[45]

More recent work points out that even among these purposes, primitive money will not necessarily be used in all the ways we might expect. In the heroic literature of the early Germans, rings may be used for gifts in connection with marriage, with reconciliation, with recognition of overlordship, or as a reward for loyalty or for service (whether past or expected); as prizes for wagers; or as alms.[46] All these uses fall under the category of means of payment, but because of the nature of German society, they are not the payments to the state that we think of when we speak of Greek society. In general, it appears that in societies whose money has no commercial use, by far the major purpose that primitive money serves is bride-wealth.[47]

The position to which we have been brought makes it clear that the invention of *money*, as an economist or an anthropologist would understand it, has little or nothing to do with the invention of *coinage*. Many different items may serve, have served, and still do serve the purpose of money. Their development has taken place in many different places and very likely through many different paths. The existence of money seems, in fact, to be a regular development in societies that have reached a certain level of economic development.[48] Beginning in Asia Minor, in India, and in China,

---

44. For a description of Polanyi's working group, see Polanyi, Arensberg, and Pearson, v–x. For a brief outline of his theories, see pp. 22–25. On the term "economic anthropology," which was becoming current at the time, see Herskovits, v–vi.

45. "Our money is 'all-purpose' money . . . Early money is . . . special-purpose money." Polanyi, "The Economy as Instituted Process," 264, 266. Similarly, though less categorically, see Quiggin, 4, and Einzig, 428–30. See further Dalton, "Primitive Money." Melitz has raised serious objections to this formulation, though scholars continue to think that there is validity to it (see Pryor, 151). See appendix 1 for my own discussion.

46. See Sommerfeld, 155, for a list of a number of expressions showing the way a person's rings establish and reflect personal worth and social honor.

47. Pryor, 169.

48. See Pryor, 163–71, on the strong correlation between level of economic development and the presence of money.

other forms of money have been replaced by coins—flat pieces of metal with a device on them that asserted (and in many instances created) their value. We can speak of the "development" of money, but not properly of its invention; we can speak of the invention of coinage, but that is not at all the same as the invention of money.[49]

⦿ A CONCEPTUAL REVOLUTION

Viewed in the perspective of human development that I have traced, the invention of coinage seems almost a triviality, a technological innovation that simplified and broadened the use of money that had developed over millennia. For an economist, that perspective is valid and even essential. An economist who would deny the name "money" to the various items that perform monetary functions throughout the world of primitive and peasant economies would seriously misapprehend the similarity of function that is hidden by a difference of substance.

This is the case for an economist, for whom the term *money*—however problematic its definition—is a term of science, used without reference to the conceptual world of the people studied. Whether the Eskimos are using money, special-purpose money, a "premonetary form," primitive money, or primitive valuables is a question that the economist approaches without asking the Eskimo's opinion of the matter.

This cannot be the approach of a historian. Money is a concept that is used and understood today, but has not always been so used.[50] Many of the basic concepts of our economic worldview—purchase, inflation, net worth, and liquidity, to mention a few—depend for their definition on the idea of money. One of the central propositions of this book is that when we speak historically, *the invention of coinage was the invention of money:* that is, the concept that we understand as "money" did not exist before the seventh century B.C.E., when coins were first minted. There surely had been many items before that we may recognize, correctly, as money; there were even places, as we shall see, where a single item performed all the functions that we associate with money. Never before, however, had these items been conceptualized as money, for money to the Greeks, as to us, was the measure of all things,[51] something different in nature from all the valuables that might represent it.

---

49. This is stated clearly by Will (210) and again by Alföldi (1:63).

50. That items performing monetary functions must necessarily have preceded the concept of money was already stated by Simmel (119–20).

51. πάντα γὰϱ μετϱεῖ (Arist. *Eth. Nic.* V 5.10 [1133a 20–21]).

From the Greeks onward, we find a new way of speaking and of thinking. Now a person might state the entirety of a household's possessions in terms of money, as no member of a premonetary society would ever do. Money was not just an item, like gold, silver, rubies, or cattle, that made up a part of a person's wealth; money *was* wealth.[52] When Greeks spoke of coins as a physical object, they called them *nomismata*, "customary things,"[53] or sometimes *argyrion*, "the silver thing." The first term may date from the first time when a Greek state issued coins; the second may be a translation of the term that applied to silver in the Near East, whether the silver was being used as jewelry or as money.[54] When the Greeks spoke of money, they had no term available, neither from the days before coinage nor from their Phoenician trading partners. They used the term *chremata*, "useful things"—a term that had formerly referred and could still refer to all the goods that a person might possess.[55]

The invention of coinage came at the end of a long process of the monetization of Near Eastern society. The technology of making coins was trivial and had been available for a long time—surely more than a millennium. Coins were not a case where technology transformed history, for technology was not the driving force here. What was new, at least to the Greeks, was the underlying concept.

For Lydians and Phoenicians, perhaps, the difference between coins and the other forms of silver that they had been accustomed to use was little more than a quibble. The Greeks, however, who had had only very primitive forms of currency, thought of coins as they had never thought of those items in which they had once traded, evaluated, and paid. An idea that had grown up in the East at a time when Greece had had no need for it suddenly dawned on the Greeks when coins appeared. It was a time when the Greeks were in a period of economic and intellectual expansion for which their relatively primitive economic concepts did not provide an adequate basis. The concept of money, which appeared with the invention of coinage, organized their economy with an efficiency and elasticity that had no parallel among their contemporaries. Precisely because of their economic back-

---

52. For Aristotle's opinion of this idea, see p. 175.

53. The term is derived from νόμος, "custom" or "law." Perhaps the closest English parallel, at least from an etymological point of view, is the phrase "legal tender." For a more nuanced, if more adventuresome, suggestion, see von Reden, *Exchange*, 177.

54. Akkadian *kaspu*, Hebrew *keseph*. Arabic indeed has a word for money, and the word is *dirham*, a derivative of the Greek *drachma*.

55. Von Reden (*Exchange*, 175) notes that "the absence of a name for the phenomenon of money in Greece suggests that it gradually emerged rather than being imposed from outside."

wardness, they had no sufficient preexisting conceptual structure to compete with or subordinate the idea of money. The new concept changed radically their patterns of behavior. In some fields, this happened immediately; in others, more slowly. In some fields, it happened completely; in others, only partially; in yet others, hardly at all. From the Greeks, the concept passed to their neighbors, and although I shall not, in this book, attempt a universal history of monetization, the penetration of money into human society has been both broader and deeper than its inventor could ever have imagined.[56]

The idea of money did not come upon the Greeks in a vacuum. Its uses had been developed in the East; the way it was understood was deeply rooted in concepts of exchange, justice, and reciprocity that had developed in Greece before the first coins were ever seen.[57] It not only transformed their society but conquered the societies with which they came in contact. It undoubtedly brought with it new opportunities and strengths, which were probably in large part responsible for the cultural and military success of the Greeks no less than for their economic prosperity.[58] It continues to influence us today and to conquer vast new territories, often with a cruelty and efficiency that few mere human tyrants could match.

This book will tell the story, insofar as its author is able, of the development of money both in the Near East and in Greece up to the invention of coinage and its widespread adoption by the Greek cities, the only communities that adopted it wholeheartedly at its first appearance. I shall then discuss its penetration into various aspects of Greek life and its effect on them, concluding with some general observations, which may, as good history should, have some usefulness for helping us understand our own situation.

---

56. There have been setbacks; see Cipolla, "Primitive Money," for an account of how and for what reasons Dark Age Europe almost reverted to an entirely nonmonetary economy.

57. On the conceptual background, which only seems "monetary" in retrospect, see in particular Will, 210–26; von Reden, *Exchange*.

58. Merkelbach's wide-ranging essay gives an indication of this, though its enormous chronological range and tendency to slip into the inventionist fallacy (see particularly pp. 23–24, where he seems both to acknowledge the earlier possibility of the phenomena he describes—in fact, some of them are clearly attested certainties—and to speak as if coinage had created them) prevent his occasional piece from doing more than touching the surface.

2 QUESTIONS AND CONTROVERSIES

EVEN MORE THAN OTHER historical events, the invention of coinage is an occurrence whose aspect depends upon the attitudes we bring to it and the questions we ask of it.[1] Economists, historians, and anthropologists may each reasonably claim it for their own portion and may indeed treat with scorn those who, without the expertise of their field, presume to trespass upon it. It would be naive to hope that this book can escape such scorn, but I can at least attempt to inform the reader about some of the basic questions and controversies that produce the varying aspects under which the invention of coinage can be seen.

THE LEVEL OF THE ECONOMY: PRIMITIVISTS AND MODERNISTS

In some passages Athenians appear to be businessmen with a thoroughly monetized view of themselves and their world.

> Gentlemen of the jury, my father left two factories, each of them a decent-sized business: thirty-two or -three sword makers worth five or

---

1. "The field of economic anthropology is split between the substantivists . . . the formalists . . . and the Marxist approach . . . This makes it difficult for the outsider to find his way about in the field and evaluate what is going on" (Muhly, "Copper Ox-Hide Ingots," 80).

six hundred drachmas apiece, the least of them worth not less than three hundred, from whom he got an income of three thousand drachmas per year free and clear; then sofa makers, twenty in number, who were security for a loan of four thousand drachmas, who brought him twelve hundred drachmas free and clear and about a talent of silver lent out at twelve percent, from which the interest every year came out to more than seven hundred drachmas. This was the active property he left behind . . . Besides this, there was ivory and iron, which were used as raw materials, and sofa-quality wood worth eight thousand drachmas and gold and clothing, my mother's jewelry . . . And all these were left at home; there were also a maritime loan of seven thousand drachmas to Xuthus, two thousand and four hundred at Pasio's bank, six hundred at Pylades', one thousand six hundred deposited with Demomeles, the son of Demon, and about a talent lent out at two- and three-hundred-drachma loans.[2]

A similar impression is given by Thucydides' account of how Pericles encouraged the Athenians to go to war with the claim that "in general, one is victorious in war by intelligence and by monetary superiority," after saying which he enumerated the financial resources at Athens's disposal. When we read such passages as this, we seem to be in an economic world smaller than our own but rather similar in its outlook and its preoccupations.

When we attempt, however, to apply modern economic ways of thinking to these texts, we are soon struck by how rare it is to find any such thought in the texts themselves. Sir Moses Finley noted that in the presentation just quoted, Demosthenes treated his father's property with no concept of such things as amortization and depreciation: he seems to presume that the sword makers should all have kept producing the same number of swords forever, without getting old and without their tools ever wearing out.[3] His distinction between active and inactive property is not at all the distinction

---

2. Dem. 27.9–11. For a detailed consideration of the estate and some of the problems in estimating its value, see APF, pp. 126–33.

3. There might be some slight possibility of defending Demosthenes against this charge; his statement that the revenues were "free and clear" [ἀτελεῖς] (literally, "free of taxes") might perhaps be taken more broadly to mean "after deducting expenses" (although I know of no such usage of the word), and nothing in Demosthenes' text requires us to believe that these expenses would not have included amortization and depreciation—that is, the regular replacement of ill or aged slaves and worn-out tools. Finley's comment is not based so much upon Demosthenes' words as upon the absence of these concepts from Greek literature in general; the most alarming example is Xenophon's *Ways and Means*.

that we would make between invested capital and wealth held for consumption: he classes the raw materials for the factories together with his mother's jewelry.[4] If the ancient Greek economy was much like our own, the Greeks themselves seem to have been most uncharacteristically obtuse in their understanding of it.

A hundred years ago, the coexistence in the sources of a good deal of modern-seeming activity with a very primitive grasp of basic business concepts had already led to a division of historians of the ancient economy between those who saw it as basically modern in its organization, however imperfectly the literary sources may have understood it, and those who considered it to have been a primitive economy, chiefly agrarian, whose rudimentary trade and finance tend to deceive scholars into seeing in it something more familiar than they should.[5] The father of the "primitivists," Karl Bücher, insisted on seeing the ancient economy as a "household economy," each of whose individual households constituted a more or less independent unit, supporting itself from its lands and interacting with other households only marginally.[6] J. Hasebroek's later study took more careful account of the extent of commerce in ancient Greece but argued that it was the domain of outsiders, metics, and foreigners, not usually an essential function of the polis and not an important factor in determining policy. Other scholars, notably Eduard Meyer and Michael Rostovtzeff, have held the opposite, "modernist," viewpoint. In recent decades, Sir Moses Finley's broad and well-argued works (most notably *The Ancient Economy*) have made primitivism the dominant opinion, but dissenters remain.

METHODS OF ANALYSIS: FORMALISTS, MARXISTS, SUBSTANTIVISTS, AND CHAYANOVITES

It is obvious that modernists will find modern economic analysis congenial as a tool for understanding the ancient Greek economy. Those who hold, in Rostovtzeff's words, "that the economy of this period was distinguished

---

4. Finley, *Ancient Economy*, 116.

5. A selection of early twentieth-century contributions to the debate was made easily available in Finley, *Bücher-Meyer,* but the controversy continues to our day.

6. "A penetrating study . . . must reach the conclusion that *the national economy is the product of a historical development that lasted a thousand years, and it is not older than the modern state. Before its development humanity throughout long periods of time managed its affairs either without commercial exchange, or by forms of barter of products and of payments that can not be said to belong to a national economy*" (Bücher, 90–91, reprinted in Finley, *Bücher-Meyer;* emphasis in original, translation my own).

from the modern economy only quantitatively, not qualitatively,"[7] will hardly doubt that the ancient economy was subject to the same rules, however imperfectly understood, that govern our modern world. There is, in theory, nothing to prevent a primitivist from holding the same opinion: modern economists, after all, consider their models to be appropriate, if properly applied, to all forms of human production and consumption. It must immediately be admitted that the ancients, of course, applied no such analysis to their own undertakings, so that the economic analysis of the ancient economy in modern terms would seem to offer a fertile field for scholarly endeavor. In fact this field has been ploughed only lightly. Historians prefer (and indeed, ancient sources dictate) an analysis with less mathematical sophistication than modern economics demands, while economists, lacking for the ancient world the kind of data that are their normal bread and butter, usually prefer to begin their histories with the medieval period or later.[8] In fact, if the primitivists are correct in their belief that trade was of marginal importance in the ancient world, the entire apparatus of modern economics must be reinterpreted in order to apply it fruitfully to the ancient world: we will speak of exchanges within the family, of "costs" and "profits" to which we will assign monetary values although the ancients would not have done so, of "supply-and-demand equilibrium" in markets of very restricted temporal and geographical extent. It is by no means certain that such a reinterpretation could not be pursued successfully,[9] but primitivist scholars have generally preferred paradigms other than those developed for the analysis of modern economic systems. Those who follow modern economics they call "formalists"; the primitivists themselves have ranged in other pastures.

Marxism, which divides human economies into various "modes of production" that follow one another in evolutionary sequence, is more congenial to a primitivist approach than is more orthodox economic analysis. Locating ancient Greece in the "slave mode of production," however difficult for the uninitiated, clearly distinguishes the ancient Greek economy from our own, and the ubiquity of ancient slavery, in productive work as well as in personal services, provides a strong case for such a classification.[10] The starting point

---

7. Rostovtzeff, 334 n. 1.

8. See appendix 1, p. 219.

9. As was urged by Smelser, 175–77; and cf. Gunderson, who makes a start in that direction.

10. For two different arguments as to why ancient Greece should be considered a slave society, see Finley, "Greek Civilization"; de Ste. Croix, *Class Struggle*, 51–52.

of Marxist interpretation is that economic classes, their behavior and their conflicts, are by far the most important factor in historical explanation. These classes are defined by their relationship to "the dominant means of production," not by the prestige that they or their society may attach to their position: athletes or entertainers, no matter how fabulously rich, would not be considered by Marx to be members of the ruling class unless they had purchased a business (in our days) or land and agricultural slaves (in antiquity). Different modes of production entail not only different forms of labor but different goals for individuals; the individual's desire to maximize profit, for example, which is the basis of classical economics, is for Marxists a characteristic peculiar to the capitalistic economy.[11] Marxist scholarship of the ancient world was given a new respectability by Geoffrey de Ste. Croix's *The Class Struggle in the Ancient Greek World,* which brought a depth of analysis that earlier Marxists in this area had not achieved and a wealth of documentation that few ancient historians of any persuasion could match. There may not be many who have been brought to orthodox Marxism by their study of the classical world,[12] but the analytical tools developed by Marx are not likely to have exhausted their usefulness for historians of this epoch.

By far the most influential revisionist economic theory for ancient historians has been that of Karl Polanyi, a theory now referred to as "substantivism." Polanyi insisted that until very recently, economic behavior was always "embedded" in society as a whole.

> The outstanding discovery of recent historical and anthropological research is that man's economy, as a rule, is submerged in his social relationships. He does not act so as to safeguard his individual interest in the possession of material goods; he acts so as to safeguard his social standing, his social claims, his social assets. He values material goods only in so far as they serve this end.[13]

Polanyi did not claim that primitive man was any less self-serving than his modern counterpart. As he saw it, after the anthropological studies of Bronislaw Malinowski "the mystical 'individualistic savage' was now dead and buried, as was his antipode, the 'communistic savage.' It appeared that not so much the mind as the institutions of the savage differed from our

---

11. And so not to be expected in the ancient world: see Andreyev.
12. Except, perhaps, Marx himself: see de Ste. Croix, "Karl Marx," 12–13.
13. Polanyi, *Great Transformation,* 46.

own."[14] The economic functioning of these institutions was not based on the simultaneous functioning of interconnected markets, with exchange mechanisms and supply-and-demand equilibriums that permitted the circulation of goods throughout the society. It was based, in general, on either *reciprocity* or *redistribution.*

In *reciprocity,* the individual hunts, farms, or otherwise works to produce a product, which may then be given to a relative, clansman, or other address dictated by customary rules. The recipient may not repay the gift directly, but somewhere in the society (or perhaps in a neighboring one), there is a person or group of persons who give produce to the donor. The producer works not directly for the goods produced but for the societal prestige of being a good producer; this in turn, but very indirectly, may result in getting more physical goods, but under normal circumstances, that is not the goal.

It should be noted that the term *reciprocity,* as used by Polanyi, does not apply to what we would call ordinary exchange; on the contrary, it is opposed to the kind of trading that goes on in a market. Polanyi's reciprocity is the fulfilling of social responsibilities in such a way that everyone is a giver in certain situations, a receiver in others. Marshall Sahlins distinguishes three kinds of reciprocity: generalized reciprocity (you give if you have, take if you need, but there is no calculation of relative values), balanced reciprocity (a trade should be fair), and negative reciprocity (you try to get the best of the deal).[15] Polanyi's reciprocity belongs under Sahlins's category of generalized reciprocity, but even there it sits uncomfortably, for Sahlins's way of describing the matter disembeds the economic question from the society, putting us back into the situation where the relevant question for the individual is how to get a return, not how to fit into society.

The sort of organization described by Polanyi as "reciprocity" may be seen through other glasses. In a challenging paper, Annette B. Weiner holds that the organization whereby each individual produces for some other individual can more properly be seen not as "reciprocity"—a sort of vast generalized trade taking place throughout the society—but, rather, as "reproduction," the constant labor for "the renewal, revival, rebirth or recreation of entities previously reproduced."[16] Weiner, however, has not yet found her Finley, and her theory has not yet been influential in the field of ancient history.

---

14. Polanyi, *Livelihood,* 51.

15. Sahlins, *Stone Age Economics,* 191–96. Donlan ("Reciprocities") cites Homeric examples for all three types.

16. Weiner, 71.

In the form of *redistribution* most relevant to our discussion, products are given to a central figure, normally a chief or other important man; he collects vastly more products than he can possibly use, and may indeed be expected to demonstrate his wealth by ostentatiously letting them rot or destroying them. He is also expected, on the other hand, to offer feasts, help, and other forms of largesse, so that much of the produce eventually gets redistributed throughout the society, with everyone receiving a share according to what the society considers appropriate.[17] It should be noted that redistribution can be managed either for the maintenance of societal solidarity or for the accomplishment of external goals, whether of the ruler or of the group as a whole. In the first instance, redistribution is a form of pooling resources; in the second, it is a form of mobilization.[18] Although these two forms can be distinguished, it will be obvious that different observers may judge differently which we have in a given case and that, moreover, one form of redistribution can slip into another, as the history of the Soviet Union has demonstrated.[19] Polanyi, who spoke of redistribution in relatively benign terms, was not thinking of societies in which redistribution is a form of mobilization.

In his early work, Polanyi mentioned a third form of organization, which he called "householding," the organization of the self-sufficient household, village, or manor;[20] in his later work and in that of his followers, little is made of this third method, which is generally subsumed under the category of redistribution.[21]

The strong indictment of modern economics contained in Polanyi's thought—the claim that modern economics, whether capitalistic or communistic, leaves the individual alienated by addressing physical needs in isolation from the social integration that is essential to every human being—has had, so far, relatively little effect on modern society; but Polanyi's approach

---

17. Shares, of course, are not necessarily equal: see, for example, Farb, 137–40.

18. I use the term *mobilization* in the sense in which it was first proposed by Smelser (179–82). The definition offered by Earle (215)—"the recruitment of goods and services for the benefit of a group not coterminous with the contributing members. Examples: tribute, taxation, and corvée labor"—makes a presumption, in my eyes not always legitimate, that the group to whom the goods and services are paid is necessarily using them for its own benefit rather than for the benefit of the society as a whole.

19. There are other forms of redistribution; Earle (215) distinguishes four, subsuming under the category of mobilization both phenomena just described.

20. Polanyi, *Great Transformation,* 53–55.

21. So in Earle, 215.

has been widely applied to the study of premodern societies, with differing effects. For the primitive economies studied by modern anthropologists, the substantivist framework has become a major and perhaps the dominant approach to the subject, changing permanently the terms of discussion even by those who reject Polanyi's most dogmatic assertions.[22] It has been applied to ancient Greece—partially by Finley (who attended Polanyi's seminars at Columbia University), rather more so by Paul Millett, David W. Tandy, and others. Here, it has been very influential—M. M. Austin and P. Vidal-Naquet placed near the beginning of their *Economic and Social History of Ancient Greece* a section entitled "The Economy in Greece Is Embedded in Society"—but it has not succeeded in driving other models from the field, largely because by the classical period the existence of markets in Greece is, as Polanyi knew,[23] incontrovertible, so the most that can be claimed is that other forms of economic integration may have existed side by side with it.

In studies of the ancient Near East, Polanyi's claims (particularly about the absence of markets and the prevalence of other forms of exchange) have been less successful. Although here, too, Polanyi raised questions that have permanently changed the terms in which scholars conceive of ancient history—in particular, we no longer take for granted that a society necessarily supplies the needs of its various members by trades among them, and surely not necessarily by the kind of free-market trade that characterizes the modern West—those who deal at first hand with hieroglyphic and cuneiform documents have not found in them the kinds of structures that Polanyi suggested they would.[24]

Recent studies of ancient agriculture have made much use of the ideas of the Russian[25] economist Alexander Chayanov, who claimed that the classical cost-effectiveness model for economic activity could not properly describe the working of a peasant farm.[26] For the peasant, Chayanov insisted,

---

22. See, for example, the discussion of Berdan and that of Narotzky (42–98).

23. Polanyi, "Aristotle," 83–87; cf. Finley, "Aristotle," 14 n. 45.

24. See pp. 41, 46–49.

25. He did his most influential work after the revolution, but I find it hard to call him a "Soviet" economist, since he disagreed with Lenin and was arrested in 1930 by Stalin, after which he was never heard from again.

26. For Chayanov, a "peasant farm" was one worked by a peasant family without the help of hired labor, whether or not the family actually owns the farm; this is different from the American term "family farm," which refers to a farm owned and managed by a single family, which may or may not employ a certain amount of hired help in its cultivation.

the balance of supply and demand and the desire to maximize profit are inapplicable concepts; the central equation that determines the amount of labor expended and the output produced is the equilibrium between the satisfaction of demand, on the one hand, and the drudgery of labor, on the other.[27] The monetary cost of labor is irrelevant, since the peasant does not use hired labor; on the other hand, the peasant works the land relatively few days in the year, so that where the supply of land is sufficient, one can always produce more by working longer or harder.[28] What limits the willingness to do so is the extent to which the advantage to be gained justifies the extra effort; this consideration may make the peasant insensitive to considerations that would carry great weight from a cost-effectiveness standpoint.[29]

Recent work has tended to find Chayanov's analysis more useful than classical analysis for describing the world of ancient agriculture. Chayanov was writing particularly about the economy of the self-sufficient peasant family, and he recognized that the analysis he developed described only a sector of the broader national economy. The national economy, as he freely admitted, included large sectors for which more orthodox economic analysis was appropriate, and he devoted attention not only to the peasant sector itself but also to the interface between it and other sectors. For all that, since subsistence agriculture[30] was a dominant, though sparsely documented, feature of ancient economic life, Chayanov's theories, barely noticed in the West until recently, have now come to exercise a signal influence.[31]

---

27. The problem that Chayanov was analyzing may be familiar to readers of novels as the problem with which Levin struggled in Tolstoy's *Anna Karenina*, and there is a certain similarity between Tolstoy's analysis and the economically much more sophisticated ideas of Chayanov. For a description of the situation out of which both analyses grew, see Thorner's remarks in Chayanov, xi–xiii.

28. Chayanov, 72–84. Chayanov (110–17) recognized that this fact of Russian peasant life would be less applicable in places where land was in short supply, as it surely was in ancient Greece.

29. See Chayanov (79): "It is exceedingly significant and entirely of a pattern that an increase in worker's output caused by an increment in numbers of consumers does not cause a parallel increase in well-being, and in some budget inquiries (Novgorod) *even leads to a reduction in it*" (emphasis in original). Cf. ibid. (80), "*The annual intensity of labor declines under the influence of better pay*" (emphasis in original)—again a result directly the opposite of that predicted by classical economics.

30. Whether it is properly called "*peasant* agriculture" is chiefly a matter of definition: Millett, "Hesiod," 90–93.

31. See, inter alia, Sahlins, *Stone Age Economics*, 87–92; De Neeve, 15; Gallant, 35. For its application to other societies, see the essays in Durrenberger, none of which deal with the classical world. Salisbury (88–89) notes that the data of Sahlins, "Intensity," do not confirm Chayanov's principle.

◉ USE VALUE AND EXCHANGE VALUE

I mentioned in chapter 1 that money may serve as a standard of value and that, indeed, many have seen this as being its essential defining feature. This plausible statement hides a great uncertainty as to precisely what constitutes the value of an object. It is clear to every sane adult that a fruit tree has, under normal circumstances, a higher value than a pebble; but why is that so? If money is a measure of value, precisely what is it measuring?

Aristotle recognized two sorts of value, one appropriate to the specific item itself and one not so.

> The use of every commodity is double. Both uses, it is true, belong to the thing, but not in the same way; rather, one is specific to the thing and one is not—as, for example, a shoe has a wearing use and an exchanging use. Both of these are uses of a shoe; and a person who exchanges with somebody who needs a shoe in exchange for money or food is using the shoe as a shoe, but not in its specific use, for it does not exist[32] for the sake of exchange. The same applies in the case of other commodities.[33]

In this passage, Aristotle is not developing a comprehensive theory of value; his observation is designed as a starting point for the distinction between "natural" exchange (whose goal, wealth, has a natural limit when the person's needs are fulfilled) and the unnatural exchange practiced by tradesmen, which seems to have no limit. His words, however, served as the basis for most of the discussion of the meaning of value before the advent of modern economics,[34] and since the first modern economists built on their predecessors, a good deal of his influence can still be detected today.[35]

The question of value, however, had already undergone a subtle change at the time that Aristotle was writing. Aristotle, who is bringing into question here the very legitimacy of market trade, does not consider exchange value to be the "true" value of an item; on the contrary, he considers the use

32. οὐ γὰρ ἀλλαγῆς ἕνεκεν γέγονε. The perfect γέγονε refers to its specific and permanent purpose; Aristotle is not unaware that it did indeed "come into existence" [ἐγένετο] for the sake of exchange, for the shoemaker, not the customer, made it. On the significance of the perfect, see Sicking and Stork, part 2, particularly their summary on pp. 168–70.

33. Arist. *Pol.* I 9.2–3 (1257a 6–14).

34. On this, see the excellent surveys of Langholm (on Aristotle's influence on scholastic economic theory) and Monroe.

35. See, for example, Meikle, 1, 15 n. 11, 180–200; Polanyi, *Great Transformation*, 54. Polanyi considered the distinction just quoted to be an insight deeper than any achieved by classical economists.

value to be natural and proper. Where market trade has become prevalent, however (and this must have been true already in Aristotle's time, as we can indeed see from the orators),[36] exchange value becomes the dominant concept—so much so that it is hard for people to understand by such a phrase as "that is worth a thousand dollars" anything other than "one could get a thousand dollars by selling that."

Where market trade is not the prevalent method of circulating goods, what a person means by an item's worth may be based on other standards. When Homer tells us that every tassel of the aegis was worth a hundred oxen,[37] he was not contemplating the possibility of the goddess's running low on cash and coming down to the marketplace to try to replenish her herds by selling a few tassels from her shield. In a nonmarket economy, there is no easy referent to establish the proper exchange value of an item. One may praise the value of an old woman by quoting the price that was paid for her when she was a young maiden.[38] Although her value has surely declined since then, nobody has estimated it in the interim, and she is not for sale. Even where actual exchange takes place, very many factors may intrude that would be unlikely to have much weight in the marketplace. "Tribesmen engaged in bargaining," Einzig writes, "have often no means of knowing how far the price they ask or offer corresponds to the correct price arising from the total supply and demand in their community. Very often theirs is an isolated transaction, and neither party knows how much the next door neighbour would give for their goods. As for the cost of production, any possible comparison between the working time spent on the one good and other is bound to be quite rudimentary."[39]

On the other hand, when speaking of value in the abstract, a person in a nonmarket economy may not think in terms of exchange at all. Many items, among them the most important, are not usually involved in any form of exchange.[40] We still use nonmonetary value terms in situations where ex-

---

36. I have in mind such passages as the evaluation of Demosthenes' father's estate quoted at the beginning of this chapter; there, the valuation of items seems to take for granted that they should be considered at their "market value," that is, the amount of money that one could receive in exchange for them. Even Polanyi (*Great Transformation*, 54) stated that Aristotle wrote "at a time when Greek economy had made itself dependent upon wholesale trading and loaned capital"—a statement so sweeping that many ancient historians would consider it to reflect too modernist a view of the Greek economy at the end of the classical period.

37. *Il.* 2.448–49.

38. *Od.* 1.431.

39. Einzig, 416.

40. Forde and Douglas, 25.

change is obviously inappropriate: the ritual statement of the referee at the beginning of a prizefight, "May the best man win," does not contemplate an evaluation of who is "best" in terms of the price that each would bring if sold as a slave (nor, for that matter, in moral terms). People whose lives are less dominated by commercial transactions than our own may slip from one criterion to another without noticing it. This is the mode of thought that allows Pindar to say that water is best but gold shines like a blazing fire in the night, standing out in a great man's wealth.[41] It is hard to think of a single criterion that could produce those two particular items for ranking one after the other.

● ECONOMIC THEORIES OF VALUE

With the rise of the market, the concept of price comes to dominate thought about value, so that modern economists' discussions of value deal essentially with the question, What determines the price at which a given commodity is bought and sold? In the investigation of this question, much light has been shed by economic thinkers, particularly over the last two and a quarter centuries. The parts played by *utility, need,*[42] and *scarcity*[43] have been threshed out;[44] a brilliant insight called *marginal utility* has helped explain such paradoxes as the fact that luxuries cost more than necessities;[45] a lasting controversy over the place of labor in creating value, never properly put to rest, continues to exercise economists and, on occasion, even politicians. These matters are extremely interesting for people who want to know how a monetary economy functions, and Greek thinkers had important and influential things to say about them, though modern economics, like modern biology and physics, has developed far beyond Aristotle. In spite of that, the

41. Pindar *Olympian* 1.1–2.

42. Both ideas originate with Aristotle's statement at *Eth. Nic.* V 5.11 (1133a 25–27) that "everything has to be measured by one thing . . . and this thing is in reality *chreia*, which holds everything together."

43. This idea, too, was helped along by the medieval translation of *chreia* as *indigentia*. See Langholm, 16, 39, 42–46. For the various translations of *chreia* into modern languages, see Langholm, 46–47 n. 25; "demand" first appears as the English translation in 1819, more than fifty years after Adam Smith's *Wealth of Nations*. For an attack on the idea that Aristotle was referring to demand in the modern sense, see Meikle, 28–42. As Meikle notes, Finley ("Aristotle," 8 n. 22) was already suspicious.

44. They are not—it should go without saying—agreed on by all economists: Marxist economists, in particular, give more credit to the labor theory of value that Marx favored, while functionalists tend to emphasize scarcity.

45. For a clear, concise, and readable description of marginal utility, see Whynes, 67–71.

discussion of the factors that go into price determination does not form part of this book, for their importance arises in a money economy, and the point at which the Greeks achieved a money economy is the point at which this study ends.

THE VALUE OF A COIN

If economists remain divided on the question of precisely what gives a commodity its value, there can hardly be a clear-cut definition of what gives a coin its value, for the value of a coin clearly depends on the value of a commodity—either the metal of which it is made or the commodities for which it can be exchanged. In point of fact there has been a vacillation throughout history between these two understandings of coinage. According to the first possibility, a coin is simply a measured piece of precious metal; the image or inscription on the coin is a guarantee of the weight (and usually the fineness) of the metal. By this understanding, a coin made of a base metal would be practically worthless and would reflect ill on the authority that issued it. According to the second possibility, the coin is merely a token, taken by a person in return for a valuable commodity in order to be exchanged for another such. Its worth has nothing to do with the substance of which it is made; as long as it is acceptable in the marketplace, it may be made of base metal or even, as the Chinese first discovered, of paper. Such money is known as *fiduciary money*; today, practically all coins are fiduciary money.

It is reasonable to presume that the first coins were produced not as tokens but as pieces of bullion of guaranteed weight and fineness.[46] Throughout the Greek world, coins were normally made of silver, at more or less precise weight and at the highest level of purity obtainable.[47] It was not virtue but economics that prevented Greek statesmen from debasing their coins: since no one state controlled the Greek world, a debased coinage, with no value outside of the boundaries of the issuing state, would have made it difficult or impossible for the citizens of that state to import the things they wanted. In times of dire need, fiduciary coins might be issued, like the debased Athenian coins about which Aristophanes complained in the Peloponnesian War;[48] and in the exception that proves the rule, the Ptolemies,

---

46. That was not true of China, where a coin's value depended from the beginning on its markings, not its weight. On the uniform fineness of the earliest coins, see p. 99.

47. Kraay, *Archaic and Classical*, 9–11.

48. Aristophanes *Frogs* 718–37.

who ruled over a large and generally autarkic empire, issued, in addition to gold and silver coins for foreign trade, bronze coins that circulated locally as a fiduciary currency.[49] The emperors of Rome, on the other hand, whose control over their economic area was enormous, could debase the currency at will to finance their expenditures, a procedure that eventually led, in the third century c.e., to an inflation that has no parallel in Greek history.[50]

◉ THE FUNGIBILITY OF MONEY

A point that must be stressed, and in which coin differed from earlier media of exchange or measures of value, was its fungibility: one coin was like another, and any coin could be exchanged for anything else. It was precisely this aspect of coinage, one that we take for granted, that made it possible to see a coin as we see money, as "the incarnation of economic value."[51] This way of seeing things, as I argued in chapter 1, was what was new in the concept of money that developed with coinage, but it took a long time for its implications to work themselves out. It was immediately obvious that a coin could be exchanged for wheat or for a pot. It took longer to discover that coins could buy power, victory, or the hearts of one's countrymen.[52]

◉ THE EMBEDDED ECONOMY

I have already mentioned that Polanyi insisted that all economies before the nineteenth century were embedded in their societies, relying on the structure of society to direct a person's desire for social standing into channels that would benefit the group as a whole. Since the work of Finley, ancient historians have generally accepted the idea that the Greek economy was embedded in its social institutions and that, in that fact, it was different from the modern economy. There has been, however, a good deal of confusion

---

49. See Mørkholm, 295. There may have been some precedent for this in the debased tetrobols of Macedon, for which see Kraay, *Archaic and Classical*, 142–43.

50. This is not to say that inflation was impossible or unknown in Greece. Heichelheim (2:139; 3:31, 33, 36–38) detailed what he took to be secular trends, though other scholars, most notably Reger, have doubted that any such wide-ranging movements can be identified. The debasement of coinage, however, permits inflation on a massive scale that no mere evolutionary development can match.

51. The phrase is that of Simmel, 101.

52. On this last—and on its novelty even as late as the end of the fifth century b.c.e.—see Xen. *Mem.* 2.5.2–3, where the value of a person's friendship is given a cash equivalent.

about exactly what that embedding meant and how thorough it was. Austin and Vidal-Naquet, as already noted, saw embedding as a general feature of the Greek economy throughout its existence; Tandy sees a movement toward disembedding in the eighth-century archaeological remains and in Hesiod;[53] for Leslie Kurke, Pindar is already trying to "reembed" the economy in the early fifth century;[54] for Edmund M. Burke, we find only the "onset of disembedding" in late fourth-century Athens.[55] None of these scholars would doubt that the economy of Lycurgan Athens was very different from that of Homer, Hesiod, or Pindar; their disagreement seems not so much to be an argument about the facts of the Greek economy as a haziness about exactly what constitutes an embedded economy.

The salient characteristic of a disembedded economy is probably *the anonymity of economic transactions.* When I buy an item by clicking on an icon at a Web site, pay for it by entering my credit-card number, and receive the item by parcel post, I generally do not know at all with whom I am transacting business. Even this transaction is not entirely anonymous: the owner of the Web site has probably recorded my name or card number, may notice if I am a regular customer, and treat me accordingly. Nevertheless, the extent to which such a transaction can be subordinated to noneconomic social norms is minimal; it is a very different procedure from the potlatch by which a Chinook man would give away everything he had, gaining thereby a social status that was worth more to him[56] than all his physical wealth ever could be.

The truth is that every economy, including our own, exhibits a certain amount of embedding in the social milieu. "Market activity," writes Thomas Rawski in a brief but persuasive discussion, "does not occur in isolation but depends on institutions ... [It] also reflects ideas and values. If Japanese feel that prestigious corporations should never dismiss long-term employees, while Americans believe that it is fair for hard-pressed businesses to dismiss employees but not to reduce wages for the remaining workers, these contrasting visions of equity and property surely leave their mark on employment

---

53. Tandy, 112–38, 214, 230–31. Tandy is speaking only of the first stages of disembedding; he considers a truly dominant market system not to have existed before fourth-century Athens (124–25).

54. Kurke, *Traffic,* 225–56.

55. Burke, "Economy," 201.

56. On the potlatch, see the essays in McFeat, 72–133. A thoroughgoing formalist could see the advantage gained as an economic one, because the people who received gifts, now obligated to the donor, would give him help with his livelihood as well as with his social status; but to see the potlatch as an economic exchange is to narrow our focus to the point of myopia.

arrangements in Japanese and American companies."[57] The pursuit of personal economic gain is not entirely absent even in primitive societies; the pursuit of social position, even through the sacrifice of wealth, is present and even prominent in the most market-dominated of societies. The question of embeddedness is not an either-or question but a question of degree.

The relativity of embeddedness makes it possible for different scholars to see disembedding at virtually every period of Greek history. There is no doubt that economic transactions tended, as Greek society developed from the archaic age to the classical and the Hellenistic, to be more a matter of immediate mutual economic benefit and less a form of discharging social obligations. The invention of coinage certainly facilitated this change, which may, however, have been propelled more by simple population growth than by any technological or cultural development. We can see transactions becoming less embedded as early as Homer and Hesiod; we can still see coined wealth being spent—even lavished—for the achievement of social status down through the liturgies that supported the Athenian democracies and through euergetism, the private expenditure for the public welfare that continued and flourished throughout the Hellenistic period.[58]

57. Rawski, "Economics," 9–12. This section of Rawski's essay contains enough examples to convince the most hidebound believer in laissez-faire that there is no truly disembedded economy. Indeed, Polanyi himself (*Great Transformation*, 3–4) said that there could not be for any great length of time.

58. See p. 128.

Money before Coinage

The Ancient Near East

IN THE BRONZE AGE, the Near East was by no means what an economist would consider a moneyless society. All ancient Near Eastern societies had a conventional standard of value, and many had a standard of payment, usually precious metals or a specified grain. The standard of payment was always "primitive money," never coin,[1] and it did not always perform all of the functions that coin was later to perform. The economic details varied from place to place and from time to time, but Egypt, Mesopotamia, and the Levant had all reached high levels of economic sophistication before the Greeks did. If Greece was the cradle of coinage and Lydia its birthplace, the societies of the Near East were its ancestors. A short[2] survey will show the economic background in which primitive money developed more and more into something very closely approaching modern money.

---

1. See appendix 2.

2. Scandalously short, certainly, to an Egyptologist or Assyriologist, but giving a proper account of the economies involved would require a digression of truly Herodotean proportions. My intention is only to mention those factors that were significant in the development of the concept of money.

○ EGYPT

Our economic information about Egypt before the introduction of money comes chiefly from the time of the New Kingdom (i.e., the Eighteenth through Twentieth Dynasties), about 1567–1085 B.C.E. Information for the centuries between this time and the Greek archaic age is less abundant, but what we have indicates that the picture I shall sketch here still obtained in the seventh century, when coins were being invented.[3] Egypt was at this period—and aspired to be at all periods—a vast empire whose population was supported chiefly by peasant agriculture, with a governmental class supported by a wide-ranging redistributive system. Produce came to Pharaoh's storehouses in huge amounts and left those storehouses to accomplish Pharaoh's purposes.

One important purpose, peculiar to Egypt and begun immediately at the beginning of a pharaoh's reign, was the preparation of his monumental tomb. The mortuary temple of Rameses II (built far from his actual tomb, in the eventually vain hope of misleading grave robbers) contained storage space for some 16,522 cubic meters of grain, enough to support a medium-sized city for a year.[4] The builders of the actual tombs were supported by the state—at a level that provided more applicants for the jobs than there were positions[5]—in a hidden workers' village. Like modern soldiers, they enjoyed regular rations:

> Grain ration of the gang of the 3rd month of winter: the 3 captains, each one 3½ khar,[6] makes 10½ khar, 39 men, each one 3 khar, makes 117 khar . . . [7]

The workers were supplied with grain, fish, vegetables, water, wood, and pottery; with occasional issues of dates, cakes, and beer; and with periodic bonuses including sesame oil, salt, natron,[8] and beef. A certain

---

3. See R. Parker, 49–52 (= P. Brooklyn 16.205). Cf. Menu, 255–57.

4. Kemp, *Ancient Egypt*, 192, fig. 68. Cf., however, Kemp himself, "Granary Buildings," 131, for some of the difficulties of such a calculation.

5. Bierbrier, 27.

6. A *khar* is approximately forty-eight liters: Wolfgang Helck in *LDÄ* III, col. 1201, s.v. "Maße und Gewichte."

7. Černý, *Community of Workmen*, 236 (= O. DM 141, 1–2), with references to many similar texts.

8. A naturally occurring sodium salt, among whose uses were mummification and ritual purification. Rolf Gundlach in *LDÄ* IV, col. 358, s.v. "Natron."

amount of clothing was issued, though not enough to fill all the community's requirements.[9]

Another of Pharaoh's important purposes—a purpose that made the strong centralized monarchy so essential to Egypt—was to hoard stores of produce that could maintain the population during years when the Nile flood was insufficient. Needless to say, these stores served also to support Pharaoh, his household, his army, and his bureaucracy.[10] Money was not needed for these transactions. Taxes were collected in kind and recorded with no concern for their comparative value:

> Things exacted, the impost of all the people and serf-laborers . . . which King Usermare-Meriamon,[11] life, prosperity, health, the Great God, gave to their treasuries, storehouses and granaries as their yearly dues: . . .

Copper	26,320 *deben*[12]
Royal linen, *mek*-linen . . . various garments	3,722
Yarn, *deben*	3,795
Incense, honey, oil, various jars	1,047
Shedeh and wine, various jars	25,405
Silver . . . for the divine offerings	3,606 *deben*, 1 *kidet*
Barley . . . 16-fold *heket*[13]	309,950
Vegetables, bundles	24,650
Flax bales	64,000
Water-fowl . . .	289,530
Bulls, bullocks . . . of the herds of Egypt	847
Bulls, bullocks . . . of the lands of Syria	19[14]

Although it lived much longer than some of its modern imitators, this vast system of state appropriation and redistribution was not as all-encompassing

---

9. Bierbrier, 40. This was of course, a highly favored village.

10.˙ Kemp, *Ancient Egypt*, chap. 3.

11. Rameses III, ca. 1186–1154 B.C.E.

12. A *deben* of silver is about 13.6 grams; a *deben* of copper is twice as heavy. A *kidet* or *kite* is one-tenth of a *deben*: Wolfgang Helck in *LDÄ* III, col. 1202, s.v. "Maβe und Gewichte."

13. One one-hundredth of a *khar*, that is, slightly less than half a liter (*LDÄ* III, col. 1201).

14. P. Harris I, col. 12, quoted here from Breasted, 4: nos. 227–29; Grandet has produced a voluminous and up-to-date edition, in which this passage will be found at 1:237–38. This famous papyrus is one of our principal sources for the economic history of Egypt in the Eighteenth and Nineteenth Dynasties. The list of taxes from the tomb of Rekhmire (see n. 31 in this chapter) is similarly innocent of evaluation.

as its masters pretended. A system of regional government and the endow-
ment of religious centers that played a significant part in local administration
introduced a considerable degree of local adaptation, variation, and, it must
be admitted, confusion.[15] Local magnates could deal with the needs of their
localities:

> I was a worthy citizen who acted with his arm. I was a great pillar in
> the Theban nome,[16] a man of standing in the Southland. I nourished
> Imyotru[17] in years of misery. Though four hundred men were in straits
> through it, I did not seize a man's daughter, nor did I seize his field. I
> acquired ten herds of goats, with herdsmen for each herd. I acquired
> two herds of cattle, one herd of asses. I acquired all kinds of small
> cattle. I made a 50-cubit boat, another of 30 cubits. I gave Upper
> Egyptian barley to Iuni, to Hefat, after Imyotru had been supplied.
> While the Theban nome traveled [downstream] and upstream,[18] I
> never allowed Imyotru to travel downstream and upstream to another
> nome.[19]

Even with local structures to complement it and compete with it, the
bureaucracy can hardly have supplied all the wants of every Egyptian. In the
community of workers that built the Pharaohs' tombs, the relatively well
supplied workers did a good deal of work on the side,[20] both to provide for
exchange among themselves and to have something to take down to the
riverbank for trade.[21]

Private deals were sometimes simply swaps, with no clear statement of
value.

> What the draughtsman Neferhotep gave to Haremwia: one wooden
> stela of Nefertari, while he gave to me one chest in exchange for it. Also I
> decorated two coffins for him . . . and he made one bed for me.[22]

---

15. Kemp, *Ancient Egypt,* 235–38. Kemp's chapter 6, mistitled "The Birth of Economic Man"
(for he seems to consider "economic man" to be universal), is the best capsule survey of the
ancient Egyptian economic system known to me, and I have based much of my discussion on it.

16. One of the administrative subdivisions of Egypt.

17. His town.

18. In search of food.

19. Lichtheim, 1:89.

20. Barbara Lesko, 20–23.

21. Andrea McDowell, 46; Kemp, *Ancient Egypt,* 252–55.

22. Bierbrier, 60.

Credit might be extended, though we generally know about it only in cases where there were difficulties with collection:

> Reminder of the workman ———— to the mistress ————. The scribe Amennakhte, your husband, took from me a coffin saying that he would give the calf for it, but he has not given it down to this day. I mentioned it to Pe'okhē and he said: "Give me a bed in addition to it and I will bring to you the calf when it has grown up," and I gave him the bed. There is neither the coffin nor the bed down to this day. If you give the calf, send it, and if there is no calf, send the bed and the coffin (back).[23]

In this case, the calf was the price of the coffin, and raising the calf to maturity was the price of the bed. It is unlikely that the values of the items on the two sides of the trade were carefully calculated in silver or copper equivalents; one person needed a coffin, the other one needed a calf, and they traded. This is the sort of barter that Mill envisaged, although the possibility of credit has made it more practical than he realized.

We find, moreover, exchanges where calculation of value seems to be taken for granted:

> Year 17, first month of the summer season, day . . . under the Majesty of king of Upper and Lower Egypt, Lord of the Two Lands Usima'rē'miamūn, son of Rē' Ra'messes-ḥek-Ōn.[24] On that day the workman Menna gave the pot of fresh fat to the chief of Medjay[25] Mentmose who said: I will pay for it to you in barley from this brother of mine who will be responsible. He is my guarantor. May Prē' keep you in health, so he said to me. I have reported him three times in the court before the scribe of the Tomb Amennakhte, (but) he has not given me anything to this day. And behold, I reported him to him in year 3, second month of the summer season, day 5, of the Majesty of king of Upper and Lower Egypt, Lord of the Two Lands Ḥekma'rē'-setepnamūn, son of Rē', Lord of appearances Ra'messes-

---

23. Černý, *Community of Workmen*, 351 (= O. Berlin 12630).

24. Again Rameses III. The differences in transliteration throughout this chapter reflect differences among the translators.

25. A formerly nomadic people who served as a sort of police force: Černý, *Community of Workmen*, chap. 20.

ma'aty-miamūn,[26] that is 11 years (later). He took an oath by the Lord, saying: If I do not pay him for his pot before year 3, third month of the summer season, last day, I shall receive a hundred blows of stick and shall be liable to pay the double, so he said before the three domestic captains, the external agents and the whole gang.[27]

Here, Mentmose's promise "I will pay for it to you in barley" is quoted without any mention of how much money was to be paid. The plaintiff or the scribe who wrote down his complaint must have presumed that the official to whom the complaint was made would know or could at least easily ascertain the barley equivalent of a pot of fresh fat.

The Egyptians were capable of much more sophisticated transactions. Houses and animals were regularly sold for a price quoted in silver or copper. In reality, however, it was rarely silver or copper that changed hands. Somewhere around the time of Rameses II, in the thirteenth century B.C.E., a housewife by the name of Erēnofre deposited in court as follows:

> In year 15 . . . the merchant Rē'ia approached me with the Syrian slave Gemniḥiamente, she being (still) a girl, and he said to me: Buy this girl, and give me a price for her. So he said to me. And I purchased the girl and gave him a [price] for her. I will now state in front of the authorities the price that I gave for her:
>
> 1 shroud of Upper-Egyptian cloth, makes 5 *kite* of silver;
> 1 blanket of Upper-Egyptian cloth, makes 3 1/3 *kite* of silver;
> 1 *djayt*-garment of Upper-Egyptian cloth, makes 4 *kite* of silver;
> 3 *sdy*-garments of fine Upper-Egyptian cloth, makes 5 *kite* of silver;
> 1 dress of fine Upper-Egyptian cloth, makes 5 *kite* of silver . . .

Erēnofre continues to enumerate various other items taken from friends and neighbors—some bronze vessels, beaten copper, a jar of honey, and shirts—to make up the total price of four *deben* and one *kite* "of silver in objects of all kinds."[28] Here, we have elements that we had not seen previously: a merchant, a price calculated in silver (other documents use copper or grain

---

26. Rameses IV, ca. 1154–1148 B.C.E.
27. Černý, *Community of Workmen*, 282–83 (= O. Chicago 12073).
28. Gardiner, "Lawsuit," 141–42 (= P. Cairo 65739); Černý, "Prices," 907.

as a measure of value),[29] and a list of commodities every one of which has a recognized price. Parallels could be multiplied, and have been.[30]

Erēnofre was living at the height of pharaonic power, when the "redistributive" powers of the royal palace were enormous. The detailed (if partial) tax list from the tomb of Rekhmire, the chief minister of Thutmose III more than two hundred years earlier,[31] gives us some idea of what a pharaoh's power was, and it is clear that the power of Rameses II was not less than that of his predecessors—nor, for that matter, was it less than that of his successor, Rameses III, for whose reign the Harris papyrus shows that the redistributive system was alive and well. Nevertheless, the king did not supply the needs of his subjects so completely as to make household trade or professional traders obsolete.

For all that, we are still in the world of barter. To get the price she had offered to pay, Erēnofre threw together anything on which she could lay her hands. There does not seem to have been much surplus in her own house: one shroud, one blanket, one apiece of two different articles of clothing and three of a third is the sort of inventory that suggests to us a woman looking through her closet to see what she can part with. A purse full of coins or even a household store of silver, into which she could dip to produce the four *deben* and one *kite* of silver that she had agreed to pay for her slave girl, had no place in Erēnofre's mental universe. Even of everyday goods, her house did not have much surplus.

From her neighbors, however, in addition to one apiece of some common household items, we find ten shirts from "the steward of the house of Amūn, Teti," and "from the *wēb*-priest Ḥuy-Pinḥas, 10 *deben* of beaten copper"— quantities that suggest that in the temples, at least, there were surplus articles held for trade. Those who could afford to do so engaged in true commercial manufacture, producing items for trade, at least on a small scale.

> You must get Hety's son Nakht and Sinebniut to go down to the town of Perhaa and cultivate for [us] 20 (?) arouras[32] of land on lease. It is with the cloth—which has been woven where you are—that they

29. Janssen (514–23) discusses the observable criteria for when one standard was used and when another in the Deir el Medina documents.

30. The major work on this subject remains Janssen, though his work deals only with documents from a single (and singular) village.

31. Breasted 2: nos. 663–762.

32. An *aroura* = ten thousand square cubits = 2,756.5 square meters: Wolfgang Helck in *LDÄ* III, col. 1200, s.v. "Maβe und Gewichte."

shall secure its lease. If, however, they have gotten a good value in exchange for the emmer which is in Perhaa, they shall apply it there also so that you no longer be concerned with the cloth about which I had said, "Weave it! After it has been evaluated in the village of Nebeseyet, they should take it and rent farmland for what it (the cloth) is worth."[33]

Great houses often had traders—never people of high status—whose job it was to manage such exchanges.[34] They had an eye out for an advantageous trade: "Do not drink water in the house of a merchant," 'Onchsheshonqy advises his son; "he will charge you for it."[35] In the grave-robbing scandal of the Twentieth Dynasty, whose investigation has left us much valuable information, we find traders receiving items of gold and silver, presumably as middlemen for the poor robbers, in whose hands such items would have been suspicious.[36] The wealthy houses did not have to bother "making up a price"; they often paid in real gold or silver.[37] The very fact of grave robbery—apparently an established profession, if not an everyday or a respectable one—implies that the robbers could count on finding people who could exchange the very varied items that they would take from the tombs for other things of more value to themselves.[38]

Trade was developed in ancient Egypt far beyond anything that Mill would have imagined possible within a system of barter. Certain ideas that are basic to money were present: that everything can be valued according to a single standard, that items have a regular price, and the use of precious metals as a standard. People who traded could tell a good price from a bad one. The letters of Hekanakht, a prosperous farmer of the Eleventh Dynasty,[39] are full of attention to the subject: "If, however, they have gotten a good value in exchange for the emmer . . .";[40] "Have then 20 arouras of land

---

33. Wente, no. 68 (= P. Hekanakht 1), pp. 58–59.

34. Kemp, *Ancient Egypt*, 244, 257, and note 259: "Trading was akin in status to making sandals. Rich people enjoyed the benefits of trading but did not pursue it as an occupation, whilst the idea that the activity could bring wealth and position on its own terms was literally unthinkable to all concerned. There were no merchant princes just as there were no princes of sandal-makers. Officials—'scribes'—maintained the monopoly of power, prestige and wealth. It was not a conspiracy. The attitudes were held, so one imagines, unthinkingly."

35. Glanville, 39; cf. n. 194 on the translation.

36. Peet, *Great Tomb-Robberies*, 90.

37. Kemp, *Ancient Egypt*, 257.

38. For the items taken by thieves, see Phillips, 163–65.

39. He lived under Sankhare Mentuhotep, ca. 1998–1986 B.C.E.

40. Wente, no. 68 (= P. Hekanakht 1), p. 59, quoted earlier.

cultivated for us on lease . . . (paying) in copper, in clothing, in northern barley, or [in] any[thing] else, but only if you shall have gotten a good value there for oil or for whatever else."[41] In another passage, he apparently advises selling a bull whose price has risen by half.[42] There is surely a sense in which we can call Egypt a monetized society, at least within the framework of primitive money that I sketched in chapter 1.

Still, however, we have not arrived at the concept of money as we know it.[43] The evaluation of items in terms of copper, silver, and gold in no way required that those items actually be used for the trade: the various functions of money had not yet coalesced in ancient Egypt. Even where precious metal was hoarded, and even when it was prepared in forms convenient for hoarding (rings, coils, bars), the Egyptians do not seem to have bothered to prepare it according to any regular weight;[44] when the time came to trade, it could be weighed on the spot. Much less do we have the equivalence of wealth with the precious metals themselves. Hekanakht, just quoted, had to have his cloth brought to the village to be evaluated, and as we saw at the beginning of this chapter, enumerations of treasure emanating from the royal house describe each item (often along with pictures or sculptures) without any thought of calculating its silver equivalent. The Egyptian economy was sufficiently developed to maintain a society that knew some long periods of stability, and it managed to maintain its sense of continuity even through disruptions. It did this without a unified sense of money as wealth. The great wealth of Egypt was normally in the hands of the state and the temples, and it was not held or even calculated in money.

BABYLONIA AND ASSYRIA

The history and culture of Egypt, though by no means static or uniform, nevertheless lend themselves to connected narrative and general descriptions; both the relative strength of the central government over long periods of time and the cultural continuity of the lower Nile Valley produced a society that we describe as "Egyptian." Such a claim cannot be asserted so

---

41. Ibid., no. 69 (= P. Hekanakht 2), p. 62.

42. Baer, 19.

43. This was the clear conclusion of Janssen (545–50), though he ends with a salutary warning against drawing broader conclusions: "For a more profound study of Egyptian 'money' the time does not yet seem to be ready. Far more material is required to prevent our falling into the trap of preconceived theories which are so widespread among students of the origin of money."

44. See the weight graph of the el-Till hoard in Kemp, *Ancient Egypt*, 245, fig. 82; and contrast the practice in Old Babylonia, below, p. 45.

categorically for Mesopotamia. In the valleys of the Tigris and the Euphrates, one state succeeded another as various indigenous dynasties established a greater or lesser hegemony and as various foreign conquerors or immigrants had more or less influence. These states do not have a single continuous history. Many factors are constant: the primacy of agriculture as the basis of the economy, the organization around greater or smaller urban centers, and a scribal tradition whose astonishing conservatism survived the rise and fall of empires and even the demise of the language in which it arose.[45] Nevertheless, one cannot presume that there is a continuous economic history of Mesopotamia: what was true of one age and one culture was not necessarily true of another. Were I to describe each of the various states that arose, I should have to devote an entire book to background before returning to my story. I shall leave, of necessity, many things unsaid. The reader is warned not to presume that an innovation mentioned in one age must have continued into later ages; things did not necessarily work that way in Mesopotamia.

If Egypt was of all ancient countries the most self-sufficient, Mesopotamia, on the contrary, was a land dependent upon trade from the earliest times, and trade was developed there to a high degree. The river valleys in which the great civilizations developed were entirely alluvial soil washed down by rivers, chiefly the Tigris and the Euphrates. The soil was rich and productive, particularly when irrigated by man-made canals, but it was utterly lacking in stones and metals; nor were there any trees to speak of except date palms and poplars, which are not appropriate for timber. Buildings could be made out of mud bricks, but agricultural implements could only be made by importing metals, stones, and timber from the neighboring areas, in exchange for the barley, dates, and sesame oil that the plain produced in abundance.[46]

From at least the end of the third millennium B.C.E., probably before the first Greeks ever entered the peninsula that bears their name, Mesopotamian

---

45. For a forceful argument for the essential unity of Mesopotamian civilization, see Oppenheim, *Letters*, 1–53, and van de Mieroop, *Ancient Mesopotamian City*, 7–9. Note, however, that Oppenheim does not deny the contrast with the unity of Egyptian history; he uses "the term 'Mesopotamian civilization,' . . . just as we may use the term 'European civilization' . . . [which] emphasizes its inherent unity without minimizing the diversity that the several distinct regional formulations and the multiphasic development of that civilization produced within the geographical and temporal limitations mentioned" (1–2).

46. Leemans, *Merchant*, 1. Van de Mieroop (*Ancient Mesopotamian City*, 30–31) doubts that long-distance trade was as indispensable as is generally asserted, but he does not deny that it was an important feature of Mesopotamian life throughout the historical period.

merchants and functionaries estimated the value of each item in silver, gold, or barley, and the evidence seems incontrovertible that these items at least sometimes functioned not simply as theoretical standards, as they did in Egypt, but as true media of exchange, being taken by one party to a trade not because he wanted them for himself but because they were generally acceptable as payment to buy something else from somebody else.[47] The importance of exchange is also indicated by the introduction, by royal edict, of standard measures: "I made the copper bariga-measure and standardized it at 60 silas. I made the copper seah-measure, and standardized it at 10 silas . . ."[48]

The actual relationship between silver and barley was not a simple one; sometimes one was used, sometimes the other.[49] Obviously, silver is more convenient for large transactions and barley for small ones, but this is not the whole story.[50] There seem to have been times and situations when prices were calculated in silver but paid in barley or other commodities, and other times and other situations when the opposite was the case. From the early second millennium, the temples and palaces tended to keep their treasure in silver, necessitating middlemen whose profits were turned into silver;[51] but this does not mean that silver became a universal currency. During the third dynasty of Ur,[52] the possession of silver does seem to have been spread rather broadly throughout the population, and even accounts kept in barley may represent payments in silver;[53] workmen, however, were regularly paid in barley, with a ration of wool once a year and other items when there was a surplus or on special occasions.[54] For many transactions, for which the accounts at Ur reached a high level of sophistication, balanced silver ac-

---

47. The attempt of Karl Polanyi ("Marketless Trading") to deny the existence of primitive market trade, a theory that had until recently carried the field in analysis of the primitive Greek economy, has fared much worse among Assyriologists: see Veenhof, 348–400; Muhly, Review, 174–75; Yoffee, 4–6; Powell, *"Wir müssen,"* 8–11. For a recent judicious overview of the attitudes of Assyriologists toward the issues discussed in chapter 2, see van de Mieroop, *Cuneiform Texts,* 108–23.

48. Roth, 16. The inscription is from the laws of Ur-Nammu (sometimes attributed to his son, Shulgi), king of Ur in the late third millennium B.C.E.

49. For a brief overview, see Ebeling in *Reallexikon der Assyriologie* III, p. 198, s.v. "Geld."

50. Powell, *"Wir müssen,"* 14–15.

51. Van de Mieroop, *Ancient Mesopotamian City,* 157.

52. Ca. 2100–2000 B.C.E. For Mesopotamian dates of the third and second century B.C.E. I follow the "middle chronology," conveniently available in Hallo and Simpson; since all the dates under debate are in any event well before the invention of coinage, the precise chronology does not concern us.

53. Lambert, 80–82; and see now Steinkeller, pp. 92–97, 133, and van de Mieroop, *Society and Enterprise,* 209.

54. Waetzoldt, 118.

counts were kept, although we cannot be sure whether the merchants involved actually used silver.[55]

A few centuries later, during the Old Babylonian period,[56] silver seems to have been a rarity among the general population, so that prices quoted in silver may well have been paid in other media.[57] Loans were made sometimes in silver, sometimes in grain or even other commodities;[58] the interest on a silver loan might be a measure of barley,[59] and the principal itself might be repayable in a commodity other than the one borrowed.[60] In Ur during this period, we find the merchant Ea-nāṣir amassing the capital he needed by collecting contributions of silver rings, baskets, or headbands.[61] This is not quite the way Erēnofre put together the money to buy a slave girl, but it is clear that in Ea-nāṣir's mind, the need for capital did not immediately translate into a need for a given weight of silver. From a similar date but a different place, a merchant from Mari asks his employer either to send him five minas of silver to Emar or to pay an agent in Mari sixty *ugar* of barley for the same amount of silver.[62] In Ur at this same period, we find silver being turned into coils by weight—overwhelmingly, though not exclusively, five shekels—although the texts make it clear that a good deal of leeway was allowed for variations in the weight.[63] Both the high value—five shekels of silver would buy a good deal of barley—and the inexact weights make it clear that we are dealing not with "currency" but merely with a convenient way to keep silver available for exchange. These coils do not seem to occur in later periods.[64]

In the Neo-Assyrian period, during the first half of the first millennium, first copper and then silver were used as standards, and bronze also makes a

---

55. Snell, 58–60.

56. Ca. 2000–1600 B.C.E.

57. Nemet-Nejat, 267.

58. Skaist, 104–7 and passim.

59. Ibid., 109–13.

60. Ibid., 45 n. 47.

61. See Van de Mieroop, *Society and Enterprise*, 137.

62. Van de Mieroop, *Ancient Mesopotamian City*, 170–71 (= Oppenheim, *Letters*, no. 37, pp. 98–99); cf. Durand, 160–63. The merchant is presuming a higher price for barley in Mari than he could get at Emar, which is presumably the reason that he was in Emar in the first place.

63. At any rate, this is what I conclude from Powell, "Contribution," 216–17, where the real weight is often either more or less than the intended weight and the authors of the texts were aware of the difference. Powell (217–18; cf. 228–30) attributes the lack of precision to the fact that the silver would at any rate be weighed at the time of exchange; I would also surmise that its uses were not necessarily in the kind of commercial exchange for which small variations were significant: see below pp. 183, 207.

64. Powell, "Contribution," 219.

brief appearance,[65] but payments were normally in kind;[66] somewhat later, in Babylon of the seventh and sixth centuries B.C.E., the situation seems to have changed again, with the texts specifying carefully the kind of silver to be paid.[67] Farmers, of course, would regularly pay with agricultural products rather than precious metals: "In the month Addar he will repay the silver in its principal amount. He will repay it entirely from his onion-patch."[68] There is much work still to be done before we can understand why a given document speaks in terms of silver, barley, tin, or dates and whether in each case the substance mentioned should be considered a currency or merely a commodity,[69] but there is no doubt that silver, barley, and sometimes other items performed monetary functions in Mesopotamia.

The most thoroughly commercial set of documents we have are those from Kültepe (ancient Kanesh) in Anatolia, dating from the Old Assyrian period in the nineteenth century B.C.E. and written in the Old Assyrian dialect. Some fifteen thousand tablets, most still unpublished,[70] show the activities of a dynamic colony of Assyrian businessmen, engaged in an active and profit-oriented trade, chiefly designed to procure silver and gold for the "houses" (moderns are tempted to call them "firms") whose agents traded in Kanesh. Their use of precious metals was certainly chiefly commercial,[71] and this particular colony in this particular era was surely using silver in a way that we would call monetary and, in fact, downright capitalistic, even though, as we shall see, there were steps in the development of money that had not been taken.

That the merchants of Kanesh were using silver as money is not simply a modern definition; the traders themselves spoke in terms that were unmistakably terms of money purchase, not of swapping. In swapping, each side gives a commodity; in purchase as we practice it, only one side (the seller) gives a commodity, while the other side gives "money," something taken not for its intrinsic value but because it will be acceptable in trade. An Old Assyrian never said, "I will buy silver in exchange for my slave,"[72] although

---

65. Radner, 129, 139–54.

66. A. K. Grayson in *CAH*³ III, part 2, p. 215.

67. Oppenheim, *Ancient Mesopotamia*, 87; cf. Veenhof, 360.

68. Van de Mieroop, *Ancient Mesopotamian City*, 207, from Wunsch, 2: p. 103, no. 124, a late Babylonian text.

69. See the comments of Skaist, 31–32.

70. Larsen (*City-State*, 50–55) gives a brief description of these documents and the circumstances of their discovery and publication; the number fifteen thousand is from Kuhrt, 20.

71. Veenhof (349–51), against Polanyi ("Marketless Trading").

72. Veenhof, 359–60.

he might say, "I will buy silver in exchange for my copper."[73] It is now clear that there were instances many hundreds of years before Homer where Assyrians, at least, saw their exchanges as sales of a commodity for money, not as symmetrical exchanges.[74]

Markets, in the sense of fixed places for retail trade, certainly existed in ancient Mesopotamia; in fact, Pryor's cross-cultural survey notes that "few societies have ever been found that have no type of market exchange at all."[75] At Ur, agricultural products were sold in the harbor, and archaeological remains suggest the existence of retail trade, though no texts record it.[76] The Old Assyrian documents from Kanesh speak of prices at the *kārum*, the "quay" (more precisely, the quarter set for foreign traders),[77] and in some of them, the use of *maḫīrum* to designate a place where trade took place seems unambiguous.[78] In the Old Babylonian period, too, there were fixed places for buying and selling,[79] and there was apparently a "Market Gate" at Babylon itself.[80] A thousand years later, Assurbanipal, king of Assyria, brags about the cheap price that camels brought "at the Market Gate" in his land; a Neo-Babylonian document mentions barley being sold there.[81] These marketplaces do not seem to have dominated the economic life of their cities as the agora dominated the Athenian economy, nor is it likely that any Mesopotamian market offered the variety of goods on which Athens prided itself;[82] but Polanyi's complete denial of the existence of markets in the Near East[83] is no longer maintained, even by his supporters.[84]

Not only marketplaces but market prices—that is, commonly accepted prices for certain goods that fluctuated with supply and demand—existed

73. Kienast, no. 32 (p. 47). The writer had obtained the copper by trading tin for it, apparently by barter with no "medium of exchange" between them. Similarly, the Old Babylonian document summarized in Leemans, *Letters,* 194–95, speaks at one point (§5) of buying silver for gold, in the next section of selling gold for silver.

74. Veenhof, 359–60.

75. Pryor, 110.

76. Van de Mieroop, *Society and Enterprise,* 200.

77. So Larsen, *City-State,* 230–41.

78. Veenhof, 389–400.

79. Renger, 113.

80. Powell, "*Wir müssen,*" 9–10.

81. Röllig, 289.

82. Though the range of merchandise was by no means contemptible: ibid., 292–94.

83. Polanyi, "Marketless Trading" and "Ports of Trade."

84. Oppenheim, *Ancient Mesopotamia,* 128–29; Renger, 113. One of Polanyi's chief arguments was the *mot* attributed by Herodotus to Cyrus, king of Persia, which I quote on p. 177. Such a comment would hardly be taken today as an unproblematic source of information for the entire Near East: see, in general, Edith Hall, 56–100.

in ancient Mesopotamia. Merchants knew what the items they had could fetch, and no less than the Egyptians, they could tell a good price from a poor one.[85] There is evidence of price fluctuation as far back as the third dynasty of Ur,[86] and long-term fluctuations that are by no means negligible can be observed in the price of barley from the twenty-fifth century B.C.E. through the fifth.[87] Royal decrees as far back as Hammurabi and before attempted to regulate wages and prices,[88] and kings boasted (we cannot tell how honestly) of the low prices in their prosperous reigns.[89] By the late Babylonian period, astronomical records also recorded what kinds of produce a shekel would buy at the time of each entry.[90] Scarcity regularly

---

85. Silver (74), citing Kienast, no. 32 (see n. 73 in the present chapter), writes: "Along the same line, a merchant in Anatolia informs a business associate that the price of copper (in terms of silver) has been driven up by the arrival from Ebla of numerous copper-seeking merchants. He adds: 'Within the next ten days they will have exhausted its (the palace's) copper. I shall then buy silver (that is, sell copper) and send it to you.'" From Silver's way of quoting the text, one might have concluded that the merchant in question was holding out for the higher price that he could get when the palace had no more copper to sell, in which case he had quite a clear grasp of the law of supply and demand; but it is at least as likely that Kienast is correct in stating that he had to wait because he was legally or politically forbidden from competing with the palace as long as the latter was still selling. Nor is it correct that the merchant states that the price "has been driven up." He says that the Eblaites are buying it at a certain price, which we—and surely he and his associate—can see is a very high one, but this is not at all what Silver makes of it. If the price had "been driven up," that would mean that there was a regular set of copper buyers, all of whom were now paying more to compete with the Eblaites, by the law of supply and demand. But the merchant neither says nor implies any such thing. The Eblaites came with a lot of silver and needed a lot of copper; other copper purchasers, if there were any, may simply have waited quietly for a better opportunity or bought some other metal instead. In general, Silver (73–144) attacks Polanyi's theses point by point with a mass of evidence that he has culled assiduously but not evaluated critically, so that much of his evidence turns out upon examination to be inconclusive, irrelevant, or misunderstood. See, for example, his misunderstanding (75) of the Euneos episode (quoted on p. 76) or his collection, without evaluation, of "evidence for coinage" (126–28; cf. appendix 2 in the present study). Cf. the article of Mayhew, Neale, and Tandy.

86. Kozyreva.

87. Powell, "Price Fluctuations," 88–94.

88. See Roth, p. 26, paragraph a (Laws of Lipit-Ishtar, ca. 1930 B.C.E., rents), pp. 37–38 (Laws of X, ca. 2050–1800 B.C.E., listing wages, interest, rents and prices of land), pp. 59–62 (Laws of Eshnunna, ca. 1770 B.C.E., prices, wages and rents, interest), pp. 126–32, paragraphs 239, 242/3, 257–58, 261, 268–77 (Laws of Hammurabi, ca. 1750 B.C.E., wages and rents). These are "legal" texts, which may well have represented the scribal traditions more than the practical or even the legal reality. On this hotly debated question, see Finkelstein; Bottéro; Westbrook; as well as Roth, 4–7. For a comparison with attested rates of hire, see Driver and Miles 1:469–78.

89. Luckenbill, p. 16 (Shamshi-Adad); Edzard, p. 154, n. 817 (Sin-kashid).

90. The texts, from 652 to 165 B.C.E., are published by Sachs and Hunger, with a short description of the price material at 1:34. Of course, only the earliest texts predate coinage; it is noteworthy that the introduction of coinage seems to have no effect at all on the way in which the prices are recorded.

brought about a rise in prices; the collapse of the third dynasty of Ur was accompanied by a famine in which grain rose to sixty times its normal price.[91] Long-term fluctuations were rare but not unknown, with the significant exception of iron, whose price in silver in the Old Babylonian period was thousands of times more than it would be in Babylon a thousand years later.[92] The Babylonian economy was still not, as it would become in the Hellenistic period, dominated by a market where prices changed each day; but it was not immune to the law of supply and demand.[93]

Silver often served for payments to the state,[94] but where it was in short supply and narrowly distributed through the population, it could not serve for all of the large areas of the economy that were taxed. What we know about the taxation system indicates that payments were overwhelmingly exacted in kind and that the wealth thereby accumulated was redistributed rather than being exchanged: the Assyrian and Babylonian palaces, like the Egyptian, took what they needed and gave it to whom they pleased.[95]

The silver of the Near East had never been coined; it was weighed at each transaction, and the scale was an essential accessory to every sale. All silver was equally valuable; rings, bars, and broken bits of silver could be thrown equally into the balance. Indeed, if the weight turned out uneven, one could always chop up an item to make the scale balance. This *Hacksilber* (fig. 3) is perhaps the clearest indication of the extent to which silver had become money for the Babylonians.[96] Whether a shekel of silver consisted of a wire, half a ring, or a piece chopped off an ingot seems to have

---

91. Jacobsen, 41–42.

92. Powell, "Price Fluctuations."

93. On the interpretation of the price fluctuations in the later Babylonian texts, see Slotsky; Temin.

94. This function varied; the earliest reformer of history, the Sumerian king Urukagina, relieved boatmen, fishers, farmers, and herdsmen of the requirement to pay their dues in silver. The various legal documents quoted in Roth often prescribe that offenders are to "weigh and deliver so-and-so many shekels of silver," but the verb that she translates etymologically as "weigh and deliver" need not in fact imply that any actual transfer of silver (rather than its value) was envisioned. Occasionally, it is grain (Roth, p. 26 [Laws of Lipit-Ishtar]) or even lead (ibid., p. 156, etc. [Middle Assyrian Laws]) that is to be "weighed and delivered."

95. See, for example, C. J. Gadd in *CAH*[3] II, part 1, p. 193 (Old Babylonia); Postgate, 206–12 (New Assyria); M. A. Dandamaev in *CAH*[3] II, part 2, p. 261 (New Babylonia). In this last period, the value of the items was estimated in silver, which suggests that in late Babylonia the palace may have collected what it could get and then traded it for what it needed.

96. Although I am speaking here of Mesopotamia, the phenomenon of *Hacksilber* is broadly distributed throughout the Near East, including Egypt, before and even after the introduction of coinage.

Fig. 3. *Hacksilber.* These rods, coils, and odds and ends are part of the Tell-el-Amarna hoard. (© Copyright the British Museum.)

meant as little to the Babylonian as the difference to us between a dollar bill and four quarters.

The use of *Hacksilber,* however, was not simply a matter of collecting odds and ends the way Erēnofre had done. Just as wealthy Egyptians hoarded items for purposes of treasure or trade, so Babylonians kept stores of silver for purposes that can only be called monetary. These hoards regularly included rings and coils that probably were not jewelry but simply a convenient and easily divisible way to keep and carry silver.[97] More striking is the "chocolate-bar ingot"—very widely found in hoards of *Hacksilber,* pre-portioned bits of silver snapped off a larger ingot much as pieces of chocolate are snapped off a larger bar.[98] When necessary, these bits of silver

97. The presence of silver in these easily usable forms distinguishes the regular *Hacksilber* hoards from such collections as that described by Themelis, where "[t]hose pieces which show signs of manufacture are bent and/or crumpled . . . [and] it would be no simple matter to straighten out and rework such pieces" (Bjorkman, 22). See, in particular, the illustrations in Themelis, 160, 164.

98. For an accessible and admirably concise description of *Hacksilber,* see the article of Christine Thompson.

could be weighed, placed in a bag or tied in a cloth, and sealed with a seal that identified the amount contained.[99]

The practice suggested by these finds is very similar to Herodotus's story that Darius, king of Persia, would melt his subjects' tribute into a pottery jar until the jar was full, then, when in need of money, break off as much as he needed.[100] The *Hacksilber* hoards, however, usually have their silver preserved in much smaller pieces, more appropriate to everyday trade than to the financing of a great empire.

In a sense, then—in almost every sense—Mesopotamia used money and had been using money for a millennium before the Greeks discovered it. Silver, or its alternatives, was a universally recognized standard of value; it was a potential and, in many circumstances (in particular, long-distance trade), a real medium of trade; it was valued for its exchange worth as well as for its commodity value; it could be a "price," while what one got in exchange was the "merchandise." There was no significant function of money that could not be performed by silver or by one of the alternative substances that were occasionally customary.

There was still, however, a step that the Assyrians and Babylonians had not taken. Silver, whatever its commercial function, was still only silver: there was no visible distinction between silver serving as money and silver serving as jewelry or utensils. Indeed, for this very reason, its functions could be and in various circumstances were served by other metals or even by grain, without any sign of inconvenience (fig. 4). Silver was an effective medium of trade, and since the Mesopotamians were a trading people, it played an important role in their lives; but it had not yet become an identifiable item that represented nothing but money. Because of this, its effects were limited to the sphere of its use: silver that arrived in Asshur did not remain there and spread through the population; rather, it remained in the hands of the merchants who had brought it until they made new purchases with it.[101] It never became, as coins eventually would, synonymous with wealth itself. It could not have done so, if only because too few people owned it. For this reason, the Babylonians never thought of silver as we think of money.

---

99. See p. 223.

100. Hdt. 3.96.2.

101. "The normal procedure is that almost all the silver and gold arriving in Aššur was used for making purchases, as the analysis of the 'caravan accounts' in Larsen [*Caravan*], 97ff. shows." Veenhof, 350, n. 466.

Fig. 4. The Shalmaneser stele. The burden of the second figure from the lower left, who is carrying what may be silver and gold to Shalmaneser (king of Assyria, 858–824 B.C.E), is sometimes reproduced as a "forerunner of coinage." A glance at the whole obelisk shows, as its text states, that the precious metals were only two among many valuable items. (© Copyright the British Museum.)

● PHOENICIA AND ISRAEL

The eastern shore of the Mediterranean Sea had many cities that thrived on trade, and here, too, silver served as both a standard of value and a medium of exchange, never coined but weighed.[102] The varying local weights tended with time to be standardized, but not by coinage: on the contrary, it was the stone that was placed on the other side of the scale that was made standard and eventually even guaranteed with the king's seal.[103] Occasionally, other items served as media of exchange.[104] Here, too, as in Babylonia, barter also thrived,[105] side by side with "monetary" purchase.

The sea allowed the Phoenicians to trade with many peoples with whom they had no common language. Herodotus describes the procedure of the Carthaginians in Africa.

The Carthaginians tell, too, of a land in Africa and of people who dwell beyond the Pillars of Hercules; and when they visit this people and unload their cargo, they place it out in a row upon the beach and then board their ships and raise a smoke. The natives, seeing the smoke, come to the seashore, and then put down gold in exchange for the goods and retreat back away from the goods. The Carthaginians come on shore and look, and if the gold seems to them to be worth the goods, they take it and go away; if it seems not to be worth it, they board their ships again and wait, while the others approach and add more gold to what they have already put down, until they persuade them. Neither side cheats; they themselves do not touch the gold before it equals the worth of their goods, nor does the other side touch the goods before the Carthaginians take the gold.[106]

We cannot tell whether this kind of trade, plausible enough and paralleled in other sources from later periods,[107] was practiced by the Carthaginians'

---

102. Gen. 23:15–16, in which Abraham weighed *(wayyišqol)* to Ephron the Hittite as the price of the Cave of Machpelah "four hundred shekels of silver, current money with the merchant," is often quoted.

103. Balmuth, "Monetary Forerunners," 26, 29–30.

104. Pettinato, 186–88; Wiseman, p. 14; Heltzer, pp. 76–77.

105. Pettinato, 185–86 (though here one side of the exchange is regularly silver in the documents); Wiseman, nos. 52–56, 58, 61–62, 72; Heltzer, chap. 2, table 1, nos. 2, 5, 6, 12, 21, 22, 23, 25, 44, 45, 48, 49, 56, 94.

106. Hdt. 4.196.

107. The fundamental monograph of Grierson was superseded by the article of John A. Price, who discounted many of Grierson's examples but retained enough to show that the phenomenon was real.

Phoenician forefathers as well nor how widespread it was. The parallels adduced stem from the old world, mostly from Africa;[108] it is not a universal that occurs in all appropriate situations. Nevertheless, it is a striking example of the extent to which international trade may develop with primitive means, and it would seem that even the gold mentioned by Herodotus as a medium of payment need not have been a necessary accompaniment of this "silent trade."[109]

In Syria and in Canaan/Israel, as in Mesopotamia, silver served trade in all the forms that money could take; but silver still was not all there was to wealth. The Bible records that Pharaoh "entreated Abram well for her [Sarai's] sake: and he had sheep, and oxen, and he asses, and menservants, and maidservants, and she asses, and camels," and that "Abram was very rich in cattle, in silver, and in gold"; his son Isaac "had possession of flocks, and possession of herds, and great store of servants, and the Philistines envied him"; his grandson Jacob received for his salary only sheep and goats, but "the man increased exceedingly, and had much cattle, and maidservants, and menservants, and camels, and asses."[110] Jacob had obviously converted his sheep into other items, but it is noteworthy that he had not converted them into precious metals. Solomon's wealth is described by the list of things he used, not a monetary equivalent.[111] Gold (fig. 5) is quoted by weight,[112] but other items are quoted with it without equivalences.[113] Hundreds of years later, when the prophet Elisha rebuked his servant for taking gifts, he asked, "Is it a time to receive money, and to receive garments, and oliveyards, and vineyards, and sheep, and oxen, and menservants, and maidservants?"[114]

---

108. Pliny, however (*Natural History* 6.88), speaks of trade between the Ceylonese and the Chinese, on which see next note; cf. John A. Price, 77, 85–89. Kurimoto's examples do not seem to match Price's stringent criteria for "real" silent trade.

109. Pliny speaks of goods, not gold or silver, being put down in return for the items offered for sale (*merces positas iuxta venalia*).

110. Gen. 12:16, 13:2, 26:14, 30:43. I quote from the King James Version not for literal accuracy, but because it is likely to be most familiar to the reader.

111. I Kings 4:22–23, 26, 28.

112. I Kings 9:28, 10:10, 14.

113. I Kings 10:10–12 (the Queen of Sheba's gifts); cf. 22, 25. A price might be mentioned when there was an actual sale, as with the horses that were brought for Solomon in Egypt (I Kings 10:29). The relevance of these passages is what they show about the economic concepts of the author and of his audience; whether the reader believes the author's information to be accurate or not does not affect the observation.

114. II Kings 5:26. Here as in some other places, the King James Version uses the word "money" to translate the Hebrew *keseph,* "silver." *Keseph,* while it remained the only word for "silver," did get the additional meaning of "money" when silver became money. The translator's

Fig. 5. Gold circlets found in Samaria and dated to the beginning of the fourth millennium B.C.E.: precious metal was hoarded in convenient shapes eons before coinage. (Courtesy of the Israel Antiquities Authority.)

That there were more things than just a plethora of silver that might make up wealth was not a new concept; as early as the end of the third millennium B.C.E., Ur-Nammu had expressed himself similarly.[115] What is noteworthy is that even where silver performed all the functions of money, it still had not become the unique measure of wealth. Many years later, Aristotle would say that many people consider wealth to be "plenty of coin";[116] no Israelite restricted wealth to plenty of silver. In a functional sense, money

---

considerations here are presumably stylistic, not historical. Note that the actual gift had been only silver and clothing.

115. "I did not deliver the orphan to the rich. I did not deliver the widow to the mighty. I did not deliver the man with but one shekel to the man with one mina [i.e., sixty shekels]. I did not deliver the man with but one sheep to the man with one ox" (Roth, p. 16).

116. Arist. *Pol.* I 9.10 (1257b 8–9). Aristotle himself gives a wider definition (*Rhet.* I 5 1361a 11–16).

already existed in the Levant long before coinage; but the conceptual change by which a person's wealth was to become synonymous with an amount of silver had not taken place there, any more than it had in Mesopotamia.[117] Silver and gold were much, but they were not yet all.

117. Nor did it take place quickly and thoroughly even after the invention of coinage. Cf. the expression of Rabbi Yosi ben Qisma's interlocutor in the *baraita* quoted as Mishnah, *Abot* 6:9: "I will give you a thousand thousand golden dinars, *and precious stones and pearls.*" This expression is very different from the ones we find in Genesis. The "useful" categories of slaves and cattle have been supplanted by precious stones, presumably because wealth is now thought of as small things of great value that are hoarded in chests. Nevertheless, the victory of coinage is not yet, in Judaea, as complete as it seemed to be in fourth-century B.C.E. Greece, where wealth was regularly quoted in talents, minas, and drachmas.

4 GREECE BEFORE MONEY

The Bronze Age

BRONZE AGE GREECE was far behind its Near Eastern contemporaries in
economic sophistication. As far as we can tell, it had no regular standard of
value. Gold was important to the kings of Mycenae; not for nothing did Homer speak of "Mycenae rich in gold," and visitors to the National Museum in
Athens are still astonished today by the wealth and workmanship of the gold
masks, jewelry, armor, and trinkets that were buried with the kings. None of
this, however, was currency, and the palace account books, which have been
opened to us by the accumulated effort of a previous generation of scholars
capped by the brilliant decipherment of Michael Ventris, show clearly that
these kings managed their accounts without the use of currency at all.[1]

This was not due to any heroic disdain of bookkeeping; on the contrary,
the records are meticulous in their detail.

> Dexeus: at Damnio- in Ku-ta-to, 56 rams, 16 ewes, twenty-eight of
> last year's rams. (*DMG* 69 = Df1119)
> Women of Knossos (for the *ki-ri-te-wi-ja* women): ration for one
> month, 12,000+ liters of wheat. (*DMG* 89 = E 777)

---

1. For the various items that have on occasion been identified as Bronze Age money, see
appendix 2.

At Pylos: due from Dunios: 2220 liters of barley, 526 liters of eating olives, 468 liters of wine, fifteen rams, eight yearlings, one ewe, thirteen he-goats, twelve pigs, one fat hog, one cow, two bulls. (*DMG* 96 = Uno2)
And similarly the village (will give): 240 liters wheat, 72 liters wine, two rams, five cheeses, 4 liters fat, one sheepskin. (*DMG* 171 = Un718)

The records deal with much smaller amounts than do the inscriptions of Pharaoh's ministers, as we should expect from a society whose greatest centers covered only a few acres; they are also more detailed than the Egyptian records. A close reading of the documents makes it clear that behind them lies a reasoned, if primitive, assessment of the land, the people, and the resources.[2] Money, as one can see, is not one of the things recorded.

The most striking series of tablets is the Ma series from Pylos,[3] apparently an assessment, listing for each village six different commodities, always in the same order and always in the same proportions:

For Ti-m-to-a-ke-e: 24 of *146; 24 of RI; 7 of KE; 10 *152; 5 of O; 500 of ME.

Delivery: 21 of commodity *146, 2 are o[wed]; of RI;[4] of KE; of O; of ME.

Item: the bronzesmiths do not give 1 of *146, 1 of RI, 10 of ME. (*DMG* 176 = Ma123).

The word "delivery" (*a-pu-do-si* = ἀπύδοσις) in line 2 shows us that we are dealing with items that are payable to the palace; the amounts delivered and the "exemptions" in line 3 (*o-u-di-do-si* = οὐ δίδονσι) add up to the sums in the top line, indicating that the top line is giving us the amount ideally payable, that is, the assessment. We have, in short, a tax document, describing what the community is supposed to pay, what it has paid (with some still "owed" [taking the "o" to stand for *o-pe-ro* = ὄφελος, "debt"]), and what, for whatever reason, it does not pay. There are six different items, presumably six different commodities, in the tax; they are always listed in the same order. The identification of each of the commodities is not certain, but the

2. On taxes, see the text immediately following; for the principles of land assessment, see de Fidio, *I dosmoi;* for the regularity of food rations, see de Fidio, "Razioni."
3. *DMG* 173–82, pp. 289–95. The Knossos Mc series (*DMG,* pp. 301–3) is similar.
4. The scribe does not give the total "delivered" for most of the commodities on this tablet. Since three of them do not appear on the next line either, the editors presume that they were paid in full.

striking matter is the proportion among them, which remains the same from tablet to tablet: the proportion is always 7:7:2:3:1.5:150. Some localities pay more, and some pay less, but the proportions do not vary. Apparently each village was assessed for all the commodities, in the same proportion, no matter what the local conditions. Although occasionally exemptions are mentioned (in the round proportions of 20, 30, or 50 percent), the sums are not transferable: no village paid one commodity in place of another. If the king of Pylos demanded barley, he did not take olive oil in its place; nor, it would seem, was there any general medium of payment that would be acceptable. The Mc series of Knossos shows us another such law, with four different commodities, but apparently on the same principle of taxation, with no substitution of one commodity for another.[5]

Not only was there no universal medium of payment that was acceptable to the palace, but there is no evidence even for a theoretical unit that might have served to establish the relative values of different items. Today, we find no difficulty in speaking of a dollar's worth of cheese; Erēnofre in Egypt, when purchasing a slave girl, offered her price in terms of silver, though she paid a mixed bag of household items;[6] the Homeric heroes estimated the values of tripods, armor, and serving maids in oxen.[7] But on the tablets of Bronze Age Greece, the items paid, owed, or given are always defined by weight or by volume, never by value.[8]

This does not necessarily mean that the Greeks of the Bronze Age were incapable of estimating relative values. They did exchange goods, as I shall shortly mention, and although goods may be exchanged by mechanisms other than evenhanded trade, it is neither impossible nor implausible that the Mycenaeans, like their contemporaries, engaged in exchanges in which

---

5. De Fidio ("Fiscalità") gives the most complete discussion of the tablets, though it will be apparent that I am not convinced by her belief that the entire system was based on a system of equivalences in which one sheep or four oxen equals one *medimnus*, a claim not, on the face of it, borne out by the Mycenaean evidence she adduces and at variance with the entire principle behind the Ma and Mc tablets. Cf. Lejeune, "La série Ma" and "Sur la fiscalité"; Olivier; Shelmerdine, "Pylos Ma Tablets" and "Mycenaean Taxation."

6. See p. 39.

7. See pp. 69–71.

8. Chadwick (cf. *DMG*, p. 406) saw an "equivalence" between cloth and wheat in Un1322 (now *DMG* 319); but as he seems to acknowledge in *DMG²*, the tablet is in too fragmentary a condition to support any certain interpretation, and Chadwick's explanation is not without its difficulties. In the absence of any parallel, we certainly cannot take it to indicate the use of grain or cloth as a standard of value. It may, as he suggests, record an exchange, although the context, insofar as it is comprehensible, does not seem to support that thesis; but even if so, such an exchange need not be any more than barter. Cf. Lejeune, "Vocabulaire économique."

they calculated carefully how much of one commmodity was worth exchanging for another. What the Ma and Mc tablets show us, however, is that this kind of calculation was not, as it was for later Greeks and as it is for us, a habit of thought that came naturally. There is no basis for asserting that the Mycenaeans could not decide how much oil was worth trading for an amphora of wine, but the fact that the calculation could be made does not seem to have made them think that it did not really matter whether it was wine or oil that one had in the storehouses. Their wealth, in their eyes, was not fungible.

The tablets record little, if anything, about trade, and this fact is not an accident of preservation. The great palaces did not support themselves by trade; as the tablets have amply demonstrated, they supported themselves by a comprehensive system of exactions from the villagers and workmen over whom their kings ruled. The villagers presumably lived—as most Greeks (and, indeed, most settled peoples) lived throughout the ancient period—by subsistence agriculture, growing on their own land most of what they needed. The workmen did not produce their own food, but they do not seem to have been paid directly for their work. They received allowances of food and of raw materials, and it is not unlikely that many of them ate, if not at the king's table, at least at his expense in the palace.

The economy, in short, was a redistributive one like that of Egypt, on a much smaller scale but on the same principle, with the central authority taking a large part of the produce for itself and allotting it as it saw fit. This was by no means the entire story of the Mycenaean economy. In a perceptive and carefully reasoned article, Paul Halstead has demonstrated that significant portions of the Mycenaean economy took place outside of the sphere of the palace economy entirely. At Pylos, it would appear that production of pottery was slowly centralized, but not at the palace: a few workshops eventually produced all of Messenia's pottery, but they did not work under royal patronage.[9] The nonpalace economy is undocumented, and there is nothing to tell us what mechanisms may have operated in it. As in Egypt, there was presumably a certain amount of trade between individuals; one may surely doubt whether anybody lives a long life without exchanging, at some time, an item that is not required for something of a neighbor's that seems more attractive. It has been observed that weights are often found in domestic contexts, far from the palace, suggesting that both production and trade were less centralized than might have been thought on the basis of the

9. Galaty, 75–82.

tablets alone.[10] These weights are not ipso facto proof of decentralized trade, since there are other mechanisms by which items can change hands;[11] but trade is certainly one of the most obvious reasons for wanting to ascertain an item's precise weight. (Gift giving, for example, can take place without a scale.) Still, this trade was not the mechanism by which the Bronze Age Greek received his daily bread, and we shall probably never know whether it involved any medium at all or was simply a matter of barter.

One form of trade certainly was practiced by the Mycenaeans, and that was international trade. The gold of Mycenae was not mined in the Argolid, and Mycenaean pottery has been found in various places around the Mediterranean.[12] It would seem that the merchants themselves did their business on foreign soil: we know of no foreign Bronze Age emporiums in Greece, but we do seem to find Mycenaeans in Cyprus, Rhodes, Miletus, and Ugarit.[13] We can only speculate what their method of trade was; it may well have been dictated by the customs of the foreign place where they did business. It has been suggested that trade with outsiders took the form of noble gift exchange, but that can be no more than conjecture.[14] Not surprisingly, the primary recipients of foreign goods were the major Mycenaean centers, from which a certain amount percolated out to smaller communities.[15] Such of their imports as modern excavators have found were chiefly luxury items designed for kings and nobles; copper and tin were imported in bulk.[16] All of this may mean that the Mycenaean merchants were agents of the kings just as the palace workmen were, though other explanations are possible.[17] Whatever the practice of the merchants may have been, they certainly did not turn gold or anything else into a currency in Knossos and Pylos.

---

10. Michailidou.

11. See the more detailed consideration of possibilities in Rehak and Younger, 136–40.

12. Though rarely far inland. For a brief and accessible account, see Vermeule, 254–58; cf. Mylonas, 210–11. For an account still brief but somewhat more detailed, see Immerwahr. Cf. Taylour, 148–65, whose conclusion, however—that "commercial enterprise . . . was the . . . driving force . . . that raised them from a humble status to a position of unimagined wealth and power" (165)—seems to go far beyond what the evidence will bear.

13. Immerwahr, 7–12. Their numbers should not be exaggerated; cf. Courtois, particularly his conclusions (216–17).

14. Killen, 262–65. The Egyptian parallel he quotes on p. 263 is more relevant than the Homeric parallels, in view of the severe discontinuity between Mycenaean economic institutions and Homeric ones.

15. Cline, xvii.

16. Dickinson, 251.

17. See Vermeule, 257, 346 n. 5.

The Mycenaeans, then, seem to have had no uniform medium of payment or uniform standard of value, and if they had any normal medium of exchange, it was so marginal as to have escaped our notice. One thing they did have, however, and that was treasure. The palaces themselves were vast storehouses, and if the gold of Mycenae was found more in its graves than in its palaces, that testifies only to the human nature of the warriors who looted the palaces before burning them.[18] This gold was practically all made into jewelry of often exquisite workmanship; not only was it not made into coins, but it was not kept in ingots, nor chopped up into the *Hacksilber* that characterizes the Mesopotamian hoards. There can be no doubt that the Mycenaean kings placed great importance on wealth and particularly on visible wealth; their accumulations of gold, silver, ivory, spices, and many more pedestrian items were designed to make their regal state lasting, visible, and impressive. They did not do this by storing up coins; they did it by accumulating the most various items. It may be considered certain that gold and ivory were prestige items and were many times more valuable for their weight than barley or even oxen, but they were not the only items that the Mycenaean kings used for accumulating and storing wealth. They served a function, but they were not money.

---

18. Indeed, many of the graves themselves were looted; the marvelous artifacts are due chiefly to a few lucky finds of places that had escaped earlier grave robbers.

HOMER

5

Tripods and Oxen

ONE OF THE ACHIEVEMENTS of Sir Moses I. Finley[1] was to demonstrate that the Homeric poems describe a society understandable in terms of modern anthropology and that the society described was not the society that produced the Linear B tablets.[2] Finley presumed that, "allowing for anachronisms and fictions, the society revealed in the poems existed in the centuries following the end of the Mycenaean age."[3] He may have

---

1. Finley, *World*, and n. 3 below.

2. On the relationship of Homeric society to "Mycenaean" society, see Finley, "Note," printed as an appendix to the first revised edition of *World* but omitted from the second revised edition (New York: Viking, 1978) on the grounds that "today it is no longer seriously maintained, though it is still said often enough, that the *Iliad* and *Odyssey* reflect Mycenaean society" (10; I cite from the 1991 Pelican edition). The historical events recounted by Homer are not relevant to us; Finley himself doubted that the Trojan War had ever taken place. See, in brief, Finley et al., "Trojan War."

3. Finley, *World*, preface to 1967 edition (Penguin Books, Harmondsworth, 1967), 10. See, however, the spirited objections of Snodgrass, "Homeric Society," and Finley's response (to an earlier version) in the second revised edition of *World*, 154–58. Snodgrass's objections undoubtedly carry weight; the question of whether we must call the background to Homer a "composite society" as Snodgrass does or dismiss the problems with a concessive phrase ("allowing for anachronisms and fictions") as Finley does is perhaps a judgment of degree. The coherence of even observable societies should not be exaggerated: it has been said with no less plausibility that

presumed too much. There is considerable uncertainty about when and even how the Homeric epics were composed. We cannot state clearly when, if ever,[4] the society that they seem to take for granted may have existed. The epics themselves, moreover, like any literary creation, are likely to present a schematic,[5] idealized or polemical[6] view of a society whose realities may have been a good deal more various and more ambiguous than the poet allows.

Whatever society can be viewed through the Homeric poems, it was not one that existed before the end of the Bronze Age: Homer mentions iron in similes and for various implements,[7] though he knows that the warriors he describes wore bronze armor. He knows there are things that have changed since the time of the heroes of whom he is singing. His anachronisms must, to some extent, reflect the world he knew.[8]

Much more than metallurgy had changed. Not only had the great Bronze Age palaces been burned, but the kingdoms themselves had fallen apart. The most eloquent evidence is linguistic: whereas the Bronze Age kings had been called *wanax,* the kings of archaic Greece were called *basileus,* a title that had been only a subordinate one in the Bronze Age.[9] In Homer, the transition is not yet complete; a king may be called either *anax* (the *w* has dropped out of our texts, as it later dropped out of the language) or *basileus,* but it is significant that although a god might be called *anax,* he would never be called *basileus*[10]—just as we continue to speak of divine kingship but would not dream of worshiping the "President of the Universe." In short order, however, even this distinction vanished. Hesiod did not hesitate to call the

---

"the culture of any society at any moment is more like the debris, or 'fall-out' of past ideological systems" (Turner, 14, quoting from the art critic Harold Rosenberg and quoted, in turn, by Kurke [*Traffic,* 88] and now by me).

4. See previous note, and more recently Cartledge, 686–93 (contra); Raaflaub (pro).

5. "The communities of Dark Age Greece developed along different lines and at different rates. There is no such thing as a monolithic '9th-century Greece' to which Homer can be compared. As late as the 5th century, Greeks could time-travel simply by visiting their neighbors, and the contrast would have been far more striking in the late 7th and early 6th centuries when sites such as Olympia and Delphi began to attract visitors from throughout Greece, potential audiences of Panhellenic epic." Erwin Cook, citing (*inter alios*) Morgan.

6. Morris, "Homer," 120–29.

7. *Il.* 4.123, 485, 18.34, 23.30, 851; *Od.* 19.494 and elsewhere.

8. If the epics are the work of more than one author, the world of each one may have been somewhat different. Even Finley's view does not, of course, demonstrate a single author; at best, it suggests that if more than one person was involved, they shared a similar cultural milieu.

9. *DMG* 120–22, 408–9.

10. Page, *History,* 188, citing Wackernagel, 3:209–13, who without the aid of Linear B, already drew the conclusion that ϝάναξ was the older word.

king of the gods θεῶν βασιλεύς,[11] and the classical poets show none of the earlier sensitivity.[12] Local strongmen, not necessarily the only ones in a city,[13] were now the highest officials the Greeks knew; and as I shall show, the economy reflected their shrinking horizon. The society Homer knew or imagined was later in time than the world of the Mycenaean palaces but was demonstrably more primitive.

● HOMERIC PAYMENTS

The Homeric heroes made payments for various reasons: to ransom a captive, to appease an enemy, to reward athletic prowess, and for the ubiquitous exchanges of gifts by which heroes honored each other and established their own worth. In a striking part of the scene of the city at peace on Achilles' shield,[14] two talents of gold are offered not to the party that would win the law case but "to the one among these [i.e., among the elders judging the case] who would speak the straightest judgment."[15] Nowhere, however, was there any single medium of payment. Metal, particularly in the form of cooking utensils, was the most favored item, and it was the one that came to the lips of a man desperately offering a ransom to an enemy about to cut him down.[16] Metals, both precious and base, also figure prominently in the prizes that Achilles offered at Patroclus's funeral games.[17] These were not money and were not offered as things designed to be exchanged.[18] Many other goods could serve, but only, of course, "prestige goods"; no number of cucumbers could ransom a hero.[19] Priam offered Achilles clothing, ten talents of gold, two tripods, four cauldrons, and a goblet that he had been given by the Thracians: this last (and probably most valuable) item was treasured not merely for its worth but for its history.[20]

---

11. *Theogony* 886, 923; cf. also the quotation of the *Cypria* in Athenaeus VIII 334c and *Hymn. Hom. Dem.* 358.

12. Pindar *Olympian* 7.34; Aeschylus *Agamemnon* 355.

13. On this, see Drews; Carlier.

14. *Il.* 18.497–508.

15. On this see Sealey, 92–93, 100–105.

16. Χαλκός τε χρυσός τε πολύκμητός τε σίδηρος (*Il.* 6.48, 10.379, 11.133).

17. *Il.* 23.

18. We, too, of course, often prefer to offer gifts and prizes in kind rather than in money—which is only to say that not even our own society is entirely monetized: see p. 198. For a discussion of modern gift-giving practices and a comparison of the modern gift economy with the market economy, see Furnham and Argyle, 191–202.

19. On "prestige goods," see p. 77.

20. *Il.* 24.228–37; cf. Finley, *World*, 120–23. Although Finley describes this "historical" value of an item in terms that make it seem primitive, it is in fact well known to all of us. The baseball that

The choice of goods for payment was not a matter of indifference. When Agamemnon, who had angered Achilles by appropriating his captive and concubine, Briseis, wished to appease his anger, he offered him

Seven tripods never touched by the flame, and ten talents of
  gold,
and twenty shining cauldrons, and twelve horses,
stout prizewinners, who carry off prizes with their feet.
A man who had such things would not be unpropertied,
nor would he be unwealthy in precious gold,
as much as the single-hooved horses bring me as prizes.
And I will give seven women who know how to do excellent
  work,
Lesbians, whom I chose out of the booty when I myself took
  well-built Lesbos,
who outdo the entire race of women for beauty.
These I will give him, and along with them will be the one
  whom I took then,
the daughter of Briseus: in addition, I will swear a great oath
that I never went up to her bed nor slept with her
as is customary among people, men and women.
All of these will be ready immediately; and if in the future
the gods should grant that we sack the great city of Priam,
let a ship be brought and heaped up with plenty of gold and
  silver
when we Achaeans divide the booty,
and he himself will choose twenty Trojan women,
whoever are the most beautiful after Argive Helen.
And if we should arrive in Achaean Argos, the udder of the
  earth,
he shall be my son-in-law; and I will honor him equally with
  Orestes,

Babe Ruth hit for his sixtieth home run has been sold for a good deal more than the cost of the string and glue of which it is composed, and by the time Mark McGwire hit his seventieth, each ball pitched to him was marked to identify it in case it should be the lucky one. Hotel owners who used to advertise "George Washington slept here" meant that not as a testimonial but as an attraction. It is customary for the President of the United States to use more than one pen for signing important legislation, in order to give more than one honoree the gift of the pen with which the bill was signed. The U.S. Capitol flies a different flag each day, which is then given away, often to a school, as being more valuable than an ordinary flag.

my dearly beloved, who is being brought up in great abundance.
I have three daughters in my well-built hall,
Chrysothemis and Laodice and Iphianassa,
of whom let him take whichever he wants, without bride-price,
    for his own,
to the house of Peleus; in addition, I will give gifts of
    reconciliation,
very many, such as no one ever gave to his daughter:
I will give him seven well-appointed cities,
Cardamyle and Enope and grassy Hire
and holy Pherae and deep-meadowed Antheia
and beautiful Aepeia and vine-clad Pedasos.
All are near the sea, very near to sandy Pylos;
in them dwell men with many sheep and many cattle,
who will honor him as a god with their gifts
and will pay him shining tribute under his scepter.[21]

Homer is, of course, a poet, and one cannot doubt that his enumeration is more attractive than a modern judge's laconic "three million dollars of punitive damages"; but the difference is more than just poetry. The dollars with which we pay each other for insults and damages are interchangeable: one dollar is like another, and we sweeten an offer simply by offering more money. Agamemnon does not think that way. His gift is carefully, if generously, calculated to offer Achilles amends for all the insult that he offered when he took Briseis for himself. He begins, indeed, with the usual tripods and cauldrons, but by adding more, he admits that ordinary gifts will not suffice to redress the balance. The horses are not only honorable possessions but will add further honor to their owner by winning prizes, a fact Agamemnon does not neglect to mention. The women from Lesbos are not only hardworking but beautiful, and the offer would not be complete without them: he must return to Achilles more than he took, and what he took was not a bronze tripod. A million tripods would not have made his offer reasonable without the women of Lesbos. Briseis herself is mentioned last, because she is, of course, the most important: she must be returned intact, and that is the reason for the great oath, although there had been no apparent reason for Agamemnon to abstain from her in the height of his earlier pride. The further stipulations guarantee that Achilles' honor will

---

21. *Il.* 9.122–56, 264–98.

become greater and greater with the Achaeans' fortunes: the tripods, cauldrons, and horses become an entire shipload of gold and bronze, and the seven women of Lesbos become the twenty fairest of the Trojans; then the shipload becomes entire towns, and the slave women become the daughter of the king himself, offered for free without the bride-gifts that a groom must ordinarily bring. This is the way Homeric heroes make payments—not through a single "medium of payment" of which a large enough amount will pay for anything, but by offering gifts both prestigious and appropriate.

It has been argued[22] that Agamemnon's offer is insulting, because it is so grossly out of proportion as to emphasize Agamemnon's superiority, and that what he should have offered was "to return Briseis with a public apology and a fitting compensatory gift." But gifts in Homer are never hostile; the Eskimo proverb that Donlan quotes ("Gifts make slaves, just as whips make dogs"), if he understands it correctly, has no archaic Greek parallel.[23] On the contrary, the nobles have urged Agamemnon to appease Achilles, and none of them suggests that the proffered gift is likely to have the opposite effect. The goddess had, in fact, quelled Achilles' initial anger with precisely such a promise.[24] The offer is an offer of peace; its gross disproportion is appropriate to the gross insult for which it is an apology, to the enormous valor of Achilles and to the urgent need of the Achaeans. It is nevertheless true, as Agamemnon (who says so, 9.160–61), Odysseus (who omits those words in speaking to Achilles 9.299), Achilles (who refuses the offer), and Donlan (who notices all this ["Duelling with Gifts," 332]) all recognize, that the peace offered is a peace in which Agamemnon's position as leader of the kings is maintained and thereby strengthened, and that is what Achilles refuses to accept.

Sacrifices to the gods were similarly calculated. As Diomedes wreaks havoc among the Trojans, Helenus sends word to have Hecuba choose "the dress that she considers to be the most charming and the greatest in the house and by far the dearest to her," to place on the goddess's knees. She is also to promise a sacrifice of twelve heifers if the goddess will protect Troy: as in Agamemnon's case, she is to offer a smaller present out of what is immediately available, a larger present in case of success. The value of the

---

22. Donlan, "Duelling with Gifts," 330–33.

23. Ibid., 339 n. 14. Donlan seems to have misunderstood the proverb. Whips do not turn men into dogs; they make dogs docile. Similarly, says the proverb, the way to make a slave docile is to give gifts. This does not claim that a free person is transformed into a slave by receiving a gift.

24. *Il.* 1.212–14.

dress for its purpose is explicitly determined not by any "market value" but by how precious it is to its owner. Hecuba did as she was told, but the goddess was not persuaded.[25]

Even here we can see the difference between a Homeric hero and a Phoenician merchant. For the Phoenicians, silver traded hands by weight; not only was one ring like another, but half a ring would do just as well if that was what was needed to make up the weight.[26] Agamemnon offers not only tripods but "tripods never touched by the flame." The sheen of new bronze interests him. One can scarcely imagine Agamemnon chopping up a tripod to make the weight come out evenly.

● STANDARD OF VALUE

This does not mean that Homer was incapable, as the Mycenaean Greeks seem to have been, of measuring the relative worth of disparate commodities. Lycaon was able to say that he had been ransomed for three times as much as the price for which Achilles had sold him;[27] Achilles told the doomed Hector that no one would save his body from defilement, "not if they were to weigh ten or twenty times as great a ransom and bring it here and promise more as well."[28] Homer had, as the Linear B legislator does not seem to have had, a regular standard for deciding how much of one commodity was worth a given amount of another.

The standard was the ox. A slave-woman was offered as a consolation prize for the losing wrestler at the funeral games of Patroclus; "they estimated her at four oxen."[29] Eurycleia, on the other hand, had been bought by Laertes for "twenty oxen's worth,"[30] while Lycaon, a king's son, was sold by Achilles for a hundred oxen's worth and fetched three times as much in ransom.[31] We find bronze armor valued at nine oxen, a tripod at twelve, and gold armor at a hundred.[32] There is no reason to consider these valuations to

---

25. *Il.* 6.84–101, 286–311.

26. This is not to imply that the Phoenicians were utter Philistines. *Hacksilber* hoards may contain jewelry, but it is not chopped into pieces. Coins, however, were at first fair game: see p. 107. Nebuchadnezzar was not above chopping up the brass pillars and vessels of the Temple at Jerusalem (II Kings 25:13; Jer. 52:17), but the behavior of temple plunderers cannot be taken as a norm of daily life.

27. *Il.* 21.80.

28. *Il.* 22.349–50.

29. *Il.* 23.705.

30. *Od.* 1.431.

31. *Il.* 21.79–80.

32. *Il.* 6.236, 23.703.

represent any sort of regular exchange value of which we can speak: the very fact of their belonging to heroes of epic poetry would warn us against that, without considering the questions of economic history involved. But they do indicate that for Homer an ox was a unit of value, as a dollar or a pound is for us.

Of course, no physical ox needed to be present for the Achaeans to estimate how many oxen a woman was worth; even when a sum was paid, no oxen need have changed hands.[33] Laertes had bought Eurycleia for twenty oxen's worth, not for twenty oxen;[34] Eurymachus, trying to buy the suitors' lives from the returned Odysseus, offered to have each suitor pay for what he had eaten and add to that "a price of twenty oxen's worth" [τιμὴν . . . ἐεικοσάβοιον].[35] One could even speak of the value of items that obviously could not be bought: as noted earlier,[36] Homer says that each tassel of the aegis was worth a hundred oxen,[37] although that was not meant, even in imagination, to be a "market value."

It goes without saying that less important items could not have been valued in oxen, but we do not know how they were estimated, if at all. A dog may have had a value, too, but its value was simply unheroic.[38]

If my earlier conclusion that the economies of the great Bronze Age palaces had neither fixed media of payment nor standard of value is correct, the Homeric age, whenever it may have been, seems to show clear progress toward a monetary society, though it was still nothing like Babylonia or Phoenicia. This is at first glance paradoxical, for there can be little doubt

---

33. This is not to suggest that oxen or livestock in general were not as good a medium of payment as any other. Iphidamas had given a hundred head of cattle and promised a thousand sheep and goats for the bride he did not live to marry (see *Il.* 11.242–45), and some of the Achaeans used oxen to pay for Euneos's wine (*Il.* 7.474; cf. below p. 76).

34. ἐεικοσάβοια δ' ἔδωκεν (*Od.* 1.431), not, for example, ἐείκοσι βοῦς δ' ἀπέδωκεν. I do not know, however, why Finley (*World*, 67) says, "he would never have traded the oxen for a slave"; slaves were prestigious enough items to be offered as athletic prizes (*Il.* 23.263, 704–5), and oxen as well as slaves could be traded for wine (*Il.* 7.474–75).

35. *Od.* 22.55–59. Since one could hardly afford to bid too low when Antinous had been killed and Odysseus's bow was strung, Eurymachus added to the offer an unlimited amount of metal, "bronze and gold, until your heart is softened." Odysseus, of course, was not won over.

36. P. 28.

37. *Il.* 2.448–49.

38. The spits (ὀβελοί; cf. LSJ, s.v. ὀβολός [II]) of later Greek coinage obviously suggest themselves, but although they seem to have served later as a (somewhat limited) medium of exchange, they are not mentioned in Homer or anywhere else as value tags: see pp. 83–88. There may perfectly well have been items beneath estimation. Even today, it takes a bit of computation for a person to give a money value for a single paper clip, and Homer's audience need not have put a price tag on every item.

that the Homeric economy in general was much more primitive than the economy of the Bronze Age had been. The names of professions are much more general, indicating less specialization of labor; the palace bureaucracy, so evident in the Linear B tablets, is reduced to a few servants of general function; the comprehensive bookkeeping has given way to a society only marginally literate.[39]

The paradox is noteworthy, for the existence of primitive forms of money is usually correlated with sociological complexity.[40] In Greece, however, it was probably precisely the collapse of the earlier structure that led to the development of primitive money. The administrators of the redistributive palace economy needed to know how much barley the king needed, and how many sheep; how much or how many of each he would have to provide to each of the people dependent upon him, whether free or slave; but they did not have to make the calculation of how much barley was worth a single sheep. (Often, of course, such a calculation would be absurd,[41] for no number of sheep will suffice to serve as seed to produce next year's harvest, and no amount of barley will clothe a person through the winter.) The palace could take in payment what it needed or wanted or what its dependents could give; it need take nothing else. When the palaces had been burned and their far-flung bureaucracy dispersed, there will have been more need for exchange. The Homeric heroes did indeed have to weigh the value of a slave against the value of a tripod; if this seems to us a step toward the concept of money, it is not for that reason a sign of an expanding economy.

○ GIFT EXCHANGE

We should not fall into the trap of believing that increased exchange of goods necessarily implied the practice of commerce, that is, trade for profit. There were traders in the Homeric world, as there had been in the Mycenaean, but when speaking of traders, we are not speaking of heroes. Heroes exchanged gifts, surely, and one good gift deserved and expected another; but gift giving was not trade. Finley's words on the subject have often been quoted.

It may be stated as a flat rule of both primitive and archaic society that no one ever gave anything, whether goods or services or honours,

39. Finley, "Note on Homer," 165–66.
40. Pryor, 163–71.
41. As Aristotle noted, *Eth. Nic.* V 5.14 (1133b 18–20); cf. Meikle, 28–42.

without proper recompense, real or wishful, immediate or years away, to himself or to his kin.[42]

Finley, however, significantly overstated the matter. Oswyn Murray offers a corrective.

> It seems to me that we mislead ourselves with the idea that this is a reciprocal relationship. In general, what we call gift exchange is in fact the giving of a gift to a person; and the reciprocal aspect if it is present at all may not materialize until perhaps a generation later. In Homer, there is only *one* example of a true gift exchange (Glaucus and Diomedes); all other examples are of gifts being given. The expectation may well be that one day you will receive a gift in return, but that is not the primary aspect of the ritual.[43]

None of this precisely contradicts Finley's point, but it does help to put it in perspective. In fact, even Finley's claim about "primitive and archaic society" does not correspond to the evidence of other societies, where Pryor's cross-cultural survey found that one-way transfers—transfers in which nothing at all tangible was given in exchange—were almost as common as exchanges.[44] This, too, does not quite contradict Finley, for Finley was willing to include recompense "real or wishful, immediate or years away, to himself or to his kin," which on examination is a statement about presumed psychology of long-dead people, not a meaningful statement about primitive (or any other) society. It states no more than the belief that nobody gives something for nothing, a belief that many people hold about other societies and even about all societies,[45] but one that is neither proven nor disproven by Homeric gift exchange.[46]

Whether, in fact, a gift was equivalent in value to its countergift would

---

42. Finley, *World*, 64.

43. Murray, comments on Coldstream in Hägg, 207.

44. Pryor, 5, 27–37, 69–101.

45. Pryor (35) offered as a "poignant example" of exchanges that were not expected to be balanced the dating practices of the 1940s in America, "where the boys paid all the expenses of the date and received very little or nothing in return." This comment apparently stirred up a hornet's nest among those who read his manuscript, requiring a long and interesting footnote justifying his claim, of which the part relevant to us is his despair of being able to speak meaningfully about the intangibles involved: "The difficulties in deciding whose company benefited the other more illustrates the absurdity of introducing social invisibles to 'balance' such transactions and of refusing to recognize the transactions as a [one-way] transfer."

46. On the related belief that everything can be bought, see pp. 198, 205.

depend on the circumstances. Agamemnon's offer to Achilles, which was not so much a gift as an indemnity, was out of all proportion to the value of the woman Agamemnon had taken, but in other circumstances, gifts, although surely not appraised as market-goods are, would be more closely commensurate. When Diomedes met Glaucus on the field of combat and spared him because they were familial guest-friends, they exchanged armor, but Glaucus's wits were taken away, "for he exchanged with Diomedes, son of Tydeus, gold armor for bronze, a hundred oxen's worth for nine oxen's worth."[47] Diomedes was on the rampage, and it was presumably prudent for Glaucus to offer him the better of the deal, but it was insane to offer something so utterly disproportionate. Many explanations have been advanced for Glaucus's mistake and for Homer's choosing to tell of it,[48] but there is no doubt that his utter disregard for the relative values was not normal or appropriate behavior.[49]

This is not to say that gifts in Homer were analogous to the occasional gifts we give on birthdays, anniversaries, and holidays. Gifts were a very serious matter that determined a good deal about the honor both of the giver and of the recipient.[50] In those circumstances where custom suggested or demanded that a superior reward or support his underlings, the granting of the gift emphasized and strengthened his superior status; where, on the other hand, gifts were offered as a recognition of superiority, it was the recipient whose status was enhanced. Honorable deeds done in return for gifts were more honorable than those done out of moral duty, as Phoenix explained to Achilles.[51] Even when a gift was unwelcome, it could not be refused with propriety.[52] The gifts were valuable, and indeed a good deal of wealth must have circulated through the giving of gifts.

Even so, gifts between heroes were gifts of luxury items. One hero might give another a tripod or a cauldron, but the barley to be cooked in it was not a proper gift. Gifts between heroes, furthermore, were traded not for profit but for honor; no hero made a living by trading other heroes' gifts. The heroes lived in peacetime off their slave-managed estates and the "gifts" of their

---

47. *Il.* 6.234–36.

48. I generally follow Donlan ("Unequal Exchange"), though I am not convinced that it was a momentary panic that motivated Glaucus. See further Scodel, Fineberg, and others too numerous to mention.

49. *Pace* Bowra (68), who thought that Glaucus's generosity did him credit.

50. For a clear and succinct description of the different situations that demanded gifts and their meaning for status relationships, see Donlan, "Unequal Exchange," 268–71.

51. *Il.* 9.597–605.

52. *Od.* 18.287.

peasants[53] and friends;[54] if these were insufficient, they made their living in the manner befitting heroes—by robbery, piracy, and plunder.[55] The plunder was, indeed, disposed of by sale,[56] but sale of plunder is not commerce, though plunder and commerce were more closely connected in the world of the heroes than they are in our own.[57]

⊚ TRADE AND COMMERCE

In speaking of trade, we must distinguish two entirely different phenomena. Some trade is merely exchange between two people, each of whom needs what the other has: items worth one hundred oxen could be very valuable to Achilles, perhaps for their use value (he had an army to feed or at least to feast) or for their prestige value, while Euneos of Lemnos, a king at peace, had no army but had a palace in which Priam's son Lycaon would be a prestigious servant. In an exchange of this sort, there need be no calculation of profit: whatever items Achilles could get for Lycaon were better than holding on to a prisoner who had to be guarded. Achilles will, of course, have tried to get the most oxen's worth he could, but he did not need to worry about their possible exchange value. He was taking the oxen (or whatever he got) not to exchange but either to slaughter and feed to his soldiers or his retinue or to hoard as treasure. No stigma attached to trade of this sort. When Odysseus's patron goddess appeared to his son, Telemachus, in the form of their family friend Mentes, she pretended to be traveling to Temesa with a cargo of iron that she planned to exchange for copper.[58]

---

53. These were not, of course, voluntary; see *Od.* 13.13–15 and Finley's comments (*World*, 96) on the sense in which such a "gift" differed from taxation. Hesiod's contemptuous references to δωροφάγοι βασιλῆες (*Works and Days* 38–39, 263–64) show a peasant's-eye view of "gifts," though the context here shows that Hesiod is speaking not of feudal dues but of gifts given in the hope of receiving favors: see M. L. West's note to line 39. Achilles' contemptuous jibe at Agamemnon (δημοβόρος βασιλεύς, ἐπεὶ οὐτιδανοῖσιν ἀνάσσεις Hom. *Il.* 1.231) shows both that the expression was a commonplace (Kirk, ad loc.) and that the necessity of submitting to such treatment was disgraceful for those who suffered it.

54. As a rule, nobles gave each other luxuries, not necessities; but oxen were both prestigious and edible, and villages with the peasants themselves could be given as gifts, as Agamemnon promises Achilles in *Il.* 9.149–56. The prospect of getting gifts could be a reason for undertaking or prolonging an enterprise (*Od.* 15.82–85; cf. Donlan, "Unequal Exchange," 272–73).

55. *Od.* 3.71, 9.39–52, 252, etc. Thucydides (1.5) already noted the respectability of piracy in Homeric society. See Ormerod, chaps. 1–2; Finley, *World*, 63, 68–69, 95 (cf. 117–20); Ferone, 32; and, in particular, the well-chosen words of de Souza (17–23).

56. See *Il.* 21.35–41, 102, 454. On the last passage, see p. 151, n. 10.

57. See p. 89.

58. *Od.* 1.182–84.

There was nothing unheroic about this; this was trade, not commerce, and Mentes would bring back from abroad something desirable and unavailable at home.

There is another form of trade, and Homer knew it. If Mentes had resold the copper at home among the Taphians in order to end up with more iron than he began with, the entire procedure would have been contemptible, and worthy of a Phoenician. In another passage from the *Odyssey*, Euryalos taunts Odysseus by supposing him to be a "ruler of sailors who are merchants, mindful of his freight, and observant of his provisions and his eagerly grasped profits."[59] Euryalos says nothing of the kind of cargo his merchant was carrying, whether prestigious or not: what he emphasizes is that the merchant looks carefully to the cargo he takes out and the one he brings back and is eager for a profit.[60] That is commerce, not simply trade, and would have been despicable even if he were trafficking in gold.

The disdain for commerce has two sides. One is the inherent unfairness of the trade: since the merchant goes home richer than he started, he must somewhere have been cheating the people with whom he dealt. No less important is the way in which he accomplishes his aim: he keeps his eye on his own benefit.[61] He is keeping his eye on what the other is ignoring, on the small difference between the price at which he has bought and the price at which he sells. This kind of attention to detail is not only unfair (for its entire purpose is to take advantage of the other party) but undignified. For a nobleman to calculate precisely the values of the gifts he gives and receives would be beneath him, and it follows from this that in an exchange between a merchant and a noble, it is precisely the ignobility of the merchant that allows him to get the better of the noble, contrary to the Homeric sense of nature and justice.[62]

Despite its disdain, the Euryalos passage and its vocabulary prove that commercial trade was well established in Homer's time. Homer disapproved and may have thought it an innovation, but it was there.[63] We may be sure, furthermore, that those who practiced it did not consider it shameful,

---

59. *Od.* 8.162–65.

60. My colleague Gabriel Danzig points out correctly that *losing* in trade, as Glaucus does to Diomedes, is even worse. Homer's heroes were not, alas, the only people for whom being a scoundrel was less of a disgrace than being a fool.

61. Κέϱδος, the term that Euryalos uses and that I have translated as "profit," is any advantage accruing to oneself, as opposed to ὄφελος, advantage for another (de Jong).

62. On the later developments of this attitude, see pp. 183, 207.

63. Redfield, 30–32. As for the goddess, Redfield suggests that she is being less than respectable, but Homer does not suggest that.

though their opinions are not expressed by Homer. Homer's values, even to the extent that they are consistent, were not necessarily the values of every member of the society.[64]

The heroic kind of one-way trade, like the sale of plunder, needs no special medium of exchange; even the profit-making trade of the Phoenicians could be managed by sailing from place to place and trading well. It is perfectly clear that there was no such medium in the Homeric world. In the only actual "market" scene in the *Iliad*, Jason's son Euneos of Lemnos had sent Agamemnon and Menelaos "personally" [χωρίς] a thousand measures of wine, after which the Achaeans "wined themselves" [οἰνίζοντο]—

> some for bronze, some for shining iron,
> some for hides, some for entire oxen,
> some for slaves; and they set a plentiful supper.[65]

Homer did not necessarily mean for us to believe that the thousand measures of wine sent to the Atreidae were then resold to the soldiers; Euryalos would have scoffed at that, and Homer probably would not have approved. Rather more probable seems the suggestion of Stanley that the thousand measures were a "gift" to the kings, in return for which the kings allowed the Lemnians to set up a temporary market to sell the rest of their wine. Such gifts to rulers by would-be traders were the normal practice during the last centuries of the Chinese Empire.[66]

It has been noted that certain items are repeatedly mentioned in Homer as gifts, whereas other items, equally useful or more so, are not. This points to a phenomenon, found in many societies, whereby certain (usually more prestigious) items pass from hand to hand according to one set of rules, while others (usually less prestigious) have a different set of rules entirely. It is quite possible that just as the nonprestige goods were not given as gifts,

---

64. In *Od.* 19.282–90, Odysseus, pretending to be the Cretan prince Aethon (not, as both Malkin and Erwin Cook would have it, a "lying bastard": cf. Joseph Russo in Heubeck on 19.181), tells Penelope that Odysseus knows better than all mortal men how to make profits and is surely now wandering around amassing them in order to come home wealthy. Malkin (89) takes this story and that of Mentes to indicate that no stigma attached to trade among aristocrats, but he has not noticed that Mentes and Euryalos are speaking about different kinds of trade and that Odysseus in book 19 does not mention trade at all. Κέρδος, which Odysseus does mention, is any advantage to oneself, and here it surely means not profit by trade but noble gifts (Erwin Cook).

65. *Il.* 7.473–75.

66. Stanley, 8–9. On this view, the word χωρίς would mean "separately," and ἔνθεν (line 472) would refer not to the χίλια μέτρα mentioned just before but to the ships of line 467.

the prestigious ones were not traded except for other prestige goods. (They certainly were traded, as we see in our passage and in *Odyssey* 1.184.) On the basis of this, Finley postulated that Homeric society distinguished "prestige goods" from "nonprestige goods" and that the latter could not be exchanged for the former.[67]

In every society, undoubtedly, prestige attaches to certain items more than to others, and exchanges usually involve items of similar prestige value: a woman may easily exchange a ruby ring for a sapphire, but we should pity her if we knew that she had exchanged her ruby ring for food to feed her family. Where, as in our society, the trade is indirect—she sells her ring for cash, then uses the cash to buy food—the exchange may be less obvious and so less difficult, so that the distinction between prestige goods and nonprestige goods is less sharp.

This said, we must admit that the Euneos episode, where "a plentiful supper" is paid for by metals and oxen, does not quite support Finley's description. The most prestigious items may not be here—by "bronze" and "iron" Homer may be imagining raw metal, not tripods and cauldrons— and wine is probably not the least prestigious of foodstuffs, but the impression is that the distinction between prestige goods and nonprestige goods is a matter of degree, not one of two exclusive categories. If cucumbers could not be exchanged for captives, it may be that ox hides could be exchanged for either.

Be that as it may, the Euneos episode makes it clear that when Homeric Greeks bought and sold items, they did so by barter. Tripods made good presents, and oxen were a good way of measuring the value of an item, but neither tripods nor oxen served the Greeks as a universal medium of exchange.

○ VALUE AND PRICE

Behind the distinction between the standard of value (the ox) and the medium of exchange (which might be anything) lies another distinction: a value was not necessarily a price. That is to say, the quotation of a value does not necessarily mean that the item could actually be gotten for the value stated. Items might, indeed, be evaluated for exchange—at least so it would seem from Homer's statement that Glaucus was insane to trade his hundred-ox gold armor for Diomedes' nine-ox bronze—but that was not the only reason

---

67. Finley, *World*, 120–23.

for stating a value. When Achilles offered a bronze tripod for the winner and a slave woman for the loser, Homer must tell us the value of each, because a younger, stronger, more beautiful or more highly born woman might have been worth more than a tripod.[68] It does not mean that Achilles would necessarily have agreed to trade either of them for their "value." We do not know what the basis for establishing a value may have been, nor did the Achaeans themselves necessarily have any very developed rules for such an estimation.[69] Once established, a value could be quoted in spite of the fact that it was no longer even conceivably a price: when Eurycleia was an old maid, she was still a slave for whom Laertes had once paid twenty oxen's worth, and the price once put on her made her a special slave long after her beauty had faded.[70]

Treasure for Homer, as for the Bronze Age kings whom he claimed to describe, consisted of various "prestige" items, not tallied up by weight or by number but held for their innate value, a value that might be much more than either their use value or their exchange value. The value, as already mentioned, might be greater for having belonged once to an important personage, or for having been given on an important occasion; it did not derive from use, and indeed, treasure does not seem to have been meant for use. Homer often describes the heroes feasting; never does he suggest that they brought out tripods and cauldrons of special pedigree for the purpose. Nevertheless, it *could* be used, and a rare enough item might be. For the shot-put at Patroclus's funeral games, Achilles offered the iron weight itself as the prize, announcing:

> Get up, you who would win this prize, too.
> Even if his rich fields lie very far off,
> he will have it even for five years as they come around,
> using it; for his shepherd or farmer in need of iron
> will not go into town, but, rather, this will supply him.[71]

The shot, first an athletic accessory, as it had been in the hands of its previous owner,[72] was to serve as a prize (and a more valuable one, presumably, for having belonged to so illustrious a predecessor), but its owner

---

68. *Il.* 23.702–5. These are the only prizes for which Homer gives a value.
69. See p. 28.
70. *Od.* 1.429–33.
71. *Il.* 23.831–35.
72. *Il.* 23.827.

would eventually use it for shears and plowshares. Iron was too rare a commodity to be held indefinitely in the treasure-house.[73]

When every item had its own history, no two items were really the same. A theoretical ox might measure whether two items were commensurate in value, so that the parties trading them would be striking a fair bargain, but it could not measure the matters that were most important in deciding to trade. Do I want what the other person has? Is he an equal with whom I should trade or is he one to whom I should give a gift to establish a future relationship? Is he a dependent to whom I should give gifts that he needs or a superior to whom I owe a portion of my produce? Usually, items are exchanged in Homer not because the sides need each other's items but because the circumstances require a gift or an exchange. That determined, the secondary consideration is to decide what items are appropriate to the occasion.

It is significant that the items that counted as treasure, even if not meant to be used, were functional: Gerloff to the contrary,[74] the Greeks of Homer had no interest in hoarding items whose only value was prestige. Nothing suggests that their attitude toward trade would have been different. A coin or a cowrie shell would have meant nothing to Achilles. Homeric Greece did not simply lack a standard medium of exchange; the entire concept that an otherwise worthless item would gain a value by being accepted in trade was still foreign to the Greeks. Greece not only lacked money; it did not yet conceive of money.

---

73. That one man, even a hero, could be imagined to throw as much iron as his estates could use in five years speaks tomes about the limited penetration of iron into Homeric Greece. Finley (*World*, 68) learns a similar lesson from the Mentes episode: "So crucial was the need for metal that even a king could honourably voyage in its search." But Mentes' voyage was not the sort of trade that degraded its practitioners, as noted on pp. 74–75.

74. See p. 10.

6 THE ARCHAIC AGE

Cauldrons, Spits, and Silver

IF THE POST-MYCENAEAN AGE had been one of geographic retrenchment, with local dynasts taking the place of the regional palaces, the period that we call "archaic," from the eighth century to the sixth, was one of expansion. Many new or abandoned sites were settled. The number of burials seems to have risen steeply, strongly suggesting that population, too, was rising. The extent of the population growth is debatable,[1] but the archaeological remains leave a clear impression that the number of people inhabiting the Greek communities was significantly larger than it had been for centuries.

With more settlements and more inhabitants in each settlement, there is likely to have been a good deal more interconnection among the cities. In 776 B.C.E., the first clearly attested date in Greek history, the first Olympic Games were held; the very existence of a Panhellenic festival indicates that the ties

---

1. Snodgrass (*Archaeology and the Rise*, 10–16) saw a veritable population explosion for late Geometric (eighth-century B.C.E.) Athens, and he found similar information (*Archaic Greece*, 19–25) for the Argolid. But Morris (*Burial*, 156–58) pointed out that the evidence suggests that much of the difference in burial statistics results from the fact that in the Dark Ages only the most important people were buried. Snodgrass himself has admitted that his own original estimates were too high (Hansen, "Note," 9). Nevertheless, the general opinion remains that there was a significant growth in population: see Snodgrass, *Archaeology of Greece*, 192–93; Sallares, 62–63, 84–94; Tandy, 19–58; Jonathan Hall, 216, 221.

between cities, disrupted at the end of the Bronze Age, were being renewed. The Panhellenic shrines themselves, at Olympia and at Delphi, became important places of contact for the communities, which were still quite various in their social forms.[2] Styles of pottery and of metalwork show less local variation, another indication that the Greek settlements were once again in contact with each other.[3] What can only be called an explosion in metallurgy indicates that the international trade that provided the metals had revived.[4]

The rise in population brought with it a new social organization. The old Mycenaean citadels, long since abandoned, were once more brought into use, or new ones were established. Around these citadels, communities, at first simply groups of villages, grew into what the Greeks called poleis—not, by our standards, large cities, but unmistakable urban centers where people lived together, exploited the surrounding countryside, and managed their affairs with a greater or lesser degree of independence.[5] A group of peasants and herders[6] eking out a marginal living from the land had turned into an interconnected community.

This community was not a revival of the old Mycenaean centers. Although the archaic Greeks knew that kings of Mycenae and Pylos had once ruled over many lands, they had no inkling of how they had done so. The feudal dues that had supported the palaces, the bureaucracy that had administered them, and the syllabic script that had kept their accounts had all been forgotten, as Homer's epics eloquently show. The poleis of archaic Greece were a new development—perhaps a Hellenization of the city-state organization that predominated in Israel, Philistia, Phoenicia, and northern Syria; perhaps an improvised structure growing out of the heroic households of the Dark Age under the pressure of increasing population; perhaps a bit of each. It cannot be doubted, however, that the poleis, facing new and conflicting demands and opportunities both at home and abroad, must have required a much more complex mechanism for meeting the needs of their citizens. The redistributive system of the Mycenaean palaces no longer

---

2. Morgan.

3. Snodgrass, *Dark Age*, 68–84, 419–21. If I refer to Snodgrass in these remarks in preference to the many other excellent books that have been written on the archaic period (most of which can be found in his bibliography), it is because he provides, while the others presume, the argumentation on which the statements here made are based.

4. Snodgrass, *Archaic Greece*, 49–54. For the sources of the metals that the Greeks used, see Healy, chapter 3.

5. This point is worth noting. As we see from the Linear B tablets, the Mycenaean kingdoms had united many cities under a single government, as our states do.

6. Snodgrass, *Archaeology of Greece*, 188–209.

existed and was not revived; the simple measures of gift giving, plunder, and communal feasting were not adequate to the needs of an urban community, even a small one.[7]

UTENSIL MONEY

At first, the economic vacuum seems to have been filled by a continuing elaboration of the "primitive money" of Homeric society. To Homer, tripods and cauldrons had been gifts or prizes, but although Agamemnon might promise Achilles "twenty shining cauldrons, untouched by the flame," nobody seems to have thought of *demanding* a number of cauldrons as a fine or a deposit. Indeed, Homer's interest in their quality shows clearly that Agamemnon's cauldrons lacked at least one characteristic of money: they were not interchangeable with each other.[8]

By the eighth century in Crete, it would seem, things had changed. The mentions of cauldrons in the inscriptions of the Pythium at Gortyn are very fragmentary, but numerous:

- posit one hundred [cau]ldrons e[ach-
. . . to redistribute . . . should break up [a hundred?] cauld[rons . . .
- [to b]e under oath for [t]en cauldrons-
- [let them se]t down fifty c(?)[auldrons-
- [cauld]rons each-
- six [c]auldrons of th[e-
- [twen]ty cauldrons-
- [let them set do]wn fifty [cauldrons-
twenty cauldr[ons-
- to set down f(?)ifty caul[drons for e]ach. If the serving *kosmos* should not pay in, he h[imself] and the *titas* [shall o]we if he should not pay i[n-
- for each one to set [d]own a cauldron. The same man shall not be *kosmos* within three years, nor *gnomon* within ten . . .
- [whoever] stirs up [the law suit] shall set down five cauldrons, and if there should co[me -][9]

---

7. For a broader picture of the economic expansion of these centuries, see Starr, *Economic and Social Growth.*

8. Cf. p. 69.

9. *IC* IV 14 g–p. Cf *IC* IV 1.3 d–f; 5.2; 8 e–f; 10 f–h, s–t, a*–b*, p*; 11 h–i; 21.7–8. Note Guarducci's comments at *IC* IV, pp. 41–42 and on the various inscriptions, as well as her article

Exactly what is going on in any one of these sentence fragments is most unclear, but it is hard to escape the impression that cauldrons, as inconvenient as they may seem to be, were functioning as a medium of payment in Gortyn, in which fines could be assessed and deposits demanded. One might suppose that the cauldrons are mere shorthand for "a cauldron full" of some more convenient article such as barley, but that is not likely. A cauldron (λέβης) is not a vessel of fixed proportions, and the Greeks of the archaic period seem to have been able, as were their Bronze Age ancestors, to measure volume with a regular system of measures, none of which was ever called a "cauldron." Although it may seem odd to demand that each citizen be ready with what can only seem to us the inventory of a small housewares shop, it may be that these payments were envisaged only for those citizens of the upper class from which the magistrates came, people with "tripods in their house and abundant cauldrons."[10]

For lesser people, smaller utensils would do; and at a number of sites, iron spits have been found in contexts that strongly suggest a use as currency.[11] Spits are sometimes found in burials, much as later Greeks buried coins with their dead.[12] Plutarch claims that spits were once used as money,[13] and the Greek language supports him: the smallest silver coins of the classical period were indeed called *oboloi,* "spits," and six of them made a *drachme,* or "handful" (fig. 6).[14] There are, in fact, stone receptacles designed to hold spits, and

---

"Tripodi, lebeti, oboli." I have not included the single mention of a tripod in these inscriptions (*IC* IV 8 a–d), because it is not clear that the τρίποδα ἕνα mentioned there as a penalty is really fulfilling a use any different than it would have in Homer. The square brackets in the text represent, as normal in epigraphy, letters not legible on the stone. My rough translations here necessarily gloss over many difficulties in the Greek.

10. [Hom.] *Hymn. Herm.* 61.

11. See Courbin, "Dans la Grèce."

12. Stevens, 227. These spits may, however, have been simply items for use in characteristically upper-class settings, like the firedogs that are sometimes found with them (Tandy, 159–61).

13. Plut. *Lysander* 17.5. Cf. *Etymologicum Magnum,* s.v. ὀβελίσκος; Pollux 9.77. Tod ("Epigraphical Notes," 58–59) adds Plutarch's comment (*Fabius Maximus* 27.3) that Epaminondas left behind "nothing but an iron spit" when he died. This comment is perhaps suggestive, but both Breglia (*Numismatica antica,* 188) and Bernadotte Perrin (3: p. 197 in the Loeb translation) go too far in taking this as proof that spits were still being used for money in Epaminondas's Thebes.

14. This etymology is ancient (Plut. *Lysander* 17.3) but accepted by the moderns (Frisk, s.v. δραχμή; Chantraine, s.v. δράσσομαι). Kraay (*Greek Coins,* 314) notes that the term *drachme* itself supports the derivation of obol-coins from spits, "for though six tiny silver obols were the equivalent of a drachma, they certainly did not fill the hand, whereas six iron spits were as many as the hand could comfortably grasp"—a perceptive observation already made by Heracleides of Pontus (*apud* Orion of Thebes, ed. Sturz, p. 116, s.v. ὀβολός, quoted by Svoronos [194]) and repeated by Plutarch (loc. cit.). The suggestion that a drachma was a handful of copper coins (Prakash and Singh, 55) founders on the fact that copper coinage was a late invention in Greece

Fig. 6. Six spits make a handful. (From Svoronos, p. 197.)

they hold precisely six. Why spits should have come in "handfuls" is not a question that I am able to answer. The modern "table service for six" is designed to accommodate an ordinary-sized family and a guest or two, but it is not clear that any ideal-sized group would be best served by the animals roasted on six spits. That was, however, the standard grouping of spits, and

(see p. 116). The precise weight of a drachma shows a geographical variation that probably reflects differing local weight standards going back to the Dark Age or the early archaic period; but this does not require us to believe, as Carradice and Price (91–93) would have it, that the term *drachma* itself once referred to the weight of a handful of grain.

that was the number of *obeloi* that later made up a *drachme,* when both expressions had become the names of silver coins.[15]

It is not clear whether there was any place where all the differing utensils—tripods, cauldrons, spits—served as money; different places may have either established or inherited from an earlier period the custom of using particularly this or that item.[16] The Gortynian inscriptions, as we have seen, regularly mention cauldrons; spits seem to come entirely from places that formed part of the sphere of influence of Pheidon of Argos.[17] The concept of utensils as a medium of payment seems to have been widely spread throughout Greece; the particulars may well have varied from place to place.[18] If utensils were a currency, they were probably only a local currency. For that matter, given the difficulty of transporting large utensils, they were hardly appropriate for anything more.

An interesting and revealing anecdote is told by Herodotus about the courtesan Rhodopis. Some people, says Herodotus, think that Rhodopis had built one of the pyramids, but they are wrong. Rhodopis was indeed brought to Egypt, and plied her trade successfully:

She made a lot of money, enough to make her Rhodopis,[19] but not so much as to reach such a pyramid. For anybody who wants can see a

---

15. By a process of semantic differentiation, the Athenians called a spit an ὀβελός and the coin an ὀβολός, but the difference in vowel does not mask the common origin of the two words.

16. I omit from my survey the often cited fourth-century inventory from Chorsiae in Boeotia published by Platon and Feyel. In each of three sanctuaries, the Thespians had at some time dedicated cauldrons and "handfuls of spits" [ὀβελίσκοων δάρχμαι], and the number of cauldrons and the number of "handfuls" was always the same. Platon (Platon and Feyel, 162–63) suspected that these items had been dedicated at the time when cauldrons and spits lost their monetary functions. Kraay ("Interpretation of *Ath. Pol.*," 5) went further and noticed that the largest number, thirty-five, was precisely half of an Aeginetan mina. This, however, is overinterpretation; the number thirty-five is not necessarily more significant than the three sets and two that the other sanctuaries contained, and it is surely not impossible that the cauldrons and spits were simply sacrificial kitchen sets, with one cauldron cooking the amount of stew, soup, or meat that would accompany six roasted animals.

17. Courbin, "Dans la Grèce," 227.

18. Such was the case with the utensil money of China (see p. 235) and with the utensil money of northern Germany, as documented by Sommerfeld, 61–155.

19. I do not follow Rosén's ingenious ὡς ἀνεῖναι ῾Ροδῶπιν "enough to free Rhodopis": both the change of subject and the repetition of Rhodopis's name seem awkward according to this reading, and it seems an extreme and un-Herodotean stretching of terminology to say that the money freed Rhodopis rather than that she freed herself with the money.

tenth of her money down to this day, and he can see that she cannot have been able to dedicate any great amount of money. For Rhodopis conceived a desire to leave a memorial of herself in Greece, making something that nobody else had hit upon and left in a sanctuary, and to dedicate it to Delphi as a remembrance of herself. So out of a tenth of her money, she had a lot of ox-sized[20] iron spits made, as many as her tithe allowed her, and sent them off to Delphi, where they even now are still piled up behind the altar that the Chians dedicated, opposite the temple itself.[21]

There is presumably a basis in fact for Herodotus's claim that the spits in question were still visible at Delphi in his day.[22] He seems, however, to have believed that Rhodopis herself had been paid in some other medium, presumably coins, which she then exchanged[23] for the spits she dedicated. Herodotus, who (unlike Plutarch) was not aware of the monetary use of spits, imagined them to be a purchase intentionally bizarre,[24] but in view of what we have already seen, it would seem more likely that the spits themselves had been her accumulated treasure, whatever her particular tariff may have been.

How many spits were in Rhodopis's pile? We can only guess. There were certainly more than ten. If the pile contained a hundred, it rivaled the greatest dedication of spits known to archaeology.[25] But even if we presume it to have

---

20. If they were really βουπόροι, "ox-piercing," then they were probably somewhat longer than the meter and a half that Courbin found to be common for "monetary" spits; but neither Herodotus nor Courbin can be pressed too precisely on this point. See n. 22.

21. Hdt. 2.135.2–4.

22. Since Fehling (and cf. Stephanie West, 15–16, for some worthwhile cautions), it cannot be stated categorically that Herodotus actually visited any of the places of which he claims firsthand knowledge. Fehling himself (16) doubts even Delphi, which has always been considered one of Herodotus's chief sources. Not everyone has been convinced (cf. Dewald and Marincola; Pritchett, *Liar School*), and even if Herodotus had only heard about them second hand, there is little reason to doubt that the spits existed. Herodotus is somewhat confused about the identity of this Rhodopis, as the ancients noticed: see H. T. Wade-Gery in Payne et al., 1: p. 259.

23. The participle ποιησαμένη could equally well mean that she "made for herself," but there seems no reason to saddle Herodotus with a theory of some other kind of iron money that Rhodopis then forged into spits.

24. Spits were of course used in temples, and some spit holders have been found, as well as the "Pheidonian" mass mentioned in n. 25. I do not think that these examples justify von Reden ("Money," 173) in taking Herodotus's tale to show "the Thracian freedwoman . . . betray[ing] hilarious ignorance" by thinking that her dedication was remarkable. I agree with Jeffery (124) that it was the number of spits that was remarkable, though I do not follow her in doubting entirely their monetary significance.

25. That ascribed to Pheidon at the Heraeum in Argos (on which see p. 101), Courbin ("Dans la Grèce," 218) estimated the total number of spits at ninety-six.

been a thousand, making her total worth ten thousand spits, she had not amassed an amount of wealth very great by later standards. Ten thousand obols, in classical Athens, made somewhat less than sixteen minas, a respectable but unremarkable dowry for a citizen woman.[26] That such wealth should have been considered legendary strongly suggests that when utensils were money, there was not very much money to be had.[27]

Another point to be noted about Rhodopis's spit-money is that it was not easily convertible. Where large sums of money were needed, precious metals seem never to have lost entirely their hold on the Greeks; bronze tripods and cauldrons, too, were worth a good deal more than iron spits. Even if Rhodopis had amassed ten thousand spits, it is not clear that anyone would have given her a mina of silver for them. Silver, insofar as it was used, was a more prestigious item[28]—gold certainly was[29]—and it is very likely that it would be hard to find a person willing to take spits for silver. This observation, though, entails another: utensil money, unlike later silver, does not seem to have allowed a person to pass easily to a higher social class simply by amassing a lot of utensils.

The use of utensils as a medium of exchange was a development indigenous to the Greeks—their neighbors show nothing comparable[30]—but was by no means peculiar to them. The use of spades, sickles, and other utensils (normally metal ones) is independently attested in many societies.[31] These items are always primitive money, serving only some of the purposes we associate with money. They are hoarded, like Homer's tripods; they are given as gifts, as bride-price, as ransom; and they are offered as prizes. The person

26. See the table in Schaps, *Economic Rights*, 99. Nor should we suspect that the spits themselves were worth more in Rhodopis's day than later. On the contrary, the ratio of iron to silver was strikingly low at the time of the introduction of coinage, as Courbin ("Dans la Grèce," 219–27) has demonstrated.

27. See further appendix 3.

28. In fact, silver—much less mentioned in Homer and much less found in Bronze Age sites than gold—is never mentioned as an item of exchange (H. Neitzel in *LfgrE* 1216, s.v. ἄργυρος [B]; cf. Forbes, 26). In Homer, silver items always belong to important heroes or to gods (H. Neitzel in *LfgrE* 1211, s.v. ἀργύρεος [1a]).

29. On the archaic prestige of gold as opposed to other metals, see Kurke, *Coins*, 41–64.

30. As Breglia (*Numismatica antica*, 180) correctly observes, the rings that were often used as money (see above, pp. 42, 45) were not essentially pieces of jewelry but simply a convenient form of metal appropriate for carrying and preweighing. As such, they cannot really be considered utensil money.

31. For an excellent example of what can be concluded from archaeological evidence alone, see Sommerfeld, who deals with finds from north Germany dating from the Bronze Age. He notes (3–4) that there are indications of sickles having been used as money at Kanesh (see above, p. 46), but at no other time or place in ancient Mesopotamia.

who has them is wealthy; the person who gives them is generous. But they are not generally tokens for market exchange; they are both too valuable and too bulky for that purpose. It is hard to imagine that utensils could have served as the basis for a market economy in Greece.

Utensils in Greece, in fact, were never made for the purpose of exchange. There is some evidence of local standardization of the size of spits in Argos,[32] but this is as likely to have been for culinary purposes as for monetary ones.[33] Utensils that were valued by unit need not have been standardized according to weight or dimension.

Anthropology offers another interesting observation: when utensils come to function for exchange in a large way, they tend to lose their usefulness. The knives that circulated as money in China[34] were useless for cutting; the sickles that were hoarded in Germany in the early and middle Bronze Age ceased to be functional in the late Bronze Age, and it is presumed that this is when they changed from hoarded wealth into true utensil money.[35] This phenomenon is not accidental. Where utensils are accepted "by tale," one knife being equal to another, there is no need to make a high-quality knife for monetary use. The useless knives, by Gresham's law,[36] are the ones that circulate, until all monetary knives are useless, stylized versions of the utensil.[37]

In archaic Greece, there is no evidence that such a thing happened. The spits that have been found in contexts suggesting monetary use are long, heavy, and useful, as Herodotus thought Rhodopis's spits to be. If archaeology has produced any stylized, useless cauldrons and tripods, I am not aware of them. The only reasonable conclusion is that the use of utensils as money had not progressed very far in archaic Greece. They did not, in our terms, use spits for money; they simply traded in spits.

○ FOREIGN TRADE AND WEIGHED SILVER

Had the Greeks lived in a world where no more sophisticated system was known, perhaps they would eventually have developed a complex monetary system based on utensils. But the Greeks lived in a world where other societies

---

32. Courbin, "Dans la Grèce," 219–22.

33. Strøm, 47–50.

34. See appendix 2, p. 235.

35. Sommerfeld, 271.

36. That bad money drives out good (see Chown, 16–17). The law applies to primitive money as well as coins, as Einzig (413–15) demonstrates.

37. The process is not necessarily gradual. In China, spade coins and knife coins appear at once, apparently by governmental fiat, without any intermediate stage.

had elaborated the use of money much more completely than they had. Greeks in the archaic age traded in foreign lands, and if they did not reach the sophistication of the Mesopotamians, they nevertheless used agents, kept records, understood how to turn a profit, and very likely had methods of arbitrating commercial disputes, as we learn from a few letters, written on lead, that have been discovered from this period.[38] Nobles were interested in luxuries that they pursued in voyages whose nature might be mercantile or piratical depending upon the circumstances that they met; they were likely to travel far and to carry a large freight that they had amassed from their estates. Peasants might try to change an agricultural surplus into a more lasting form of wealth by sailing abroad during the seasons when the farm could be left alone.[39] They would carry a smaller freight and would not sail far, since they could not abandon their farm for long. From these two types of archaic trade, not without benefit of the example of the Phoenician traders whom Homer had so despised, there arose a new form of more specialized trade, carried out by independent merchants whose status was not as high as that of the Homeric heroes but who were not simply the opportunistic peasants that Hesiod advised.[40] These merchants, the *emporoi*, traded more widely and more professionally than either heroes or peasants had done, in a wider range of commodities, mostly consumable items that were perhaps luxuries for some but not for everyone and items whose availability could play a not unimportant role in creating the demand for them.[41]

The Phoenicians had used precious metals as a medium of trade for centuries, and as their own international trade revived, the Greeks must have done so, too, at least when dealing with the Phoenicians. The only literary evidence we have for this dates from the late archaic period but still probably represents a situation before the introduction of coinage. The Aristotelian *Constitution of Athens* informs us that "the laws of Solon that are no longer in use" frequently use the phrase "to spend out of the naucraric silver"[42]—that is, out of silver that was in the charge of the *naukraroi*. We

---

38. Jean-Paul Wilson; his presumption (50) that the presence of local witnesses on a contract presupposes the existence of a local mercantile court is not impossible but could use more direct evidence.

39. For the peasant trade, see Hesiod *Works and Days* 618–94. For both peasant and noble trade, see Mele—who calls (following Homer and Hesiod) the noble trade *prexis*, the peasant trade *ergon* (cf. Tandy, 62–83)—and Murray, 69–76. The centralized nature of *prexis* commerce is shown by the standardized amphorae in which the produce was carried (Whitbread, 20).

40. Mele, 92–107.

41. Foxhall, 300–308.

42. [Arist.] *Ath. Pol.* 8.3.

know little of these *naukraroi,* but their name ("ship chiefs") indicates something to do with shipping, whether commercial or military, and the words quoted indicate that they had a store of silver out of which they made expenditures.[43] The one attested use for the "naucraric silver" is for the expenses on the road of sacred ambassadors to Delphi.[44] There can be little doubt, then, that the Greeks were well acquainted with the use of silver for payment and, presumably, for trade.

Silver had made little impression, as we have seen, on their internal dealings,[45] but the Greeks were probably aware that what they were doing with utensils within the polis was the same thing that they were doing with silver when dealing with foreigners. In the meantime, however, a new development had occurred in the form that precious metals might take.

○ THE STAMPING OF METALS

The value of precious metals in the Near East depended, in any given transaction, upon two intrinsic qualities:[46] the weight of the metal traded and its fineness. The history of weight is not irrelevant to the history of coinage, but it suffices here to point out that by the time of Greece's archaic age, a more or less standard system was in place throughout Mesopotamia and the Levant.[47] Weight could be ascertained by anybody with a scale and an honest set of weights, and indeed, the scale was the normal appurtenance of the trader.[48]

Fineness—that is, the percentage of the metal that was actually silver or gold—was harder to ascertain. It was well known that some kinds of silver and gold were better than others,[49] and traders might be particular about

---

43. For a good summary of what is known and what can be conjectured about the *naukraroi,* see Rhodes, 151–53.

44. *FGrH* 324 F 36 = Schol. Aristophanes *Birds* 1541.

45. Kroll ("Silver" and "Observations") argues that Athens had an internal silver bullion economy in Solon's day, and Grandjean (406) suspects the same. For my reasons for disagreeing, see Schaps, "Conceptual Prehistory," 96–100.

46. I mention "intrinsic" qualities because the price also depended, of course, on supply and demand.

47. See M. A. Powell (in English) in *Reallexikon der Assyriologie* VII, pp. 508–17, s.v. "Masse und Gewichte"; cf. p. 44. There was, of course, a limit to the standardization possible, as Powell notes (op. cit., p. 509). The Greek system was based on the Near Eastern: the name of the mina is Semitic, and its divisions (the stater) and multiples (the talent) are parallel to the Semitic equivalents (see Kroll, "Observations," 80).

48. See, for example, Lev. 19:36; Ezek. 45:10; Hos. 12:8; Amos 5:5; Prov. 11:1, 20:23. Cf. Jer. 32:10.

49. Gen. 2:12; cf., e.g., Kienast, no. 32, line 22.

the quality of metal they would accept.⁵⁰ As early as 710 B.C.E. in Assyria, the "silver of Ishtar of Arbela" seems undoubtedly to have been first-quality silver and to have circulated as such. The texts do not indicate how one recognized the goddess's silver, but they do make it clear that its circulation was not restricted to transactions involving her temple. The most plausible presumption, although archaeology has produced no palpable example, is that the temple refined its silver to a certain fineness and put some sort of stamp on the resulting ingot. Other temples seem to have done the same, and the temple of Arbela had copper ingots as well, also of known quality.⁵¹

There is no need to presume that the temple administrators were demonstrating an interest in the public welfare or the promotion of trade by smelting and stamping their silver; most likely, the stamp of the temple was intended as a sign of ownership, like other such stamps that are found in the Near East slightly earlier.⁵² But once these ingots had been given in payment to anyone with whom the temple did business, their recognized fineness will have given them a premium in trade. This does not mean that they would have driven out more pedestrian grades of silver from the market—on the contrary, Gresham's law tells us that they were more likely to be hoarded— but a customer of sufficient importance could insist on them, turning the temple's mark of ownership into a guarantee of value.

---

50. Lipiński, "Les temples," 567–68; Oppenheim, *Letters,* no. 12 (= *UET* 5, 81) and no. 147 (= *CT* XXII, no. 40). Note that neither letter takes it for granted that only fine silver would be acceptable, though the second mentions a royal edict; not every transaction and apparently not every customer was held to the strictest standards. Abraham paid Ephron silver, "current money with the merchant" (Gen. 23:16). Silver (128) seems to have been misled by the translation into suspecting the presence of a merchant's mark on the silver, but the Hebrew is ʿober la-soḥer, "passing to the merchant": the merchant here is receiving the silver, not giving it. Since neither Abraham nor Ephron was a merchant, the Targum is presumably right in taking it to mean that it was of such a quality as to be acceptable to any merchant anywhere.

51. Lipiński, "Les temples," 565–88.

52. Notably the seal of Barrekub, found in Zinjirli and dated to 730 B.C.E. (Andrae, p. 73, and Tafel 38b). Balmuth ("Monetary Forerunners," 28–29) initially recognized the inscription, scratched on a rather large disk, for a mark of ownership; later ("Remarks," 5–6), she changed her mind, and in "Critical Moment," 296–97, she saw in it "the critical moment when, by the transfer of a seal's inscription to the disc, currency acquired the guarantee whereby it became coin." But there is no indication that the disk, which weighs about half a kilogram, was ever meant to be currency at all, and coins did not become current in this area until centuries later. Christine Thompson (50) states that the disks were designed for storage of wealth, not exchange, and Professor Balmuth has told me that she is now convinced. Similar in date is a famous jasper seal found at Megiddo with the inscription "belonging to Shemaʿ, servant of Jeroboam," once reproduced on Israeli paper money but now, according to Balmuth ("Critical Moment," 296), "presumably lost." The seal was first published by Watzinger (2:64–67) and is more easily available in Avi-Yonah and Stern 3:854. Balmuth considers it similar in appearance to later coins, but such visual similarities are notoriously misleading.

There was nothing particularly important about this development as far as Assyria was concerned. The temple's ingots, even if stamped, were no more than good-quality silver, such as had been available in various places at various times. It will have been the business of a merchant to recognize them and to know good silver from bad, but there was nothing revolutionary about them. They may have come in convenient sizes—a *maneh* or half a *maneh* would be usual weights—but they were hardly standardized, and it is hard to imagine that a merchant would have failed to put them on his scale before accepting them.[53] A bar of fine silver was a good thing to have, but these ingots were not the only silver around or the only fine silver that had been seen. The nature of what the Assyrians considered money—that is, what they called "silver"—was not affected.

---

53. Lipiński ("Les temples," 578) suggests that the Arbela ingots may have had a reliably fixed weight, but his evidence is very slender, and he cautiously adds the words "en théorie." Cf. my p. 45, n. 63, on the vague standardization of Babylonian coils.

7 THE FIRST COINS

THE EARLIEST DATABLE COINS were made neither of gold nor of silver nor of copper. In the British Museum's excavations of the Artemision at Ephesus during 1904–5, ninety-three small pieces of metal were discovered, all but two of them conforming to the Milesian weight standard and most of them struck with an image on one side. Nineteen of these were a hoard found inside a pot. The largest weighed half of a Milesian stater; the smallest weighed only one ninety-sixth of a stater, a mere seventh of a gram. They are made of electrum, an alloy of the gold and silver that occur naturally in the area of Mount Tmolus and were anciently panned out of the Pactolus River that flows past the Lydian capital of Sardis.[1]

Two of these items were not coins at all but merely "dumps," small blobs of metal dropped onto a surface and cooled there. Three more were marked on one side with a sign known to numismatists as an *incuse square*, the mark of a hammer designed to make a deep impression when used to strike soft metal.[2] Four more pieces show an incuse square on one side and a pattern of striations on the other. The other coins continue to show an incuse square on one side,

---

1. The entire hoard was published by Barclay V. Head as chapter 5 of Hogarth, *Ephesus.*
2. Göbl (1:149) presumes that these items must have had a design that was either ineffectively transferred or worn away with time, "for an incuse strike without a design into which it is supposed to drive the metal is senseless"; but see the text immediately following for Kraay's reconstruction.

Fig. 7. One of the earliest electrum coins, showing the lion's head and the incuse square. (Collection of the Israel Museum, Jerusalem. Exhibit and photo © Israel Museum, Jerusalem.)

but on the other, in place of (or, in a few cases, in addition to) the striations, an intaglio design of a lion's head, goat's head, beetle, or other device now appears (fig. 7).[3] Numismatists have seen in this variation the actual invention of coinage, right before our eyes: first a goldsmith prepared preweighed bits of metal;[4] then he or someone else had the idea of striking them with a hammer to make an impression that would test whether they were electrum all the way through.[5] Since a small drop of metal is likely to slip away from the hammer, it was better to score the surface on which it was struck so as to hold it in place; this will have produced the striated items. Finally, the producer could identify himself by a sign carved into the surface on which the coin was struck, which would reproduce itself as an embossed pattern on the coin.[6] Some decades would pass before Greek mints added a design to the hammer as well, producing a coin with two faces, one on the side struck by the hammer and the other on the side that lay against the anvil.[7]

---

3. A full list of the thirteen types represented in the Artemision deposit can be found in Kraay, *Greek Coins,* 22.

4. I am not sure, though, that the dumps are correctly taken as an early stage of money. They could as well be bits of metal prepared for striking but not struck. A further problem is that of the two dumps, one of them is an eighth of a stater, a weight not otherwise testified for this coinage, which was based entirely on thirds, sixths, and fractions thereof.

5. See, however, Le Rider, 50–51, for a new explanation of the incuse squares.

6. Barclay V. Head in Hogarth, *Ephesus,* 88–89; Kraay, *Greek Coins,* 20–22.

7. Numismatists refer to the more important image (usually bearing the head of a deity or of the ruler or the heraldic emblem of the city) as the "obverse" and to the other side (often

Some of the coins of the Ephesus hoard were found beneath the recon-
structed Artemision, to which Croesus, king of Lydia, was known to have
contributed.[8] According to David Hogarth, the original excavator, the structure beneath which they were found was only the second of four buildings
on the site, of which Croesus's temple was the fourth, so that two shrines
were built and destroyed after the coins were deposited and before the
temple was rebuilt in the time of Croesus. Both the quantity and the excellent condition of the jewelry found with them convinced Hogarth that these
were not items accidentally dropped or lost but items intentionally placed
there, a "foundation deposit" placed beneath the floor of the second temple
when it was built. Since Lydia was conquered by Cyrus the Great in 546
B.C.E. and since the Artemision was not built in a day, these coins must have
been lying there beneath the floor for quite a while before the middle of
the sixth century. Hogarth—suggesting that of the two stages of building
before Croesus's temple, one corresponded to a Cimmerian attack that he
dated about 660 B.C.E.[9]—estimated their date around 700 B.C.E.[10] E. S. G.
Robinson, reviewing all the finds, showed that although most dated from
the seventh century, the latest of them could be dated from the beginning of
the sixth century.[11] The coins, which were very various in type, were surely
not all minted just before being deposited or lost in the Artemision, but they
cannot be taken as proof for the existence of coins for more than a few
decades before they were first put there, giving a date somewhere around the
year 620 for the minting of the first coins.[12] A serious attack on this dating
was mounted by Liselotte Weidauer, who preferred, on grounds that are
chiefly stylistic, a date at the beginning of the seventh century.[13] Robinson's

---

including some letters to indicate the ethnic name) as the "reverse." Normally, the obverse will
have been the anvil side, as that was less easily damaged: Jones, s.v. "obverse and reverse."

8. Hdt. 1.92.1. Cf. How and Wells, ad loc.; Hogarth, *Ephesus*, 5–8, 232–46.

9. Shortly thereafter, in "Archaic Artemisia," Hogarth admitted that this date was too early.
Subsequent scholars were not agreed on more than that the date falls somewhere in the mid–
seventh century, a consensus that held the field until Bammer's excavations (see n. 15).

10. Head in Hogarth, *Ephesus*, 74–93, particularly 92. Martin Jessop Price (9 n. 16) argued
that the temple destroyed by the Cimmerians may have been on a different site, so that the
deposit would have been *after* that event.

11. Jacobsthal, 85, 90–93.

12. So Robinson ("Ephesian Artemision," 164–65; cf. "Date").

13. Weidauer, 72–109. Her arguments have not convinced English-speaking numismatists,
who generally consider stylistic arguments uncertain and prefer the more precise, if more restricted, methodology based chiefly on establishing connections among the various dies used for a
given style of coin. The two articles of Donald Kagan, upholding the older chronology before
Weidauer's monograph, were no more successful.

dating was accepted by most numismatists,[14] but more recent excavations have demonstrated that the building that Hogarth took for an early temple is in fact the latest building on the site, apparently that of Croesus himself, so the archaeological context can guarantee only that the coins are earlier than about 560 B.C.E.[15] It is unlikely that the last word has been said in this controversy.[16]

Where were these coins minted? That they are made of electrum suggests a Lydian origin, particularly since Xenophanes, who lived in the sixth century, is quoted as having written that the Lydians were the first to strike coins,[17] and Herodotus may say the same.[18] The contribution of Croesus to the rebuilding of the temple makes Lydia a likely source for coins found under its floor. The varying types, however, make it unlikely that the kings of Lydia were directly responsible for their production, since there can have been at most only two or three kings from the time coins were invented until the fall of Lydia. Twenty known coins have the letters .WALWE., which raised the exciting possibility that we could have the name of Alyattes, the father of Croesus; but two other coins, from the same source, have the letters .KALI., which cannot possibly refer to any known Lydian king.[19] The prevailing opinion is that the types embossed on the coins identify not the reigning king but the producer of the coin.[20] Those coins bearing a lion, the symbol of the Lydian royal household, may have been issued or at least guaranteed by the king's authority.

⊚ WHY WERE COINS INVENTED?

We shall never know for certain. The inventor, of whose name we are utterly ignorant and whose era and nationality we can only approximate, will never

---

14. Vickers's suggestion that the earliest coins are as late as the 540s has not found supporters.

15. Bammer, "A *Peripteros*" and "Les sanctuaires." Howgego (*Ancient History*, 2) had already noticed the implications of Bammer's findings. Bammer ("A *Peripteros*," 150) also denies that the coins belonged to a foundation deposit.

16. It was already unlikely when these words were first written, and now Le Rider has offered new arguments for preferring a date not before 590–580.

17. *Apud* Pollux 9.83. Xenophanes is the oldest author to be quoted on the subject. Pollux (loc. cit.) offers other candidates as well, not all plausible. See W. L. Brown, and after him Kagan, "Pheidon's Aeginetan Coinage."

18. Hdt. 1.94.1. But it had already been noted by Six (210 n. 69) and, more recently, by Balmuth ("Remarks," 3) that Herodotus's words can also be taken to mean only that they were the first to strike a bimetallic currency, which is certainly true.

19. Wallace, ".WALWE. and .KALI.," with references to earlier literature.

20. See Breglia, *Numismatica antica*, 42; Furtwängler, 157–58.

tell us. The question, however, has a certain fascination, and there is a certain amount of evidence that makes some of the many hypotheses advanced more probable than others. The hypotheses may be grouped into two families: those that take coinage to have been a response to a need for a uniform and reliable medium of payment (the ideas differ on the sort of payment envisioned) and those that take it to have been a response to the problematic nature of electrum itself.

It is not, on the face of it, likely that coins were designed, as Paulus thought,[21] merely to facilitate retail trade; the smallest electrum coins were too small in dimensions and perhaps too valuable[22] to be practical for the smallest purchases. Nor is it easy to see who would have been likely to issue coins for such a purpose. The traders in the local marketplace would not have been influential enough in the palace to have produced such an innovation on the part of the king; if, on the other hand, we take it to have been the merchants themselves, perhaps goldsmiths, who struck the first coins, it is hard to see what advantage they would have gotten out of it, since it is hard to believe that the volume of trade at this date was such that a given coin would ever be likely to return to the merchant who originally marked it.[23]

Aristotle's presumption that it was international trade that suggested the necessity of coinage is also unlikely. Long-distance trade had been going on for centuries (indeed, for millennia) without the need for coinage.[24] More tellingly, no early coinage seems to have circulated far from its place of issue until the end of the sixth century, a certain indication that the earlier coins not only were not invented for international trade but were not even used for it when available.[25] The first coins to be spread widely were those of Thrace and Macedon, countries not in the forefront of commerce but rich in silver; the "owls" of Athens soon followed.[26]

Other theories have been proposed. R. M. Cook, noting that the most likely use a state would have for small, standardized sums of precious metal would be to make small, standardized payments, suggested that the first

---

21. For the ideas of Aristotle and of Paulus, see pp. 5–7.

22. R. M. Cook, 260. Kraay (*Archaic and Classical,* 318 n. 2) calculates that the ninety-sixth of a stater would have been worth about two Attic silver obols. This sum was sufficient—even in fifth-century Athens, when coinage was much more abundant—to reimburse the citizens at the ecclesia for a full day's work lost ([Arist.] *Ath. Pol.* 41.3; cf. Rhodes, ad loc.).

23. R. M. Cook, 260.

24. See pp. 43–47, 53, 61, 74–75, 81.

25. Kraay, "Hoards," 76–85, 88.

26. Ibid., 82–83. Even the famous Aeginetan turtles occur in quantity only within the vicinity of Aegina: see ibid., 78–79.

coins were struck to pay mercenaries.[27] This, however, is to bring the retail trade hypothesis in by the back door, for the prestige value of these small and standard coins cannot have been great, and if they were not generally acceptable in some kind of exchange, it is hard to see why mercenaries should have risked their lives to accumulate them.[28] Even less attractive is the theory of M. J. Price that the earliest coins were designed to be "bonus" payments, parting gifts for employees, "far more akin to gifts (or medals) than to coins as we know them."[29] It stretches the imagination to think that one-seventh of a gram of electrum, a mere speck in a person's hand, could serve as a medal, particularly if it had no value in trade.

Colin Kraay generalized the "mercenary" argument by suggesting that the earliest coins were designed to be "legal tender" for all payments both by and to the state: "Among receipts may be mentioned . . . harbour dues, . . . fines and penalties, and any other taxes. Payments will have included those occasions on which a surplus was divided among the citizens . . . , the pay of mercenaries or soldiers, salaries paid to experts, and expenditure on public works . . ."[30] This succeeds in broadening the uses of coinage, but I doubt that it suffices: would all the workers on a public building be willing to be paid in a small piece of metal that would be useful to them only insofar as they could give it back to the government that gave it? Some nineteenth-century corporations practiced such a policy, paying their workers in scrip that only the company would accept as payment; but these corporations—who gained no love from their workers for this policy—also ran a "company store" where the workers could buy the goods they needed. If coinage was not a medium for retail trade, state payments are not likely to have made it acceptable.

The second family of explanations sees the origin of coinage in the problematic nature of electrum itself. The gold panned from the Pactolus is quite variable in its contents, varying today from 17 to at least 24 percent silver, with the rest being mostly—but not entirely—gold.[31] Electrum, much more than the silver ingots of the temple at Arbela, could use a stamp that indicated where it had come from and who was responsible for it.

The earliest electrum coins, in fact, are not simply disks of the metal that flows down the Pactolus. They are much poorer in gold than the electrum that

---

27. This suggestion was also supported by Bogaert ("Encore," 127–28).
28. Martin Jessop Price noted further that if mercenaries were the recipients, the coins should have spread more widely than they did.
29. Martin Jessop Price, 7.
30. Kraay, "Hoards," 89.
31. Waldbaum, 186; Meeks, 100; Cowell and Hyne, 172.

could be gotten from the river, and it has been suggested that this very difference provided the motivation for their invention, a literally royal scam by which the king's treasury passed off as real electrum metal that it had debased with a good deal more silver than it should have.[32] We do not, in fact, know at what value these coins may have circulated, but the practice of giving coins a nominal value that is slightly higher than their value as bullion has been a normal one throughout the centuries; it is known as *seigniorage* and is justified as the means by which the issuing authority reimburses itself for the costs of minting the coins. The reader will not be surprised to know that the markup usually leaves the mint not only reimbursed but with a tidy profit.

Seigniorage, however, is not likely to have been the reason for the first coins. Seigniorage can only succeed if the coins are actually accepted in the marketplace at their stated worth, and that is precisely what could not be guaranteed when they were first minted, with no previous custom of taking a coin at its face value. The markup, moreover, was too great: the royal coinage apparently had a consistent fineness of 54 percent gold, a difference so great as to be visible to the naked eye.[33]

The uncertain value of electrum, however, is likely to have been a real problem in Lydia. A sixth-century inscription from the very temple where the earliest coins were found indicates that large donations were made in silver and gold, not in electrum, and we must presume that these metals, not their uncertain alloy, provided the standard by which value was measured.[34] Robert Wallace suggested that the coinage was fixed to an arbitrary value, applicable to all coins regardless of their actual gold content.[35] It is probably true that the electrum generally used in coins was often, as it continued to be in later years, of variable fineness;[36] more recent work, however, has indicated that the royal coinage of Lydia was quite regular in its ratio of gold to silver.[37] It appears likely, then, that the type was indeed intended as a

---

32. Bolin, 11–45.

33. Cowell and Hyne, 172. Cf. Wallace, "Origin," 388: "There is sufficient difference in color between coins of 60% silver and coins of 40% silver to result not in standardized issues, but in endless doubts and disputes over particular coins."

34. *IE* 1; cf. Furtwängler, 158.

35. Wallace, "Origin," 392–93.

36. Bolin, 24, table 2. But Bolin's figures are based chiefly on Hammer, that is, on specific gravity alone, an insufficient criterion when other metals are involved, as they usually are, or when air bubbles are present (Wallace, "Origin," 386 n. 14). Kraay ("Composition") provided more precise information on twenty electrum coins in the Ashmolean. For later Greek issues, see Figueira, 93 n. 3.

37. "The gold contents of the coins are very consistent (a necessary requirement for coinage), with all but two of the British Museum's royal types within 1% of the average of 54%" (Cowell and Hyne, 172).

guarantee, though the guarantee could at first indicate no more than "this is gold from so-and-so's shop." Such parallels as can be found would seem to indicate that the earliest stamps were private indications of ownership that were understood by those who dealt with it to indicate the quality of the metal; eventually, however, the royal lion indicates that the palace stood behind the currency, whether or not it was directly involved in its minting.[38]

Whatever their antecedents and whatever the motive behind their minting, the first coins were surely an innovation. They were not a mere extension of the kind of stamp that may have adorned the ingots of the temple at Arbela. The temple had stamped ingots of a pound or more, whereas the heaviest coins of Asia Minor weighed no more than half an ounce. The coins of the earliest datable hoard came in no fewer than eight denominations, from halves to ninety-sixths of a Milesian stater. The motivation behind the "cutting" (to use the Greek term for what we call "striking") of such coins must have been quite different from the motivation of the temple of Arbela in casting its ingots. Ingots of a pound or so are a convenient way in which to store silver, and they were probably made for that purpose. Small and minutely subdivided weights of electrum, however, were undoubtedly made for payment, not for storage.

For what sort of payment? Perhaps indeed for payment to the state, but retail trade must have been present in the background, as Herodotus states.[39] When I stated that retail trade was not likely to have been what brought about the invention, I said so because for the most common forms of retail trade, electrum coins were not useful; they were too valuable. For those larger-value trades where electrum would be used, however, coins solved a problem that surely came up in commerce as much as anywhere else. The first coins probably changed hands by weight; Head's idea, rarely quoted, that the smallest denominations were designed as makeweights to bring a scale into balance, remains the most probable explanation.[40]

The coins must have been popular, for they continued to be produced in Lydia and even imitated in Lydia's Ionian neighbor cities. It is not as clear, however, that they succeeded in standardizing the value of electrum. Croesus, the last king of Lydia, eventually ended the electrum issue and began to mint coins of silver and of gold. The process used, as uncovered in the Sardis excavations, involved technology that was not new but that had previously

---

38. Holloway; Furtwängler.
39. Hdt. 1.94.1.
40. Head in Hogarth, *Ephesus,* 88.

been used only to burnish the surface of naturally occurring metal. It was probably the need to give the coins a reliable fixed value that led the Lydians to refine their metal throughout, producing coins of solid gold and of solid silver, whose value would withstand a tester's chisel.[41]

For all that, it was not in Lydia that coins were to find their future. They may have had a considerable effect on the economy and society of the Lydians, but we have no way of knowing that. In 546 B.C.E., Cyrus of Persia defeated Croesus, and the Lydian kingdom disappeared forever.[42] The life of its people, whatever it may have been like, has been covered by the ages.

⊙ THE SPITS OF PHEIDON OF ARGOS

The earliest hoards contained electrum coins apparently issued by the Greek cities who were neighbors and subjects of the kings of Lydia. The idea of coinage seems at first to have been a local phenomenon, restricted to the west coast of Asia Minor; but that soon changed.

The *Etymologicum Magnum*, a compilation of a twelfth-century antiquarian, includes the following brief account.

> Pheidon of Argos was the first of all people who coined money, in Aegina; and giving the coins and taking the spits in return, he dedicated them to Hera of Argos.[43]

The excavators of the Heraeum at Argos had the good fortune to come upon one of those thrilling but dubious discoveries, a find that seems to match an otherwise uncertain story. They found a large bundle of iron spits and a large iron object in the shape of a giant spit, whose weight may once have been the same as that of the bundle of spits. The spits themselves were stuck into a mass of lead, putting it beyond doubt that they were meant to be left there forever, not used for any sacrificial purpose or for any purpose at all. The spits are just the right size for six of them to make a handful.[44]

There remain, as always, many questions. The date of Pheidon himself is

---

41. The process of refining gold at Sardis has received its definitive treatment, as of this writing, by Ramage and Craddock.

42. Croesus's coinage, however—not the old-fashioned electrum coinage, but the gold and silver series that he seems to have commenced shortly before his fall—continued into the Persian period until it was replaced by the darics and sigloi issued by the Great Kings (Kraay, *Greek Coins*, 31–32).

43. *Etymologicum Magnum*, s.v. ὀβελίσκος.

44. Waldstein, 1:61–62, 77, with fig. 31 on p. 63; see my fig. 6, p. 94.

uncertain: the *Marmor Parium* puts him as early as 895–893 B.C.E.,[45] and Ephorus, apparently the origin of the story that it was Pheidon who invented coinage, seems to have placed him around the middle of the eighth century.[46] Either of these dates would be too early for the introduction of coinage. Herodotus, at the other extreme, makes Pheidon's son a suitor for the hand of Agariste, daughter of Cleisthenes, who was tyrant of Sicyon in the first third of the sixth century.[47] This date is more appropriate for the earliest coinage, though only if we are willing to grant that Greek states were minting coins of pure silver before Croesus did;[48] the question is multifaceted, and scholarly opinion remains divided.[49]

Even if the introduction of coins can have taken place in Pheidon's lifetime, it is not at all clear that Pheidon—or any ruler—was responsible for it.[50] If, moreover, the hundred or so spits found[51] were all the spits of Argos, their monetary use must have been limited indeed. All the archaeological evidence thus far indicates that the first coins were not struck in Argos, in Aegina, or in Europe at all, and other sources mention Pheidon as an originator not of money but of a system of weights or measures.[52]

Nevertheless, the suggestion is more than tempting that the Heraeum dedication dates from the time when silver coin was first substituted for iron spits. It becomes even more tempting when we consider the discovery of an inscription of similar age from Perachora near Corinth that begins, "I am a drachma, white-shouldered Hera . . ." The rest of the inscription is irretrievably mutilated, but it has been suggested that this drachma was a coin identifying itself as being equivalent to a "handful" of the old spits, a dedication designed to show the public what a drachma was now to be.[53] Paul

---

45. *FGrH* 239 A 30.

46. Jacoby, ad loc. (= *FGrH* II B, 684). Ephorus was a historian of the fourth century B.C.E.

47. Hdt. 6.127.3.

48. The earliest Aeginetan coinage that can be securely dated is from the Persepolis foundation deposit of about 511 B.C.E., but it is universally accepted that Aegina had been minting for some time before this (Kraay, *Archaic and Classical*, 43). How and Wells's belief (ad loc.) that Herodotus's date is too *late* for the earliest coins is based on Hogarth's dating (see above, p. 95), which is no longer widely held, and on a presumption, which archaeology has not confirmed, that Greek coinage began in the course of the seventh century.

49. See, in particular, Tomlinson, 81–83; Kelly, 94–111; and the broader bibliography cited in Tausend, 1 n. 2.

50. See W. L. Brown; *contra* Courbin, "Dans la Grèce," 224 with n. 5.

51. See Courbin, "Dans la Grèce," 218.

52. Hdt. 6.127.3; Strabo 8.355. Cf. Th. Lenschau in *RE* XIX, cols. 1943–44, s.v. "Pheidon" (4).

53. See Milne, 18–19, with the unprovable conjecture that the Corinthian drachma was at first fixed according to the "Pheidonian" standard, then changed to the new, lighter Corinthian standard, at which time the inscribed stone was reused for building material.

Courbin added another consideration with the observation that the spits found in the Heraeum may be seen as evidence of a uniform weight and length for spits in the Argolid, a phenomenon that he took as evidence for their monetary function.[54]

If these finds are correctly interpreted, then there was in Argos[55] a conscious, governmental decision to replace the primitive utensil money that had been serving as a means of exchange and payment with coins; but other explanations are possible. The dedication of the spits, even when accompanied by an oversize iron "model spit" of the same weight, may easily date from the period of utensil money without necessarily being evidence of its demonetization; the drachma that announced itself at Perachora may have been merely a group of six spits;[56] approximate standardization of size and weight of spits may have functional reasons as well as governmental ones (and indeed, true utensil money need not have a fixed weight). In fact, the story as recorded in the *Etymologicum Magnum* is hardly believable, for a simple reason: if Pheidon called in all the spits (that is, all the money) in his realm, gave silver in return for them, and then declared the spits worthless and dedicated them to the goddess, he will have left himself with neither silver nor spits, having reduced his wealth by an amount equivalent to the entire supply of money in circulation. This is perhaps not inconceivable, but it is not the way Greek tyrants were known to behave.

Perhaps a more likely suggestion is that Ephorus's story is not an account to which the spits bear independent witness but, on the contrary, a rationalization of the spits themselves, an explanation like that by which Herodotus explained the spits behind the altar of the Chians at Delphi, which were said to be the dedication of Rhodopis. Even if we restrict ourselves to this less imaginative reconstruction, it is clear that coins appear in Greece in the sixth century, shortly after the electrum coins of Lydia.

The substitution of coins for spits and cauldrons was in a certain sense an innovation, since coins themselves were a new phenomenon; but in a larger historical perspective, it was merely a matter of borrowing and adaptation. Silver had been used from time immemorial in the Near East as a medium of exchange and a standard of value. Its use in Asia was much more widespread than its use in Greece had ever been, and its cultural meaning was much broader, approaching very closely what we now mean by the word *money*. In

---

54. Courbin, "Obéloi d'Argolide." Courbin ("Dans la Grèce," 225) did not, however, believe that Pheidon had "demonetized" the spits.

55. Of course, the idea of a *Panhellenic* "governmental decision" would be anachronistic.

56. As H. T. Wade-Gery in Payne et al., 1:257–61, argued.

the growing Greek poleis of the archaic period, exchange and payment played an ever greater role. At first, Greek society had developed its own indigenous "money"; but the invention of coinage made the precious metal of the East so convenient of use that the Greeks came to adopt it themselves.[57]

The Greek coins were silver, not electrum; the electrum coins of Asia Minor were a local phenomenon, due to the presence of mixed gold and silver lodes in the valley of the Pactolus River. European Greek cities had either silver or, much more commonly, no precious metal at all; it was neither necessary nor sensible for them to mix gold and silver to imitate the Asians. The change to silver indicates that coins, even if they had begun as a solution to the problem of the variability of electrum, had come to be appreciated as what they now were: a countable unit of value. A few cities continued to mint electrum—the electrum staters of Cyzicus remained a popular and trusted coinage down to the fourth century—but the future of coinage, in Greece, was in silver.

◎ THE SPREAD AND ASSIMILATION OF COINAGE

For the Greeks, there can be no doubt that coins were an idea whose time had come. They continued to be produced; they spread over a wider and wider area; and undoubtedly, they circulated from hand to hand. States large and small began to mint coins; by the end of the sixth century, more than one hundred mints had operated in the Greek world.[58] Most of these issues were small and circulated locally; for international trade, it may be doubted whether coins were at first any better than any other form of precious metal for an exchange medium. As for local trade, not every polis had a marketplace so developed as to need small coins, and many did not mint small change.[59]

---

57. I do not agree with Kurke's suggestion (*Coins,* 303–4) that silver was adopted because it was a metal with a more middle-class ideology than gold. Silver had been the main medium of international trade throughout the eastern Mediterranean when Athens had been a village, and it needed no ideology to make it preferable to gold, which was too rare and too valuable. This does not require us to deny that Athenian ideology may have preferred the more "democratic" (and "Attic") silver, but unlike Kurke (304 n. 11), I do not see this question as "a chicken-and-egg problem" whose answer "is impossible to know."

58. Holle, 1. The body of Holle's thesis includes an area-by-area review of these mints.

59. Kraay, "Hoards," 76–85, who regards "the triangle formed by Corinth, Rhodes and Crete . . . as a currency area (like S. Italy or Sicily), within which Aeginetan coinage was to be found in quantity, and outside which it occurs in numbers no greater than those of many other coinages" (79). He is even more dismissive (79–80) of the ostensibly wide circulation of Corinthian coinage. The coins undoubtedly traveled and are often found far from their point of origin, but they are rarely a major part of the total silver in a hoard.

Fig. 8. An Athenian owl tetradrachm. The owl's face has been dented with a chisel to test whether the coin was solid silver. (Photo courtesy of David Bar Levav, Jerusalem.)

Thrace and Macedon, where silver was mined, were silver-exporting areas, and the coins of these areas are sometimes found in large numbers in hoards outside of Greece in the late sixth century.[60] Aegina, which had no silver mines of its own, was the first state of Greece proper to mint coins in large quantity, and its coins are found over a broad area, though they are numerous only in hoards from the Cyclades and their vicinity.[61] The first issues of Athens, the *Wappenmünzen,* included many coins of small denominations, and the basic coin was a didrachm; with the latest of the *Wappenmünzen,* those with a gorgon's head on them, the basic coin of Athens became a tetradrachm, twice as heavy as the old coin and better adapted to use as an international currency. This is presumably when Athens began to use coinage as a way of exporting the silver of the Laureion mines; with the famous owl coins that soon followed (fig. 8), Athenian coinage came to be the dominant coinage in the entire eastern Mediterranean.[62]

The adoption of coinage was not a matter of any state initiative by which earlier forms of money were forbidden; on the contrary, precoinage items probably functioned side by side with coins throughout the sixth century. This was not simply a matter of variation from place to place; even within a single polity, the new money took some time to drive out the old.[63] But drive

---

60. Ibid., 82–83. In the fifth century, they were generally displaced by Athenian owls.
61. Ibid., 78–79.
62. Ibid., 80–82, 87; Kroll, "From Wappenmünzen," 13–17.
63. Von Reden, "Money," 156–61.

it out it did, until the time was reached, by the end of the sixth century, when "money" to a Greek meant "coins."

The Phoenicians, the Carthaginians, and the Egyptians continued to run their economies and their trade without coins. It has generally been thought that there was a lag of centuries between the Greek adoption of coinage and its spread to the Near East. To my knowledge, it has not hitherto been noticed that numismatic scholarship of the last few decades has closed this gap. It now appears that there was no massive circulation of Greek coinage in the Near East until the Aeginetan turtles, which were soon supplanted by the Athenian owls. At first, the coins arriving from Greece presumably sufficed for their main purpose, which was to be traded back to Greeks for other commodities; but when the volume of Athenian coinage dwindled in the 470s and 460s,[64] their Levantine trading partners filled the vacuum. The relative paucity of Near Eastern coinage and its failure to spread inland for two or three more generations[65] show that the barbarians struck coins for the Greek trade, not because they had come to think, as Greeks did, that silver that was not coined was not really money. The earliest Phoenician coins were minted slightly before the middle of the fifth century.[66] Judaea followed yet later, and its early coins were imitations of Athenian owls.[67]

Not only did these peoples not mint coins of their own; at first, they did not even treat the Greek coins as anything more than lumps of silver, to be cut up like anything else if necessary to even up a balance (fig. 9), a practice that they continued in the fifth and even the fourth centuries.[68] They may have recognized that this silver was of reliably good quality; the Babylonians, who were not yet minting coins, refer to them often, distinguishing them from mere *Hacksilber,* though the latter remained their dominant commercial money.[69] Even the Persians, who took up the minting of coins from the

---

64. For this phenomenon, see Starr, *Athenian Coinage,* 81–84.

65. In the fourth century, but not before, Tyrian and Sidonian coins were exported widely; Elayi and Elayi (386) attribute this to a decrease in the production of Attic coins, whose place was filled by Phoenician coins.

66. At Byblos, according to Elayi and Elayi (386); Betlyon is now out of date. Tyre, Sidon, and Arwad began to coin soon afterward: Elayi and Elayi 89–90, 240–41, 363–65.

67. Meshorer, 1:13–18. Loewe (147–50) claims that the expression ṣeror naqub in Haggai 1:6 implies that coins were in common use in Judaea as early as 520 B.C.E., but he admits that the term might also apply to a bundle of *Hacksilber* and that coins themselves in that period in the Near East were still treated as *Hacksilber* (cf. Kraay, "Hoards," 84).

68. Robinson, "Find," 106; Balmuth, "Jewellers' Hoards," 30; Kraay and Moorey, 229–31.

69. On the transition from the use of uncoined silver to the use of coins in Babylon see Vargyas, "*Kaspu ginnu,*" "Silver and Money," and Vargyas, *History of Babylonian Prices,* 24–34, 42–44, 46–51, cf. 21 n. 116, and Le Rider, 30–35.

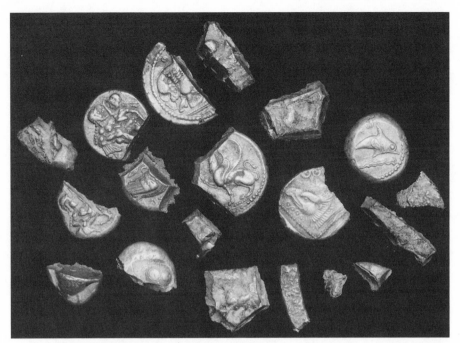

Fig. 9. The Jordan hoard: whole coins, chopped fragments of coins, and fragments of silver. (Photo courtesy of the Ashmolean Museum, Oxford.)

defeated Croesus, seem to have used them chiefly, if not exclusively, in the vicinity of the old Lydian empire.[70] The Carthaginians, who did not mint coins until the end of the fifth century, began the practice on Sicily, where they were in constant contact with Greek colonists who had been minting coins for generations; they may have needed the coins to pay mercenaries.[71] The Etruscans, also a commercially active people, were yet later.[72] Among the Greeks, however, even those who did not mint their own coins—on Crete, for example, coins seem not to have been minted before the fifth century and were widely produced only from the end of the fourth[73]— apparently used the coins of other states, speaking of them in monetary terms, from the time that they came into general use.[74]

---

70. Schlumberger; Carradice, "'Regal' Coinage," 89–90. This view, however, has now been challenged by Vargyas, "*Kaspu ginnu,*" 249–60.

71. Ameling, *Karthago*, 188–89; Jenkins and Lewis, 18.

72. Howgego, *Ancient History*, 2.

73. Stefanakis, 257–60.

74. Ibid., 249–57; von Reden, "Money," 158–59.

Why were coins so exciting to the Greeks and so uninteresting to their neighbors? The answer is surely that they filled a need peculiar to Greek society. The Phoenicians had no need of innovation to encourage trade; they had been dealing freely in silver for centuries. The scale was their identifying mark, and to collect all silver simply to put a stamp on it and return it was not anything they needed. Egypt was a society in which trading played only a limited role, and its own mechanisms of trade sufficed for that role; as for payments to the government, they were arranged in well-established patterns, and replacing them with coinage could have added only confusion. It was Greece that was searching for new forms of government and administration to manage the new complexity of the poleis and new ways of organization to maintain its people, and coins made that administration and that organization simpler and more manageable than spits and cauldrons could have done.

Both the ease with which the new coins could change hands and their uniform value made them peculiarly appropriate to Greek ideas. An aristocratic society whose values were cemented by reciprocity both in gift giving and in hospitality produced an outlook that saw many of the most basic human relationships as matters of exchange. Coins could be subsumed into a preexisting worldview in which giving and taking were essential ways of defining and reinforcing the social order, ways that also offered a means for moving up or down within the social order. To meet one's needs, reward one's friends and dependents, and establish one's own independence and power by means of exchange was behavior congenial to the archaic Greek.[75]

The uniform value of coins and their almost unlimited exchangeability met a real need in Greek society. In a world where class conflicts were sharply felt and the moral authority of the wellborn was not taken for granted,[76] coins offered a basis for evaluating worth and behavior at every level of society—a basis more universal and more subtle in its distinctions than the oxen of Homer. The conventional way of evaluating behavior in terms of exchange became the basis for a new and more broadly based morality, in which the relative claims of the poor and the well-to-do could be evaluated against each other and given a proper weight and recompense.[77] In a sense, then, coinage was a way of giving each person what was proper, very much a continuation of traditional Greek ways of thought; in

---

75. Von Reden, *Exchange*, passim; "Money," 161–76.

76. Even, perhaps, by the nobles themselves: see, for example, Sarpedon's words to Glaucus in Hom. *Il.* 310–21, urging him to fight in order to justify his enjoyment of noble status.

77. Will, 214–26.

another sense, as we shall see, it was subversive of traditional distinctions, denying by its very universality the inherited structure of the society into which it was introduced.[78]

There were more prosaic advantages to coinage in Greece. Retail trade was undoubtedly one. It is true that many poleis do not seem to have minted small-denomination coins, and that many Greek states had no markets at this stage or even a century or two later.[79] But rather more of the first Attic coins occur in small denominations than in large, and numismatists have also noted that small coins are more likely to have disappeared through wear or to have been ignored by archaeologists and by treasure hunters—and are, for that matter, less likely to have been hoarded and buried in the first place.[80] In the Athenian agora, where coins recovered are mostly coins dropped by their owners, the small denominations predominate.[81]

We should remember as well that trade in archaic Greece held a limited place chiefly because of the absence of a convenient mechanism for it. For the kinds of trade for which a Greek would have accepted six spits, a silver drachma would now do; for small bargains of a single spit, one may easily suppose that a single spit was still available. The introduction of coinage was not the invention of a medium of exchange but simply the introduction of a medium that had previously been used only for large amounts and for foreign trade into much smaller amounts and local trade. That the use of coins did not immediately and everywhere penetrate to the lowest levels[82] may not be surprising. The situation was, however, to change decisively, for an invention can make for itself a place that had not been there before.

When the Greeks began to use silver obols instead of spits, it is not likely that they intended more than to find an easier medium to pass from hand to hand when necessary and to hoard when possible. Convenience, however, can be destiny. We may see it in our own day. Modern art and music have been radically transformed since it has become possible to produce a perfect representation with a camera or a symphonic performance with a recording.

---

78. See pp. 114–20. Kurke (*Coins*, particularly 41–64, 299–336) believes that coinage was considered by the aristocracy an illegitimate innovation, while it was adopted by the demos as a metaphor for the equality of citizenship. Von Reden ("Money," 168–76), while rejecting Kurke's class conflict, admits that coins were a problematic metaphor for the Greeks: the idea may have been rooted in old Greek ways of thought, but it was not without revolutionary implications.

79. R. M. Cook, 259–60; Kraay, "Hoards"; Kraay, *Greek Coins*, 317–18.

80. Holle, 187–88. Holle notes, however, a local distinction: Asia Minor seems to have used small-denomination coins much more widely than did mainland Greece.

81. Kroll, *Greek Coins*, 4.

82. See p. 105.

The art of penmanship has withered since the typewriter made it possible to produce crisp and legible copy in a fraction of the time. More significantly, the place of images, music, and writing in our lives has expanded enormously simply because they are easily available. Coins, too, though superficially only a convenience, made the behaviors that they enhanced—trading, paying, evaluating, and hoarding—a much larger part of Greek life than they had ever been.

8   Money and the Market

THE MONETIZATION OF THE MARKETPLACE appears to have been immediate (a matter of decades at the most) and total. Nowhere in the historical record after coins have been invented do we find local markets being run by barter. Everything sold in the marketplace was sold for a price, and the price was expressed and expected in coins. As we have seen in his story of Rhodopis,[1] Herodotus was unaware that iron spits had ever been used as a medium of exchange. By the mid–fifth century and probably well before that, market trade implied coins.

The two, in fact, seem to have grown up together. The physical location of the market was in the general place of meeting for citizens, the agora. This was the place where speakers addressed the people (ἀγορεύω), and the same[2] was now the place where people bought wares (ἀγοράζω). This last verb had been unknown to Homer's vocabulary:[3] on Achilles' shield, in the "city at peace," the people are gathered in the agora to adjudicate a dispute, not for commerce.[4] With the development of retail trade, however, the place

---

1. Pp. 85–86.

2. Or nearly the same. The central agora itself seems, at least in Athens, to have been set aside for public buildings, with the "commercial" agora crowding in on it from all sides: Thompson and Wycherley, 170–71.

3. The same is true for all the derivatives of ἀγορά as "marketplace": Chantraine, s.v. ἀγορά (3).

4. Hom. *Il.* 18.497–508. My colleague Gabriel Danzig points out that Lattimore is anachronistic in 497 when he translates, "The people were assembled in the market place."

Fig. 10. Markings on the bottom of an oinochoe; designating twenty (ΔΔ) painted (ποι{κιλαί}) vessels for a drachma and four obols (⊢||||). (Courtesy of the Shefton Museum, Newcastle.)

of public assembly (for that is what the word *agora* means) was the obvious place for sellers to look for customers, and by the archaic era, the term *agora* meant both a political center and a market.[5] Today, the commercial meaning has won out entirely, and a modern Greek agora is simply a market.

---

5. See, in particular, the observations of Miller (219–23). But I believe that he is being anachronistic in putting the development of the commercial agora before the political. The literary evidence, as mentioned in the text, indicates the opposite.

The classical agora of Athens, as traced by its public buildings, seems first to have developed in the course of the sixth century, either simultaneously with the first Athenian coins or shortly thereafter.[6] It may well have been the result of city planning: although the impressive buildings were later constructions, the agora from the beginning seems to have been laid out over the same general area and with the same general plan that later defined it.[7] The place in which Athenians had previously congregated was hardly remembered by the Athenians and has not been securely identified to this day.[8] The agora grew up in the Kerameikos, the potters' quarter, and excavations have found evidence of potters' waste from as far back as 1000 B.C.E., but there are no other signs of commercial or industrial activity before the growth of the agora itself.[9] By the middle of the sixth century, the activity of potters and painters seems to have increased almost tenfold,[10] and as the sixth century progressed, the agora seems to have become a true commercial center, without ever losing its position as the chief gathering place for citizens.[11] By the middle of the fourth century, one could buy there

> figs, marshals of the court, grape bunches, turnips, pears, apples, witnesses, roses, medlars, haggis, honeycombs, chickpeas, lawsuits, beestings, curds, myrtle, allotment machines, blue cloth, lambs, water clocks, laws, indictments.[12]

Not everything that went on in the agora was an innovation. We must distinguish between crafts and trade. Long before the sixth century, the production of pottery was in the hands of professional craftsmen. The pres-

---

6. Schaps, "Monetization of the Marketplace." Miller (224 n. 4) doubts that the agora has any connection at all with the Peisistratids; he thinks it is earlier, a product of the early sixth century.

7. Von Steuben, 33–37.

8. Thompson and Wycherley, 19. For the archaic agora, the most impassioned advocate was Oikonomides. Miller (214) brings strong and perhaps conclusive arguments for locating it on the north slope of the Acropolis, as suggested earlier by Robertson (157–68).

9. Thompson and Wycherley, 170–71.

10. See Webster, *Potter and Patron*, 1–3.

11. Aristotle disliked this and thought that there should be a second agora, untainted by commercialism. He recommended "what is called a free market, as is the custom of Thessaly" (Arist. *Pol.* VII 12.4–6 [1331a 30–b 4]).

12. Eubulus, *PCG* fr. 74, quoted in Athenaeus XIV 640b–c. Eubulus is musing on the location of the law courts and all the public buildings in the agora near the market stalls. It has been suggested that two characters are speaking here, with one delivering the "straight" lines ("figs . . . grape bunches, turnips, pears, apples . . .") while the other interpolates ("marshals of the court . . . witnesses . . . lawsuits . . ."): see *PCG,* ad loc.

ence of a blacksmith among the gods suggests, as we should have presumed on our own, that ironwork, too, was a specialized profession. The same conclusion might be drawn from Achilles' boast that the dependents of the man who won his iron shot "will not go into town, but rather this [the shot] will supply him."[13] It need not, perhaps, be the case that these crafts were the only means of support for those who practiced them; it is possible that potters and blacksmiths were merely peasants who had a special skill, and whatever profits they derived may have been a matter of gravy rather than bread and butter. The straightforward understanding of Achilles' words, however, seems to point in the other direction: that the usual procedure for a peasant who was "in need of iron" was to go into town, where he would find the blacksmith in a particular place.[14] Hesiod, indeed, knows the smithy and warns against wasting too much time there.[15] Iron forging is a particularly difficult craft to move, requiring as it does heavy equipment (anvil, bellows, and a heavy hammer), and it would not be surprising if blacksmiths were among the first to ply their trade in a fixed place, where their customers sought them out, although Achilles' boast also suggests that if the iron were available, forging itself might be done with local talent.[16] The existence of a potters' quarter before the agora suggests that pottery, too, was an urban craft, whose practitioners could live in town without having to tend fields at all. We do not know how they were paid, but there are various possibilities. There may have been other independent crafts in addition to pottery and metallurgy.

We must distinguish not only between craftsmen and tradesmen but also between different kinds of tradesmen. International exchange, in which people exported what they had in abundance to obtain what they lacked, dated from the Bronze Age; the practice of international trade for profit was already known to Homer and Hesiod. The one trade of which early epic makes no mention is retail trade, where a single trader buys from various producers and then resells to individuals. We cannot state for certain that such trade did not exist in Homer's time: he had no need to mention

---

13. *Il.* 23.835; cf. p. 78.

14. This is the conclusion of Donlan ("Homeric Economy," 651), although he points out that carpenters would presumably be mobile, since they worked on buildings.

15. Hesiod *Works and Days* 493–95; cf. Hom. *Od.* 18.328–29.

16. Alternatively, one might understand that blacksmiths usually came to their customers, but iron was only available in town; a middle suggestion would be that the blacksmith made rounds for small jobs, such as sharpening tools, but took major jobs in the shop. In Hellenistic Delos, it seems that the blacksmiths themselves usually, but not always, provided the iron: see, for example, *IG* XI 158A 80–81, 161A 67–68, 163A 61–62.

anything so unheroic,[17] and Hesiod was writing for farmers. Archaeology shows us no archaic shops, but the wooden stalls of shops rarely leave a trace, and traveling peddlers leave yet less.

We cannot, then, prove that there was no retail trade before coins were invented; but what we have seen suggests that if there was any, there was not much. The utensil money of Crete and the Argolid was, as we saw, neither abundant nor highly developed; the archaic marketplace of Athens vanished without a trace both from the landscape and from the memory of the people. Herodotus may or may not have been correct in believing that the Lydians were the first to practice retail trade, but it is noteworthy that he thought of the trade itself as being an innovation.[18] By the classical period, there are not only retailers but wholesalers, and laws to regulate them.[19]

Innovators or not, the grain dealers who bought from farmers and from ships, the shopkeepers who bought pots from various workshops, and the innkeepers who supplied food to wayfarers were all making a profit, and they were doing it in a way that would have been a good deal more difficult before the invention of coinage.[20] If their trade had roots in the past, it must have grown very quickly once coins were there to help it along.

THE MARKET AND THE LAND

Retail trade itself was at the root of other developments. The growth of the agora, of course, was in large part both a result and a measure of the multiplication of shops and shopkeepers. More than that, it was the agora that made possible the growth of the city itself. The possibility of making a profit by buying and selling in the agora meant that a landless citizen, even if he

---

17. That Euryalos taunts Odysseus by calling him an international trader, not a shopkeeper (Hom. *Od.* 8.162–65), does not demonstrate anything; Odysseus was obviously the victim of a shipwreck.

18. Hdt. 1.94.1. That he mentions it in one breath with the minting of coins, however, is not very significant, since by his day that would have been an obvious connection. Kurke (*Coins,* 3) builds an entire book on the collocation of these items (along with the Lydians' custom of prostituting their daughters and their playing the same games as the Greeks). I find the list unremarkable, but there is much more to Kurke's book than her starting point.

19. Lysias 22. Not every trade is likely to have had wholesalers as the grain trade did. The Mishnah (*Demai* 2:4; *Baba Bathra* 5:10; *Kelim* 12:1) uses the Greek term *siton* (= Greek σιτώνης; cf. LSJ, s.v.) for a grain wholesaler, whence Modern Hebrew has taken the term *sitonai* for any wholesaler.

20. In fact, inns in Greece now developed into a popular and common institution, much more important than the "travelers' houses" that had existed in Mesopotamia: Rosenfeld, 134–37. (Firebaugh's anecdotal account, though there is real scholarship behind it, is seriously outdated, and Kraynak's unpublished thesis was not available to me).

was not a trained craftsman, could earn enough to keep himself alive. No less significantly, it meant that there was a regular place for him to buy his food and an established way to go about it.

We have no way of knowing how many people made their living in the agora or how many sellers were simply peasants disposing of a surplus, though it is worth noting that Aristotle considered farmers, no less than shopkeepers and tradesmen, to be characteristic of the commercial agora.[21] It is certainly true that at later times, selling in the agora was one of the refuges of the poor.[22]

By the fifth century, one could conceive of such a strategy on a communal scale. Themistocles suggested that in case of war, the Athenians could abandon their rural land entirely and resist all comers from the ships, an idea that obviously envisioned procuring all of Athens's food from abroad. Themistocles himself fortified Athens's harbor, the Piraeus, with this in mind;[23] his successors went further and built the Long Walls to connect the harbor with the city. From behind these walls, Pericles, at the beginning of the Peloponnesian War, implemented Themistocles' strategy, bringing the rural population inside the walls and allowing the Spartans to ravage the land. In the crowded conditions, a frightful number, Pericles included, died of a plague, but they did not starve. How they actually supported themselves—whether by foreign imports or from the land itself once the enemy had gone home—is not recorded, and a strong case has been made for the idea that the devastation could not have been so great as to destroy their livelihood entirely.[24] This may well have been the case, but Thucydides does not offer it as having been Themistocles' rationale, nor do we hear of Pericles giving such an argument. In Athens, the idea of a livelihood had become sufficiently divorced from the land that its leaders, at least, thought they could maintain the state without it indefinitely.

The possibility of living away from the land lay, in turn, at the root of a larger revolution. In Homeric times and probably in archaic times, not every item was available for exchange. The items that Agamemnon offered to Achilles for his wounded pride were not things that he would have sold at

---

21. Aristotle (*Pol.* VII 12.4 [1331a 34]) includes farmers among those he would exclude from the "free" agora. Chremes, in Aristophanes' *Ecclesiazusae* (815–22), on the other hand, seems to have come to the market for a commodity-to-commodity trade: he sold his grapes, then took his coins straight off to the barley market to buy barley. Cf. Markle, 154–55.

22. Aristophanes *Thesmophoriazusae* 447–48; Dem. 57.31–36.

23. Thuc. 1.93.7.

24. Hanson, *Warfare and Agriculture*, 131–73; cf. 245.

any price, though he would give them away under appropriate circumstances. As we have seen, too,[25] it is likely that there was a certain prestige gradation, so that not every currency bought every commodity. The circulation of iron spits may normally have been limited to a certain class of items, and it would seem unlikely that a peasant with some extra produce to dispose of could expect to get silver, even in small quantities, in return for it. Land may not have been alienable at all, though that is a subject of great uncertainty. Exchange meant finding the appropriate item to give in return for what one wanted.

Money did not work that way. An essential characteristic of money was that it was exchangeable for anything, great or small. It may have taken time for this to be appreciated: many Greek cities, as already mentioned,[26] did not at first mint coins smaller than a drachma, and the earliest electrum coins need not have been designed to purchase things for which precious metal would not earlier have been used. But as money came to be available anywhere it was wanted, in any denomination, there can be no doubt that silver coins could buy anything at all, from gold jewelry to sardines. Bronze or copper coins, it should be noted, did not appear for another century thereafter and never achieved the importance that they had at Rome.[27]

To the extent, then, that Homeric society had distinguished prestige goods from nonprestige goods, money subverted that distinction: money could buy anything and could be gotten in exchange for anything. It followed that even a peasant or a shopkeeper could amass enough money to buy the most prestigious of goods; and it followed from this that the possession of those goods, which was now open to everybody, no longer distinguished the best from the worst. The honor of Achilles and Diomedes was greater in proportion to the gifts they were given;[28] no classical Greek would have defined his honor in that way. Wealth, indeed, conferred honor, but the wealth was now measured by quantity, not quality.

Yet more: the opening up of new and individual roads to wealth broke the circle of dependency that reinforced the distinction between rich and poor. In Homeric society, the *basileus* both received gifts from his dependents and bestowed gifts upon them: "a house and a plot of land and a much courted wife" was what the swineherd Eumaeus would have expected from

25. P. 76.
26. P. 104.
27. Kraay, *Archaic and Classical*, 252–53.
28. P. 73.

Odysseus.[29] The wealth and success of the *basileus* was not only conceded by his dependents but actively desired by them, for his success and wealth were the success and the wealth of the whole community, dependents included.[30]

It is easy to see that this kind of relationship is self-perpetuating and leads to a society whose leaders are, like the Homeric *basileis*, leaders by virtue of hereditary right. This social construct, too, is undermined by money and the market. A landless man or one whose land is insufficient may, perhaps, still apply to the noble for "a house and a plot of land and a much courted wife"; but he may also simply go off to try his luck in town. He does not need the *basileus*, and to the extent that he does not need him, he is likely to chafe at the gifts by which he is expected to support him. The retail market, of course, was not the only safety valve open to a landless man: he might go down to the sea as an overseas trader or join an expedition of colonization. Both options were risky, and the second removed him permanently from the community. The marketplace, in comparison, might provide a living for a person divorced from any patron but still a member of the polis.

The availability of the market as an alternative source of livelihood was all the more important because of the overpopulation that had beset Greece since the archaic era.[31] The colonies with which the archaic Greeks tried to solve their population problem were based on agriculture and international trade, the two great means then available in Greece for making a living. Retail trade could not by itself provide more food for the landless; but by giving them an opportunity to amass silver, it made them potential—and in Athens, at least, very real—beneficiaries of the international trade that would once have served only the powerful. Where the Mycenaeans had imported luxury items to adorn their kings, the Athenians imported grain to feed their urban poor.

Trade was not necessarily practiced as an alternative to agriculture. A farmer whose land did not suffice to feed his family could perhaps trade in

---

29. *Od.* 14.64; Hoekstra (ad loc., in Heubeck et al., vol. 2) considers the swineherd's hopes for a "much-courted" wife to be "rather unrealistic and presumptuous," but even if we ignore the traditional nature of epithets, there is no reason why a poor girl may not have many poor suitors. On the dependent relationship, cf. Redfield's discussion (33–37).

30. This is normally taken as being a sign of Homer's aristocratic prejudice, and it may be so; but modern parallels from Africa suggest that it is an accurate description. See Schapera, 175–76, 184. Tandy (101–6) underlines the importance of this attitude to a redistributive economy. We may add that it is no less important to subgroups that function redistributively (such as a gang of thieves) in a larger economy that may be organized on other principles.

31. In modern Africa, land shortage has often been the factor forcing natives to adopt a money economy, as described by Schapera (184–86) and Gulliver (444–46).

the marketplace during the long periods of agricultural slack. A more prosperous one might use the same opportunity to sell a surplus there, enabling
him, perhaps, to buy more land and increase his standing yet more. Hesiod's
advice to would-be seafarers recommends times when they would not be
needed at the farm. The trader whom he imagines is a farmer who will not
leave until the grain harvest is over and will have to be back home in time to
harvest the grapes and plant the next year's crop.[32] As already mentioned,[33]
this form of commerce was eventually supplanted by the more professional-
ized *emporie*,[34] but the new merchant still offered the farmer a means to turn
his crops into money.

In another world and time, in the later Middle Ages, the increasing use of
money and the increasing power of merchants were important factors in
the breakdown of manorial ties, and it will be obvious that they may have
performed a similar function in Greece and notably so in Athens, where
Solon is said to have forbidden debt-bondage and thereby to have freed
the poor.[35] That the poor did not fall back into a situation where "there is
not ought left in the sight of my lord, but our bodies, and our lands"[36] was a
basic precondition to the development of the Athenian democracy and may
indeed have been connected with the existence of alternative ways of making
a living. Retail trade was not, however, the only such alternative, and the
existence of serfdom in Attica before the *seisachtheia* is not as certain as it is
sometimes presented.[37]

It is not only the universal buying power of money that subverts ties of
dependency by offering the poor independence; it is also its anonymity, which
offers power to those excluded by birth. The gifts offered to a Greek hero were
valuable, as we saw, not only for their exchange value or their use value but for
their history. The shot that Achilles offered as a prize had belonged to the hero
Eetion; Achilles had taken it as plunder "with the rest of his possessions"[38]
after killing its owner. The shot reinforced Achilles' position of preeminence
not only because of its inherent value but because of what it said about

---

32. Hesiod *Works and Days*, 663–65, 678–88; Mele, 16.

33. P. 89.

34. *Emporie* was the practice of the *emporoi* described above, p. 89.

35. [Arist.] *Ath. Pol.* 4.5, 6.1.

36. Gen. 47:18.

37. Hammond, "Land and Society," on the one hand, and, on the other the heterodox but
provocative article of Rihll. The *seisachtheia*, enacted by Solon in Athens (probably when he was
archon in 594/3 B.C.E.) was the cancellation and prohibition of debts that turned the debtor into
the serf of the lender.

38. *Il.* 23.829.

Achilles himself: it was a physical reminder of his martial prowess. When Polypoetes threw it the furthest and won it, the shot gained another story, one that emphasized both Polypoetes' great strength and his connection with the great Achilles. Even when it was used for a plowshare, the farmer who used it would remind both himself and others of his own connection with Polypoetes and of the importance of the lord he served.

No coin was like this. Coins would not be countable if they were not essentially identical. They had a value in exchange, but the value was not tied up with their history. They said nothing about their owner, and the items bought with them were similarly anonymous. This did not mean that a person with a treasure-house full of coins was not a powerful person; but it did mean that power could now be achieved and exercised without the prestigious activities that had once been the occasion of transferring prestige goods. Wealth, and hence power, were open to people who would not have been invited to lead the raid against Eetion or to compete for Achilles' shot. Callias, the richest man of classical Athens, was known as λακκόπλουτος, "pit rich," because he was said to have found his enormous wealth in a pit; those who called him so seem to have had no clearer idea of where his money came from.[39] It does not seem to have mattered, nor to have prevented Callias from playing an influential role in Athenian politics.

For both these reasons—the freeing of the poor and the creation of nouveaux riches—money tends to be subversive of hereditary rights, as the aristocrats of France discovered in the last centuries of the Old Regime. The history of the late archaic age in Greece is the story of the crumbling of oligarchies. This development was already underway before coinage had been invented; the Cypselid tyrants of Corinth and the Orthagorids of Sicyon were seventh-century phenomena.[40] Nevertheless, it is more than probable that money and the market had their share in continuing the process and in changing the entire concept of oligarchy. Throughout the classical period, neo-oligarchical

---

39. Plut. *Aristeides* 5.7–8; *Suda*, s.v. λακκόπλουτον. Cf. schol. Aristophanes *Clouds* 64; Athenaeus XII 536f–537c = Herakleides F 58 Wehrli. The "obvious rationalization," as J. K. Davies puts it (*APF*, p. 260), is that he had made his fortune through the Laureion mines, information corroborated by Xenophon (*Ways and Means* 4.15) and Nepos (*Cimon* 1.3).

40. For the date of the Cypselids, Servais's treatment has won general acceptance. On the chronology of the Orthagorids, I follow, in its essence, the reconstruction of Hammond ("Family"), against that of Mary White, which seems to me to force the text of the Rylands papyrus beyond what is reasonable. White would move the beginning of the Orthagorid dynasty down to 610, perhaps after the very earliest coins (which were, of course, not in Sicyon but in Lydia), but hardly late enough to make coinage a factor in undermining the oligarchy. At any rate, it seems clear from Herodotus that the roots of the Sicyonian revolution were chiefly ethnic rather than economic.

movements were based on restoring an oligarchy of wealth, never of pedigree. The power of birth, once broken, did not revive.

The new freedom undoubtedly came at the price of a weakening of the traditional bonds of society, and it dissolved them in both directions. Just as the poor had opportunities for survival that did not require their masters' assistance, the wealthy had less need for the loyalty of their dependents: their wealth could purchase advantages from anyone, not only from those with traditional ties to their estates. If a Eumaeus of the classical age was freed from his master's dependency for a house and a plot of land and a much courted wife, his master was also freed from any need to provide such a thing. Liberation, by definition, dissolves bonds, and a later generation, in Aristophanes' *Clouds* and in the trial of Socrates, sometimes questioned whether the dissolution of bonds had perhaps proceeded too far.

There was one Greek state that did maintain an economy based on the brutal exploitation of dependents by a small and hereditary class of fighting but nonproducing citizens. That state was Sparta, and for centuries, Sparta refused, apparently on principle,[41] to adopt a silver currency.

● INFLATION

It is not very meaningful to ask whether the invention of coinage caused inflation. The growth of markets that accompanied the use of coins meant that questions of value that might be judged by various standards were turning into questions of exchange value, so that when we compare precoinage and postcoinage prices, we are dealing with figures that are not entirely comparable. That said, we must admit that a person with goods to exchange could probably get more silver for them after the invention of coinage than before. This is, on the face of it, a paradox; in other places, the adoption of a monetary economy, by increasing greatly the demand for silver, causes prices to fall, not to rise.[42] With the invention of coinage, however, an increasing demand for silver was matched by an enormous increase in the velocity with which it circulated. In Homeric times, silver was a prestige item, and it was hoarded, not freely exchanged. A person wishing to trade for silver before the invention of coinage seems to have had to offer a good deal to justify parting with so important an item. Coins, which were made to pass from hand to hand, conferred no special prestige and were more freely given.

---

41. See Hodkinson, 96.
42. Wordie, 65–69.

Coins circulated as silver had never done before in Greece—indeed, as even spits do not seem to have done. At the beginning of the fifth century, moreover, there was a great increase in the amount of silver available, when a major discovery of silver at Laureion provided the basis for a vast volume of Athenian silver coins, which were exported far and wide. A passage in Plutarch seems to indicate that there was a time when a drachma—perhaps a drachma of silver, perhaps a handful of spits—was in some way considered the equivalent of a sheep.[43] That would never be the case again.

⊙ TRADERS AND POLITICS

Money, we may reiterate, did not create trade, but it marked the beginning of a new age of commerce in Greece. Commerce did not supplant agriculture: most poleis were still supported by their surrounding countryside,[44] and even Attica, the city most notably dependent on imported grain, maintained a numerous and influential peasantry.[45] Even the most committed modernist cannot claim that Athens, the queen of Greek commerce, had a commercial class whose political importance approached that of the Roman *publicani*,[46] much less the bourgeoisie of the last few centuries.[47] But traders were no longer marginal to the community. The tax law gave Athenian citizens preferential treatment as retailers.[48] The laws that were made to protect the grain supply of Athens[49] were designed to protect consumers,

---

43. See appendix 3.

44. Aristotle's claim (*Pol.* I 8.7 [1256a 38–40]) that "the largest part of the human race lives from the land and from cultivated crops" means at least that; from the context, it is clear that he does not simply mean to say that most people eat the produce of farms, which would be a truism. He may mean to say that most people support themselves by agriculture, which would be an even more interesting statement and may well have been true. Finley's discussion (*Ancient Economy*, 123–49) is still a good introduction to the topic, although the nature of the relationships between town and country has been elucidated much further by more recent studies.

45. For the percentage of its grain that Attica imported, see Noonan as well as Garnsey, "Grain for Athens," disputing the higher figures of Jardé. Whitby argues that Athenian policy was to encourage generous supply or even an oversupply of grain.

46. The *publicani* were wealthy Romans who collected public revenues under contract to the state. On the nature of their influence, see Badian, 82–118, whose analysis may also offer some good indications of why Athenians of proportionally comparable fortunes never exercised significant political influence.

47. De Ste. Croix, *Class Struggle*, 41–42. De Ste. Croix points out correctly that the Roman *equites* themselves were in no way a commercial class. Cf. Finley, *Ancient Economy*, 47–50.

48. Dem. 57.34; cf. Whitehead, *Ideology*, 77–78. This was distinct from the *metoikion*, the twelve-drachma annual tax on every foreigner who remained in Athens for an extended period: Whitehead, op. cit., 7–9, 75–77.

49. And of other communities: see ML 30.

not traders, but they presupposed a class of traders capable of feeding a significant part of the population on a regular basis. Laws were made, prices were fixed, and officials were appointed[50] to regulate commercial practice. The commercial agora that crowded the political agora kept the new class of retailers very much in public view, and Aristophanes could even joke that a politician could win over the Athenian public if he could only lower the price of sardines.[51]

This development caused some disquiet among the Greeks. In archaic Sparta, Theognis inveighed against the people of wealth but no breeding; in the fourth century, we find an Athenian's citizenship being impugned on the grounds that his mother sold ribbons in the agora.[52] Aristotle dealt with the matter more analytically. He blamed the pursuit of money for the perversion of society and saw in commerce and even more in usury an unnatural and parasitic way of gaining one's livelihood. There may have been other voices, but our sources do not preserve them.[53] The malaise that the sources express continued to be heard throughout the life of Greece and Rome and long thereafter. At Rome, senators were forbidden to engage in commerce. In France, it was only with the Revolution that traders came to exercise real political power. Even then, the feeling was not dead: the nation of shopkeepers[54] had the last laugh on Napoleon, but Karl Marx, the bitterest of all opponents of the merchant class, remains influential even after the fall of the USSR.

---

50. [Arist.] *Ath. Pol.* 51, with Rhodes's commentary ad loc.; J. Oehler in *RE* I cols. 883–85, s.v. "Agoranomoi"; Garland, 76–78.

51. Aristophanes *Knights* 624–82. Cf. van Leeuwen (on line 645) on the volatility of prices of small fish. On the precise identification of the fish called ἀφύαι (line 645) and τριχίδες (line 662), see D'Arcy Wentworth Thompson, s.vv.

52. Theognis, passim; Dem. 57.30. Demosthenes puts in his mouth the obvious rejoinder that the existence of the tax on metics shows that, on the contrary, the agora was the peculiar preserve of citizens, but the fact that the charge could be made suggests that there were many who doubted that a true Athenian citizen would so lower himself.

53. It is a priori unlikely that retailers themselves considered their calling to be shameful, though that is indeed the attitude of the speaker of Dem. 57.30–31, who nevertheless states that the laws prohibit speaking ill of a citizen because he or she works in the agora. Whitehead (*Ideology*, 116–21) found no sources speaking well of *banausia* (roughly, the career of an artisan); neither, apparently, did Ehrenberg (114–15) for *kapelia* (retailing). For the philosophers, see Schaps, "Socrates."

54. The phrase seems already to have been proverbial at the time of Adam Smith, who uses it at IV.vii.iii.

9 THE MONETIZATION OF POLITICS

○ PEISISTRATUS

Peisistratus was an Athenian of good family and connections, who had distinguished himself in the Megarian war. Being politically ambitious, he organized a party around himself; being unscrupulous, he succeeded in persuading the Athenians to supply him with bodyguards. With the aid of these "club bearers," he established himself as tyrant of Athens.

In time, however, his enemies made common cause against him and brought about his expulsion. Having learned something about politics, he bided his time until he could make himself a good alliance. The time came, as it generally will in politics. He allied himself with the Alcmeonids, one of the two factions that had opposed him. Cementing his alliance by a marriage, he returned to power.

The marriage ran into problems, and Peisistratus was again expelled. A less persistent man might have decided to cease pursuing a tyranny that he could not hold; even Peisistratus, according to Herodotus, considered that course, but his son persuaded him otherwise.[1]

Settling at first in the flourishing city of Eretria, he moved to the area of

---

1. Hdt. 1.61.3.

Mount Pangaeus, which was out of the way but rich in gold and silver.[2] He cultivated important friends in other cities, and he raised money—some of it, surely, from his friends, but his time in Pangaeus must have given him more than fresh mountain air. After ten years of exile, he returned with an army that may have included a good number of mercenaries;[3] at his appearance, old supporters and probably new ones as well deserted to his side.[4] He defeated the army of Athens and returned to power, with no need now for the other parties. The Alcmeonids may have gone into exile, but it appears that they eventually resigned themselves and returned to take crumbs from the ruler's table.[5]

Peisistratus was, as aspiring tyrants must be, an innovator. His first rise to power showed resourcefulness in building a party of his own and using the institutions of the state to undermine it; his first return showed the ability to maneuver that characterizes unprincipled seekers after power. His final return showed doggedness and careful planning, but there was a new twist. In the world of Homer and probably in the world of the archaic oligarchs, wealth had followed power: it was the lord of the land to whom goods flowed and to whom others looked for benefits. No one suggests that Peisistratus ruled over any city during his second exile, but he used his time to amass wealth through political contacts and very possibly through mining connections, though it would probably be fruitless to speculate what sort of connections those might have been.[6] His wealth and that of his friends provided him with an army large enough to invade Attica; the size and impressiveness of that army must have been important factors in encouraging his local supporters to desert to him. The liquid wealth[7] that Peisistratus

2. On the mines of Pangaeus, see Hdt. 7.112; E. Oberhummer in *RE* XVIII cols. 589–92, s.v. Pangaion. But see n. 6 below.

3. So says Herodotus (1.61.4) of the Argives, who are said at [Arist.] *Ath. Pol.* 17.4 to have numbered a thousand. The latter source says they followed him because of a connection by marriage; Lavelle (*Sorrow*, 109 n. 76) takes this as a contradiction to Herodotus, whose account he explains by "fifth century Athenian disdain of the Argives." There is no real contradiction; soldiers may fight for pay under a leader who follows political advantage.

4. Hdt. 1.62; [Arist.] *Ath. Pol.* 15.2.

5. The chief sources for Peisistratus's rise are Hdt. 1.59–64 and [Arist.] *Ath. Pol.* 13–15. For the exile of the Alcmeonids, see Hdt. 1.64.3 and Greg Anderson; for their return, see *IG* I[3] 1031, with the editio princeps of Meritt (pp. 59–65) and the article of Eliot and McGregor.

6. No ancient source claims that he actually owned the mines or that the mines themselves were the source of his wealth, as was pointed out by Lavelle in his review of de Libero; what is important to us is that the money he made there, whatever its source, provided the basis for his successful return.

7. It is not probable that this wealth consisted of coined money; although the coins of northern Greece seem to have been the first to have circulated widely beyond their immediate

had amassed in his exile proved stronger than the landed power of his enemies.

Peisistratus could not have maintained the state out of his own resources; a tithe[8] on all agricultural produce supplied him with the wherewithal to maintain the city well, to destroy his enemies, and to provide for the sacrifices.[9] Perhaps remembering that hungry people were open to outside influence, Peisistratus did not neglect the economic life of the Athenians. It was probably during his tyranny that the new agora was established,[10] and toward the end of his last tyranny, the *Wappenmünzen* appear, a series of coins mostly of small denominations, more appropriate for the marketplace than for international trade. The silver in these coins was of various sources; whatever Peisistratus's connections with Pangaeus, it did not give him a plentiful source of fresh silver from the mines of Thrace.[11] It was probably under the rule of his sons (though there is a good deal of debate as to the precise date) that Athens began to mint larger coins for export, at first featuring a Gorgon device and later the famous Athenian "owls." These were minted from the native Attic silver of the Laureion mines, and Athenian coins spread throughout the Greek world.[12]

The use of wealth to establish personal power was nothing new; it was the everyday practice of the archaic Greek nobility, operating through a system of gift giving that was a part of the ritualized friendship and reciprocal obligations through which alliances were established and maintained.[13] This

---

area of origin (Kraay, "Hoards," 83–84), the time of the earliest mints there is itself only about the middle of the sixth century, the time of Peisistratus's second return (Kraay, *Archaic and Classical*, 131).

8. Or more likely a twentieth: Thuc. 6.54.5 (speaking not of Peisistratus himself but of his sons); [Arist.] *Ath. Pol.* 16.4 and cf. Rhodes, ad loc.

9. Thuc. 6.54.5. The suggestion of Spahn (200–202) that this tithe was formally a religious levy is attractive. I am more hesitant about his conclusion (203) that it was mostly paid in coin.

10. See p. 112.

11. Gale, Gentner, and Wagner, 29–32, 49. The one obol of *Wappenmünzen* type that they examined was apparently from Laureion silver.

12. For the problems of the precise dating of the owls, see Raven, with the bibliography in his footnotes; Price and Waggoner; Kroll, "From Wappenmünzen"; Kroll and Waggoner. For their distribution, see Kraay, "Hoards," 80–82. Note also Kraay's observation (83) "that North Greek coins were being dispersed in quantity long before owls, and that therefore, the idea of dispersing locally mined silver in the form of coins came to Athens from North Greece." Kraay continues, "We may hazard a guess that the Pisistratids, who spent their exile in Macedonia just at the time when this practice was beginning, brought the idea back with them to Athens." The reservations of Howgego ("Ancient States," 3) do not invalidate Kraay's guess, though they emphasize the fact that it remains only a guess; more damaging to it is the opinion of Kroll and Waggoner, now generally accepted, that the owls are not likely to be earlier than the very last years of the tyranny.

13. On which see Herman and now Mitchell.

kind of alliance was at the basis of tyrannic power throughout archaic Greece,[14] and it had been the basis for Peisistratus's first exile and his first return.[15] On his second return, however, Peisistratus seems to have secured a more reliable income, and to have spread it widely without the specificity of personal gifts and binding relationships. He had hit on something that worked, for a while, better than the elite alliances that had once served him and then disappointed him.

⊙ THE ALCMEONIDS

Money had become power, and the Peisistratids knew it. It would appear that their rivals either knew it as well or quickly learned it. The Alcmeonids tried traditional methods at first, raising an army of exiles and attempting to force their return; they were defeated. Like Peisistratus, they now turned to a more indirect method of restoring their influence.

What they undertook was nothing less than the rebuilding of the Delphic sanctuary, the first building project known to us that was let out by contract. The sanctuary had burned down and had not been replaced for decades;[16] its reconstruction was now entrusted to the Alcmeonids. The money involved (three hundred talents, according to Herodotus)[17] was enormous. Whatever precise part the Alcmeonids played in the contract or contracts,[18] they were considered to have gained both money and prestige from the project. This was undoubtedly a form of aristocratic competition,[19] and the Alcmeonids will have enhanced their position simply by the honor that accrued to them for achieving the project and achieving it grandly, building a marble face on

---

14. Scheid-Tissinier.

15. Hdt. 1.60; [Arist.] *Ath. Pol.* 14.4. Cf. *FGrH* 323 F 15 (= Athenaeus XIII 609c–d).

16. Pausanias 10.5.13; Eusebius *Chronicon* p. 103b Helm: their dates are almost in agreement, ca. 548–547.

17. Hdt. 2.180.1; cf. 5.62.3. It is noteworthy that the contribution of Pharaoh Amasis was given in alum, not in coin. The twenty minas of the Naucratites on the other hand, were more likely given in silver, as Stein (ad loc.) noticed long ago: twenty minas of alum, as Pomtow (333 n. 1) also said (though without drawing the same conclusion), was strikingly little for a prosperous trading community. How and Wells's judgment (ad loc.) that "more probably H. intends to contrast the liberality of the king with the meanness of the Greeks" is only comprehensible when we consider that twenty minas is less than ten kilos, "an astonishingly low contribution from what must have been a large and prosperous population" (Lloyd, 3:233).

18. The contract was presumably let out not to the entire Alcmeonid clan but to certain of its members. See Schaps, "Builders," 81–82.

19. This is emphasized by Stahl (129–33).

the temple where the contract had specified only *poros* stone.[20] To an extent, we are seeing here only the kind of aristocratic *kydos* that the Homeric heroes had pursued in more dangerous competitions.

Herodotus's description of their work as a contract, however, surely implies that the enterprise was undertaken with a view to profit as well. The precise way in which this money furthered the Alcmeonids' political purposes is variously reported.[21] Some fourth-century historians believed that they had used the money to raise their own mercenary force,[22] but this, though a natural presumption in the fourth century,[23] is not very likely. Had there been any such force, Herodotus, who was very partial to the Alcmeonids, would not have omitted their presence from the description of the tyrants' overthrow.[24] Nor is it likely, though Herodotus claims so in the name of "the Athenians," that the Alcmeonids bribed the Pythia to urge the Spartans to intervene.[25] Their very visible presence at Delphi over a period of years, employing dozens or perhaps hundreds of people and expending large amounts of money on the temple, would have been enough to make their opinions about the Athenian political situation seem very persuasive in Delphi.[26]

What interests us is not the particular way in which this contract was

---

20. Hdt. 5.62.3. Even if, as Philochorus says (*FGrH* 328 F 115) and as is perfectly likely, the work was not completed until after the overthrow of the Peisistratids, it would not have taken long for visitors to Delphi to see the difference after a generation of desolation.

21. The best and fullest discussion of the historical questions and of the use to which the money was put is still that of Jacoby (*FGrH* III b (Supp.), 449–54). Parke and Wormell (1:143–47) prefer to suspect the later historians of anachronism, chiefly because "there is no place in the Herodotean account . . . for money at all, except for bribing the Pythia." This argument ignores, however, the word μισθοῦνται at Hdt. 5.62.2, which clearly means that the Alcmeonids got and managed money; and it ignores 2.180 entirely. What Herodotus does not tell us and probably did not know is how the money was used.

22. [Arist.] *Ath. Pol.* 19.4; cf. schol. Dem. 21.144 (vol. 9, p. 623 Dindorf). Isocrates (15.232) puts a different twist on the story, claiming that Cleisthenes persuaded the Amphictyons "by words" (λόγῳ) to lend him the money; he is listing individuals who helped the people by their eloquence.

23. Forrest, 282.

24. Stahl (121–33) also doubts that money could have been used to support troops at this period. This is, however, uncertain, as Stahl himself admits, and it is undoubtedly characteristic of Herodotus to play up the anecdote and play down the more ordinary matters of politics and war. What Peisistratus seems to have done successfully the Alcmeonids could surely at least have tried.

25. Hdt. 5.63.1.

26. This is stated—not for the first time—by Eric W. Robinson, but his claim that the construction of the temple was itself the "bribe" to the Pythia seems to me to stretch unnecessarily the meaning of Herodotus's words. There is nothing unlikely about the idea that a story circulated in Athens and was perhaps even put into circulation by the Alcmeonids themselves that made their influence more direct than it need have been.

turned to political advantage but the fact that a powerful noble family, trying to increase its influence when it had lost control of the state, went about the matter by undertaking an enterprise that involved the collection, management, and expenditure of large amounts of money. This was by no means a matter of simply buying influence, but it was not exactly the way the Homeric nobles had gone about their competitions. The expenditure of personal fortune on public munificence, particularly on impressive public buildings and temples, was to become a major form of aristocratic competition and political influence in monetized Greece.[27] In the Hellenistic period, it became probably the most important method by which wealthy citizens and local magnates defined and cemented their influence. Scholars refer to this phenomenon as *euergetism,* and it has received its definitive treatment, for now, from Paul Veyne.[28]

◉ BRIBERY

The successful use of money to undermine the Athenian state had sinister implications that did not escape the Athenians who ejected the Peisistratids, and although they placed no limit on wealth, they did establish in their new constitution safeguards against any citizen's accumulating enough power to make himself tyrant. Another sinister side to the relationship between money and power was bribery.

It is hard to imagine what bribery would have meant in Homeric times. The Homeric heroes were themselves the state. What was paid was paid to them (or in their terms, "given" to them), and they owed no one an accounting. Gifts were given to them publicly, and receiving them was not only condoned but honored. "Bribing" a feudal lord to have him do your bidding was then, as at other times, a sign of the lord's superiority. It was shameful only to the briber and only because he had to buy cooperation instead of forcing it.

Underlings could not be bribed in the classical sense, at least not on the grand scale. One might offer them something they needed and so get their cooperation or even persuade one of them to betray his lord; a woman might be seduced.[29] These were dangers, but they did not change materially

---

27. On the earliest signs of this and of how a poet could reconcile work for pay with aristocratic ideology, see Kurke, *Traffic,* chaps. 7, 10.

28. Veyne, 185–373.

29. Hom. *Od.* 15.415–75. A man could surely be seduced as well, but Homer does not give examples. Homer likewise offers no examples of the disgraceful sophistication of our modern

the status of the underlings. The prestige possessions that identified the powerful were not available to them. There was, perhaps, nothing to prevent a clever thief from stealing into Achilles' treasury and spiriting away dozens of bronze tripods. To a hero of the requisite social status, such an exploit would be permissible, though dangerous, if Achilles was his enemy. But it is hard to imagine what a common man would have done with all those tripods or how he would justify their being found in his possession. If he could maintain his possession of them by force, that very fact would place them among the powerful people whose successful exploits brought him honor; but if not, the tripods themselves would be of little help to him.

A new conception of the community changed the situation.[30] A polis was not identical with any of its citizens, even the greatest, and gifts given to an individual were not respectable if he was thereby to act in his own interests against those of the state. Put bluntly, in the *polis,* everybody was an underling—a noble idea, perhaps, but one that meant that the most powerful people in the state could now be bribed. The most honored statesmen of Greece were accused and sometimes convicted of accepting bribes; in one of the most famous cases, the Spartan king Leotychidas was forced into exile shortly after the Persian War by charges of bribery, "having been caught red-handed there in the camp with a sleeve full of silver."[31] It was not something that would have been conceivable for a Homeric king, because the Homeric king would have taken the silver openly, and his honor would have been the greater for his having done so.

The new conception of the state made bribery conceivable; the anonymity of money, which I mentioned in chapter 8,[32] made it possible on a grander scale than ever. There was now no limit to the bribe that might be offered, and a person of minor significance might hope to obtain great wealth (and thereby, perhaps, power) by selling clandestine services that could not be sold openly. The distinction between prestige possessions and ordinary possessions had been blurred, and it was now possible to bribe a commoner with princely gifts. Not every commoner could resist.

Nor was it clear that he should resist. The ancient aristocratic attitude by which gifts were tokens of friendship and honor did not die with the introduc-

---

intelligence agencies (and the Philistines, Judges 16:5), in which men employ women to seduce other men; but cf. Notopoulos, 140, for a modern Cretan epic example.

30. On the way in which a new apparatus was built to manage the money that was now conceived of as belonging to the polis rather than to individuals, see Schaps, "Builders," 82–89.

31. Hdt. 6.72. For other Spartan examples, see the note of How and Wells, ad loc.

32. P. 119.

tion of coinage; it remained normal behavior at the courts of kings and tyrants.[33] Unlike modern laws, which forbid or severely restrict the acceptance of gifts by public officials, the law of Athens treated as criminal only the case in which "anybody . . . as an orator does not say what is best for the democracy of the Athenians because he accepts money."[34] It was not criminal to accept the gifts so long as they did not cause a person to use his influence disloyally.[35] In practice, this could leave a large area of uncertainty, for the rules of *xenia* (guest-friendship) obliged the recipient of gifts to reciprocate by being helpful to the donor when needed, and the line between the rules of friendship and the demands of patriotism could be hard to draw in practice and even more debatable in hindsight.[36] It is hard to establish how common bribery was in Greek politics, but the suspicion of bribery hung over the Greeks and their leaders in many a dubious situation.[37]

⊙ FROM PEISISTRATUS TO CIMON TO PERICLES

If Peisistratus had shown the power of money in recruiting soldiers to subvert the constitution, it should not surprise us to read that he knew how to use it to maintain his position. He was, as other tyrants were, a patron of the arts, but his patronage had a populist slant: he seems to have fostered the Great Dionysia, and under his regime the tragic competition was first instituted.[38] His public buildings must have offered a livelihood to many Athenians who would otherwise have been dependent upon nobles—that is, upon other nobles.[39] He is said to have offered loans to the poor and, in general, to have comported himself "more like a citizen than like a tyrant."[40] Another man might have learned a different lesson,[41] but Peisistratus's behavior was well attuned to the spirit of equality that had been growing in Athens

---

33. For this reason, accusations of bribe taking were usually connected with embassies to Macedon or Persia: Perlman, 224–26.

34. Hypereides 3 *(For Euxenippus)* 7–8; cf. 1 *(Against Demosthenes)* 24–25.

35. Perlman, 224; Harvey, 108–13.

36. Mitchell, 181–86.

37. Harvey, 89–102.

38. Pickard-Cambridge, *Dithyramb*, 76–77. On the unlikelihood that Peisistratean patronage of the arts had a directly propagandist slant, see Blok.

39. Fritz Schachermeyr in *RE* XIX cols. 188–89, s.v. "Peisistratos."

40. Μᾶλλον πολιτικῶς ἢ τυραννικῶς ([Arist.] *Ath. Pol.* 16.2). That, according to the same source, he contrived to make a sizable profit on the loans does not and very likely did not detract from the impression of liberality, as long as he was careful not to reduce his debtors to the depths of penury.

41. As Henry VII, who after collecting an army and conquering the throne of England, was noted for his parsimony and his care to increase the royal treasure. There is more than one way to use money to enhance one's power.

and that was to continue after his death. His behavior was also the traditional way for a noble to bind his underlings to himself.[42] His sons, remembered by the Athenians as being less affable and generous, suffered the common fate of tyrants' successors: one was killed and the other expelled.

We cannot say[43] whether Peisistratus's example was remembered or whether opportunity itself was a teacher, but it was not necessary to be a subversive to use money to political effect. The first to have done so in a way that draws our sources' attention was Cimon, son of Miltiades and leader of one of the factions of Athenian politics in the years after the Persian War. Theopompus's description, as reported by Athenaeus, is memorable.

> Cimon of Athens placed no guard over the fruits in his fields and his orchards, in order that any of the citizens who wanted could come in, pick the fruit, and take it if they needed any. Then he made his house open to everybody and regularly supplied a cheap meal for many people, and the poor Athenians came in and dined. He also took care of those who asked anything of him each day, and they say that he took around with him two or three young men with small change and instructed them to give it to anybody who asked him. They say that he also contributed to funerals, and they also say that he often did this: whenever he saw one of the citizens ill-dressed, he would order one of the young men who accompanied him to exchange clothes with him. From all of these acts, he won his reputation and became the first of the citizens.[44]

Theopompus lived more than a century after Cimon, and there is probably some exaggeration here;[45] in particular, the Aristotelian *Constitution of Athens* describes his generosity as having been restricted to his demesmen, a rather more likely way for a noble to insure his political base.[46] Yet Cimon's reputation was not Theopompus's invention; already in the fifth century, the comic poet Cratinus had called him "divine and most hospitable and best in everything."[47]

---

42. Millett (*Lending and Borrowing*, 51) already noted this.

43. Though Theopompus seems to have been willing to say it: see Connor, *Theopompus*, 32.

44. *FGrH* 115 Fr. 89 (= Athenaeus XII, 533a–c). Cf. [Arist.] *Ath. Pol.* 27.3. For a comparison of the sources and what each was trying to do with the information, see Schmitt Pantel, 180–86.

45. Wells (138 n. 1) suggests further that "the supposed universal readiness of Cimon to make his attendants change clothes with any poor Athenian citizen is probably only a generalization from gifts made to Cimon's old comrades in arms in certain definite instances."

46. On this see Whitehead, *Demes*, 305–13.

47. Plut. *Cimon* 10.1 = Cratinus, *PCG* fr. 1.

Cimon, the wealthy scion of one of the great houses of Athens,[48] was behaving simultaneously as a reactionary and an innovator: supporting and increasing his dependents by largesse as the Homeric nobles had done, he was also using his liberality to curry favor with the people as Peisistratus had done. As the orator Gorgias put it, Cimon made money to use it, and he used it to be honored.[49] In both he succeeded better than any democratic politician had done before.

Cimon's formula, however, was not a formula that others could use: the ground had been pulled out from under it. The generosity of the Homeric nobles had been based on an identity between themselves and the state that was granted by their underlings no less than by themselves. Income flowed into their houses as a matter of right, and when they distributed some of it—and we need not entertain the hypothesis that they normally distributed any very large percentage of it—they gained a reputation for generosity. Cimon could distribute what he had, but he could not control the flow of incomes: taxes now went to the state, not to the nobles. As commander, he was in charge of disposal of booty on the battlefield and could, to a certain extent, turn that to his advantage;[50] but once the booty was brought home, it, too, belonged to the state,[51] which had a right of ownership just as if it were an individual.[52] What had been, in Homeric times, a self-perpetuating system that left the noble houses ever richer had become a flow of money whose final destination was the state, so that a wealthy politician like Cimon could dissipate his fortune in pursuit of power but could not replenish it.[53]

A politician whose personal wealth did not reach that of Cimon could not even compete by dissipating what he had. Another approach was needed. The Aristotelian *Constitution of Athens*[54] says that an Athenian by the name of Damonides[55] suggested the winning strategy: "to give to the multitude what

---

48. The story told by Plutarch (*Cimon* 4.4) and Nepos (*Miltiades* 7.6) that his father died a state debtor was disposed of by Meyer (2:25–27), whom Blamire (91) follows.

49. Κτᾶσθαι μὲν ὡς χρῷτο, χρᾶσθαι δ' ὡς τιμῷτο (Plut. *Cimon* 10.5 = DK 82 B 20), a very Gorgianic use of parallelism and assonance.

50. Plut. *Cimon* 10.1; cf. Blamire, ad loc.

51. On the legalities of the situation, see Pritchett, *Greek State at War*, 1:85–92; cf. 5:398–401.

52. Descat, 233, distinguishing between the terms *demosion* and *koinon*.

53. He was not the last to try: Nicias followed a similar course in the latter years of the fifth century (see p. 136), as did Aristophanes, son of Nicophemus (whose property was the subject of Lysias 19) in the 390s. In the fourth century, on the contrary, the rich tried to hide their wealth: John K. Davies, *Wealth*, 88–105.

54. [Arist.] *Ath. Pol.* 27.4; cf. Plut. *Pericles* 9.1–3.

55. So, at least, in our manuscripts of the *Ath. Pol.*; many scholars have identified him with Damon, a famous theorist of music who was among Pericles' teachers. See von Jan in *RE* IV, col.

was their own," that is, to distribute largesse out of state moneys. Damonides did not exactly use this strategy; he offered it to Pericles, who made it his own. Of course, the state moneys were not Pericles' to distribute, so he could not simply follow Cimon's example and "order one of the young men who accompanied him" to change cloaks with a poor man or give him a present out of the state coffers. He could, however, propose legislation distributing the public moneys in various ways: for a fund that subsidized attendance at festivals and for a daily wage for jurors. As Damonides foresaw, Pericles got a reputation for liberality just as if it had been his own money. It was later claimed that he was at one time called to put his money where his mouth was and had to go so far as offering to pay for all his distributions himself,[56] but there is no reason to believe that he ever actually had to touch a penny of his own money to defeat Cimon in generosity to the poor.

At a later stage of his career, Pericles was the author of another method of distributing wealth, when he initiated a large-scale building program that remains the pride and glory of Greece to this day. This was not necessarily intended, like Franklin D. Roosevelt's New Deal, to finance poor relief by creating jobs; the buildings themselves were their own justification, for the greatness of the city was a source of pride to all its citizens.[57] In fact, expensive public works were regularly undertaken by ancient states when there was a large enough volume of money in circulation.[58] The Parthenon and the Propylaea need not be the result of Pericles' brilliance as a social legislator, but they testify eloquently to the success of his policy of amassing wealth in the hands of the state—a policy that meant chiefly the efficient enforcement of the tribute of Athens' allies, of which I shall speak later.[59]

Pericles' new-style liberality restored, in its own way, the circular flow of resources that had characterized the archaic nobles. The Athenian state did not take from its citizens a regular portion of their produce as the nobles had, but it did have its established sources of revenue, from various taxes and enforced contributions, and it could apply its revenues to offering its poorer citizens the kind of help they had once expected from their betters. The citizens, in turn, could establish new taxes if necessary, perpetuating the

---

2072 s.v. "Damon (17)", Kirchner in *RE* IV, col. 2075 s.v. "Damonides (1);" *APF* p. 383; and the list of sources in Chambers ad [Arist.] *Ath. Pol.* 27.4.

56. The offer, according to the story, was not accepted: Plut. *Pericles* 14.

57. See, e.g., Thuc. 2.41.1–4, although Pericles here does not explicitly discuss the physical aspect of the city.

58. As observed and demonstrated perceptively by Giglioni (221).

59. Pp. 138–43.

system indefinitely as the archaic nobles had done and as Cimon could not do. It is not surprising that Pericles had and has many imitators in this practice. The rich, at least, called them demagogues.

The new demagogy was not just a new name for a system no different in essentials from the archaic one. The demagogues had much less freedom with the public moneys than princes like Odysseus or Agamemnon had had with their own. Moneys spent were subject to public scrutiny, and every politician had his enemies ready at least to criticize. The demagogue could only spend so much money and in such a way[60] as he could convince enough people was desirable. To spend it on himself was always illegitimate. Of course, a clever politician can always find ways to conduct public affairs to private advantage,[61] and a corrupt one may, if he can get away with it, take bribes or embezzle public funds, but the politician in a democracy is never in the position of the archaic noble or the feudal chief, whose public position is enhanced and whose honor is increased by a lavish and conspicuous personal lifestyle.

Alcibiades, indeed, tried to build a career as a democratic politician on an unashamedly aristocratic lifestyle. He combined his extravagance with public generosity and argued before the people that his lavishness added honor to the state.[62] He was not without success, but both in his lifetime and afterward, he was regarded with suspicion, and his profligacy was not remembered to his credit. We do not find this kind of flamboyance in fourth-century politicians.[63] The fourth century was undoubtedly more suspicious of oligarchs, but this is not the whole story. Once the state, rather than the local noble, had become the milch-cow of the poor, a person's visible wealth no longer increased his desirability as a protector the way it once had. Cylon in the seventh century had tried to parlay an Olympic victory into a tyranny;[64] Alcibiades in the late fifth could still claim that his victory was good for the state, but the fact that he had to make the argument at all shows the change in situation. A democratic politician, even a wealthy and noble one, did not make the people's resources truly his own.

This meant that the state probably gave back to its citizens a much larger percentage of what it had taken from them than the nobles had ever given.

---

60. This is presumably why, as Schmitt Pantel (194–96) observes, Pericles proposed not straightforward giveaways but rewards to citizens for the performance of their civic duties.
61. The definition of politics according to Bierce (222).
62. Thuc. 6.16; cf. Schmitt Pantel, 196–201.
63. Millett, *Lending and Borrowing*, 90.
64. Thuc. 1.126.3–4.

Paradoxically, it also meant that the state's exactions were the more resented, since both the amount to be collected and the way of distribution were matters of public discussion and disagreement. Moreover, the fact that it was state money that had to be given away in view of all required the politician to give it away according to rules: two or three obols a day for each dicast, public maintenance for the descendants of the tyrannicides because of their service to the state. The paternal relationship of the archaic rich to the poor, in which a poor man expected simply to be given what he needed by the man whose estates he worked, was not reproduced by the relationship of the demagogue to the people. A demagogue could not simply give you help for no other reason than that you needed it. Tyrants could behave that way, and so, to a certain extent, have various political bosses in modern democracies. Both tended to draw their support from poor people who felt themselves excluded and defeated by the democratically established rules; the principled and the wealthy have always considered such practices corrupt.[65]

One did not have to be a noble to copy Pericles' example, and it has often been observed that Pericles was one of the last of his breed. Whereas the men who dominated Athenian politics in the fifth century—Miltiades and Cimon; Xanthippus; Pericles; Thucydides, son of Melesias—had been aristocrats of noble family, those who came after them were usually not so.[66] Cleon certainly, Hyperbolus probably, and Cleophon possibly were far from poor,[67] but their wealth came neither from ancient pedigree nor large landholdings but from factories where their own slaves or their fathers' had worked. Wealth based on status and on landed property had been supplanted by wealth based on money.

That wealth may have freed its owners from other cares and given them the leisure and perhaps the education to pursue politics, but that pursuit no longer required personal largesse. The state money provided the wherewithal for a politician to curry favor with the masses, and the state machinery

---

65. On the modern practice, see James Q. Wilson, 258–316.

66. The obvious exception was Alcibiades, mentioned earlier. The oligarchs of 411 and 404 were of course aristocratic, but it is not clear that we must consider them as regular leaders of Athenian politics. Connor (*New Politicians,* 175–98) argues forcefully that it was precisely their exclusion from and disillusionment with Athenian politics that drove them to revolution. See, however, the comments of Lewis in his review (89–90). It cannot be denied, in any case, that men like Critias were not the normal leaders of the ecclesia, and many leaders of the revolution of 411 seem to have had surprisingly obscure origins.

67. See *APF* 8674, 13910 (and cf. the comments of Camon, 191 n. 11); Connor, *New Politicians,* 152–53.

provided a mechanism that was available to anyone with the requisite skills. In theory, even a pauper, if skilled enough in speaking or administration, might rise to political prominence, and in due time, this happened too.[68]

Personal generosity was still appreciated and might be turned to political advantage. It is worth noting that the only politician of the new generation who is said to have made it a major part of his policy was Nicias, the most conservative of nouveaux riches.[69] Later politicians bragged about their generosity and expected jurors and sometimes even voters to show them favor because of it, but their generosity was a matter of liturgies and donations to the state, not personal gifts that bound individuals to the benefactor.

◎ THE APPARATUS OF STATE MANAGEMENT

The recirculation of wealth now went through the state by means of money. That meant, on the one hand, that personal resources were no longer very important and, on the other hand, that the state machinery itself had become much more complex. As has been observed by others, not every person was capable of overseeing the finances of the state or of making intelligent budgeting proposals.[70] The comic and oligarchic objections to the new politicians are regularly claims of dishonesty, not of incompetence: if anything, the comic heroes of Aristophanes tend to see men like Cleon as being much too competent in the management of money. When state finances became a serious problem, dominance in the state went to those who could manage the finances well. This seems to have been the case for a brief period in the middle of the fourth century, during the ascendancy of Eubulus,[71] and perhaps again under Lycurgus, when Athens's sun had set and Alexander's had risen.[72] Already more than a century earlier, the management of money had opened up new avenues to the management of the state. Now, when times were difficult, the management of the state's money could become the management of the state itself.

---

68. John K. Davies, *Wealth*, 117; cf. *APF* 3263.

69. John K. Davies, *Wealth*, 116–17.

70. On this aspect of the late fifth-century democracy, see Andrewes, "Mytilene Debate," 83–84; cf. Kallet-Marx, "Money Talks."

71. The fundamental treatment of Eubulus remains that of Cawkwell.

72. See Burke, "Lycurgan Finances," whose arguments, however, rest on sparse information and dense reconstruction.

10 WAR BY OTHER MEANS

AS IN ALL OTHER SPHERES, so in war: the invention of coinage did not make possible the impossible. Money pays the soldiers, supplies their food and weapons, and may often buy off their enemy, but all of these problems can be met without money. Here as elsewhere, the invention of coinage made the possible much easier and so changed the way in which things were done, until war, too, came to be a matter of money—as, to a large extent, it still is.

○ THEMISTOCLES

It had never hurt a ruler to be rich, and to use one's wealth to pay soldiers was only reasonable; Peisistratus's care of state revenues, once he had returned to power, was perhaps only a matter of increased attention to matters that must have occupied every ruler to some extent. Themistocles, however, turned wealth into military power on a new scale.

Two years after this, in the archonate of Nicodemus[1] [483/2], when the mines in Maroneia came to light[2] and the city had a surplus of one hundred talents from the business, some suggested that the money should be divided up among the people. Themistocles, however,

---

1. On the name, see *AO,* p. 58.
2. For this translation, see von Fritz and Kapp, 167 n. 59.

prevented that, not saying what he would use the money for, but proposing to lend a talent to each of the hundred richest Athenians. Then, if they were satisfied with the way the money had been spent, it would be charged to the state; if not, they could get the money back from those who had borrowed it. Getting the money on those terms, he had a hundred triremes built, with each one of the hundred citizens building one. These were the ships with which they fought at Salamis against the barbarians.[3]

The fairy-tale theme of asking for money and not revealing its purpose is hardly likely; more probable is Herodotus's version that Themistocles urged building the ships for use in the war against Aegina (in which, he adds, they were never employed).[4] It was, however, these ships that gave Athens the basis on which to defy Xerxes.[5]

The use of the silver to finance the ships did not, perhaps, have anything directly to do with the fact that the silver could be (and presumably was) minted into coins. A Levantine monarch could also have had ships built for silver, had he had the forethought and the ambition of Themistocles; Darius would have chopped the requisite amount of silver out of the jars in his treasury.[6] This use of money was, however, new to Greece and could not have taken place until the introduction of coinage had made buying and selling the normal way that goods changed hands. A hundred and fifty years earlier, the state could perhaps have enriched itself by taking the silver for its own purposes, but it is not likely that it could have gotten a hundred ships of war built in a short time simply by distributing silver.

● THE DELIAN LEAGUE

The interchangeability of money and military strength was grasped immediately by the Athenians. Directly after the war, when the allies sought a new and

---

3. [Arist.] *Ath. Pol.* 22.7.

4. Hdt. 7.144.1–2. According to Herodotus, two hundred ships were built. Polyaenus (1.30.6), whose story is closely parallel to that of the *Ath. Pol.* in its phrasing, agrees with Herodotus about the reason advanced.

5. For the way Athens outfitted ships before Themistocles, see Jordan, 5–16, and Thomsen. Jordan notes the expression of Pollux 8.108 (δύο ἱππέας παρεῖχε καὶ ναῦν μίαν), but when he says (10) that "the word for 'supplied,' pareiche, would seem to mean 'provided the money for' the ships," he is projecting the use of money for war back before the time when it is attested. Thomsen (147) admits that "we do not know anything for certain about the construction of warships at Athens in the period of the naukraric system," but he also prefers the theory that the naucrary "financed the construction" of the ship.

6. See p. 51.

permanent basis for the alliance, Aristeides the Athenian set up the Delian League on principles that no Spartan would have been likely to lay down.

> When the Athenians had taken over the leadership in this way, . . . they determined which of the cities had to provide money against the barbarian and which ships, for their pretext was to retaliate for what they had suffered by laying waste the king's land. Then, for the first time, there was established among the Athenians a magistrature called the *hellenotamiai* [treasurers of Greece], who received the *phoros*—for that was what the payment of money was called. The first *phoros* that was assessed was four hundred and sixty talents. Delos was their treasury, and their meetings were held there.[7]

That the war against Persia should be continued was not surprising, and that the states that fought the war should seek a more permanent structure for their alliance was only reasonable. What was utterly new was that the structure set up should be a treasury and that the contribution of most members of the alliance should be money.[8] There could be no clearer recognition of the principle that wars are waged with money.[9] The determination "which of the cities had to provide money . . . and which ships" takes as its basis the equivalence of money and ships, the equation of money with its value.[10] This is precisely the conceptual revolution of which I spoke in chapter 1.

This was not the final stage in the monetization of war: in a sense, it was only the beginning. For one thing, only naval warfare had come under the sway of money; hoplite campaigns continued to be short affairs, the economic burden of which was borne by the soldiers individually. This was not

---

7. Thuc. 1.96.

8. Kallet-Marx (*Money, Expense, and Naval Power*, 6) notes the novelty in literature of Thucydides' emphasis on surplus wealth as the basis for Athens's power. It was a new theme in literature because it was a new development in the world, but the actions of Aristeides make it clear that Thucydides was not the first Athenian to realize it.

9. It is striking, indeed, to note that modern alliances seeking a permanent structure seem to have been less conscious of the importance of finance: both the Articles of Confederation under which the United States were first governed and the more recent charter of the United Nations created central organizations critically enfeebled by their lack of a secure financial base.

10. The point is all the stronger if the editors of *ATL* are correct in believing that Aristeides' original assessment assessed *everybody* in monetary terms, then, having decided which states should contribute ships, converted their money assessments into ships; but as long as that is just a hypothesis, it can only show that the *ATL* editors themselves thought in monetary terms. See *ATL* III, pp. 236–43; *contra* Meiggs, 63–67.

to change until the latter years of the Peloponnesian War, when "total war" required new extremes of dedication.[11]

Even in naval warfare, the intrusion of money had just begun to make itself felt. The founders of the Delian League had grasped the equivalence of money and ships, but that equivalence, as I have noted, is in certain respects an illusion. Precisely because money is not the same as ships, the assessment itself changed the balance of power among the allies. The Athenians came to dominate the alliance.

> ... and for this the allies themselves were responsible. For because of their aversion to campaigns, most of them, in order not to be away from home, had themselves assessed to bear the due expense in money rather than ships, and the Athenian fleet grew out of the expenditure that they contributed, whereas they themselves, when they revolted, found themselves unprepared and unexperienced for war.[12]

There is no need to suspect the Athenians of having purposely encouraged the allies to contribute cash in order to enervate them.[13] The acceptance of money in place of military service was itself an innovation, and an extremely reasonable one in a situation where many of the states could not reasonably be called upon to man even a single ship or to part with a significant portion of their manpower on a permanent basis. The sapping of the allies' power came about naturally, a result of the fact that money, though it measures value, is never truly identical with the things it can buy.

⊙ LITURGIES

The building of the fleet had been financed by an extraordinary find in the silver mines of Laureion; its maintenance, however, required a regular system of management and finance. For this, the Athenians used a system that

---

11. See Kallet-Marx, *Money, Expense, and Naval Power*, 10–12. For Kallet-Marx (12), "it was the introduction not of naval power per se (which was not new to the fifth century) but rather of naval *arche* . . . that required the massive infusion of money into the military sphere." The battle of Salamis, however, was made possible only by a "massive infusion of money," despite the fact that it was only a single campaign. What was new was the relatively facile translation of money into ships that Themistocles pioneered; this, in turn, made possible a fleet that could hold its own against Xerxes' and that could dominate the Aegean Sea for seventy years.

12. Thuc. 1.99.3.

13. As Plutarch (*Cimon* 11.2–3) seems to imply, though he does not say so directly; cf. the comments of Gomme in *HCT* I, pp. 284–85.

they had already begun to use for financing at least one festival[14] (and that, according to the story just quoted, they had used for building the fleet in the first place): each of the wealthiest citizens of Athens was made trierarch, required to outfit and command a trireme for one year. This system succeeded in harnessing aristocratic wealth and aristocratic competitiveness to the service of the state; in the fifth century, it must be presumed that the tribute from the empire continued to subsidize the fleet. But Athens was to its empire as a nobleman was to his dependents: Athens's ability to provide protection was a function of its ability to continue to receive its aristocratic due. When, in the fourth century, Athens no longer ruled an empire, the liturgies became more and more difficult to maintain. At first, the trierarchy, the most onerous of the liturgies, was replaced by a system of shared responsibilities; soon afterward, the festive liturgies, too, came under attack.[15] Since the rich did not receive any financial benefit from the liturgies, they avoided them more and more. One cannot milk forever a cow that one does not feed.

⊙ THE BUILDING PROGRAM

From the first, the Athenians administered the money. The *hellenotamiai* were Athenian officials, answerable to the Athenian government like all other officials;[16] if they ever had to offer an accounting to the assembled allies, we never hear of it.[17] A decree of which we possess only a fragment enforced the use of Athenian weights, measures, and coinage throughout the empire, though it apparently did not forbid the use and even the production of other weights, measures, and coins as well.[18] In the year 454/3, the treasury

---

14. The city Dionysia. On the various "civilian" liturgies and their dates of origin, see John K. Davies, "Demosthenes on Liturgies."

15. On the trierarchy, see Jordan, 61–93; on the *choregia* (the production of performances at the dramatic festivals), see Pickard-Cambridge, *Dramatic Festivals*, 86–93.

16. They surely were required to present their accounting to the *logistai* from 454 on, as described in *ATL* III, pp. 13–14. Gomme's presumption (*HCT* I, p. 273) that that had been the case from the start is reasonable.

17. *HCT* I, pp. 272–73. For that matter, there is precious little evidence that the assemblies of the allies ever took place: see *HCT* I, p. 280; but cf. *ATL* III, p. 262 n. 91.

18. I am following here the opinion of Figueira on this much debated decree (*IG* I³ 1453; ML 45), whose date—whether in the forties or the twenties of the fifth century—has also been hotly disputed: I refer the reader to Figueira for the relevant bibliography. While there is still room for much debate, I agree with Figueira that the hoard evidence, which he surveys thoroughly (19–197), indicates beyond doubt that there was no period at which Athens forbade its allies to mint their own coins, a conclusion that reduces considerably the significance of this decree. *IG* I³ 90, even more fragmentary and of utterly uncertain content, nevertheless testifies to the continued interest of the Athenian assembly in the orderly management of currency exchange.

itself was moved to Athens, and there can be little doubt that the funds contributed were held together with other Athenian state funds. Pericles did not scruple to use the funds for his building program, and according to Plutarch, the matter caused some complaint.

Pericles' enemies reviled his policy in the assemblies, screaming that the demos had a bad reputation and was ill spoken of for having transferred money that was the common property of the Greeks from Delos to itself. The most respectable of all their claims against their accusers, that they had removed the common treasury from there and were keeping it in a safe place from fear of the barbarians—that claim Pericles had removed; and it appeared that Greece was being treated with terrible outrage and unmistakable tyranny, when it saw money that it had been required to contribute for the war being used by us to gild and make up the city like a gaudy woman, hung around with expensive stones and images and thousand-talent temples.[19]

Pericles was not at a loss for an answer.

So Pericles taught the demos that they owed no accounting of money to the allies, since they fought for them and kept the barbarians from them, when the allies did not contribute a horse, nor a ship, nor a hoplite, but only money—money that belongs not to the givers but to the receivers, if they provide that for which they take the money.[20]

We can by no means take this exchange to be a true reflection of a fifth-century debate. Ancient historians after Thucydides did not feel themselves bound by "what was really said" nor even required to inquire after the matter. In the passage at hand, a number of apparent inaccuracies and anachronisms strengthen the presumption that the debate presented was the invention either of Plutarch or of some other source already far removed from fifth-century Athens.[21] In particular, we have no contemporary evidence that there was any organized opposition in Athens to the exploitation of the empire for its own enrichment, although the great building program

---

19. Plut. *Pericles* 12.1–2.
20. Plut. *Pericles* 12.3.
21. See Andrewes, "Opposition." Note also the observation of Stadter (145) that this particular passage is written in a highly embellished style typical of Plutarch at his richest.

certainly had its opponents.[22] The terms familiar to us from fifth-century debate speak not so much about the rights of the allies as about excess and luxury leading to disease and corruption.[23] The words just quoted were surely written half a millennium after Pericles, and we have no guarantee that Pericles or his contemporaries considered the moral questions involved.

Still, the "debate" is worth our attention, for it defines clearly the conflict between two concepts of economic government. Pericles, in the first part of his answer, has put the city in the position of the archaic nobles, to whom all goods flowed by right and against whom there was no grounds for complaint as long as they looked after the needs of those under their care. His attackers, on the other hand, have taken the newer view that common money belongs to the community and that nobody has a right to touch it except as the community authorizes. We saw in chapter 9 that the second view was taken for granted in Pericles' time with regard to the internal management of state finances; the first view may well have continued to seem appropriate for international relations, where the self-interest of one's own state is considered a virtue.

The second claim put in Pericles' mouth—that the money belongs to the receivers "if they provide that for which they take the money"—is a claim of another sort, putting Athens in the position of a seller in the marketplace, entitled to make a profit as long as the goods are provided. From a monetary point of view, there is nothing anachronistic about this: the market in Athens was surely developed to the point where elementary rules of sale were universally acknowledged. From a rhetorical point of view, however, one may doubt whether the fifth-century Athenians saw themselves as selling their services to the allies for profit. That surely is not the way Thucydides presented the picture. The legitimacy of profit, so problematical for Homer, was not yet accepted for all relationships and at all levels in the fifth century.[24]

● THE PELOPONNESIAN WAR AND AFTERWARD

When a war that threatened their existence finally came to the Athenians, it was entirely characteristic for them to face it with a clear eye on money, and that is how Thucydides presents Pericles' attitude on the eve of the

---

22. Ameling, "Plutarch," 50–52.
23. Kallet-Marx, "Diseased Body Politic."
24. See von Reden, *Exchange*, 117–23.

Peloponnesian War.[25] Money, however, was not all to the Athenians: well aware of how they had reached their position of power, they never considered staying at home while others did their work for them. "Most matters of war," Thucydides quotes Pericles as saying, "are won by intelligence and by monetary superiority."[26] He expected the Athenians' monetary resources to be decisive when combined with their own efforts.

There were mercenaries in the war; sometimes—as in the expeditions of Aristeus to Potidaea and Brasidas to Thrace—they comprised a large proportion of the fighting force.[27] More significant was the investment involved in building and maintaining a fleet, an investment that became crucial in the last ten years of the war, as Athens and Sparta found themselves competing at the court of Persian satraps for the Great King's money. This money, without which the Spartan fleet could never have been maintained, was a decisive factor in the Athenian defeat.

Here again, a lesson once learned was not unlearned, and Persian money continued to be influential in Greek politics thereafter. The Corinthian War was financed heavily by the Persian satrap Tithraustes; as Agesilaus, king of Sparta, left Asia, he is said to have commented that he had been driven out "by thirty thousand Persian archers"—the archer portrayed on Persian coinage.[28] When the satrap was persuaded to move his bribery to the other side, the states of Greece found themselves obliged to agree to the Peace of Antalcidas, conceding to the king of Persia the rights for which their fathers had shed their blood a century earlier. At Salamis, money had made it possible for Athenian ships to conquer the Persian; a hundred years later, when the Greeks were more deeply divided, Persian money was able, with only the most modest recourse to ships or to weapons, to reconquer what had been lost.

This did not make money the ultimate arbiter of war. Alexander conquered the Persians despite their money; money was and is only one of the potent resources with which war is fought. It can allow an otherwise

---

25. Thuc. 1.141.2–5, 142.1, 143.1–2; 2.13.2–5.

26. Thuc. 2.13.2. That Archidamus of Sparta seems to be more categorical (ἔστιν ὁ πόλεμος οὐχ ὅπλων τὸ πλέον ἀλλὰ δαπάνης, δι᾽ ἣν τὰ ὅπλα ὠφελεῖ, Thuc. 1.83.2) reflects his situation, where a sea attack on Athens was inconceivable without great expense (ἄλλως τε καὶ ἠπειρώταις πρὸς θαλασσίους, ibid.).

27. Parke, 15–16.

28. Plut. *Agesilaus* 15.8; *Artaxerxes* 20.4; *Moralia (Apophth. Lac.)* 211b. This was, of course, the typical comment of a ruler faced with hostility that he cannot comprehend or credit; the war was not simply a matter of Persian bribery. Nevertheless, the fifty talents (Xen. *Hell.* 3.5.1) will surely have helped to encourage disgruntled states to dare open revolt.

exhausted nation to fight on: it allowed both Sparta and Athens to keep up the Peloponnesian War when the armies with which they had started the conflict had been lost. The lack of money can force a nation to give up a fight that it would otherwise wish to continue. But tactics, skill, and force of will still count for much in war, which is why the richest nation on earth is never quite as all-powerful as its financial resources would seem to dictate.

◉ MERCENARIES

The most obviously monetized factor in war is the mercenary, a monetized soldier; but coinage is not necessary to entice a man to serve in another man's army. "As long as there were wealthy masters," wrote H. W. Parke, "there were also masterless men who for need or greed or adventure would sell their swords and even their lives."[29] Achilles, as we have seen,[30] knew how to sell a captive for a good price, and war provides plenty of opportunities for enrichment other than salary. Alcaeus's brother had served with the Babylonians, surely not from patriotic zeal;[31] various tyrants had had bodyguards, who may have been paid, though the privilege of eating at the tyrant's table may have sufficed for them. I have mentioned[32] the Argives who served with Peisistratus; Herodotus calls them mercenaries, and it is not unlikely that they were promised some reward for their service, since they presumably did not imagine that they would be allowed to sack Athens in case of victory. The question of what precise recompense they did get is not likely to have occurred to Herodotus; in mid-sixth-century Greece, it probably was not coins. This is the first explicit statement that mercenaries were used by a tyranny,[33] and even Herodotus does not state that these mercenaries remained in Peisistratus's service once the battle was won.[34] Being a popular leader, he probably had no need of them.

The introduction of coinage did not, at first, bring about any great increase in the number of Greeks who served as mercenaries. Throughout the fifth century, the armies of Greece remained citizen armies. Campaigns were brief and fought on land; Athens, the one power that was almost constantly at war, did begin paying its soldiers during the fifth century, but it

---

29. Parke, 3.
30. P. 69.
31. Alcaeus fr. 350 LP. For the date, see Page, *Sappho and Alcaeus*, 224: this is approximately the time when coins were invented, but no one suspects Nebuchadnezzar of using them.
32. P. 124.
33. Parke, 8–9.
34. Lavelle, *Sorrow*, 109–10.

did not, at first, use foreigners.[35] Those Greek mercenaries who fought during the years before the Peloponnesian War were generally in the service of Persian satraps,[36] and the coins with which they were paid were sometimes special issues designed to remind them of the fact.[37]

Initially, the pay of soldiers seems to have been conceived of as a maintenance allowance; the fifth-century sources use the terms μισθός, "wages," and τροφή, "maintenance," interchangeably.[38] For a citizen force, it would probably have been objectionable, at least at first, to suggest that the money paid was required to persuade the soldiers to do their duty. It is not impossible that people who could not maintain themselves at home would have been perfectly willing to hire themselves out simply for a regular supply of food; we must presume that Athens had no need of mercenaries as long as its citizens sufficed.

They sufficed until the Sicilian expedition. There, we find the first mercenaries employed by Athens; Sparta, with a much smaller population, had been using them for some time,[39] presumably paying them with foreign coin. They came mostly from Arcadia and later also from Crete,[40] driven by the poverty of their surroundings more than they were attracted by the prospect of wealth.[41] This point is significant, for it was here that the presence of coinage made a difference. An army that supplies itself by booty or by foraging has a very precarious existence; one that supplies itself from central stores can only function as long as it can maintain a well-organized commissariat. Money made the matter much simpler: wherever food could be bought, an army could be provisioned.[42] Where provisions were sure, army service was attractive to people whose provisions at home were less than sure.

When the war ended, many more men had become used to a life of

---

35. Pritchett, *Greek State at War*, 1:7–14.

36. Parke, 6.

37. Trundle, 34. The practice of barbarian states issuing special coins to pay mercenaries, often with imitation Athenian coins, recurs in numerous cases, and examples of the practice are also found among Greeks: Garlan, 62–68.

38. Pritchett, *Greek State at War*, 1:3–6.

39. Parke, 15–18.

40. See Willetts, 65–75, with the comments of P. Ducrey and E. van 't Dack on p. 76, for a sketch of the kind of society that produced mercenaries.

41. Ducrey, 121; Pritchett, *Greek State at War*, 5:458–59, basing himself on Fuks, "Isokrates," 30–31 n. 49.

42. Though such passages as Xenophon's *Anabasis* 5.5.6–25 show us that not every community was willing to part with enough food to feed an army, even for money: the citizens realized that money would not save them if their supplies ran out.

campaigning, and many of them had decidedly less appealing prospects in the country from which they came. The attempt of Cyrus the Younger to conquer the throne of Persia with an army of mercenaries, of whom Xenophon the Athenian was one,[43] combined the Persian willingness to employ mercenaries with the newly widespread Greek willingness to serve as such. As the fourth century wore on, mercenaries served with whoever would pay them, and military power had less and less to do with the training of the citizen body. Inevitably, the converse was also true: the citizen generals became more and more independent of the city that sent them, forming their own personal friendships and alliances and improvising strategies that would provide them with the success and the financial backing for which the city was no longer the only source.[44] As war became more monetized, the city was losing its exclusive hold on the practitioners of war.

An opposite problem was also looming: the foreign mercenaries who served Greek cities became a force to be reckoned with in politics. They did not form themselves into a political party or lobby; but their presence, when they were not fighting the city's wars, was an unwelcome one. The Thracians who had massacred the schoolchildren at Mycalessus in 413[45] were only the first example of a problem that was to become chronic: what to do with mercenaries who did not go home. Xenophon suggested that the Ten Thousand who had fought with Cyrus might found their own city;[46] Isocrates, in proposing the conquest of Persia, explicitly had in view the settling of the conquered territory by "those who now wander about from lack of the daily necessities and inflict damages on all those whom they encounter."[47]

THE HELLENISTIC ARMIES

Philip of Macedon fulfilled Isocrates' dream, with what may be considered the first successful professional army in Greece. This was by no means entirely a mercenary army; it was based, like the army of his son, Alexander the Great, on levies from Macedon and the peoples subject to it.[48] The armies of Alexander's successors continued his successful organization, adapting it to their territories. Both in Egypt and in the Seleucid Empire, a system of military

---

43. An indication that not every mercenary was a pauper.
44. Garlan, 150–53.
45. Thuc. 7.29.5.
46. Xen. *Anabasis* 5.6.15–16.
47. Isocrates 5 (Philip) 120.
48. Hammond, Griffith, and Walbank, 2:438–44, 3:86–88.

settlements provided troops for the king, without his having to pay them when their service was not required; but in both, soldiers were paid when on campaign, and mercenaries played a part that was not negligible, so that a military effort required a substantial outlay of cash.[49] Although large armies had been raised and maintained in both Egypt and Syria long before the invention of coinage,[50] the Greek way of maintaining control of the region made extensive use of coins. Money never, however, became the entire basis for recruitment, as it did in Rome under Marius or as it has in America in recent decades; much less did the Greek states become entirely dependent on mercenary armies, with military power going to the highest bidder. The monetization of war proceeded far in the Greek world—farther than in many subsequent societies—but there were steps in monetization that the Greeks never took.

The Hellenistic armies were in their general organization an innovation; in terms of their multinational composition and the broad strategic problems with which they had to deal, they were a continuation of the oriental armies that had preceded them. Like those, they eventually fell before a more highly motivated citizen-based army from the West.

---

49. Lesquier, 101–2; Préaux, 29–34; Bar-Kochva, 20–53; van 't Dack.

50. Cardascia describes a quasi-feudal form of military tenure in Achaemenid Babylon that bears some similarities to the Hellenistic military settlements. He is probably right to conclude that the Ptolemaic cleruchy "probably has Greek or Hellenistic origins" (10), but it does represent a solution without coinage to the same administrative problem that continued to face the Hellenistic kings.

11 THE MONETIZATION OF LABOR

○ THETES

There was no proletariat in ancient Greece; the use of the term *proletariat* to refer to wage earners in general is an innovation of the nineteenth century.[1] There were surely poor Athenians, and there were propertyless Athenians; but as far as is known to me, there were, until the invention of coinage, no free Athenians who worked daily for an employer who paid them a regular salary.

There were slaves. There had been slaves since the time of Homer and Hesiod and, for that matter, since the Bronze Age. For all we know, there had been slaves for eons before. When coins became available, slaves were traded for money, but they had long been being captured, subjugated, traded, and ransomed without the need of a silver disk with an image impressed on it. It is very likely that the invention of coinage facilitated somewhat the traffic in slaves and may thereby have increased it, but this will have been no more than the general increase in market trade that I noted in chapter 8.

There were also free laborers, but they were not what we would call wage

---

1. The term *proletarius* was used in prerepublican Rome to describe the lowest class of citizens, who had no significant property of their own. The economic realities of the nineteenth century restricted the term to wage earners, generally those whose wages were low.

earners. Homer speaks of *thetes*, free men[2] who worked for others and received a wage *(misthos)*.[3] They were not simply day laborers: one might contract to be a *thes* for a year "at a stated wage,"[4] as two gods were said to have done for Priam's father Laomedon, though he never paid them their wage; and a nobleman might take his *thetes*, along with his slaves, to accompany him on a journey.[5] But the terms of service as a *thes* were not those we usually think of when we speak of wage labor. Eurymachus asks if Odysseus (disguised as a beggar) might like to work for him as a *thes*,

at the furthest part of my field—and you will have a sufficient[6]
wage—
collecting stones for a wall and planting large trees?
Then I would provide you with a regular allowance of food,
and I would clothe you with garments and give sandals for your
feet.[7]

This is not a wage in our sense of the word; it is simple maintenance. The poor free man, who, for lack of land, was in danger of utter deprivation and death, could attach himself as a *thes* to a noble or to a more fortunate commoner and thereby expect food, clothing, and presumably shelter. Some scholars believe that since maintenance was simply a necessary condition of his work, he must have gotten a wage in addition; others are less generous.[8]

---

2. They are distinguished from δμῶες (slaves), *Od.* 4.644; cf. schol. BEPQ (Dindorff), ad loc.: Θῆτες γὰρ λέγονται οἱ ἐλεύθεροι μέν, μισθῷ δὲ δουλεύοντες. Ramming (98) is unwilling to rely on the other Odyssean passages (that use the verb θητεύω rather than the substantive θής) because they refer to imaginary circumstances; but this seems to carry skepticism too far. I cannot think of any parallel for the suggestion to a free man that he might voluntarily reduce himself to slavery, as Eurymachus suggests to Odysseus at *Od.* 18.357–64 that he might be "willing" [θητευέμεν] for him. Nor, for that matter, are we required to ignore, as Ramming does, *Il.* 21.445, where gods worked as θῆτες and were cheated of their wages—an impossibility for a slave, who had no right to demand wages from his master.

3. *Il.* 21.445; *Od.* 18.358.

4. θητεύσαμεν εἰς ἐνιαυτὸν μισθῷ ἐπὶ ῥητῷ (*Il.* 21.444–45).

5. *Od.* 4.644. It would, of course, be more respectable to be attended by one's (noble) friends; and although one can read Antinous's words δύναιτό κε καὶ τὸ τελέσσαι as a mere statement of possibility ("i.e., he had servants enough to man a ship with them" [S. West, ad loc., in Heubeck et al., vol. 1]), they may equally well be a sneer: "He is even capable of that."

6. Finley (*World*, 57) says that "a little of the joke lay in the words, 'you can be sure of pay'. No *thes* could be sure." But it is not certain that ἄρκιος here or ever means "sure."

7. *Od.* 18.357–60.

8. Finley (*World*, 57) seems to take the phrase μισθὸς . . . ἄρκιος to refer to the food, clothing, and footgear ("ample grain and clothes and shoes make up the store of a commoner's

Of course, what matters is not the opinion of one scholar or another nor even that of the laborer but what Eurymachus would have said when the time came to pay. The phenomenon of agricultural workers who work for their room and board is not unknown even today, and Eurymachus had not committed himself to more. Had his suggestion been more than a joke and had Odysseus taken him up on it, he would have had no better hope than Laomedon's divine *thetes* to get any real fulfillment of a vague promise. Eurymachus had promised no more than simple maintenance.

A man who needed something specific (seed corn for the next year's planting, for example, or discharge of a debt) might specify some other *misthos*, as the two gods did when they were forced to work as *thetes*;[9] but receiving a salary in addition to maintenance, as Eurymachus's suggestion shows, was not what defined a *thes*. Laomedon's behavior—he drove away the divine *thetes* with threats to sell them to a far country[10]—suggests, as does Antinous's suggestion that Telemachus might have filled out the crew of a boat with "*thetes* and servants," that the service of a *thes* was not visibly different from that of a slave.[11] Being free, of course, the *thes* could always leave, if he could find another way to ward off starvation; but he was more probably homeless himself.[12] The point of Eurymachus's raillery was the implication that Odysseus was so desperate for sustenance that he should be willing to accept. As long as he was not that desperate, his freedom, even as a beggar, seems still to have been preferable to a wage-slavery more naked than any of Marx's day.

Finley noted—and many have followed his lead—that Achilles' words to

---

goods"). Wickert-Micknat (176–77), followed by M. Schmidt (*LfgrE*, s.v. θητεύω), takes it to refer to an additional wage.

9. *Il.* 21.443–57. He might even get it, if the noble, unlike Laomedon, chose to behave honestly.

10. *Il.* 21.454, where περάαν must mean what it clearly does in *Il.* 21.40 and *Od.* 15.453 "to sell abroad," and not, as Lattimore translates it, "to carry us away for slaves." There is no reason why Laomedon should have been interested, once his city was built, in going off himself to faraway islands. He was threatening to dispose of the gods the way one normally disposed of unwanted captives.

11. It seems less likely that the suggestion at *Od.* 4.644 is to hire them for the purpose. Of course, a *thes* would probably be hired for a particular purpose, but I do not think that Wickert-Micknat (155) is justified in treating the specification of his job as a defining characteristic of the *thes*.

12. Θῆτα . . . ἄοικον, Hesiod *Works and Days* 602: The meaning of ἄοικον here is surely "without a family" (see Martin L. West, ad loc.; *contra* Nussbaum, 216 n. 3), but lack of family and homelessness were likely to go together. West's quote from Šuruppak, however ("not having a house, he does not go to his house," Alster, line 167), is inappropriate: Šuruppak is speaking of a foreign slave bought in the mountains (ibid., line 163), whom he explicitly contrasts to the more fractious freeman.

Odysseus in the underworld seem to imply that the life of a *thes* was worse than that of a slave: "A *thes*, not a slave, was the lowest creature on earth that Achilles could think of."[13] Perceptive as this remark may be, I no longer think it is true. Despite Achilles' remark, a slave was probably lower than a *thes*, but for a free man to sink to slavery was to lose his personhood entirely. In sociological terms, it was death;[14] in terms of honor and self-esteem, it was worse than death. Achilles did not say that he would rather be a slave than king of the dead either because the poet did not think he would make that choice or because the poet was not willing to debase Achilles so far as to present him, even in imagination, as a slave.

The exchange between the *thes* and his employer was a drastic one: freedom for sustenance. It seems to have been made, typically, for an extended period,[15] as indeed the circumstance of the dependent required: since he must eat every day, he required an arrangement that promised him "a regular allowance of food," not merely today's necessities. On the other side, his employer would not offer him such regular sustenance if he could not count on using him for whatever work was needed, so the *thes*, like the slave, had to be available for any sort of work that might be required. Skilled workers, *demioergoi*, performed services that were useful to many and that commanded, from one or from many, remuneration important enough to guarantee a livelihood;[16] but there were not many such people in Homer's world,[17] and *thetes* had to offer all they had. There does not seem to have been any middle ground.

⊙ DAY LABORERS

The introduction of money changed that. Again, the change came about not because a new labor relationship was possible that had not been possible before but because what would once have been clumsy and rare became simplified and common. The growth of the market might itself offer work for the poor free man. Actual selling will have required having something to sell, but some of the *thetes* may have been able to find or to borrow enough capital to begin with. Artisans were still able to make a living, perhaps a

---

13. Finley, *World*, 57; and again in *Ancient Economy*, 66.

14. See von Reden, *Exchange*, 67; for "social death," see Patterson, especially 1–14.

15. Whether a poor farmer would take on a *thes* for seasonal labor or for a longer period we cannot state: Mrozek, 14.

16. On the Homeric *demioergos*, see Finley, *World*, 55–56.

17. Donlan ("Homeric Economy," 650–51) identifies three: "the potter *(kerameus)*, the metal worker *(chalkeus)*, and the carpenter-builder *(tektôn)*"; he does not think that the other trade titles that are occasionally found identify full-time occupations.

good one.[18] Even before the development of the commercial agora, they were likely to have a fixed place of business[19] and perhaps a few helpers, slave or free. Even for those with no profession and nothing to sell but their labor, the agora was a place where many people, both buyers and sellers, wandered around with money in their purses, and many of them might have a bit of work they needed done. A man no longer needed to sell himself for a year to guarantee his sustenance. It would be enough to get a wage today. That wage itself might perhaps be stretched to pay for food for more than a single day; and whenever it ran out, the agora would still be there.

It was a misfortune, although a common one, to have to work for a living. Those who did, whether small farmers, artisans, shopkeepers, or workers, were called *penetes* (the poor), and their life was not enviable. They were distinguished, however, from the *ptochoi*,[20] those who suffered from want that they could not overcome by labor (that is, those that we today would call poor). The distinction must have been unclear at the edges. Not everybody, surely, found work every day, and a *penes* probably had more than one day when he retired hungry.[21] Still, the stark need to sell his freedom for a year was much further removed than it had been in Odysseus's day.

A person who was hired by the day was not a *thes;* the term never appears to describe a contemporary class of workers after epic. A new term, *latris*, appears for a while, and it can refer to a person hired for a day[22] or for a year;[23] later, the adjective *misthotos* takes the form of a substantive and becomes a catchall term for those who receive a wage. The *latris* may not, in some cases, have been treated much differently from a slave—Theognis advises a person to be "bitter and sweet, charming and harsh," to his slaves, *latreis,* and neighbors[24] and shows some resentment over how much a *latris* might eat[25]—but he did not necessarily have to endure such treatment every day.

---

18. There were, of course, those whose trade could barely support them, as the cripple claims in Lysias 24.6.

19. See p. 113.

20. LSJ translates πτωχός misleadingly as "beggar"; but it was not begging that defined a πτωχός, but the inability to supply basic needs: Hemelrijk, 53–54 [140–41].

21. See, for example, the worry of the boy and his father in Aristophanes *Wasps* 303–10, although the boy appears too young to work and the father too old.

22. Theognis 486: λάτριν ἐφημέριον.

23. Solon fr. 13.48 Bergk.

24. Theognis 301–2. One could, of course, as easily argue that the *latris* was treated like a neighbor or that, as Theognis's word order suggests, his position was somewhere in between. Undoubtedly, much depended upon the character of the employer.

25. Theognis 485–86: these lines are not necessarily by Theognis, but that need not concern us.

Eventually, the *thetes* ceased to exist as a category of workers. This may have happened by the early archaic period, but we cannot be sure. The term *thetes* was used by Solon for the lowest property class, those who had nothing or next to nothing. A *thes* was barred from holding any office, but there was, at least by Aristotle's day, no implication about how he made his living.[26] More to the point, we do not find, at least by the middle of the fifth century, large noble families with networks of hangers-on who could be counted on for work or for political clout. That, it would appear, had ceased to be the way for a propertyless free man to support himself.

In Athens, there were particularly Athenian ways to make a living. Those who served as soldiers during the incessant wars of the fifth century were maintained during the course of the campaign; those that stayed at home could maintain themselves with jury service or one of the other paying jobs that the state increasingly offered.[27] These people, however, were availing themselves of particularly Athenian opportunities, supplied by the revenues of the empire. Even at its height, the empire did not maintain everybody.

There were still those citizens who worked for wages to earn their living, though they appear to have been relatively few.[28] They were no longer *thetes*. Some worked for their wealthier fellow citizens: "As I hear," says one Demosthenic speaker, "many citizen women were turned into wet-nurses or weavers or grape pickers by the troubles of the city in those times";[29] the speaker's own mother worked as a wet-nurse,[30] and she must have done this at home for money, for a married woman would hardly have moved into another man's household when her husband was away on military service.

The various public building accounts of Athens mention workers in the building trades. They worked either directly for the city or for a contractor. They received a low but fixed wage, and the notable fact about this wage is that it was always stipulated either by the day, by the prytany,[31] or by the job. I know of no example in the fifth century of a free worker who contracted to

---

26. [Arist.] *Ath. Pol.* 7.4.

27. There were more than twenty thousand such jobs according to [Arist.] *Ath. Pol.* 24.3, though the figure may be exaggerated: see Gomme, "Notes," 8; Rhodes, 300–309.

28. Glotz (*Ancient Greece at Work*, 172–75) observed not only that the citizens formed a relatively small proportion of the workforce but also that their relative share declined from the fifth century to the fourth. Cf. Hemelrijk (53 [140]) for the converse, that salaried workers and day laborers were the smallest of the various groups that made up the poor.

29. Dem. 57.45.

30. Dem. 57.42.

31. One-tenth of a year. This formulation is that used in Athenian accounts, *IG* I³ 435: μισθοὶ κατ' ἐμέραν, μισθοὶ κατὰ πρυτανείαν, μισθοὶ ἀπόπαχς.

work for a full year at any job at all; nor, to look at the converse, do I know of any employer who contracted to employing a salaried laborer for a year. When there was work to be done, a person might work and get paid; when there was no work to be done, that person could look elsewhere or starve. A fifth-century worker was freer than a *thes* had been, and once the money was received, it gave the worker independence for as long as it lasted; but nobody was responsible for seeing that a worker ate throughout the year. This pattern remains, as far as we can tell, at least throughout the fourth century in Athens and during the third and second centuries in Delos. That we can speak of no other places or times is not because we have reason to believe that matters were different but simply for want of documentation.[32]

In the one place where we can trace individual workers, Hellenistic Delos, it appears that it was not the usual practice of an unskilled laborer to go out every single morning looking for work. Although the jobs to be done were very similar from year to year, it is relatively rare to find the same worker being hired on each occasion: almost three-quarters of the names appear only once or twice and never again.[33] Delos was a small island, but it would seem that when the temple managers looked for a worker, they found different people in the marketplace each time. The pattern indicated is one still found in many societies, where a man goes to work because he has run out of money or needs it for a special purpose. If he can get along on what he has, he will stay at home and tend to whatever other matters may interest him.[34] According to calculations made by Gustave Glotz,[35] a drachma a day could support a family securely, if not luxuriously, even if the worker had to buy all his necessities in the marketplace; a bachelor could get along on a third of that, which is to say that he need work only one day out of three.

This was not the only form of employment. That contractors might take on long-term jobs does not necessarily mean that they had a regular workforce at

---

32. See *IG* I³ 435; *IG* I² 472, lines 180–90 ([μι]σθὸς hυ[πογ]οῖς χατ᾽ ἐμέϱ[αν . . . μισ]θὸ[ς] ἀπόπ[αχς]); the accounts of the Erechtheum (*IG* I³ 474–79); the accounts of the Eleusinian treasurers (*IG* II–III² 1672–73); and the accounts of the Delian *hieropoioi* (*IG* XI 2 135–289; *Ins. Dél.* 290–469).

33. I hope to publish a survey of this information in a forthcoming article provisionally entitled "The Working Class at Delos." The statistic becomes more significant if we agree with Reger (49–82) that the economy of Delos was a relatively small one, whose horizons did not extend far beyond the Cyclades.

34. The casual nature of ancient free labor was noted by Finley (*Ancient Economy*, 73. Fuks ("Κολωνὸς μίσθιος," 171–73) identified the place in Athens where laborers would present themselves in the morning to be hired by people needing work done.

35. Glotz, "Les salaires," 209–10.

hand; they may have counted on finding people at the "shape-up" every morning.[36] Certain cases in the Delos inscriptions themselves, though, make it clear that there were people who worked regularly for wages, though where we see them, they are regularly skilled workers.[37] Even free workers on long-term projects, however, did not necessarily show up every day. One gang of thirty-three men working for seven days has its full complement only twice; on the other five days, two, four, twelve, fourteen, or twenty-three workers are missing. The gangs including free workers who did the fluting for the Erechtheum columns worked on less than two-thirds of the days in each prytany. The slave gangs, in contrast, worked almost every day: free men who had no compulsion to work themselves constantly did not for that reason consider themselves obliged to indulge their slaves.[38] The question of whether we should see in the partial employment of workers the blessing of leisure or the curse of unemployment would probably require us to ask the ancient Greek worker himself, which we cannot do.

● SALARIES

The first true salaried workers were the mercenaries,[39] and the fact should not surprise us: only the state now had enough capital to be able to promise a steady salary (although it still seems to have been calculated by the day), and there were no workers, at least in wartime, that the state needed more than soldiers. More to the point, soldiers could not be taken each morning from the marketplace: once they were sent out on an expedition, they had to be maintained until the expedition came to an end, successfully or otherwise. Even so, only in the fourth century did the Greeks begin to take to

---

36. *Contra* Mrozek, 161.

37. Such as Deinocrates (*IG* XI 156 A, lines 39, 71, and elsewhere), who performed odd jobs for the temple for over a decade and apparently was a citizen (cf. *IG* XI 105, line 14; 108, line 15). Mrozek (161) offers mussel fishing and "chemical" workshops as examples of "difficult and unhealthy" jobs that required regular employment of unskilled workers, but one may question whether he is correct to classify these jobs as unskilled. I know of no proof that unskilled laborers were ever hired for a long term, but I know of no proof that they were not.

38. Glotz, *Ancient Greece at Work*, 283. Mrozek (35–36) attributes this fact to the availability of work in the courts or the assembly, but there is no evidence as to what the free people were doing when not working.

39. De Ste. Croix (*Class Struggle*, 24–25) attributes a similar observation, "interesting and perfectly correct," to Karl Marx, although Marx was speaking not about the length of service but about the systematization of a salary system (Marx and Engels, III 8, p. 175 [letter from Marx to Engels, September 25, 1857]).

soldiering as a remunerative occupation; fifth-century armies worked for τροφή, "maintenance."[40] Even in the fourth century, a soldier's pay was not attractive for its daily rate. Only in the Hellenistic period would a young man, like Cleostratus in Menander's *Aspis,* take to soldiering to go and earn his fortune; and then he was counting on booty, not salary.[41]

Soldiers were not the only people to draw a salary. The inscriptions of the *hieropoioi* at Delos show that there, at least, a number of officials drew a daily salary in the third century. The architect got, normally, one and a half or two drachmas per day;[42] there were others, though not many of them, who got a regular salary, always somewhat less.[43] Scholars have expressed surprise at the fact that an important state functionary was paid no more than an ordinary skilled worker,[44] but no surprise is in order. The free skilled worker who worked every day in the year was rare—in fact, he was nonexistent, for no free man worked on festivals. The architect at Delos, in contrast, was paid for every day in the year, and although he was expected to work accordingly, it is most doubtful whether any workman at two drachmas a day got anything like the 720 drachmas per year of the architect.[45] These jobs were responsible ones, but they were plums, and they were not given to poor or unskilled workmen.[46] In fact, a good architect could command a better price,[47] and the architects at Delphi, though paid at first like the Delian architect (as a skilled worker), eventually came to draw a salary three times

40. As noted on p. 146.

41. For the information in this paragraph, see Pritchett, *Greek State at War,* 1: chap. 1.

42. Generally, an architect received one and a half drachmas between the years 250 and 200 (*IG* XI 2 287 A, line 87; *Ins. Dél.* 290, line 107; *Ins. Dél.* 372 A, line 99), two drachmas before and after that period (*IG* XI 2 158 A, line 51; 159 A, line 62; 161 A, line 83; 199 C, line 41; 203 A, line 60). Three architects got more (*IG* XI 2 144 A, line 27 [three and a half drachmas a day]; 159 A, line 63 [four drachmas a day]; 162 A, line 46 [three drachmas a day]), and one got less (*IG* XI 2 148 line 66—no salary is mentioned, but a "food allowance" comes out to one drachma and half an obol per day).

43. The summary of Homolle (477–92) has withstood the test of time and dozens of new inscriptions remarkably well. For my own plans, see n. 33 in the present chapter.

44. Homolle himself (480) noted this fact and added perceptively, "The modesty of the wage is less surprising if we calculate that all in all, with works that cost an average of about 10,000 drachmas, this comes out to a sum significantly higher than the five percent of today's architects."

45. This was already noted by Glotz (*Ancient Greece at Work,* 283 n. 1). Slaves, as noted above, might work more and even every single day.

46. We must presume that for mercenaries, too, the regularity of the employment made an unexciting wage into an attractive prospect. Unfortunately for the soldiers, they often found, as the *thes* in his time had sometimes found, that the promised wage did not materialize. Pritchett, *Greek State at War,* 1:29.

47. Glotz, *Ancient Greece at Work,* 283 n. 1.

as high.[48] Still, a daily salary was never such as to make its recipient fabulously rich.[49]

SLAVES

In the conditions of labor, money had not caused any new distinction between slave and free. Just as the *thes* had performed his work side by side with servants, so a workshop of the classical period might have slaves and free men working together.[50] The difference between them was in the terms of their service: whereas the free worker worked when he chose, a slave was a slave for life. This was probably the chief factor that prevented the growth of long-term salaried labor: if a person wanted workers who would work all the time, they could be bought. Stewards managing estates were regularly slaves or former slaves,[51] and wherever we hear of establishments employing a large labor force, it was a slave force.[52]

Slavery itself, of course, had not been unaffected by money: the slave market had expanded along with the rest of the market, and where in Homer only nobles had held slaves, in Athens slaveholding appears to have penetrated very far down on the economic scale. It did not, of course, extend to the very bottom; a cripple for whom Lysias wrote a speech had no children to serve him and could not afford a slave to take over his work.[53] Aristotle noted that the poor had to use their wives and children as attendants because they had no slaves.[54] For all that, it is noteworthy which case Aristotle considers the normal one: he does not say that the rich use slaves instead of wives and children, but that the poor use wives and children instead of slaves.

Slaves might not only work for their masters; they might work for others for pay. The pay, of course, would go to their master. It presumably covered a day's upkeep for the slave, but even if it did not, it was worthwhile, since

---

48. Glotz, "Les salaires," 214, who comments: "This time it is no longer a civil servant's stipend, but an artist's price."

49. Nor is it today. See p. 190, n. 76. Great fortunes were and are made by control of many producers, by market trade, by capital investment, by fraud, or by confiscation, never by salaried labor.

50. Burford, *Craftsmen*, 90–91; Finley, *Ancient Economy*, 79–80.

51. De Ste. Croix, *Class Struggle*, 505–6.

52. Finley, *Ancient Economy*, 73–74. None of these establishments, except for the Laureion mines, was very large by modern standards: Glotz, *Ancient Greece at Work*, 205–6, 267.

53. Lysias 24.6.

54. Arist. *Pol.* VI 8.23 (1323a 5–6).

the master had to feed the slaves whether they worked or not.[55] Some masters made a handsome profit on hiring out their slaves.[56]

It would be possible, of course, to have the slave take care of the entire job: the slave could use a day's pay for food, clothing, and lodging, and give the rest to the master. Such arrangements were indeed made: these slaves were referred to as χωρὶς οἰκοῦντες, "living apart," and their condition could indeed approach that of free non-citizens.[57] If they could manage to get by on less than their master allowed them, they could save money. Manumission was a viable option, more and more documented as the Hellenistic period progressed into the Roman.[58] As in the free population, money allowed the accumulation of small profits to be turned into an advantage large enough to effect a complete change of class.

Prostitution was not a trade that required money to make it possible, but it, too, was affected somewhat by the invention of coinage. Merkelbach's observation that a bordello was hardly conceivable before the invention of money[59] is a plausible one, though the "money" involved need not have been coins: the weighed silver of the Levant would also have sufficed. Brothels in Greece were usually collections of slave girls, and their wide distribution[60] can be seen as part and parcel of the general expansion of the market. Those who worked on their own—or for their "protectors," mothers, or even husbands—were more likely to be freedwomen or even freeborn women, sometimes driven, as today, by poverty to a life of disrepute.[61] Here, too, money may have made the passage from class to class easier: the archetypical case is that of Neaera, who was alleged to have moved from a madam's slave to a young noble's bought concubine to freedom and even a life so close to

---

55. I do not know of any legal requirement that a master feed his slave, but it was surely the norm. The frugal Roman Cato, who had a quite hardheaded attitude toward employing slaves for profit, recommended selling them when they got old or sick (*De Agri Cultura* 2.7), but even he did not suggest simply leaving them to starve. Slave owners in Plautine comedy threatened their slaves with the mill and even the rack, with "comic" abandon, but they did not suggest depriving them of a meal.

56. Xen. *Ways and Means* 4.14–16; cf. Finley, *Ancient Economy*, 72.

57. De Ste. Croix, *Class Struggle*, 563 n. 9.

58. The most important sequence of manumission inscriptions, from Delphi, stretches from the third century into the current era (*GDI* 1684–2342; *FD* III, passim), but many others show us that we are not dealing with a mere local phenomenon (e.g., *IG* II–III² 1553–78; VII 3198–3406; IX¹ 1 119–27; IX¹ 2, passim [see p. XXIX, s.v. *Manumissiones*]; IX² 1 612–43). We cannot know, of course, whether we are dealing with an increase in the frequency of manumission or with the introduction of regular methods for recording it.

59. Merkelbach, 25.

60. Herter, 71–72.

61. Ibid., 77–79.

that of a citizen that her consort could be prosecuted for having allowed it.[62] This will hardly have been the fate of most women caught up in her profession. For most of them, the conditions of employment must have changed little over time.

◉ WOMEN'S WORK

The work of citizen women was even less affected by money. Throughout the ancient period, women—the mistress of the household along with her slave girls—continued to work at spinning and weaving wool. As Judith Brown noted, women in all societies have been occupied with activities "compatible with simultaneous child watching." Brown summarizes their characteristics: "they do not require rapt concentration and are relatively dull and repetitive; they are easily interruptible and easily resumed once interrupted; they do not place the child in potential danger; and they do not require the participant to range very far from home."[63] Elizabeth Barber showed both persuasively and absorbingly that the production of clothing from fiber fulfills these conditions excellently and was the province of women from long before the dawn of the ancient world to centuries after its fall.[64] The women of ancient Greece were no different in this area from their mothers, daughters, and distant cousins.

The wool might be bought from the market, but the clothing that the women made was generally for the family's use. It could also be sold and surely was, but it seems that only a major crisis would suggest to a person the idea of turning a household into a factory.[65] Only in the last two hundred years, with the advent of the power loom, has women's work begun to be monetized. Only in the last fifty years has monetization progressed so far that it has become the norm for a woman to leave the household to work and hire replacements to take care of her housework and her children, monetizing the care of children and family.[66] The reasons for this revolution are still being debated, and it is a far-reaching change in women's lives. Perhaps no less interesting is the fact that Greece and Rome—and even the modern world until our own generation and our parents'—resisted this change long after men's work had become entirely monetized.

---

62. [Dem.] 59.
63. Judith Brown, 1075–76.
64. Barber, Prehistoric Textiles, 283–98; Women's Work, throughout.
65. Even then, it took Socrates to suggest the idea: Xen. Mem. 2.7.
66. It had long been normal for rich families to hire servants, but the women of these families did not have to work elsewhere in order to get somebody to take over their housework.

◉ THE CONCEPT OF LABOR

When speaking of the monetization of men's labor in ancient society, we must be cautious, for as far as monetization did progress, there was a long road further that neither the Greeks nor the Romans chose to take. Labor in our own society is monetized to an extent of which the ancient world never dreamed. Today, it is often the fact of payment that defines labor. We speak of a labor market, where labor is traded, like tomatoes, for money. Any paid job is labor, no matter how thorough a sinecure it may be; building one's own house or even helping a neighbor to build his is not "labor," though it may be work. The term "unemployed" describes not the person who performs no work, but the person who performs no paid work, and it took an organized movement of women to stop a man from saying, "My wife doesn't do anything," when what he meant to say was that she dedicated all of her time to cleaning his house and clothing, preparing his meals, and raising his children. Not to work for money is idleness, and millionaires and their wives may take paying jobs, for salaries that they hardly need, to avoid its reproach.

All of this was undreamed of and might well have been considered insanity in the ancient world. The ancient Greeks, even when money had become the universal medium of economic exchange, still considered the exchange of labor for money to be the exceptional case, and working for another a distasteful and perhaps somewhat shameful condition to which necessity might reduce a person. The ideal economic life was to work for oneself, producing one's own needs and providing for one's family out of one's own possession. This meant, of course, tending a farm, and it remains for us to see to what extent agriculture was affected by the invention of money.

12 Money on the Farm

FARMERS ARE AND WERE notoriously conservative. Not only their relative isolation from the trends of public opinion but the nature of their work predisposes them to continue in the ways of their fathers: plants and animals can be damaged or killed with a day or two of improper care, and one introduces innovations only with the greatest of caution. It will not surprise us, then, if agriculture was affected by money less quickly and less pervasively than was the marketplace. Well might Dicaeopolis find himself

> looking away to my farm, in love with peace,
> despising the city, longing for my village,
> which never ever said, "A great buy on coals!"
> nor "Vinegar," nor "Oil," and didn't know "A great buy,"
> but bore everything itself, without the grating.[1]

---

1. Aristophanes *Acharnians* 32–36. Aristophanes wrote not of a "great buy" but simply of people saying, "Buy coals," etc., on which Dicaeopolis comments dryly that his village was simple, χὠ πρίων ἀπῆν "and the sawing-man was not there," a pun on πρίαμαι (to buy) and πρίω (to saw): Dicaeopolis finds the hawkers' cries as unpleasant as the sound of sawing. My "great buy" is an attempt to improve on the more common translation of this pun with the English "buy-word" (Frere, Rennie, Rogers, Starkie, Douglass Parker—to quote only the translations at hand as I write), which hits the sound but misses the point.

Yet the effects that money had on the rest of society were felt in the fields as well, though it is impossible to gauge the details of their extent. The change of free labor from one of yearlong dependency to one of occasional work surely had its effect, for farms of moderate size would need helpers for the harvest at least, and if helpers were hired, they would now have to be paid; whether they were paid in coin or in kind might vary.[2] Neighbors or family might help,[3] particularly if they could be offered hospitable enough conditions,[4] but not everyone had enough of such unpaid labor available. In many states, various noncitizens who were held in some measure of subjugation might be called upon, but these, too, were not universals throughout Greece. Many families will have had no choice but to seek out workers as they needed them and to make sure they had on hand something acceptable with which to pay them.

That, at any rate, was the case with those with enough land to require help; for their poor neighbors, occasional labor and its wage could produce the difference between survival and starvation. To provide such seasonal work was in fact one of the responsibilities of the wealthy. Although the workers will never, as we saw, have received an annual wage, they are likely to have depended upon the same work being available every year in the same places, producing something of a patronage relationship, though the elaborate Roman rules of patron and client were not a Greek phenomenon.[5]

The hiring of occasional labor was not necessarily the choice for those—in Athens, a significant part of the population—who preferred and were able to spend their time in the city and to have others do all of their farming for them. Farms could be, and certainly were, rented.[6] The state rented them out for cash, which at least indicates that there were people around who had no difficulty in getting cash in return for agricultural

2. See Burford, *Land and Labor*, 190–93. The modern harvest workers whom I. T. Sanders met were paid in wheat and would only get it a month later, when the threshing was done: Sanders, 86–89, quoted by Walcot, 41–42.

3. Osborne (*Demos*, 144–46) quotes Menander (*Dyscolus* 329–31, 366–67; *Georgos*) and [Dem.] 53 for evidence that, as we should have expected, such rural mutual help was indeed the norm in Athens.

4. "In effect, since agricultural production is individualistic, the majority of men in a group work collectively for each other in turns, the output of work varying with the quantity of beer provided. If much beer is offered much work will be done: but if the quantity is parsimonious or the quality poor the work output will be reduced in proportion." Allan, 44, speaking of Africa.

5. Gallant, 164–65; Millett, "Patronage." On the existence of patronage relationships, though not legally or socially defined, see now Zelnick-Abramovitz.

6. Isaeus 11.42; Lysias 7.4, 9–10.

produce; we do not know which form of payment private individuals may have preferred.[7]

An absentee landlord could take care of his farm without having to rent it out. Most simply, he could have a bailiff manage it for him. We have no evidence with which to judge the relative frequency of various modes of agricultural labor. The easy way in which Xenophon's Socrates considers a field to be a likely source of wealth for a city dweller[8] might be imagining either renting out the farm or managing it through a bailiff; and although he uses at one place the distinction between the owner of a field and its renter as a metaphor for the distinction between a person interested in the welfare of an item and one interested only in what he can get out of it, that, too, says nothing about how common the arrangement might be. Even the anecdotal evidence on which we usually rely is particularly sparse and would in any event be unhelpful: nobody *tells* us what the proportion of slaves working in the country was, and the inferences we may draw, even if correct, can only reveal to us what the speaker's probably uninformed presumption was. Governments today compile statistics on such questions, and their findings are often full of surprises. What would be the point of trying to guess the truth from a metaphor used in fiction?[9]

For those who needed full-time workers, slaves were now the most attractive form of labor, and the growth of the slave market, together with the market in general, offered them slaves easily and cheaply.[10] For the rich, the slaves both managed the estate and worked it; for the poor, they were their co-workers throughout the year. It was money that had made slaves widely available, and to this extent, money had indeed changed the way of life on the farm.

A further change that money had brought about was simply an increase in the availability of alternative ways of making a living. The farm was still,

---

7. I do not understand why E. E. Cohen (*Athenian Economy,* 6 n. 14) brings the sources cited in nn. 6 and 8 in the present chapter as proof that "in Attica, rents for agricultural land were by the fourth century . . . *invariably* [my emphasis] paid and calculated in money, not in kind." Only one of the sources mentioned (Isaeus 11.42, which Cohen, by a copying error, cites as 9.42) tells us anything about the terms of the lease. Cohen's reference to Theophrastus *Characters* 4.5 is in error; if he means 4.3, that deals with hired agricultural laborers (μισθωτοῖς), not a hired-out farm, and again says nothing about how they were paid. The information from Hellenistic Delos (see below, p. 167), like the information from Athens, deals with rentals by the state.

8. Xen. *Mem.* 2.7.2, 3.11.4.

9. See Jameson; de Ste. Croix, *Class Struggle,* 505–6; and for a spirited but not yet conclusive ("And yet, after all this is said it must still be acknowledged that Athenian democracy was inextricably bound up with slavery on a scale unprecedented in the ancient world," 110) rejoinder, Wood (51–80).

10. On the cheapness of slaves, see de Ste. Croix, *Class Struggle,* 585 n. 1.

in the ideology that we hear over and over from various authors, the ideal way of supporting oneself, but it was not the only one available. If it became too oppressive, one could try one's luck in business, in a craft, or in emigration. What this meant for the farmers themselves was a certain decrease of pressure on the land. Farms did not have to be subdivided beyond reason to give each brother his share. If there was only enough land to support one man and his family, the other could find—and where possible, be helped to find—an alternative way of life. We find one Athenian who allegedly wanted to arrange a marriage between his daughter and his brother so as to leave their father's property whole. The brother refused, "saying that he preferred not to marry," and "having agreed even that the property should remain undivided for that reason, he lived on his own in Salamis."[11]

Hesiod's advice to a farmer to have only one son[12] was not a catchphrase we find repeated in the classical period. Exposure of infants[13] was certainly practiced, though its extent is a matter of considerable debate;[14] but the sources are clear that a girl was less welcome than a boy.[15] As long as they were children, a daughter probably cost less to raise than a son, but the dowry that the father would have to provide might convince him not to raise a daughter.[16] The prospect of dividing his sons' inheritance beyond the point of viability does not seem to have been a decisive worry. Moreover,

---

11. [Dem.] 44.10.

12. Hesiod *Works and Days,* 376–78. Finley (*Ancient Economy,* 106) asserts, "What Hesiod said . . . in the seventh century B.C. remained valid for the whole of ancient history," but he can offer no better evidence than "the frequency of foundlings in myths and legends and in comedy," a bit of literary obtuseness surprising in Finley. Many other explanations can and have been offered for the presence of foundlings in (New) Comedy and elsewhere.

13. Exposure—the refusal to raise the child—must be distinguished from infanticide. Most exposed children were probably picked up by others and raised as slaves: see Golden, 330–31; Engels, "Historical Demography," 391.

14. See the brief summary, with bibliography, of Germain (179–80). The effort of Engels ("Female Infanticide") to prove that extensive female infanticide could not have taken place was misguided: see the responses of Golden and of Harris ("Theoretical Possibility"). Engels's reply ("Historical Demography") saves him from the charge of thoughtless error but by no means proves his point.

15. Posidippus, *PCG* fr. 12; Terence *Heautontimorumenos* 626–27; *P Oxy.* IV.744 = Hunt and Edgar, 1: no. 105.

16. I must protest against the conclusion, which Golden (324–25 n. 29) ascribes to me, that a girl of Demosthenes' class would cost four minas per year to maintain. Golden apparently has drawn that conclusion by subtracting the dowry intended for Demosthenes' mother (80 minas) from that of his sister (2 talents = 120 minas) and dividing the result by ten for the ten years until the sister would reach marriageable age. There is, however, no reason why the daughter's dowry should have been equal to the mother's nor any reason why the daughter should have been maintained from principal rather than from interest, if Aphobus had invested the money as he should have.

when extra land was available for rent or for sale, the extra labor power that a son represented might encourage his father to buy or rent additional land that he would not have been able to work on his own.[17]

It was not necessary to bind oneself into debt-bondage to retain one's right to keep living on the land: there were other ways to live, if necessary. Money, in this sense, had a profound effect on the farm, though an indirect one: it was the monetization of the rest of society that allowed Attica, at least, to remain a community of small independent farmers for a period of centuries, neither becoming dominated by great magnates nor having its holdings subdivided into penury. There were surely hard times; there were presumably citizens who fell into poverty and even starved to death; there were various strategies, some more successful and some less so, by which farmers were forced to deal with threats to their survival; but there was never, at least in classical Athens, a wholesale reduction of the rural population to a situation of dependency. Of other places, we are less well informed. In the Hellenistic period, when the monarchies both exacted and spent money on a scale hitherto unprecedented, the squeeze on the peasants seems to have passed the limit of what they could deal with on their own.[18]

○ SUBSISTENCE AGRICULTURE

Money did have an effect on farming, but agriculture in Greece was never truly monetized. We need only compare the situation on the farm with that in the marketplace to realize the fundamental difference. In the market, a trader would offer a certain ware: ribbons, figs, fish, slaves, or whatever else might draw a profit. These merchandises were not mixed: not only was there no one "general store" that sold them all, but there was not even a single place where one could "do the shopping." Each merchandise had its own part of the agora, and a person would speak of being "among the fish" or "among the banks" (ἐν τοῖς ἰχθυσιν, ἐν ταῖς τραπέζαις).[19] The seller purchased merchandise,

---

17. This point is made by de Ste. Croix (*Class Struggle*, 278), with reference to feudal systems as opposed to the world of Hesiod; he does not seem to recognize that it may have applied in classical Greece as well.

18. Gallant, 182–96.

19. Aristophanes plays on this in *Thesmophoriazusae* 448–50, where the garland seller says that she managed to make a half-bad living braiding garlands "among the myrtles" [ἐν ταῖς μυρρίναις] until Euripides, "among the tragedies" [ἐν ταῖσιν τραγῳδίαις], started persuading people that there were no gods. Moderns are indebted to Sommerstein (ad loc.) for being, apparently, the first person in a number of centuries to get this joke (he translates ἐν ταῖσιν τραγῳδίαις as "away in the tragedy district").

whatever it might be, sold it at a higher price, and bought whatever was needed with the difference.

Agriculture can be pursued in the same way, with the farmer buying whatever seeds seem the most profitable, growing the most possible, selling the produce, and purchasing whatever the family needs with the profit of the sale. This procedure, known as cash cropping, is the dominant form of agriculture in the developed countries today. In classical Greece, only a rare farmer would manage the property in this way. It was not, perhaps, inconceivable: a late story tells us that Pericles sold all the produce of his lands and bought what he needed.[20] But the whole point of the story is Pericles' rejection of agriculture: he is said to have behaved in this way in order to free his attention for politics, managing the land with a minimum of effort. In Hellenistic times, when the temple of Delos rented out its farms for a cash rent for ten years to the highest bidder, the successful bidders must have been at least partially—and probably chiefly—intending to raise the crops for sale.[21] But even these farms were highly diversified, never concentrating on the single "most profitable" crop[22]—and this was not the way a poorer farmer would have treated his land.[23]

The normal use of a farm in ancient Greece was to grow crops that the family would eat throughout the year. The crops were stored, and the family supported itself from its storeroom, not from daily purchases. The farm included grain of some sort (wheat was preferable, but more often barley had to do);[24] pulses for variety, or, as we would say, for vitamins; vines for wine; sheep or goats for milk and cheese; an ox for plowing; a pig or two for the meat that was generally consumed either only on special occasions or sparingly;[25]

20. Plutarch (*Pericles* 16.3–4) writes: "He was not entirely careless of money matters, but in order that the property that he held justly from his fathers might not escape him through negligence nor cause him much business and loss of time when he was busy, he arranged it under a management that he thought easiest and most precise: he sold all of each year's produce in one lot, then managed his food and his daily needs by buying each of the necessities in the market." Burford (*Land and Labor,* 259 n. 17) observes correctly that this policy would work best if he grew a single kind of produce, but perhaps we should not take too literally the expression "all . . . in one lot" [ἅπαντας ἀθρόους]. De Ste. Croix (*Class Struggle,* 132) suspects the entire story of being a Hellenistic fabrication.

21. On the sacred estates at Delos, see Kent.

22. In modern terms, they practiced cash cropping but not monoculture.

23. In spite of the proposal of Holladay (48–49)—repeated by Rhodes (214–15) but rightly rejected by Millett (*Lending and Borrowing,* 264 n. 44)—that Athenian farmers switched to olive oil as a cash crop already in the time of Peisistratus.

24. Sallares, 313–61. With time—beginning as early as the Hellenistic period (ibid., 347–48)— barley lost ground to wheat.

25. Dalby, 23–24; Garnsey, *Food and Society,* 16–17.

and, best of all, fruit trees, which produce a crop with very little attention. Each crop would be tended in its time, spreading out the work somewhat over the year, although the alternation of wet winters and dry summers still left entire months with very little to do.[26] Each item was gathered and prepared for storage: grain and pulses were dried; grapes and olives were pressed, and wine was fermented; milk was made into cheese. Items that would not keep, such as green vegetables or fresh fruits, were simply unavailable out of season, but enough could be stored so that daily purchases would not be required. Monoculture, the growing of a single "cash crop" for sale, was probably nowhere the rule.[27]

The choice of crops reflected the purpose of farming. The olive, which produces a low yield but requires little labor, is an ideal crop for a peasant interested, as Chayanov describes, in minimizing the drudgery required to maintain the household. It is less appropriate as a cash crop, as Pliny noted, since harvesting large areas of olives requires hiring labor whose cost leaves little profit for the owner.[28] Solon and Peisistratus are said to have encouraged olive growing in Athens,[29] and the law protected olive trees with startling severity.[30] Amphoras of olive oil were the prize of the victors at the Panathenaic games, and Athens seems to have exported oil, at least in good years;[31] but the law of Solon that permitted this export and forbade the export of every other agricultural product[32] shows clearly the attitude of the Athenians about who should properly consume the produce of the land.[33]

In this, the entire conception of farming was different from that of any other business. Every person had to eat, but only the farmer owned the means for producing his own food. The ambition of an ancient Greek to own land was not unlike the modern ambition to own one's own house: as the modern worker feels a certain lack of stability as long as shelter must be paid for regularly and can be maintained only at another person's pleasure, so the ancient Greek—at least the peasant, on one hand, and the aristocrat, on the other—felt that a person whose livelihood had to be bought with

---

26. Hesiod *Works and Days* 493–503, 582–96; Walcot, 26–28.

27. Osborne, "Pride and Prejudice," 134; Burford, *Land and Labor,* 109–10.

28. Pliny *Natural History* 18.38; cf. Sallares, 308–9.

29. Plut. *Solon* 23–24; Dio Chrysostom 25.3.

30. Lysias 7 is the speech of a man on trial for his life on the charge of having destroyed the stump of an olive tree.

31. So Holladay (48) deduces from the wide distribution of plain Attic amphoras, which were presumably not exported empty. Cf. Erxleben, 394; Sallares, 304–9.

32. Plut. *Solon* 24.1.

33. This was argued by Sallares (304–9).

money from the market was something of a sojourner. A metic merchant, however prosperous, was never really "at home" in Attica the way the farmer was: he worked for others, and others supplied him with his wants. The farmer was not simply pursuing a different calling: he was out of that entire circle of existence, in a world where his livelihood depended only on himself, his land, and the gods. Without much need for cash, he was rich, for his field was his own personal horn of plenty.[34]

Of course, that imagined ideal was never truly the case. Nobody owned lands so vast and so varied that they could provide everything he wanted: Petronius's Trimalchio did,[35] but that was part of Petronius's comically exaggerated picture of the wealthy parvenu. Every farmer needed to exchange things, which he might do with or without money. If he could, he would grow somewhat more than he needed of certain crops—partly as a hedge against a bad year; partly to give to friends, neighbors, and relations; partly to sell in the market to put away money for inevitable expenses.[36] Since some years are good and some years are bad, nobody can afford to plant the minimum necessary for survival; since some people are ambitious and some are not, many people will have tried to raise enough to move their families above the level where they had to be content with mere subsistence.[37] This had been true, without the money in the middle, before the invention of coins,[38] and the combined surplus of Greek agriculture led to a nonnegligible, though still unquantifiable, international trade in wine, oil, and other agricultural products.[39] The same is true in peasant societies today.[40] Still, the ideal of "living on one's own" dominated Greek thought about farming, so that a farmer normally planned his farm in terms of his family's needs rather than in terms of maximizing profits, and his ability to do so was his pride and his independence.[41] If he had enough land, as Chayanov observed, he would work as long as the results to be obtained justified the drudgery.[42] When that point was

---

34. Phocylides fr. 7 Diehl (in *Anthologia Lyrica Graeca*) = Stobaeus IV 15.6; Philemon, *PCG* fr. 105 = Stobaeus IV 15.15.

35. Petronius *Satyricon* 38.1.

36. On the relative merits of these last two options, see Garnsey, *Famine*, 56–58.

37. This means that the picture of the "subsistence farmer," if projected too schematically, can seriously falsify the picture of ancient agriculture: Horden and Purcell, 271–74.

38. See p. 89.

39. Erxleben, 394–98; Whitbread, 22–24.

40. See Allan's very informative observations (38–48), reprinted as "The Normal Surplus of Subsistence Agriculture" in Dalton, *Economic Development*, 88–98.

41. See Fraenkel's note on Aeschylus *Agamemnon* 961 for examples, going back to Homer and Hesiod, of the recurrent identification of wealth as what one has ἐν οἴκῳ.

42. See p. 26.

passed, he was a free man, never having accepted on himself the yoke of perpetually increasing his store of coins.

Life for a subsistence farmer is different from the life of a farmer who farms to sell. Prices are less important; quality and quantity are more so. High prices mean that he can get good money for his surplus, but low prices will not cause severe distress, as long as there is enough for the family. On the other hand, getting, storing, and keeping a large enough store is a matter of great importance, occasionally even of life and death. As the new grain is still ripening and then drying and the old grain is running out, a farmer and his wife will have an anxious eye on the size of the grain heap, calculating whether it will last them until the new crop comes in. The jibes at women for "stealing from the granary" that Hesiod and Aristophanes found so witty and we find so distasteful[43] reflect the nervousness of the men at the dwindling stores as the winter wore on. The existence of money may have helped somewhat: grain could be bought in the market for money, but it would be just at this season that prices would be highest.

The women were undoubtedly no less nervous than the men, caught between the need to feed their family today and the need to see to it that enough remained to get through the winter. Not for nothing did Lysias and Xenophon put thriftiness near the top of the list of a wife's virtues. One speaker praises his wife (before her fall; he is defending himself for killing her lover) as "a capable and thrifty housekeeper, who managed everything with precision."[44] Xenophon's hero Ischomachus considered "matters of the belly" to be "the greatest point of education both for a man and for a woman."[45] The comment of M. L. West that "[w]omen stole food because they were kept half-starved by their husbands, who resented their habit of eating,"[46] while not necessarily unjust, nevertheless trivializes what was surely a very serious worry to both men and women. In fact, it was presumably not the husbands but the wives who generally determined how much was to be used at each meal—and thereby, surely, exposed themselves all the more to their husbands' criticism and mistrust. It may even have been the women who preferred to keep themselves half-starved in order to avoid their husbands' wrath or simply to feed their families.[47]

---

43. Hesiod *Theogony* 594–99; Hesiod *Works and Days* 373–75 (with Martin L. West's note ad loc.), 702–5; Aristophanes *Thesmophoriazusae* 418–23, 556–57, 811–18; Aristophanes *Ecclesiazusae* 14–15, 226–27.

44. Lysias 1.7.

45. Xen. *Oec.* 7.6.

46. Martin L. West, p. 251.

47. For such behavior in a later period, see Hufton, 91–95, 104–5.

In sum, it appears that money never truly transformed Greek agriculture. A Greek farmer worked to get his food from the earth, and the earth would accept no substitute for the seed to plant and the sweat of his brow. Once the food had grown, his wife or his slaves would make it edible and serve it to him, without exchanging it for anything else. This does not mean that he never used money. He must have tried to produce a surplus, and where he succeeded, he will have sold the surplus for money. Money played a part in his world; once it had conquered the market, he could not have gotten along without it; but the part it played was always marginal.[48]

Why did the adoption of a money economy not lead to widespread cash cropping? Cash cropping was conceivable to the Greeks; Pericles practiced it. Cash cropping, however, is appropriate only under certain conditions. One of these conditions is the availability of a cheap or slave workforce that allows landlords to extract large profits from the extensive growing of a single crop. This was present on the Roman latifundia, and there cash cropping was an important part of farm management. In more recent times, the banana republics of Latin America and their predecessors were based widely on the practice, as was the American South in the days of "King Cotton." On the western frontier of north America, in contrast, where labor was scarce, pioneer farming was subsistence farming,[49] and only in the twentieth century did mechanization, along with increasingly strict regulation and aggressive foreclosures, turn subsistence farming into a barely viable and rarely practiced alternative. Classical and Hellenistic Greece never had vast tracts of land available or such an abundant supply of slaves as the Romans got from their conquests, the Spaniards from the conquered Native Americans, and the white Southerners from western Africa. Without tractors and without cheap workers, there was a natural limit to how much land a single family could work. It was never enough to make them very wealthy, so their most reasonable strategy remained subsistence farming, using money only sparingly even when it was in plentiful supply.

The wealthier landowners raised more surplus and sold it for cash. If they were rich enough, there will have been more demands on them than the

48. This was no less the case in Ptolemaic Egypt, as Samuel observes from the papyrological evidence.

49. Peter T. White (91) writes of the situation when his father-in-law was young: "He never forgot the exciting day, once a year after harvest, when his grandfather hitched up the horses to drive a couple of miles to the little town of Greenfield, Illinois, with the wagon full of wheat. Fred Heck, the miller, would grind it into flour, keeping a bag for payment. Then to Samuel White's grocery, to leave flour for a year's supply of sugar and salt, canned goods and candy. Finally Fred Quast, the blacksmith, got flour for shoeing the horses and sharpening the plowshare."

mere sharpening of a plough or shoeing of horses: liturgies, dowries, and fines are likely to have created a very serious need for coin. In one case that we can follow, a wealthy[50] estate seems to have supplied its owner with quite a lot of cash (though not, as he of course claimed in court, enough).[51] The more striking is it that the estate in question was used for growing the staples of Athenian life: barley, grapes, and wood.·Perhaps, indeed, these were the best moneymakers one could produce from that field. It is also possible, however, that in a place where subsistence farming was the rule, the ideal of the smallholder held enough sway even over the rich to keep their marketing decisions within the realm of the possibilities dictated by the needs of the less well-to-do.

Robin Osborne has recently argued that money can be seen as a commodity, supplied by the city to the country, so "that the economic relationship between the town and country should be understood as much in terms of the need of wealthy landowners for cash as of the need of landless town residents for food."[52] The relationship between town and country, on this view, was not parasitic—as Werner Sombart, Max Weber, and, later, Finley described it[53]—but symbiotic. This is, however, to misconceive the relationship. The cash that the wealthy landowners needed was not a commodity that they used to procure their own needs; they needed it chiefly to meet the demands that the city made on them. The city exacted its subsistence from the country not by taxing the produce but by taxing the largest producers, who then had to sell their produce to pay the tax: cash, in Osborne's description, was not so much the reward of the landowner as the bridle that controlled him. In any event, both Osborne and Finley give a very schematic view of the relationship between town and country, a relationship that was in its details much subtler, as Osborne himself has elsewhere[54] gone to great lengths to show.

It will be seen that Solon was not being simply archaic when he established the census classes of Athens on the basis of agricultural yield.[55] To a monetized people—such as ourselves or all those Greeks whose livelihood was based on the city and on the sea—money is the measure of all things.[56]

---

50. The estate was not necessarily large, as de Ste. Croix ("Estate") pointed out.

51. [Dem.] 42.

52. Osborne, "Pride and Prejudice," 120.

53. Sombart, 1:142–43; Weber, 1215–17, 1349–54, 1359–63; Finley, "Ancient City," 20–23.

54. Osborne, *Demos*.

55. [Arist.] *Ath. Pol.* 7.4; Pollux *Onomasticon* 8.129–30. Cf. Rhodes, ad loc.; de Ste. Croix, *Class Struggle,* 114.

56. The miller, the grocer, and the blacksmith mentioned in n. 49 kept accounts in which the flour and the goods and services it purchased were evaluated in dollars, so the money that did not

For us, the natural way to count value is in money, and measuring wealth in *medimni* is not only perverse but dangerously inaccurate: a *medimnus* of barley, after all, may fluctuate greatly in price. To subsistence farmers, however, the measure of wealth is precisely this: how much does the land produce, and how well does it provide for the household? What amount of money might be required for an outsider to purchase the same amount of grain is a theoretical question and an irrelevant one.

The true test of the monetization of agriculture came in the first years of the Peloponnesian War. Pericles, following the Themistoclean strategy that had motivated the building of the Long Walls to Piraeus, persuaded the Athenians to adopt a policy of bringing all the rural population into the city and supporting themselves by means of their fleet.[57] The strategy worked; year after year of Spartan devastation of Athenian territory did not succeed in bringing the Athenians any closer to starvation. Like Pericles' belief that wars could be won by money,[58] his wartime agricultural strategy was tested in the most demanding of tests and passed. Wars were never the same again: nobody after the Peloponnesian War could ignore monetary questions in planning a campaign. The more striking is it that agriculture, immediately after the war and even during it, reverted to what it had been. Dicaeopolis returned to his farm, not to leave it until the twentieth century.

---

function as a medium of exchange was still present, at least conceptually, as a measure of value: "'Everybody knew the flour price,' Dad told me, 'it was in the paper every day'" (Peter T. White, 91). Such quasi-barter is not, to my knowledge, attested between Athenian farmers and townspeople, and it is quite likely that the Athenian farmer had first to sell grain to the grain dealer for cash, and only then to take the coins to pay the blacksmith.

57. See p. 115.
58. See p. 143–44.

13 Using Money to Make Money

If coins had been merely a convenience, a more effective way of transferring items from one to another, their effect on Greece would probably have been limited to increasing market trade, making trade and exchange a larger part of the society's experience. This effect they surely had; but their influence went much deeper. The conceptual revolution that identified coins with wealth turned money into an item of which one could never have too much, or, indeed, enough. Not all the Greeks subscribed to this judgment; but some did, and as their ideas became more influential, they had effects more profound than mere increase of trade.

Aristotle grasped this distinction clearly.[1] Of anything that is a means to something else one eventually gets enough, when the means is sufficient to provide what one needs. It will not take much reflection to realize that although one person's needs may differ from another's, eventually any person may have enough stoves, enough shoes,[2] enough food, or enough toothpaste. If coins are a means of exchange, a person who has enough coins to

---

1. In the following exposition, I follow closely his thought in *Politics* 1.3, though my examples and order of exposition are my own.

2. There are, of course, shoe-fetishists who cannot have enough shoes: and they precisely prove Aristotle's point, for they require the shoes not as a means but as an end.

exchange for whatever is needed will have enough; a person who has much more than needed may even find the coins burdensome, like too many pairs of shoes or too much toothpaste. When we see that people behave as if they could never get enough money, they have obviously ceased to see money as a means and, instead, see it as an end. They have, in short, confused money with wealth, and Aristotle says so explicitly.[3]

An example will make matters clearer. A man, shall we say, needs a shirt. His hen has recently brought up a nice brood of chicks, and he has rather more chickens on hand than he needs. He proceeds to the marketplace with a chicken or two, sells them for money, takes the money and buys himself a shirt, and goes home as penniless as he started. He may, of course, sell a few chickens in order to have money on hand, but he is probably better off keeping his chickens: if he wants to buy something else, he will have to go back to the market anyway, and in the meantime, coins do not lay eggs. This man has used money as a means of getting what he needs, and his transaction has been somewhat easier for not having to find somebody willing to trade a shirt for a chicken.

Other people behave quite differently. They raise chickens with no thought other than to sell them. With the money they get, they buy more chickens; these they raise, too, and sell to get yet more money. Where our first chicken raiser used money in a transaction that went from surplus commodity to money to needed commodity, the second kind of chicken raiser sees the transactions as going from money to commodity to more money. The money has become the goal, and the commodity merely a means of increasing one's money. It is, in fact, irrelevant to such traders whether chickens or clothing or, for that matter, manure is the commodity that comes in the middle. They need the chickens only as a way to make money. An outsider may not be able to tell whether the person selling a chicken is pursuing money or simply obtaining money as a means to something else; but the person knows, and the difference colors the entire behavior. Yet worse, by the ambiguity it introduces about the goal of the transaction, money tends to corrupt the nature of exchange, turning people who are seeking goods into people who are seeking money.[4]

Aristotle has some very incisive words to say about the unnatural attitude of the latter. "For it is not the business of courage to produce money but to

---

3. "People often consider wealth [πλοῦτος] to consist of plenty of coin [νομίσματος πλῆθος]" (Arist. *Pol.* I 9.10 [1257b 8–9]).

4. Meikle, 43–67, 89–95.

produce daring; nor is that the business of soldiering or of medicine, but the first should produce victory, the second health. But these people make all of these matters money producers [οἱ δὲ πάσας ποιοῦσι χρηματιστικάς], as if that were a goal and everything must aim for that goal."[5] His words have often been quoted, but people—if they can—seem to go on making money all the same.

Aristotle was not the only person to feel uncomfortable about moneymakers: a prejudice against those who trade for profit has been heard throughout the ages, from Euryalos who taunted Odysseus with the suspicion of being a merchant,[6] through many more sophisticated economic observers. Behind the prejudice, though hardly every explicitly expressed, lies a real paradox, namely, the syllogism that:

(a) a trade should be fair;
(b) if a trade is fair, both sides remain with the same value;

whence it follows that

(c) if a person can increase his capital by trade, he is cheating someone.

Modern market theoreticians have offered justifications for the paradox,[7] whose adequacy it is not my purpose to discuss, but it will be perceived at once that it is not the fact of sale or purchase that is objectionable but the fact that the commerce regularly leaves a residue in the hands of one side, something which, one may feel, should not come about if trade is truly fair. This is the difference between Euryalos's merchant, whom Homer despises, and Mentes, the noble trader of iron for copper. The trader is "mindful of his freight and observant of his provisions and his eagerly grasped profits,"[8] while his customers, less mindful and less observant, let themselves be taken

---

5. Arist. *Pol.* I 9.17–18 (1258a 10–14).

6. Hom. *Od.* 8.162–65; cf. p. 75.

7. The simplest explanation is that the merchant adds to the value of the item by making it more conveniently available to the consumer, an explanation that may fit the corner grocer better than it fits, for example, the concessionaire whose profit depends upon first preventing the producers (or others) from performing the same service. When we reach the level of stock-market speculators, who add nothing to the final product (of whose nature they may be wholly unaware), entirely different justifications, based on the idea of venture capital, must come into play. Karl Marx's labor theory of value addresses the same paradox, but without justifying the middleman.

8. Euryalos's words at *Od.* 8.163–64; see p. 75.

advantage of. The merchant who trades for profit is not merely likely to be dishonest; he is dishonest by profession, and the market in which he trades is "a place set out in the middle of the city, where people assemble and deceive each other under oath."[9]

We cannot tell when "moneymaking"—what Aristotle called chrēmatis-tikē—became a recognizable part of the life of the polis. Homer's traders-for-profit were Phoenicians, and they were engaged in overseas commerce. Hesiod complains about "gift-eating kings," but his complaint is not that they get the gifts[10] but that they give "crooked judgments" under their influence.[11] Later, when the kings are no longer the state, an oracle ostensibly given to Lycurgus and a poem of Solon's warn that love of money will destroy the polis,[12] but here it is the pursuit of private gain at the expense of the public good that is being attacked. Theognis complains that those who were once poor are now rich,[13] and within the corpus ascribed to him are hints that not everyone's wealth was gotten honestly[14] and complaints that people value wealth more than character,[15] but we do not find the kind of gibes at merchants and moneylenders that begin to appear in fifth-century Athens. Chrēmatistikē, if it existed in the archaic period, does not seem to have attracted notice. In the realm of commerce, it probably was not immediately distinguishable from the kind of trade that had been going on for generations. But in other fields, money began to produce its own professionals.

---

9. Cyrus's words in Herodotus 1.153.1, but they surely represent a Greek idea (an idea, for that matter, applied inappropriately to the Spartans about whom Cyrus is talking). That oaths are an essential characteristic of the marketplace (ὀμοῦντες codd. [a hapax legomenon], ὀμνύντες Bekker and many modern editors) may not seem obvious to us, and Rosén conjectures ὁμιλοῦντες, which seems, however, otiose after συλλεγόμενοι. To elaborate the radical distinction between simple lying and lying under oath—particularly to Herodotus's Persians, who teach their children three things only: to ride, to shoot, and to tell the truth (1.136.2)—would require a disquisition too long for this note.

10. Telemachus, at least, considers it natural for a king's house to become rich (Hom. Od. 1.392–93), and the honors that Sarpedon thinks a king has to work for (Il. 12.310–21) include some very tangible (and edible) benefits. See pp. 71–74 and, further, Martin L. West on Hesiod Works and Days 39.

11. Hesiod Works and Days 221, 264. The acceptance of gifts per se does not interest Hesiod, since he is interested not in how kings make their living but in how peasants can do so in a society ruled by kings.

12. Diod. Sic. 7.12.5; Solon fr. 4.5–6 Bergk.

13. Theognis 53–58; cf. 1109–14.

14. Theognis 145–48, 197–208, 315–18, 649–52, 753–56, 831–32.

15. Theognis 699–728, 928–30, 1117–18. For a more thorough discussion of the attitudes toward wealth from Homer to Aristotle, see Hemelrijk; Schaps, "Socrates."

◉ COINERS

Whatever else its effects on society, every invention creates a new job. The invention of the clock turned some people into clockmakers; the invention of writing turned some people into scribes or—the same job in a different medium—stonemasons who inscribed texts. The invention of coinage surely brought it about that some people would be coiners, but we know next to nothing about these people. It might, in theory, have happened that coining would have become a form of business, in which private individuals turned silver into coins that would have been accepted by the reputation of the coiner. This happened in modern times with banknotes, which were issued by banks long before they were issued by governments. It did not happen in Greece. Once coinage was generally adopted in Greek cities, the coining of money was normally a state monopoly,[16] so that the actual coiners can have been no more than workers, perhaps slaves. We are not terribly well informed about them. Their existence, in any event, was hardly a major innovation in the economy. Neither was the mining of silver, though its organization was affected, like all other state projects, by the new ways of managing public works that arose with monetization, which we have considered in chapter 11.

Some inventions may produce more than just manufacturers of the new item. The invention of printing turned writing into so large-scale an industry that a new group of professionals, publishers, eventually sprang up. Computers have produced not only computer manufacturers and salesmen but also programmers, who have turned into "software developers" as their own work is prepackaged for large-scale marketing. Money produced, in time, a new kind of professional, one who worked with money and could do with it things that a nonprofessional could not do.

◉ MONEY CHANGERS AND COIN TESTERS

The first such professionals were the money changers. No such person is attested before the fifth century, and we may question whether there was any need for money changers in the early period. Examination of the evidence of hoards indicates that throughout the sixth century, coins circulated almost exclusively in and around the place of their issue. Northern Greek coins seem to have reached the Near East in large numbers but seem not to have circulated much in Greece itself. The famous Aeginetan turtles had

---

16. For a brief account of how coins were made, see Jones, 145–47.

some international circulation, but only in the nearby area did they form anything like an international currency.[17] There may have been little enough need for coin exchange until the fifth century, when the Athenian Empire united more than a hundred cities in a league in which tribute was at first being paid from cities using various coins to a city using its own.

The first mention of money changers is in a tragic metaphor of the mid–fifth century and it captures some of an outsider's prejudices.

> But Ares, the gold-changer of bodies
> and scale holder in the spear battle,
> sends to the friends heavy
> hard-wept ashes
> burned from Ilium,
> transportable urns groaning
> with dust in place of men.[18]

Gold was not generally used for coins in Greece and might be offered in the form of gold dust: the god of war is offering the deceased's friends dust in return for their loved one, and we may perhaps see behind the famous image the resentment of a citizen offered metal or metal dust (probably, in his eyes, not enough) for a more useful, "real" product. This may not have been everybody's view of the money changer; it may not have been Aeschylus's in all situations. But it is the first Greek view we are given of a professional who deals in the exchange of precious metals,[19] and it is a hostile one.

The profession of money changer was made necessary by the profusion of states minting coins in Greece. Had silver coins been thought of in Greece (as they still were in Phoenicia) simply as stamped bullion, there would have been no need for a money changer: an assayer might have been needed to guarantee that the metal was indeed silver, but that granted, a scale would easily have revealed the weight of the silver. To the Greeks, however, recognizing money as valid was not only a matter of testing its silver content; a valid

---

17. See p. 105.

18. Aeschylus *Agamemnon* 437–44.

19. It is almost the only occurrence of the word χρυσαμοιβός in all of ancient Greek. (*Pace* Fraenkel [ad loc.], it appears also in the sixth letter of Themistocles [a late forgery], as Bogaert [*Banques et banquiers,* 47] noticed: see now Doenges, p. 154 [6.11].) It is not unlikely that the author of this letter (who attempted to Atticize, as Doenges [p. 51] notes) used the word because he had found it in Aeschylus. An actual money changer was an ἀργυραμοιβός (ibid., pp. 44–45), but that word would not have suited Aeschylus's metaphor, since a silver-changer would give you coins, not dust.

(dokimon) coin was one coined by a recognized authority, with valid markings to identify it.[20] The major source we have for a state-appointed validator of coinage requires that he determine whether the coin was "bronze underneath, or lead underneath, or counterfeit";[21] it is not clear whether determining whether a coin was "counterfeit" involved assaying the silver itself, but it surely included recognizing its markings. There were money testers in various places in Greece, sometimes appointed by the state.[22] By the fourth century, Athens apparently had a public slave in the agora—and sometimes, apparently, another in the Piraeus—who was available at all times to establish the validity of coins presented to him: he had to establish not merely that they were silver but that they were actually valid coins of Athens—or, perhaps, foreign coins with the same device.[23] Coins validated by him were true legal tender that had to be accepted in the market. The private money changer, too, must have had to be able to tell solid silver coins from base metal with a silver coating, and he undoubtedly had to be an expert in the coinage of the various Greek states if he was to tell true coins from counterfeits. He surely made a profit on his trade.[24]

⊙ LENDERS AND BORROWERS

There was far more money to be made out of dealing in coins than could be gotten simply by exchanging them. Coins, for one thing, could be lent. Loans of coin were extremely common in Athens by the late classical period, and like Darwin's Galapagos finches, they had differentiated into various different forms of loan, each filling a particular need in the society and each providing a particular advantage to the borrower and to the lender.

Lending itself was nothing new. The avoidance of lending had never been an ideal among the Greeks,[25] nor is it a reasonable one in a peasant society,

---

20. On this see Cacciamo Caltabiano and Radici Colace, who point out that the same standard was not held for Persian coinage. They take this to indicate a difference between Greek attitudes toward wealth and power and oriental ones; I would rather define the difference as being between Greek attitudes and the ones that the Greeks attributed to orientals.

21. SEG 26.72, lines 10–11.

22. Bogaert, Banques et banquiers, 44–47.

23. Stroud, pp. 168–71 (SEG 26.72). See Figueira, 536–47, for further discussion and bibliography.

24. For the various terms denoting the money changer's commission, see Bogaert, Banques et banquiers, 48–50.

25. So Millett (Lending and Borrowing, 218–20) on classical Athens; but Millett's own observations on reciprocity (27–36), based on etymology and on Hesiod, show that there was nothing particularly Athenian about this phenomenon.

where a single expensive item may more reasonably serve many households than one and where the hazards of fortune often leave a household in temporary straits from which only the help of neighbors[26] extricates its members. The exchange of goods, labor, courtesies, and favors is a regular part of rural life and lies at the basis of relationships both among equals (who reciprocate each other's favors) and between superiors and their underlings (who, being unable to reciprocate, remain permanently indebted and hence subservient to the providers of goods and services).

Interest on loans was not necessarily present in archaic Greece. In a peasant society, lending is simply one facet of the general relationship among people in a community. The loan of food[27] or of two oxen and a wagon[28]—like a present,[29] a friendly visit,[30] an invitation to a meal,[31] or even taking care of a neighbor's estate in his absence[32]—were part and parcel of the kind of favors neighbors would do for each other. To expect an immediate return in the form of interest would be churlish and would forfeit the goodwill on which the lender could later draw; not to expect the favor to be reciprocated in some later case of need would be foolish and would eventually impoverish the person who wasted favors on people who would never return them. Hesiod advises against having anything to do with people who do not or cannot return favors,[33] and we should not overestimate the communal generosity of a farmer.[34] But even while keeping an eye on one's own profit, Hesiod does not recommend demanding an immediate return on a loan. People can be expected to reciprocate; those who do not are in the most serious sense antisocial and are best avoided.

The change came gradually, and was never complete. Even in the fourth century orators might still try to arouse jurors' ire by accusing their opponents of being the kind of people who lent money at interest.[35] The most revealing statement is that of the Demosthenic speaker who finds himself constrained to admit that the jurors hate usurers like himself and to agree

---

26. Family might help too, but Millett (*Lending and Borrowing,* 140–44) is correct to observe that help from neighbors was more immediate and more regular than help from family. King Solomon (Prov. 27:10) had already made the same observation.

27. Hesiod *Works and Days* 349; Martin L. West, ad loc.

28. Hesiod *Works and Days* 453.

29. Hesiod *Works and Days* 354–55; Aristophanes *Plutus* 223–26.

30. Hesiod *Works and Days* 353.

31. Hesiod *Works and Days* 342.

32. [Dem.] 53.4.

33. Hesiod *Works and Days* 353–55. Cf. Millett, *Lending and Borrowing,* 33–34.

34. As Hanson (*The Other Greeks,* 138–39) argues persuasively from his own experience.

35. Millett, *Lending and Borrowing,* 25–26.

that in certain cases (though not his own), they are right to do so.[36] Neverthe-less, there were by that time many people who did lend regularly at interest, and a competing ideology had arisen that considered interest perfectly legiti-mate.[37] What had changed?

One difference was the increasing presence of what economists now call "productive loans," where money is borrowed not to meet an immediate need but to produce from it a monetary profit.[38] Although the Athenians did not consciously differentiate productive and unproductive loans, they did not think of them in the same way. Lending at interest was not unreasonable for a productive loan; on the contrary, it was a reasonable investment, for one would not expect a person to provide at no cost capital with which another person intends to get rich. Such loans were easily presented as prudent management of one's cash.[39] Interest on a loan for consumption might be another matter. When Apollodorus attacked Stephanus as a usu-rer, he was careful to insinuate that the loans were made to people who deserved charity.[40] Those whose class usually put them on the debtor's side will have had a different view from those who were creditors, and those in business will have had a different view from those who dealt only with nonproductive credit. Orators could pluck one string or the other by present-ing the matter in the context appropriate to their ends.

This is not the whole story, however, for loans that were made for consumption might also bear interest, often without raising anyone's eye-brow. Another change was that profit itself had become more respectable. Athens was never a sizable city by modern standards, but by the classical period, it had grown beyond the point where people knew all the individuals with whom they dealt. When dealing with strangers, one cannot simply do favors or give gifts in the hope of later recompense, so the entire relationship of reciprocal help is telescoped into a single transaction in which one side gets a needed item and the other gets a profit. Selling for a profit is the most obvious example of this, and as we saw in chapter 8, retail trade became

---

36. [Dem.] 37.53, quoted by Millett (*Lending and Borrowing*, 193).

37. Millett, *Lending and Borrowing*, 26–27. Much of Millett's book is devoted to distinguish-ing loans where interest was acceptable from those where it was not. His substantivist model causes him to ignore and even deny the world of the professional moneymakers, but for the others—whose motivations have been much less carefully studied—his analysis is perceptive and illuminating, for modern practice no less than ancient.

38. On this distinction, see appendix 4.

39. μὴ λαθεῖν διαρρυὲν αὐτὸν τἀργύριον, [Dem.] 37.54.

40. τῷ πώποτε εἰσήνεγκας, ἢ τίνι συμβέβλησαί πω, ἢ τίν' εὖ πεποίηκας . . . τὰς τῶν ἄλλων συμφορὰς καὶ χρείας εὐτυχήματα σαυτοῦ νομίζων; ([Dem.] 45.69–70).

common as soon as coins were introduced. A loan can never have quite the same anonymity as a sale, since, by definition, it requires that the parties know each other well enough for the lender to meet the borrower at least once more to collect payment; but the example of the marketplace probably helped to legitimize the idea that one might expect a profit for giving one's money to another, even for a limited time.

It would seem that the argument between primitivists and modernists has put something of a straitjacket on this subject, as if one or the other sort of credit must have been essentially foreign to the Athenians. But no compelling reason has ever been put forward for doubting that both productive and nonproductive credit coexisted in Athens, a society that was notably successful in integrating both peasants intent on having each person maintain what that person has[41] and traders intent on increasing their wealth. Since borrowing was a very common way for an Athenian to provide for current monetary needs, it would hardly be likely that either group should have avoided borrowing. If our own sources show a slant toward loans for consumption rather than for increasing one's capital, that only reflects the well-known concentration of our sources on the upper classes, who were not, in general, merchants.[42]

Another practice that was essential for the development of loans at interest was attention paid to small advantages. This sort of attention, the careful calculation of exactly what one spent and exactly what one was getting, was at the basis of retail trade and had once been considered mean.[43] Many people certainly continued to hold it so, but coinage had made this calculation much simpler, and as retail trade flourished, there were more people willing to make it regularly and to make their livelihood from it. Not only people with merchandise to sell could make a living from accumulating small profits. One could do the same with money to lend.

For these reasons, the taking of interest had become, to some people and in some circumstances, a respectable practice. The old prejudice, however, might still apply and might still be aroused. After all the reasons I have given, we must also recognize that people often hold contradictory attitudes and that the same person may view the same transaction very differently depending on whether that person is the lender or the borrower. The taking

---

41. On entering office, the archon would announce "that whatever anyone had before he [the archon] entered office, he would have and control until the end of his term" ([Arist.] *Ath. Pol.* 56.2; cf. Rhodes, ad loc.).

42. On this point, see further appendix 4.

43. See p. 75.

of interest is particularly prone to these kinds of competing attitudes, and the simultaneous existence of pro-interest and anti-interest ideologies does not necessarily depend on their being applicable to different situations.

Small Lenders

The smallest lenders lent small sums to those in need of ready cash, at high rates of interest that were probably necessary to make profitable a business that made only a small amount on each transaction. Theophrastus describes such a character, who "gives market sellers loans and exacts from them interest of 25 percent per day and goes around to the fast-food stalls,[44] the fresh-fish stalls, the smoked-fish stalls, and grabs the interest from their takings and pops it into his jaw."[45] Such characters were regularly despised: Theophrastus's character is an example of ἀπόνοια, "shamelessness."[46] The term ὀβολοστάτης—"obol weigher" or, perhaps, "obol lender"[47]—was applied to them, and, for that matter, was a generalized term of opprobrium for all usurers.[48] These small lenders plied their trade anyway and undoubtedly performed an essential service to those who needed small sums for a short time.[49] Other, less money-bound forms of credit are conceivable: modern wholesalers usually provide merchandise to retailers on credit, expecting to be paid only after sixty days or so. Those who borrow from petty usurers are precisely the people whose position is so precarious that more leisurely forms of credit are unavailable to them. These people can borrow money only from people willing to expend a good deal of effort for a small profit. The existence

---

44. μαγειρεῖα. For this meaning—by no means the only translation possible—see *FGrH* 244 F 151 (Apollodorus) = Athenaeus IV 172f–173a. For the whole range of professions that might be called μάγειροι, see Berthiaume.

45. Theophrastus *Characters* 6.9.

46. That, at any rate, is Theophrastus's own definition of the word: ἡ δὲ ἀπόνοιά ἐστιν ὑπομονὴ αἰσχρῶν ἔργων καὶ λόγων (*Characters* 6.1).

47. "Obol lender" is the more likely etymology (Korver, 113–14), but Athenians of the classical period, if they thought about it, are more likely to have understood "obol weigher."

48. Aristophanes *Clouds* 1155; Arist. *Pol.* I 10.4 (1258b 2–4). The statement of Schol. Aeschines 1.39 that the Thirty Tyrants appointed a board of ὀβολοστάται, while not likely to be accurate (the word ὀβολοστάτης was abusive and would not have been applied officially), does indicate that the word was not, as Millett (*Lending and Borrowing*, 182) suggests, limited to petty usurers.

49. Millett (*Lending and Borrowing*, 181) quotes parallels from nineteenth-century markets where petty usurers would lend dealers a bit of cash to start with at the beginning of the day, collecting it with interest at closing time. E. E. Cohen (Review, 287) is right in objecting to Millett's use of the parallel to establish that virtually all professional loans were of this sort, but there can be little doubt that the man being described by Theophrastus is just such a character as those whom Millett quotes from Glasgow and Les Halles.

of these small lenders, whatever opportunities they may have exploited, indicates that the need for coin in classical Athens reached down to the lowest level of transactions. If coinage freed a man from the need to become a *thes* in order to keep himself alive, it also produced a new class of people whose hold on him was, from the debtor's point of view, still galling.

This is not to say that the hostility toward such lenders was necessarily justified: Millett[50] aptly quotes Bentham's "question, whether, among all the instances in which a borrower and a lender of money have been brought together on the stage, from the days of Thespis to the present, there was ever one, in which the former was not recommended to favour in some shape or other, either to admiration, or to love, or to pity, or to all three; and the other, the man of thrift, consigned to infamy."[51] Modern pawnbrokers, who perform a similar function of offering credit to the poorest of people, consider themselves to be performing a valuable service, and the origin of their trade was a charitable institution, the Italian Monte di Pietà.

Not only did the small-scale lenders, as individuals, perform a valuable service to those who were enabled to stay in business by tiding themselves over with small loans; to a large extent, it was probably they who permitted the marketplace to exist and to flourish in a state whose supply of coin was, by modern standards, quite small. In a marketplace like the Athenian agora, where all trade takes place for money, the absence of coin prevents a retailer from doing business, and where the supply of coin was small, it must not have been a rare occurrence for a would-be trader to be utterly destitute of coin. Now, for a market to flourish, one needs both sellers who can reasonably rely on the buyers to appear and buyers who can reasonably rely on the sellers' being open for business. By redistributing—for a fee—the coins that circulated in the market so that any seller could count on finding enough coins to start a day's business, Theophrastus's "shameless" men were not only helping individuals but may well deserve a certain amount of the honor for keeping the market open and functioning.

The Friendly Loan

People of the sort that Theophrastus describes were by their nature dealers in petty sums. Although their rate of interest was high, they could never have gotten rich: it took too much of their time to make too small a profit, and in

---

50. *Lending and Borrowing*, 185.

51. Bentham, 107. Bentham himself (98–99) attributed this prejudice chiefly to what we should now call anti-Semitism.

any event, the class of people with whom they dealt did not have the resources to enrich them. Many people might need larger amounts of money for a wedding, a dowry, a fine, a liturgy, or simply maintaining a household whose income was not likely to come in soon enough for a short-term loan. Athens had methods of maintaining people like this, and here, too, the invention of coinage changed the nature of the institutions that had preceded it.

The simplest place for a person temporarily short of cash to seek it would be with friends (particularly neighbors) or relations. This kind of loan is familiar enough to us and probably had not been much affected by the introduction of money: the man who mortgaged land to get the money for his daughter's dowry was probably doing nothing very different from what his great-grandfather would have done, though his grandmother's dowry might not have been evaluated in terms of cash.[52] For this kind of loan, a person would not usually turn to a professional moneylender.[53] One would certainly prefer to borrow without interest if that was possible; even where it was not, one would probably find a friend or relative, who had to take into account more considerations than mere profit, a more congenial creditor than a professional lender. Moreover, friends and relatives might be willing to lend money in circumstances that a professional would deem too risky to justify the loan.

The Eranos

The most interesting form of middle-sized loan, because it has no parallel in our own world, was the *eranos*. Once, an *eranos* had been a meal whose guests brought gifts to the host.[54] In some cases, these gifts seem to have been mere countergifts that could, apparently, be stipulated in advance and demanded afterward: we find one host who was asked, "On what terms is the *eranos*?" and answered, "On terms of a horse," whereupon each guest presented the host with a horse on the day after the feast.[55] In some cases, it would seem, an *eranos* obligation would be repaid by having each guest invite the host (and the other guests) to a meal. J. Vondeling suggests that this is the meaning of

52. On the evaluation of the dowry, which generally consisted of many items more useful to the new household than mere cash, see Hans Julius Wolff in *RE* XXIII, s.v. προίξ, particularly cols. 136–39; cf. Schaps, *Economic Rights,* app. 1.

53. Millett, *Lending and Borrowing,* 145–48, 161–71, 187–88.

54. The essential study of the *eranos* is Vondeling. My discussion here is heavily based on Vondeling's, as all discussions of the subject would be if his book had been translated from Dutch.

55. *FGrH* 3 F 11 (Pherekydes) = Schol. Apoll. Rhod. 4.1515.

Telemachus's suggestion to the suitors that rather than eating at Odysseus's house and incurring an obligation that they do not repay, they should eat at each other's house in turn.[56] Among the poorer classes, the guests may have fulfilled their obligation by bringing their own food: this was surely the later practice,[57] and it is hard to see what else Hesiod can be thinking of when he says that a "meal with many guests" is "the most pleasure and the least expense."[58]

Looked at from a social point of view, the archaic *eranos* worked as a redistribution mechanism: since the feast was common, each guest partook of it freely, but the contributions were not necessarily equal.[59] More interestingly, the *eranos* could function as a form of redistribution that did not require a strong central government—an archaic-age redistribution system, not a Mycenaean one. Among nobles as among the poor, it will have reinforced mutual obligations and a sense of community.

By the classical period, however, the *eranos* had become monetized: it was a loan in which a single borrower borrowed from a group of people, generally[60] personal friends. The borrower might organize the loan, or find a friend who would take over the organization. Contributions to an *eranos* were understood to be acts of friendship and of civil piety,[61] whose recipient should not only pay them back but also be grateful to the contributors.[62]

---

56. Vondeling, 9; Hom. *Od.* 1.374–75. The same seems to be suggested by Pindar *Olympian* 1.38–39 (ἔρανον . . . ἀμοιβαῖα θεοῖσι δεῖπνα).

57. Vondeling, 15–26.

58. Hesiod *Works and Days* 722–23. Vondeling (7–9) doubts this meaning for the archaic period, but he has missed the Hesiod passage because Hesiod does not use the word ἔρανος. Vondeling is right to say that this kind of meal is not necessary among nobles, but the fact that poor people do not appear in Homer and in Pindar does not mean that there were no poor in the archaic period. In modern Israel, the custom in some circles is, as in Europe and America, for wedding guests to give the bride and groom presents that will help establish their household; in other (generally poorer) circles, gifts (usually larger) are given to the parents to help defray the cost of the wedding, and it is considered churlish to give a gift smaller than the cost of one's portion.

59. In the Pherecydes passage (see n. 55), Perseus was required, because of an ill-considered remark, to bring the Gorgon's head, while from the other guests, a horse sufficed.

60. But by no means always: E. E. Cohen, *Athenian Economy*, 208–9.

61. On the close connection between *eranoi* and *philia* and on their aspect of civic virtue, see Millett, *Lending and Borrowing*, 156–57. In Cohen's claim (*Athenian Economy* 208–9) that "there is nothing inherently 'friendly' or noncommercial about an *eranos* loan," one must stress the word *inherently*: Cohen himself acknowledges that *eranoi* were often collected from or by friends. He is wrong to state that the slave Midas's *eranoi* ([Hypereides] 5 [*Against Athenogenes*]) "could not have originated in traditional Athenian concepts of friendship" (209–10, 214), as if a slave (particularly one who operated a business!) had no friends. It was Cohen himself (73–82), who demonstrated the opposite, and the fact that *eranoi* might be used to finance a business in no way implies that their collection was not an act of friendship.

62. Theophrastus *Characters* 17.9; cf. Fox, 146–47.

Plato in the *Laws* forbade sales on credit but allowed *eranos* loans "among friends" [φίλον παρὰ φίλοις], on condition that they not be recoverable at law.[63] The *eranos* loan had become in a monetized society what the *eranos* meal had been in premonetary society: a way in which each participant contributed to a joint project. The monetary *eranos*, however, partook heavily of the idea of charity, and the word *eranos* itself eventually came to be used in that sense.[64] Other meanings, too, sprang from the old *eranos*: the term came to mean a communal meal and even a communal society with officers and rituals.[65] Whereas the monetary *eranos* was simply a loan, different from other loans only in that the creditor was a group rather than an individual, it nevertheless continued to provide one thing that the archaic *eranos* had given: a mechanism by which a group of friends could unite in a way that would help one of them, with an obligation of the recipient to repay. Among nobles, the need had been to reinforce ties of loyalty and dependence; among peasants, the most important need had been food to keep body and soul together until harvest time. In classical Athens, a person might have many needs[66] for which food alone would not provide a solution. What the old *eranos* would not provide, the monetary *eranos* did.

One noteworthy use to which an *eranos* might be put was the purchase of a slave's freedom. Both epigraphic and literary evidence testifies to this,[67] and it is a fine example of the usefulness of the *eranos* in providing credit to people whose legal position made them unpromising credit risks in the eyes of those who did not know them personally.

Commercial Lending

Free credit from friends, however, was not always forthcoming, nor was it always appropriate. Where the money itself was to be used to make a profit,

---

63. Plato *Laws* 915e; cf. Danzig and Schaps, 146 n. 8. That an *eranos* could be recovered in an Athenian court, as E. E. Cohen (*Athenian Economy*, 209) takes the trouble to prove, does not indicate that the payers of the *eranos* were not originally friends of the borrower. If Plato, who had not read *Hamlet*, did not know that "loan oft loses both itself and friend," there is no reason why we should pretend to a similar ignorance.

64. Vondeling, 160–68.

65. Vondeling, 15–26, 77–158.

66. Neaera [Dem.] 59.30–32 raised an *eranos* to buy her freedom; Nicostratus planned to raise an *eranos* to repay the people who had ransomed him from captivity ([Dem.] 53.8, 11).

67. See n. 66; Millett, *Lending and Borrowing*, 154 with n. 34. The possibility of borrowing the money for manumission should be added to the possibilities considered in Hopkins and Roscoe, 168–70.

there was no reason why the lender[68] should not expect to share in the proceeds. Some very eminent scholars have expressed the opinion that such loans were rare in the extreme,[69] but this argument has been overstated, and well answered by Edward Cohen.[70]

There were people who worked with[71] their money, lending it out where profitable. If this was a matter of lending against landed property, it could, perhaps, be carried out by anyone with money and a reasonable amount of judgment; if it was a matter of financing trading expeditions—a much riskier but much more profitable form of investment—it will have been a profession that those with no knowledge of the sea and of foreign markets would enter at their peril. In those few cases where we can identify them, private investors in maritime trade seem to have been people experienced either as traders or as financiers.[72]

Loans extended for these expeditions were extended under special terms. It was common, though apparently not required, for the ship and/or its cargo to be collateral for the loan, and interest on such a loan was normally calculated not according to the length of time between loan and repayment but according to a simple percentage established by agreement at the time of the loan and payable upon successful return. Shipwreck, on the one hand, would generally exempt the lender from repayment; on the other hand, the interest to be paid upon successful return was substantial. Although all these terms were presumably negotiable,[73] they were common because the economics of the loan demanded them. The shipwrecked merchant was unlikely to have the wherewithal to repay even principal, much less interest. The lender, on the other hand, would hardly have been willing to put money at this kind of risk if the promised return had not been large enough to make

---

68. Or, perhaps, the lenders. LSJ s.v. ἔρανος defines it as "bearing no interest" but then includes a papyrological citation (*BGU* 1165.16) "with mention of interest." Vondeling (67–70) demonstrates that there is not a single certain mention of an ἔρανος bearing interest, but E. E. Cohen (*Athenian Economy*, 208) points out, with equal justice, that there is not a single certain text to indicate that an ἔρανος did not bear interest. So we remain, for now, unenlightened.

69. This was originally argued by Finley (*Land and Credit*, 81–87; *Ancient Economy*, 141). The same position was taken by Bogaert (*Banques et banquiers*, 356–57) and by Millett ("Maritime Loans"), reiterated in Millett's *Lending and Borrowing* (229–32), a discussion worth reading for its correction of some misapprehensions about the meaning of the term *productive credit*, which properly applies only to loans in which the borrower intends to use the money for a purpose that will produce a monetary profit greater than the interest on the loan.

70. E. E. Cohen, *Athenian Economy*, 32–36.

71. The phrase is that of the retired merchant at Dem. 33.4; cf. E. E. Cohen, *Athenian Economy*, 154.

72. Millett, *Lending and Borrowing*, 191–93.

73. E. E. Cohen, *Athenian Economy*, 160–69.

it attractive. The maritime loan, in short, partook quite a bit of the nature of modern investment, in which the people supplying the money share a good deal of the risk. Also like modern investment, it will have permitted many people to enter into business enterprises that they could not have financed out of their own resources.[74]

We should not overestimate the importance of these loans. In the fourth century, when landed wealth no longer dominated the Athenian economy, there were still many ways to amass a fortune other than by means of monetary investments.[75] This is a stark contrast to modern capitalistic society, where monetary investments can, if successful, confer colossal fortunes and huge influence on their owners and are in fact virtually the only way in which the largest fortunes can be made, as Mills demonstrated long ago.[76]

Even such fortunes as were made did not allow those who made them to dominate or perhaps even significantly to influence the politics of Athens. Plato considers tradesmen and money changers unsuited for public leadership, but he never suggests that the problem is a conflict between their private interest and that of the state. He worries instead that their trade leads them to be more interested in material possessions than in the soul or the body and, moreover, that it occupies them so that they have neither leisure nor interest for politics.[77] In Isocrates' *Trapeziticus*, the son of an important foreign dynast accuses the banker Pasio of trying to cheat him of his money; throughout the speech, he presumes Pasio's motivation to have been purely financial, and he never suggests that any political interest might lie behind the banker's behavior. The reason for the difference between the ancient situation and that of the modern West was perceptively noted by Ernst Badian, who observed that wealth itself confers power only when the political structure provides it with the opportunity to do so.[78] Financial motivation did come to the fore in Athens in the mid–fourth century B.C.E., with the economic-minded leaders Eubulus and Lycurgus,

---

74. For an example of one enterprise that failed, see Schaps, "[Demosthenes] 35."

75. John K. Davies (*Wealth,* 41–72) identifies risk capital lent out at interest (60–66) as one of five new sources of wealth and not the most important. The discussion of de Ste. Croix (*Class Struggle,* 120–33) is more closely addressed to the statement made in our text, but is more selective in its collection of sources.

76. "No man, to my knowledge has ever entered the ranks of the great American fortunes merely by saving a surplus from his salary or wages ... On a salary of two or three hundred thousand a year, even forgetting taxes, and living like a miser in a board shack, it has been mathematically impossible to save up a great American fortune" (Mills, 110–11).

77. Plato *Rep.* 374a–e; *Politicus* 289e–290a; *Laws* 742d, 743e.

78. Badian, 118. He was speaking of late republican Rome.

but the Athenian state, as far as we can see, never became the servant of its bankers and merchants.

For that matter, the lenders were not necessarily and perhaps not even ordinarily citizens.[79] But they had their niche in the economy, and the money that they provided (and the risk they shared) allowed Athenian traders to undertake larger expeditions, with correspondingly larger profits and broader effect, than could have been done had the traders been left to rely on their own wherewithal.

● BANKERS

In the earlier stages of Athenian expansion, private lenders may have sufficed to supply the credit that Athenians needed to embark on business enterprises, but sometime in the course of the fifth century,[80] there arose a new business, which the Greeks called simply a τράπεζα, a "table."[81] The τραπεζίτης differed from a private lender in that he accepted deposits from people and then lent out money that was not his own,[82] a procedure that undoubtedly put at his disposal larger sums than private individuals could amass. In this sense—that the τράπεζα accepted deposits from people with money and then lent the money out at interest—it was certainly a "bank,"[83] and that has remained the meaning of the word τράπεζα in Greek down to this day.[84]

The τράπεζα was much smaller and less formal than a modern bank: the business was transacted by the banker's family and his slaves, and the τραπεζίτης was personally responsible for the money deposited. Its transactions

---

79. Bogaert, *Banques et banquiers,* 386–88; Millett, *Lending and Borrowing,* 206. Cf. E. E. Cohen, *Athenian Economy,* 70 n. 44, and the correct observation of Whitehead (*Ideology,* 117) that "citizens could find themselves in the same occupations as metics and even slaves."

80. Bogaert, *Banques et banquiers,* 61–62.

81. The modern word *bank* has the same original meaning (E. E. Cohen, *Athenian Economy,* 9), as does the Mishnaic Hebrew term *shulḥan;* the latter, at least, may be a simple translation of the Greek.

82. Dem. 36.11; E. E. Cohen, *Athenian Economy,* 8–11, 111–89.

83. Bogaert (*Origines,* 29–30, 137–44) insisted on this definition and on the claim of the Greeks to be the first to have developed the institution.

84. Various authors—E. E. Cohen (*Ancient Economy,* 23 n. 98) traces the idea back to Salin— have considered the τράπεζα more akin to a modern pawnshop. This analogy, though often repeated, is surely not a felicitous formulation: the τράπεζα accepted deposits of coin, not (or not particularly) movables; the deposits, as far as we know them, were made by the well-to-do, not by the poor; the τράπεζα did not, of course, lend money in return for the deposits or hold them as security for those loans.

were generally confidential, and one of its major functions was to hide the depositors' wealth from their creditors and from the state.[85] The business was inherently risky—the more so because of its confidential nature—and failures seem not to have been uncommon.[86]

It is possible to overstate the parallels of the τράπεζα with modern banking. The bankers did not dominate the Athenian economy, or even the Athenian credit structure, as modern banks do. Their political influence, if it existed at all, can have been only marginal and indirect. Nevertheless, they did amass and wield monetary reserves that made them the sources of funding for important undertakings, and their owners were able to amass enough personal wealth to obtain (through well-placed generosity to the state) prestige and even, in some well-known cases of slave bank managers, citizenship.[87] If one looks at the wealth available and employed by them, one can see the banks as standing at the pinnacle of the Athenian credit structure; if one looks at the breadth of their clientele, one may see them as a much more marginal phenomenon.[88] Whichever way they are seen, they are the most thoroughgoing example of a way of life brought about by money, influenced by its availability and, in turn, influencing the society in which they grew.

By the end of the classical period, coinage had insinuated itself into every level of the credit structure, from the small-scale friendly loans that would once have been offered in kind or perhaps by a shared meal and the "commercial" loans of a few obols to set up a day's small trade to the large-scale lending of banks and temples.[89] Wealthy citizens and even foreigners might be able to lend (sometimes at advantageous terms) sums of money larger than a moderate-sized polis could easily repay.[90] Credit, at least in the cities, meant credit in coin. It took the work of anthropologists in this century to remind economists that this need not always be the case.[91]

---

85. E. E. Cohen, *Athenian Economy*, 191–207.

86. Ibid., 215–24.

87. Ibid. The most famous to do so were Pasio and, later, his own slave Phormio, each of whom was manumitted and took over the management of the bank. For their careers, see *APF* 11672.

88. The first is the attitude of E. E. Cohen, a banker, while the second is that of Millett, an occasional borrower (as he writes in his introduction to *Lending and Borrowing*, xii–xiii). Without wishing to minimize the points of real disagreement in their analyses, one can recognize a certain level at which the picture depends on the angle from which it is viewed.

89. For the latter, see Bogaert, *Banques et banquiers*, 279–304.

90. Migeotte, 393–400.

91. Einzig, 47–50, 53–55, and passim.

14   Monetization
Limits and Illusions

"MONEY," WROTE PAUL BOHANNON, "is one of the shatteringly simplifying ideas of all time, and like any other new and compelling idea, it creates its own revolution."[1] Bohannon is not an ancient historian; he was speaking of the effect of the introduction of coinage to the society of the Tiv in Nigeria, and his judgment is open to the objection that Western society impinges upon traditional non-Western societies through more than one opening. "Rather than Western money," asked Jacques Melitz, "were [the Tiv] not mainly victims of their own inability to resist the lure of wives, other prestige goods, and higher subsistence standards, which the Western market cast open before them? . . . True, they blamed Western money, but they needed a scapegoat."[2] In the boiling pot of history, where many different ingredients have come together to produce the stew, we do not have the luxury of chemists, who can put each ingredient into a test tube and observe its characteristics. Monetization and Westernization always go together today, and it is hard to see which is the determinant variable.

Our own investigation is free of that particular objection. Although Greek

---

1. Bohannon, 503.
2. Melitz, 1037 n. 25.

society was undoubtedly exposed to many strong influences from the seventh century to the fourth, the influence of the modern West was not one of them. We have found that coinage affected Greek society, economy, and even politics and warfare both broadly and deeply, though neither as swiftly nor as abruptly as it swept away the Tiv's traditions. The Greeks were not, as were the Tiv, drawn into a world economy that overrode their institutions with its own; taking coinage, a new institution that had developed out of the more developed economies of their neighbors, they evolved a new economic way of thinking that eventually overrode that of their neighbors, planting influences that undoubtedly helped produce the greatness of the Greeks but that long outlived the heyday of that ancient people.

● EXCHANGE AND COINAGE

We have seen that it was by no means the invention of coinage that caused the rise of international trade. The Mycenaean Greeks had extensive international contacts that involved the exchange of goods, and the Greeks of the archaic age not only had a network of exchanges but had men who made a profession out of overseas trade. The Greeks were in commercial contact with the Phoenicians, who used weighed silver as their medium of trade, and the Greeks themselves apparently conducted at least some of their own international trade by means of silver.

In their internal transactions, the archaic Greeks had come to use utensils—spits, tripods, and cauldrons—as a standard of payment and perhaps, to a certain extent, as a medium of exchange. This use was still primitive and clumsy, in that it used real utensils, of full weight and size, the supply of which was not at all sufficient to form a basis for widespread retail trade. In fact, there is no evidence of significant retail trade before the introduction of coinage, nor do we believe that there was ever an internal bullion economy in Greece. The Greeks in the late seventh century were adept international traders, were aware of the possibilities of silver as a trade medium, and were in need of a more efficient mechanism for the increasing breadth of their own domestic economy.

Moreover, the individualism of the Greeks encouraged them to evaluate many of their noneconomic transactions and relationships in terms of exchange. The place of exchange in the economy, as opposed to reciprocity and to the redistribution that had characterized the Mycenaean economy, seems to have been large already in archaic times. Money was important to the Greeks not only in its function as a medium of payment or exchange but also as a more supple standard of value than the gross approximations of their earlier times.

With the invention of coinage, the Greeks had, for the first time, a universal standard of value, store of value, and medium of exchange and payment. They did not do anything with their coins that the Phoenicians could not do with their weighed silver, but unlike the Phoenicians, the Greeks conceived of their money as being indentical or interchangeable with the value it represented, to the extent that a Greek could identify wealth itself with "plenty of coin."[3] Once coins had been invented, Greek society underwent broad and deep changes—some immediately, some over a longer period of time. To some extent, these changes were simply a result of the greater convenience of money for the purposes to which it was put; to some extent, no doubt, the particular Greek appreciation of the universality of money, including what we have called its fungibility, changed the conceptual universe of the Greeks themselves and of all those who were affected by them, not excluding ourselves.

An expansion of retail trade was the first visible concomitant of coins. At this distance, we cannot tell which is cause and which effect, but we can say at least that the marketplace and coinage grew up together. Market trade itself had a role in relieving both the population pressure on the peasantry and the subordination of the peasantry to the nobles: the market now offered an alternative way of making a living, besides providing an outlet for surplus and a source from which to overcome shortages without incurring obligations to an agricultural magnate.

THE EXPANSION OF MONEY BEYOND THE SPHERE OF EXCHANGE

Personal labor also underwent a change. The work of artisans was changed, perhaps, only to the extent that an expanding market produced new opportunities, but those who had no particular skill were now employed under different conditions from those that had prevailed in the archaic age. Where the archaic *thes* had been personally obligated to the one who supported him, the classical *misthotos* worked at a specified job for a clearly defined wage. The introduction of contract work made the organization of large-scale projects much more common and provided a limited amount of mobility between the lowest economic class and the middle classes. At the

---

3. See p. 175, n. 3.

top of the pyramid, the most important contractors could command high sums for their services.

Since the economy is not a sealed system, but rather a particular aspect of the activities of people in society, the effects of monetization went beyond the economy itself. The possibility of procuring goods and organizing labor by means of money made it possible for wars to be waged with money. In the long run, money was often a more decisive force than strategy, tactics, weaponry, or bravery, and it has remained a potent factor to this day. Politics, too, underwent a structural change, which in some states involved the replacement of an aristocracy of birth with an aristocracy of wealth, while in others, notably including Athens, the lower classes succeeded in harnessing the state machinery to give them the power to mobilize and to employ the power of money—to make the demos wealthy as a class even though its members remained impoverished as individuals. The maintenance and proper functioning of the fiscal structure became and is today an indispensable part of the maintenance of democracy; the ability of individuals to divert, commandeer, or circumvent that machinery became and is today one of the greatest dangers to its existence.

As money became the locus of power, more sophisticated methods for dealing with it were developed. At all levels, credit became monetized, so that enterprises which had once depended on personal and social ties became available in a less personal manner. At the upper end of the credit continuum developed professional banks, whose managers could amass wealth out of all proportion to what could be gotten by the more traditional ways of earning a living. Athens, despite the opinions of some modernist scholars,[4] never fell under the political domination of these nouveaux riches, though it did on occasion find itself in need of their services and obliged to recognize those services even to the point, detestable in the eyes of the wellborn, of turning slaves into citizens—citizens whose wealth immediately put them among the foremost members of the polity. Other states, later in antiquity, found themselves less able to defend themselves against the power that could be amassed by the rich.

The importance of monetization in the achievements of Greek society must not be underestimated. Without money, the great temples, the dramatic festivals of Athens, its navy, and its democracy would have taken a very different form, if they had come to exist at all. To oversee these projects, the

---

4. Cornford, 15–24 and passim; more carefully but still exaggeratedly Thomson (79–87, 203, 325–31). Cf. de Ste. Croix, *Class Struggle,* 41.

state developed a structure of money management that both expressed and reinforced its impersonal power.[5] Armies were paid in coin, and the sale of booty required management that differed from place to place.[6] Although Alexander the Great conquered a much richer kingdom than his own, one may doubt whether he could have done so without money. Money, however, had its limits.

● THE LIMITS OF MONETIZATION

Monetization is a process with various levels and facets, not an either-or alternative. Greece in the classical and Hellenistic periods was monetized to a large extent and in many respects, but money never came to dominate its economy completely. Most notably, agriculture in ancient Greece, although affected by coinage, was never monetized into a regular and widespread system of cash cropping as it is in the modern world. Since most of the poor were probably subsistence farmers and most of the rich were landowners, certain concepts that we take for granted are not applicable to the ancient world without removing them to a level of abstraction that divorces them from history. It is not reasonable to estimate an ancient Greek's wealth in terms of an annual monetary income, nor did the Greeks themselves use such a standard, although Solon is said to have based his property classes on annual agricultural produce.[7] Few were the people who could count on a regular income in coin, and those who could were not necessarily obliged to expend that coin on their daily needs.

For the same reason, we cannot properly speak of a "cost of living" in ancient Greece. Most people did not buy all or most of their necessities; it was an unfortunate person who had to do so.[8] This fact itself means, furthermore, that even were we to translate their efforts into monetary terms, the translation would be a false one: the price paid for labor was not necessarily what it would have been had the hirable labor force included most of the population, nor was the price of foodstuffs in the marketplace necessarily the same as it would have been had the market been, as our markets are, the overwhelmingly dominant source of food for the population. We can say,

---

5. Schaps, "Builders."

6. Pritchett, *Greek State at War*, 5:401–38.

7. See p. 172.

8. "Rabbi Ḥanan said: 'And thy life shall hang in doubt before thee' [Deut. 28:66]—this is a person who buys wheat for a year. 'And thou shalt fear night and day'—this is a person who buys from a grain merchant. 'And shalt have no assurance of thy life'—this is a person who buys from a baker." Palestinian Talmud, *Sheqalim* 3:2 and elsewhere.

with some reasonable accuracy, how many days a stonecutter would have to work to buy food in the market for himself, a wife, and two children. But besides the fact that most Athenians were not stonecutters, we must also consider that his wife might well be supported by her dowry; that he might own slaves, who might, according to their assignments, abilities, age, and health, either increase the family's monetary income or drain it; that he was more likely to live in the house he had inherited (or hoped to inherit) from his father than to buy or to rent one; and that even the cost of his food and clothing would be significantly different according to the degree to which the members of his household participated in their preparation. These observations, moreover, deal only with an urban worker; we have not begun to consider the extraneous factors that would falsify a "cost-of-living" calculation for a peasant.

We are monetized to a much greater extent than the Greeks ever were. Modern agriculture is so thoroughly monetized that farmers generally do not even attempt to supply their own needs directly from the land: they raise a few salable crops or livestock and buy their food with the money. The concept of money in the abstract has become so natural to us that we no longer require that our coins be made of precious metal. Even banknotes are coming to be more and more restricted in their use, as we prefer to conduct our business by transferring abstract values without requiring any actual token to represent the value, relying rather on the records of banks and credit-card companies. The sophistication of our great credit magnates, the modern commercial bankers and stockbrokers, would make Pasio seem like a country rube; and the fortunes they amass, in the briefest span of time, would suffice to buy and sell not only Pasio's bank but the entire Athenian polity many times over.

In this situation, there is a tendency to believe that all things, at least in the modern world, can be reduced to money. When faced with the transactions of premonetary societies, we often find it necessary to translate them into terms of money to comprehend them. In our own world, many claim that everything has a price and that every transaction among people is really a sale of some sort. But even the modern world has limits to its monetization. We laugh, as the Romans laughed, at L. Mummius, who stipulated with the contractors who carted off the priceless artistic treasures of Corinth that "if they broke any of them, they would have to replace them with new ones."[9] We consider it primitive of the Anglo-Saxons to have accepted

---

9. Velleius Paterculus 1.13.4.

money as recompense for murder, and like King Solomon,[10] if offered all the wealth of a man's house for love, we should despise it.

◉ THE PARADOXES OF MONEY

The idea that cowrie shells, oxen, bronze tripods, and banknotes are all really the same thing, and that that thing, which we call money, is wealth itself, has been an enormously useful concept. It has allowed us to unite in a single concept what it is that most men (and increasingly women, though this is a more recent development) are spending their time pursuing. It allows us to compare levels of success in extremely various pursuits. Most importantly, it has created a universal incentive that can be offered to almost anyone to elicit willing cooperation, and has thus allowed us to pursue, without visible coercion, the greatest cooperative undertakings ever known. The exploration of outer space may be the most obvious example of an enormous cooperative undertaking whose participants were assembled by money, but it is far from unique. Virtually every action that we do today is in some sense a cooperative one. Turning on a car, or even eating a doughnut, also requires a huge number of people's prior activity for successful execution. Few of the people involved, if any, could have performed the job from scratch—turning iron ore into an automobile or wheat kernels into a doughnut—and rarely do we even consider the various jobs involved in it.

But money is not merely a clearer and more advanced concept than its alternatives. The concept of money and the reorganization of society that it has brought in its wake has both freed people and bound them, opened their eyes and blinded them. The paradoxes and illusions of money, often discussed by scholars and as often dismissed by fortune seekers for more than two millennia, stem in a large measure from the unification in a single concept of ideas that are not necessarily identical.

The Paradox of Possession of Money

People measured their worth by their possessions long before coins were invented and continue to do so today even in places where monetization is relatively shallow. The islanders of Yap own large stones that are their pride and joy. These stones can be moved only with the greatest of difficulty and are sold only under the greatest duress. Although small stones are exchanged

---

10. Song of Sol. 8:7.

freely, the large ones are used for display and for bride-wealth;[11] everyone knows that the possession of a stone of great size indicates that its possessor is a person of importance.[12] With no less of an eye on the pride of possession, Agamemnon promised Achilles that a man who had the seven tripods, twenty cauldrons, and twelve horses that he would give him would "not be unpropertied."[13] Money took to itself this prestige, but since money is wealth, it broadened the pride of possession well beyond prestige. A person with money was not simply prestigious or important; that person was rich, and could be thought so even if the money brought its possessor neither prestige nor benefit.

Two modern examples will illustrate the point. A man has lived his life alone and friendless, clothed in rags, covered with sores, begging his bread and eating it sparingly, living in a single room. At his death, he is found to have had hundreds of thousands of dollars, accumulated by years of begging, hidden in his mattress. Everyone who hears the story exclaims, "Why, he was rich all the time!" The exclamation is not entirely indefensible, but it surely involves an extension of the concept of wealth beyond what we usually imagine. Here, our subject derives neither physical pleasure nor prestige from his money, but we still consider him rich. On the face of it, all we mean is that he owned a lot of banknotes, although the banknotes were for him little more than colored paper, from which he never derived any tangible benefit.

The same paradox can be seen no less clearly at the other end of the apparent spectrum. A successful businessman has amassed millions or billions of dollars, some few thousands of which he has spent on a comfortable but not excessive lifestyle for himself and his family. At his death he leaves an estate of millions, most of which is taken by taxes or by legal fees. This man considered himself, and was considered by his friends and neighbors to be fabulously rich, yet his wealth consisted essentially of large numbers on statements from his bankers and his brokers, numbers that testified to money that was passed to him and that, at his death, passed from him, without having given him or his family any tangible benefit. In all his behavior and his pleasures, his life differed little from that of his neighbors,

---

11. Among the reasons why stone money was considered "women's money" was that "it stays at the estate and does not go about in social affairs, like a woman." Shell money, on the other hand, was masculine, partially "because it was given more often and thereby moved around like a man" (Labby, 39).

12. On the stone money of Yap and the question of whether or not it can properly be considered money, see Einzig, 36–40 (who answers with "a somewhat hesitant affirmative").

13. Hom. II. 9.125.

but since his monthly statements had those big numbers on them, they, he, and we consider him to have been much richer than they. This person, indeed, got prestige from his wealth, but that is not what we mean by calling him "rich," for if another man had a similar reputation but was found at his death to have had only a small bank account, we would say, "Why, he wasn't rich at all!"

One may perhaps defend our perception by saying that the two people described were wealthy in that their money opened up to them possibilities for its use, even though those possibilities were never exploited: they both were rich in that they could have achieved power and pleasure that were beyond the reach of people with less money. There is some truth in this, but it does not tell the whole story. For one thing, we consider them to have been not potentially rich but really rich. We do not think of them, for example, in the same way that we think of promising students who never achieved anything. In the case of the rich people, we say, "They were rich"; in the case of the students, we say, "They could have been great." The students, too, could have achieved power and pleasure that less intelligent people could not have, but we do not consider them to have been wealthy because of that. Moreover, if two people have the same amount of money, we consider them equally wealthy, regardless of the personal qualities, family ties, or available opportunities that may make the possibilities of one hugely greater than those of the other.

The one person in ancient literature who lives the life of a pauper while actually possessing money is Euclio in Plautus's *Aulularia*,[14] who is so obsessed with the possible theft of the pot of gold he has found that he moves it from hiding place to hiding place and is careful not to miss any possible handouts lest people guess that he has come into money.[15] He ostentatiously calls himself a poor man,[16] but that is part of the act. When a neighbor's slave gets his hand on the money, the slave immediately thinks himself "richer than the griffins who live in the golden mountains,"[17] though he is still a slave. When Euclio discovers that the pot of gold is gone, he mourns that "this day has brought me hunger and poverty,"[18] although he has lived

---

14. The *Aulularia*, like all the comedies of Plautus and Terence that we possess, is a Latin reworking of a Greek original.

15. Plaut. *Aul.* 105–12.

16. Plaut. *Aul.* 184, 196, and elsewhere. His neighbors, of course, who know no better, also call him poor.

17. Plaut. *Aul.* 701–2.

18. Plaut. *Aul.* 722.

in hunger and poverty for all of his life. He does not actually say that he had been rich as long as the gold had been buried in the ground, but he certainly implies as much.

Other Greek characters who live a poor life despite the possession of money are less appropriate parallels. The grouch after whom Menander's *Dyscolus* is named lives simply, but he simply has no use for his money, since he hates human company.[19] No more appropriate is the "self-punisher," Terence's *Heautontimorumenos*, who sold everything he had to buy himself a plot of land on which he performed grueling labor: he, too, used his money as he wished. The wealth of these people is not denied, but it is not an issue. No examples exist of people who got rich by mendicancy. The population and the volume of coinage were not so great, nor the habit of charity so well developed,[20] that a pauper could amass any great store of coins by begging.

The second kind of unenjoyed wealth also existed. A person of wide possessions who lived a simple life would have been considered by the ancients as an example not of an unimaginative nature but of piety, though he would be expected (unlike the *Dyscolus*) to expend money on helping his friends and on honoring the gods and the city,[21] but Xenophon recognized that it was also possible for money to give a man no benefit at all. At the beginning of his *Oeconomicus*, he has Socrates convince Critobulus that nothing is wealth unless it is beneficial to its possessor—an argument that leads Socrates to the paradoxical conclusion that he himself, with few possessions, is richer than Critobulus, who has plenty of everything; Critobulus, presumably with his own irony, eventually asks Socrates "to take me into your care, so that I don't really become pitiable."[22] The entire course of the discussion makes it clear that most people would be unaware of the paradox and would consider wealthy even a person whose money brought no benefit whatsoever.

Among the Hebrews, Ecclesiastes was aware of the illusory nature of possessions: "Yea, I hated all my labour which I had taken under the sun: because I should leave it unto the man that shall be after me . . . There is an evil which I have seen under the sun, and it is common among men: a man to whom G-d hath given riches, wealth, and honour, so that he wanteth nothing for his soul

---

19. On the wealth of Menander's characters, see Casson. Cf. Webster, *Introduction to Menander*, 25–26; Schaps, "Comic Inflation," 70–71.
20. Hands, 62–76, 89–115.
21. Dover, 175–80.
22. Xen. *Oec.* 1.1–2.9.

of all that he desireth, yet G-d giveth him not power to eat thereof, but a stranger eateth it; this is vanity, and it is an evil disease."[23] Here, too, the phenomenon that we occasionally see in the modern world can be identified only by the occasional polemic against it.

It must be stressed—and this is why the phenomenon just described is not an illusion but a paradox—that the measuring of a person's wealth by the amount of money the person possesses is not an absurd idea at all; on the contrary, it is an extremely useful one. When Pericles totaled up the amount of silver in the hands of the Athenians at the beginning of the Peloponnesian War,[24] he was making a very real comparison of the relative abilities of Athens and Sparta to last out a long conflict. In any consideration of a person's ability to carry out a project, the consideration of how much money one has or can amass is a vital one. When we say that Bill Gates is—as of this writing—richer than the queen of England, we are identifying a real phenomenon; but our very measure is blinding us to many differences, differences that may be obvious when we compare a commoner with a queen but that may be no less real in those cases where they are less apparent.

The Illusion That Greater Price Means Greater Value

At the funeral games of Patroclus, Achilles offered a tripod to the winner of the wrestling match and a woman to the loser. Homer, who does not state values for the prizes offered in the other contexts, takes the trouble to tell us that the Achaeans valued the tripod at twelve oxen, the woman at four. The evaluation is essential, for only the evaluation reveals to us which was the more valuable prize: a woman might just as easily have been worth more than a tripod, and, for that matter, more than twelve oxen.[25] Nowadays, we estimate an item's value in terms of its price; in this case, too, a function that exists in premonetary societies has been assumed by money.

The multifaceted nature of money, however, puts into the picture new aspects, not necessarily appropriate. For example, the price of a visit to a friend or relative increases with the distance traveled. If one Athenian woman visited her parents in Eleusis and another visited her parents in Thessaly, was the second visit of greater value? If so, was the second woman richer for having to go further? Were her children, who saw their grandparents once in a

23. Eccles. 2:18, 6:1–2.
24. See p. 19.
25. See p. 69.

year and then only after an arduous journey, richer because of that fact than their neighbors who could not afford a journey to Thessaly but who saw their grandparents every day? Odd as it seems, they will probably have thought that they were, and so will their neighbors.

One could elaborate on this. In the preceding example, the children who saw their grandparents less were thereby the richer, but had both sets of grandparents been at the same distance, we would have said the opposite, that the children who saw their grandparents more often were the richer. That, too we would have said only as long as lack of funds was not the cause—if the mothers of the children, for example, were gleaners, moving from place to place and staying with their relatives when no work was available, then the children who spent less time with their grandparents would again have been considered the richer, although they might actually have had a more difficult and unstable life because of it. In each case, the rule is the same: the person with more money, no matter what the effects of that money may be, is the richer. This paradox is well known to economists, though they have developed no theoretical basis for eliminating it.[26]

Again it should be noted that the basic idea—that greater price indicates greater use value—is one that is generally correct and extremely useful. But here again, the unification of many different concepts into a single one has produced consequences that are sometimes inaccurate and misleading.

The Illusion of Unlimited Possibilities

The physical pleasures available to any animal are limited. Too much food becomes nauseating; too much intoxicating drink leaves the drinker unconscious; other pleasures as well reach their point of diminishing return and downright impossibility. Animals who have satisfied their needs will generally spend their time either sleeping or engaged in aimless activity.[27] Money, however, is unlimited. However much we have, we could always have more.

---

26. "Economists referred to the paradox of including wages paid to housekeepers while making no allowance for housewives' services (so making it literally possible to increase national income by employing each other's wife) long before feminism became a recognised movement . . . These problems are tolerated simply because of the difficulty of doing anything else. When it becomes too obviously silly to value statistical convenience over economic sense, an adjustment is made." Hawke, 20.

27. There are, however, "cultural" activities that can occupy even satiated animals: storing food (ants, bees, squirrels), establishing and defending territory (tomcats), loud aggressive displays to establish dominance (chimpanzees). The tyrannous ability to work a creature without limit is not a characteristic unique to money or to the human race.

There is nothing special about money in this respect; it is a characteristic shared with every item that is hoarded, and once my prestige is defined by what I own, the chief reason for hoarding is precisely the fact that I can always get more prestige by gaining more of the item hoarded. Prestige is limitless: even a person who has no competitors may want to have more prestige in order to discourage potential newcomers. The use of a counter, whether cowrie shell or gold bracelet, is an entirely reasonable way of establishing and defining prestige.

Again, however, the equation of money with wealth leads to paradoxical results. The strangest of all is that the person who thinks that the pursuit of money will satisfy all needs and desires has actually entered a conceptual world in which one can never be satisfied. One can eat, drink, and otherwise amuse oneself to satiety, that is, to the point at which one wants no more; but however much money one may have, there is always more to crave. When Solon said that "there is no limit to wealth for mortals,"[28] he was recognizing the unlimited appetite for wealth; when Aristotle objected to Solon's proverb, he was not denying its reality but only its legitimacy.[29] This illusion can be seen in a positive light: money allows people to continue purposeful behavior even though their biological needs have been satisfied, saving them from a life of boredom and aimlessness. Perhaps so; it is not for that reason any less illusory.

The Myth of Infinite Fungibility

We calculate our fortunes in money, and we take it for granted that money can buy anything. I have already mentioned, however, that there are things that are not for sale. Some are simply not for sale at any price (the Grand Canyon); some would cease to exist if they could be bought (a person's moral principles); some can be bought but lose much of their value by the very reason of being purchased (love, the publication of a book, an academic degree). Other things may be available for money, but not in a way that is useful to the person with money: this is the situation of people in a besieged city, whose money can no longer buy them food, because there is no food to be had, nor favor from the enemy once they and their money have fallen into the enemy's hands. "It is peculiar," says Aristotle, "for wealth to be of such a sort

---

28. Solon fr. 13.71 Bergk, West (= 1.71 Diehl, Gentili-Prato).
29. Arist. *Pol.* I 8.14 (1256b 32–34); cf. Schaps, "Socrates." See Plut. *Pyrrhus* 14.2–8 for a famous tale of how the orator Cineas deflated Pyrrhus's similar illusion of the unlimited possibilities of power.

that a person who had plenty of it might die of starvation, as they say about Midas in the myth."[30] The extent to which money can be changed into food, drink, power, and even, when used indirectly and astutely, into more spiritual goods, is staggering, but it is not infinite. The "thirty thousand Persian archers" who drove Agesilaus out of Asia[31] showed how much money could accomplish against a trained and motivated army; Darius's defeat at the hands of Alexander showed that the power of money was not infinite. A Roman historian might consider the career of Crassus, the richest man in Rome, who counted in the First Triumvirate as an equal of Pompey and Caesar but fell at Carrhae when he tried to win the military glory that could not be bought with money. Our own times, too, have shown well-known examples both of those whose political or military endeavours foundered against superior finance and of those whose enormous fortunes could not achieve their ambitions. In the hope that my book will outlast those reputations, I refrain from mentioning them by name.

Is Money the Ideal Medium of Trade?

In some respects, certainly so: being universally desirable, it makes everything obtainable. In some situations, however, that may not be what is good for the people involved. Einzig cites "the well-known experience of Mlle. Zélie, singer at the Théâtre Lyrique in Paris, who, in the course of a tour round the world, gave a concert on one of the Society Islands, and received the fee of 3 pigs, 23 turkeys, 44 chickens, 5,000 coconuts and considerable quantities of bananas, lemons and oranges, representing one-third of the box office takings. In a letter published by Wolowski and quoted to boredom by economists ever since, she says that, although this amount of livestock and vegetables would have been worth about 4,000 francs in Paris, in the Society Islands it was of very little use to her." Einzig replies that "a local singer in the Society Islands would not have been embarrassed at receiving payment in kind, since she would have known ways in which to dispose of her takings, or store them for future use."[32] This is true but only part of the answer. No less relevant is the fact that the Society Islanders' economy, precisely because it was embedded in society, served the society and its members. Mlle. Zélie's fee made her a very rich Society Islander overnight, and as a member of that society, she could probably have flourished to the

---

30. Arist. *Pol.* I 9.11 (1257b 14–16).
31. See p. 144 with n. 28.
32. Einzig, 342.

end of her days. The economy would not have failed her. Mlle. Zélie, however, had no such interest. Just as she had received the items although an outsider, she wanted immediately to leave the society with something more easily transportable than all the local goods. It was not necessarily a weakness of the Society Islanders' economy that their barter did not make it easy for outsiders to appropriate large amounts of their wealth overnight and spirit it away across two oceans. In the Egyptian case I discussed in chapter 3,[33] Erēnofre's accumulated goods were of sufficient use to Rēʿia to make him willing to accept them, but it would not have been easy for Rēʿia to accumulate hoards of wealth in this way. Had they considered the matter, the Egyptians might have seen this arrangement as proper and desirable.

The Illusion of Fixed Value

In all of their purposes, coins may vary in value with supply and demand. When more coins are available or when fewer are needed, they are worth less in exchange, their possession confers less prestige, and—most painful for their owner—their efficacy as a way of storing value is less than complete. Still, societies in which retail trade is not widely practiced tend to maintain ideas of value over a long period of time: that a bushel of wheat is worth two bushels of barley or that a new basket is worth a basketful of figs are ideas that endure without great sensitivity to fluctuations of supply and demand, as long as these fluctuations remain within reasonable limits. Not because of anything in the nature of coins but because of the fact that before their adoption the precise calculation of value was a relatively rare procedure, values in Greece before the introduction of coinage are likely to have been generally stable.

Retail traders cannot afford this inexactitude. Their livelihood depends on the difference between the price they pay and the price they receive, and they cannot afford to be imprecise in their calculations. Their precision is often resented by those who seem to be getting the bad side of each trade, but the precision causes a fluctuation in prices that may be felt by every member of the society. Governments, when they control the money supply, often use this to their advantage, increasing the supply to pay off their debts. This method, which effectively taxes the citizens (each of whom now has less value of money than before) without having to take from them any physical item or even to notify them that they have paid anything, is obviously

---

33. P. 39.

tempting to those who can do it. The Roman emperors, who ruled over a world economy, used it on occasion, by increasing the percentage of base metal in the coins; the Greek cities generally did not, since debasing their currency meant more or less invalidating it outside of the city's boundaries.

The effectiveness of this tactic depends on the belief—known to be false, yet constantly treated as if true—that the value of money is fixed. This belief is only an indirect result of coinage, coming about as it does from the ease with which retail transactions can be carried out with coins, but it gives an enormous leverage to the person whose expertise in value fluctuations can be used to get a greater share of the society's treasure. Like the other illusions we have mentioned, this one tends to remain at the basis of people's thinking even when they know it is false.[34]

The Illusion That Money Is Wealth

The very idea that wealth is a matter of "plenty of coin" is, of course, an inaccurate one, as Aristotle argued long ago. Yet it is striking how the idea keeps recurring, at the highest levels of economic thought. Indeed, a treatise that purports to describe the fiscal management of states entirely in terms of tricks by which coin can be collected has come down to us among the works of Aristotle himself, though he is surely not its author.[35] Adam Smith devoted no small effort to attacking this idea.[36] John Stuart Mill thought it was dead.

It often happens, that the universal belief of one age of mankind—a belief from which no one *was,* nor without an extraordinary effort of genius *could* at that time be free—becomes to a subsequent age so palpable an absurdity, that the only difficulty then is to imagine how such a thing can ever have appeared credible. It has so happened with the doctrine that money is synonymous with wealth. The conceit seems too preposterous to be thought of as a serious opinion. It looks

34. Fischer, Dornbusch, and Schmalensee, in what is now a standard economics textbook, define "gold standard" as "an exchange rate and monetary system in which central banks or governments were obliged to buy and sell gold at a fixed price in terms of their currencies" (774). They know, certainly, that those who advocated the gold standard considered themselves to be fixing the value of their currency, not the price of gold; but the everyday practice of the economist makes it simpler to speak as if it were currency whose price was static, making "corrections" for its actual fluctuation only where necessary.

35. The second book of the *Oeconomica.*

36. Adam Smith, IV.i.

like one of the crude fancies of childhood, instantly corrected by a word from any grown person.[37]

Mill realized, as he wrote immediately after these words, that this idea must once have seemed very compelling. Modern economists have worked hard at creating such concepts as *gross national product* and *human and physical capital* to measure a nation's wealth by something other than its treasures of precious metal. Yet despite the fact that nobody today considers a nation's gold and silver to be its true treasure, the idea that we can measure a nation's wealth by looking at what is happening to its money—is its national currency unit rising or falling in value? are prices rising on its stock exchange?—continues, on occasion, to catch us looking at money when we should be looking at wealth. Throughout the 1970s, the oil companies of America continued to produce good profits for their shareholders. Only when the international cartel of oil-exporting nations decided to limit its exports did the Americans discover, quite rudely, that they no longer had enough of their own oil to support their economy. In the 1980s, some of the greatest American industries were destroyed: steel and television production passed out of America almost entirely, and the American automobile industry suddenly found itself hard beset by foreign competitors. But the stock market kept rising, and economists considered the period to be one of prosperity. Fortunately for America, it has not since found itself in such an emergency that it would have to know how it would compensate if foreign steel or foreign semiconductors were to become unavailable, but it would seem that the use of money as a measure, presumed to be trivially exchangeable for every other valuable commodity, has hidden some information from us.

○ THE NEW EQUALITY AND THE NEW PRIVILEGE

In the course of our investigation,[38] we saw that money was a great leveler: available to all, it could be accumulated (or wasted) to the point where a person could either transcend a low estate or forfeit a high one. Some philosophers of money have seen it as a great institution of liberation.[39] Others have seen the other side, which I traced in chapter 13: the immense power that can be had by controlling large amounts of money, in particular

37. Mill, in his "Preliminary Remarks."
38. P. 119.
39. Notably Simmel, 283–354.

by those who manipulate money to their benefit. Hesiod claimed that prudence and hard work, intelligently applied, could turn a poor farmer into a successful one, but Pasio[40] proved that the same qualities, if exercised on coins rather than on the ground, could turn a slave into a citizen magnate.

The aristocracy of wealth was and is an aristocracy that carries with it privileges far beyond the mere possession of money. A wealthy person will be listened to where an ordinary person will be ignored; favors will be done for a wealthy person that would not be done for an ordinary person; a wealthy person's interests will be protected when an ordinary person's will be trampled; and all these at no necessary expense of money, for people are willing to serve the wealthy merely for the hope of future advantage. Many people—among them artists, intellectuals, and even plutocrats—have noted the privilege of wealth with dismay.[41] Nobody has offered a plausible justification for why society should reward its bankers and stockbrokers so much more than its workers and tradesmen or even its doctors and teachers, but every effort to remove this privilege of wealth has ended by impoverishing the poor even further.

This is where the invention of money has left us. Like the industrial revolution in later years, it produced a situation in some ways far better and in other ways anomalous and even far worse than the situation it replaced. But the condition into which the Greeks found themselves propelled was not reversible. The very equivalence of money with wealth, an equivalence that made money universally desired, has given money the ability to organize human endeavors on an unparalleled scale and with an unmatchable efficiency. Those who do not have it cannot match those who do: whatever the short-term successes of the moneyless, in the long run they cannot fight those who control wealth, cannot rule them successfully, cannot compete with them successfully. Where attempted, the elimination of money has led to mass starvation and to abandonment of the economic efforts by which the enlarged population can be fed, clothed, and housed. We have gotten onto a moving train, and whatever its discomforts, we cannot safely get off.

Despite all that, I hope that my investigation has not been one of entirely academic interest. A survey of the monetization of a previously moneyless society—the first true monetization, as I have claimed, for only since the Greeks has the modern concept of money existed—demonstrates to us what

---

40. See p. 192.

41. Schaps, "Socrates"; but cf. Kurke, *Traffic*, 135–59, 165–66, 240–56, for Pindar's way of turning work for a wage into an aristocratically acceptable, socially responsible, praiseworthy and praise-generating activity.

the effects of this concept have been, what alternatives have existed, and what illusions and paradoxes it brings with it. A more lively awareness of these matters may help us to live a life whose ideas of happiness are more carefully thought out, and in the end more satisfying, than the ideas that the monetized economy offers us on its own. We cannot, while we live, leave the monetized world, and we cannot overcome it; but we may find our place more successfully if we recognize it.

APPENDIXES

The Economist and the Historian

IT HAS BEEN SAID THAT all sciences aspire to the status of geometry, a detailed and illuminating set of thoroughly nontrivial propositions all deduced ineluctably from a set of clear definitions and apparently trivial and indisputable axioms.[1] No other science has attained that status, but many of the modern natural sciences have come close, deriving observed phenomena from more or less theoretical constructs by application of rules of relative simplicity. In those fields that have produced these prodigies—physics, astronomy, chemistry, and their ilk—the rules in question are neither trivial nor indisputable; in the extreme case, they are even paradoxical or incomprehensible. These sciences derive their validity not from the intuitive acceptance of their first principles but from the accuracy with which the consequences derived from those principles succeed in describing the physical world. Einstein explained an earlier observation about the interference of light rays reflected across a table by a theory of alarming implausibility; as he worked out the consequences of his theory, he derived from it the consequence, never observed by anybody, that a star that seemed to be near the sun should appear—in a total eclipse that would make such a star visible— to be further from the sun than ordinary calculations would put it. When

---

1. Being married to a geometer, I must admit that such terms as "ineluctably," "indisputable," and even "clear" represent not the true state of geometry so much as the ideal view of it to which other sciences are said to aspire.

the total eclipse of May 29, 1919, permitted such an observation and the star indeed appeared further than it should have been, Einstein's theory was not made more plausible to the intuition, but it was validated by the accuracy of its predictions.[2]

The social sciences do not presume to aspire to the status of geometry. At their most precise, they dream of the status of physics, with rules—however implausible—that can predict accurately the behavior of aggregates of people. The validation of these rules, as in the case of physics, depends not on their inherent plausibility but on the accuracy of their predictions. None of the social sciences has come as close to this dream as has economics. On the basis of a number of definitions and presumptions (economic rationality, opportunity cost, elasticity, etc.), economists derive quantifiable and testable predictions that should, at the most optimistic hope, succeed in defining economic behavior of man under any conditions.

Success has been partial at best. Both in what the economists call "microeconomic" and "macroeconomic" behavior, human beings and even entire societies often behave in ways other than those predicted by economists, and the underlying rules are not so clearly defined and so thoroughly agreed upon that all economists make the same predictions for a given set of data. Economists often bring in "correction factors" to account for things ignored in their usual calculations, and they are aware of the limitations of their science.[3]

Still further from physics are sociology and anthropology. These disciplines have developed a technical language that includes a sort of taxonomy of societies (agriculturalists, hunter-gatherers, patrilocal/matrilocal/neolocal marriage, etc.) and are able to make, if not predictions, at least generalizations that can be tested to see how well they fit the reported data. They cannot, as economists routinely do, reduce the subject of their study to equations; while economists may be overconfident to speak of "fine-tuning the economy," sociologists have not yet come close enough to that ideal to allow them the illusion that they could "fine-tune the society."

History, the oldest of the social sciences, has not even reached the stage of taxonomy, despite efforts in that direction.[4] It has no agreed upon set of technical terms, except insofar as historians borrow them from the other social sciences. Historians, dealing constantly with documents and artifacts

---

2. Einstein, app. 3.

3. Hawke, 18–27; Rawski, "Issues," 18–24.

4. The most ambitious such effort in the twentieth century was that of Toynbee, widely heralded at its inception but rarely consulted nowadays.

of the past that speak in their own language, do not attempt to fit the past into a theoretical framework that will allow them to predict as the economist does or even to generalize as the sociologist does. In history, a careful observation of historical testimony and monuments, together with a sense—sometimes explicitly formulated but more often only implicit—of what constitutes historical causation, produces theories about the past that do not, in general, offer any predictions about the future that could validate or invalidate the presumptions. Even such generalities as historians do offer tend to come in the form of obiter dicta that are often enlightening ("Power tends to corrupt, and absolute power corrupts absolutely"; "All nations... are forever scarred by the epoch when they have been great")[5] but that are rarely testable in any meaningful sense.

This is not to say that history remains primitive whereas sociology and anthropology have advanced to a more advanced stage and economics to a stage yet further ahead. Perhaps this would be true if the scientific structure were the only legitimate way of approaching knowledge, but it is not. Scientific explanation necessarily simplifies matters, speaking of ideal cases and perfect constructs that do not quite correspond to anything in nature. Scientists, moreover, tend to see these ideal constructs even in the real world, often blinded to the things in heaven and in earth that are not dreamt of in their philosophy. It is the constant job of the historian to recall us to the facts as they appear out of the sources themselves. Historians, too, cannot help simplifying—no human brain could encode the whole of human existence, even were all of its facets recorded and available to us—but they do so, as much as possible, by the direct evaluation of the sources, seeing again and again aspects of the human condition that are not explained and often even not noticed by those whose system of postulates determine their expectations.[6]

History thus differs from economics not only in its subject matter and its

---

5. Lord John Acton made the first observation—for which alone his name is known to a host of nonhistorians—in a letter; the second is from Hugh Thomas, 33.

6. See on this the comments of the very ideological historian, de Ste. Croix, *Class Struggle* (34): "There are very great virtues in the traditional approach of the historian, the essence of which—the insistence on recognising the *specificity* of the historical situation in any given period (and even area)—must not be abandoned, or even compromised, when it is combined with a sociological approach. Indeed, anyone who is not capable (whether from a deficiency of intellect or from lack of time or energy) of the great effort needed to combine the two approaches ought to prefer the strictly historical one, for even mediocre work produced by the purely fact-grubbing historian may at least, if his facts are accurate and fairly presented, be of use to others capable of a higher degree of synthesis, whereas the would-be sociologist having insufficient knowledge of the specific historical evidence for a particular period of history is unlikely in the extreme to say anything about it that will be of use to anyone else."

methods of approach but in the basic question of what criteria validate its results. Economics, like the physical sciences to which it approaches, offers a large body of testable predictions on the basis of a small group of relatively simple presumptions; we consider it worthwhile or not to the extent that these predictions successfully describe the observed phenomena, regardless of the inherent plausibility of the presumptions. History, in contrast, depends for its validity on the internal plausibility of the explanations offered and on the extent to which they succeed in making a coherent narrative out of otherwise unconnected events.

This is the basic reason why the attacks of Polanyi and even those of the economist Einzig on the concept of *homo economicus,* the omniscient person who always behaves in such a way as to maximize personal economic advantage, are correct but misplaced. Taken at face value, the question of whether any such creature really exists is a question of small interest to the economist, just as the question of whether quarks really exist is much less important to the physicist than the question of whether the predictions that proceed from the presumption of their existence accurately describe what happens in the world. When Polanyi and the economic anthropologists who have followed and deepened his work observe correctly that people in many cultures do not do much market trading, that means for an anthropologist that these people's "economy" is not a matter independently studiable at all but something "embedded" in the larger society. For an economist, however, it means that extra factors ordinarily ignored may have to be taken into account for a proper description of the economy, but it by no means invalidates the proposition that the economist's presumptions can describe such a society, as well as any other, with reasonable accuracy.

This, at least, is the difference as experienced by most scholars in the course of their work, the sense in which what the economist is doing is fundamentally different from what the historian is doing. In another sense, both economics and history are moral and prescriptive disciplines. The economist who states that the universal pursuit of self-interest will result in the broadest benefit for the people as a whole obviously takes a stand on what kind of policies should be followed. No less does Lord Acton's observation about absolute power contain a prescriptive warning to all who have any say in defining the powers of a ruler. Polanyi's objections to disembedded economics were undoubtedly morally based, claiming that the pursuit of purely economic goals to the exclusion of others had led to a society with serious moral failings. His critics, whether left, right, or center, have had to address these moral issues. James M. Buchanan and Geoffrey Brennan go so far as to claim that the entire construction of *homo economicus* was originally conceived and is more appropriate for comparing the performance of various possible systems than for making predictions about actual behavior. Even by their claim, it is not the inherent plausibility of *homo economicus* that validates his place in their science.

The distinction I am making also explains why the invention of coinage is, as I argue in this book, an event of capital importance to history, while it is a matter of little interest to economists.[7] In fact, economic historians often ignore the ancient world almost totally. In the earlier part of the twentieth century, Herbert Heaton granted the Greco-Roman world 33 pages out of 770, while Melvin M. Knight, Harry Elmer Barnes, and Felix Flügel splurged 56 pages out of 795. By midcentury, Shepard Bancroft Clough and Charles Woolsey Cole began with the year 600, S. Pollard and C. Holmes with 1750. William I. Davisson and James E. Harper bucked the trend, beginning with a volume on the ancient world, but no other volume was ever published. In the same year, Carlo M. Cipolla's planned six-volume *Fontana Economic History* (in the end, nine volumes were published) began with the words, "Our story begins in the impoverished Europe of the eighth and ninth centuries." Rondo Cameron, speeding "from Paleolithic times to the present," allowed classical antiquity only 11 pages, and John Chown's *History of Money* began with the year 800.

This lack of interest in ancient economy is not simply a matter of style. The particularity of ancient culture, the shortage of specifically "economic" sources of information, and the absence of statistics of any kind whatsoever make the ancient world an uncongenial territory for the economist to demonstrate the principles of economics and their consequences. To the historian, it is precisely in places like the ancient world that we can see whether and to what extent the "laws" of the economist really reflect basic and universal truths about the human condition. Economists, by the nature of their science, are trained to ignore these distinctions. For them, the behavior of the Phoenician trader, who used uncoined silver, is virtually indistinguishable from the behavior of the Greek, who used coins; indeed, the entire distinction between primitive, special-purpose money and modern, all-purpose money is one of degree, not of essence.

It has even been argued, from an economist's point of view, that there is no difference at all. Jacques Melitz, in a brilliant article that has had little influence but has gone unanswered, pointed out that moderns, too, use various items for various purposes. Nobody pays for an ice-cream cone with a credit

---

7. Cf. the words of Pryor quoted on p. 8.

card or an automobile with coins; if one were to try, in fact, the seller would refuse them. It is true that we measure all these items in the notional units of dollars and cents, but there is no theoretical reason why we cannot equally well describe every item of interest to the natives of the Admiralty Islands in terms of dogs' teeth.

On the face of it, Melitz's observations are perfectly correct, yet every anthropologist who has dealt with primitive money has realized that the people with whom we are concerned are not behaving toward their money in the way that we do. Behind the differing approaches to primitive money is the difference we have observed between the economist's viewpoint and the historian's. As an economist, Melitz ignores the question of how the members of the society see the matter. The entire purpose of economics is to abstract the transactions from their apparent context in order to see the rules operating behind them. To the historian, however, all forms of modern money look similar *because we who use them see them that way.* Whether we pay with a check, a credit card, a bill, or coins, we think of ourselves as transferring "money"—in fact, as transferring "a dollar." We do not think of passing a check, for example, as giving something worth a dollar; rather, we think of it as giving the dollar itself. For this reason, it appears to us that dollars are "all-purpose"; and although one could perhaps express every item in the Admiralty Islands in dogs' teeth, the Admiralty Islanders did not think of all things as being "dogs'-teeth equivalents", and so did not use them quite this way. The terms in which the members of the society think are of capital importance to historians, despite the fact that historians themselves think in their own terms and in those of their society. To an economist, if one's analysis is correct—that is, if it produces a description of the society's behavior that fits what we observe—then it is of no interest to know whether or not the society's members think in these terms. If they do not, that merely shows that they do not understand economics; but they still behave according to its laws, just as an apple falls to the ground without having to understand the law of universal gravity.

One historian described all of history in a way that approaches the way in which natural scientists describe their own subject—describing all the observed phenomena on the basis of a hidden structure, unperceived by the people affected but ruling their behavior nonetheless. Karl Marx claimed that all history was the history of the class struggle,[8] and wrote a voluminous

8. Marx, 13. Although Marx was careful to speak of "the history of all hitherto existing society," I believe it safe to assert that the century and a half since he wrote the words have not yet

work with meticulously defined and laboriously justified terms (*mode of production, class, surplus value*) to try to build up the theoretical framework in which all history could be so described. Whether he succeeded is a question fought to this day with a violence that has long since transcended the academic, but his followers were correct in saying that he alone was a "scientific" historian, in the sense that he saw all history as an epiphenomenon behind which a set of rules of which the actors are not necessarily aware is determining what happens.[9] De Ste. Croix restated Marx's hypotheses in a less absolute formula to make them more appropriate to historians, for whom the inherent plausibility of the explanation is all.[10] Had Marx's theories achieved an accuracy of prediction approaching that of physics or even that of economics, there would have been less need for such a restatement.

The nonscientific historian and the economist, with the anthropologist and the sociologist somewhere in the middle, are all pursuing legitimate lines of investigation with, one hopes, the best tools available to them. They are, however, not only dealing with different subject matter but looking at different aspects, with the hope of discovering a different sort of truth. Economists hope for a more or less simple description that will give us a reasonable approximation of the complex truth. Historians look for as complex and nuanced a description as they can attain, in the hope of coming closer to an understanding of what that complex truth actually was. Neither goal is fully attainable, and each can benefit from the other's insights, but we cannot expect one scholar to play the other's game. I admit that the central thesis of this book—that only with the invention of coinage did the concept of money as we understand it come about in the Western world—is not a true one in the sense that the economist uses: there were things that an economist can properly call money before the concept as such had been invented. It is not (or should not be) possible for a historian to ignore the insights into human behavior that have been developed by the science of economics. It will be helpful if economists, too, will pay occasional attention to the question of whether the hypotheses on which they build their larger views really succeed in describing the world as historians alone can see it.

---

succeeded in producing a situation in which Marx would have declared the class struggle ended. Friedrich Engels, in a note to this statement in the English edition of 1888, claimed that prehistory had known classless societies.

9. The late Solomon Asch, one of the founders of social psychology, was in the habit of telling his students that Marx was the founder of modern psychology in that he was the first to claim that people's true motivation was not the one of which they are aware.

10. De Ste. Croix, *Class Struggle,* 25–28, 40–42.

APPENDIX 2

Pre-Greek Coinage

ARCHAEOLOGY CAN OFTEN REVEAL to us the prehistory of an invention. We can find the hoes of people who had no plows, the bronze instruments of people who had no iron. Numismatists and archaeologists have occasionally—though perhaps less often than one might have expected—attempted to find the precursors of coinage.[1] Various items have even been touted as being true coins.

There is no technological reason why coins should not have been minted long before the seventh century B.C.E. The technology involved would have been well within the capabilities of goldsmiths and silversmiths a thousand years earlier and more. The discovery of such pre-Greek coinage would not detract at all from the importance of the later invention, any more than the now apparently well-established Norse settlement of North America[2] detracts from the revolutionary importance of Columbus's later discoveries.

Nevertheless, an examination of the various primitive items that have at one time or another been claimed to be coins fails to reveal any clear

---

1. See, in particular, Breglia, *Numismatica antica,* 173–93.
2. See Wahlgren, particularly 121–37, and more daringly Enterline. The redoubtable Thor Heyerdahl and Per Lillieström, in a new book in Norwegian which I have not seen entitled *Ingen Grenser,* claim that the Norse settlement was much larger than generally held and that knowledge of it reached Rome, but even they cannot claim that it brought about anything like the reorientation of European culture that followed Columbus's discoveries.

example, and it may be useful to clear the air of the various hypotheses, which by their very number can create the false impression that coinage was common in the eastern Mediterranean Basin long before the Lydians and the Greeks. First, however, it is necessary to define a coin: a coin is an object, usually but not necessarily of metal,[3] which circulates as a medium of trade, and whose value[4] is guaranteed by the stamp of the issuing authority. We may thus ignore without further discussion such items as spits, rings, and sealed bags of silver, which although they served many of the purposes that coins later served[5] were not by themselves coins at all. They belong to the history of "primitive money," those items of almost infinite variety that premonetary peoples used for various functions for which our more recent ancestors used coins.

● MESOPOTAMIAN "SEALED SILVER"

Old Babylonian cuneiform texts often refer to *kaspum kankum*, "sealed silver." It has been suggested[6] that the term referred to ingots of silver stamped with the seal of a temple or a merchant. This opinion is no longer taken seriously; although we might use the verb "to seal" for the act of stamping an impression on a piece of metal, the Akkadian verb used here apparently refers only to placing things "under seal" in a container to which the seal is affixed.[7] The process and reason has now been elucidated with the help of texts from Mari. When silver was to be reused, a certain amount was given to an assayer in advance. Whatever the assayer did not use was sealed

---

3. In fact we do not, in normal usage, call anything a coin that is not made of metal: by the intentionally broad definition I offer here, a dollar bill would also count as a "coin." Nevertheless, I prefer to leave the latitude as wide as possible, since from a conceptual point of view, the material of which the coin is made is irrelevant: if it could be demonstrated that a previous nation had used wooden nickels, we should not have begrudged them the distinction of coinage because of the baseness of their material.

4. I use the term "value" advisedly. Normally, it is the weight and fineness of the metal that is guaranteed, but were I to include that guarantee in the definition, I would thereby exclude coins that like our own, are merely fiduciary currency (see pp. 30–31).

5. Rings and bracelets were particularly appropriate for hoarding and, as such, remain popular among primitive peoples today; but they have no precisely fixed weight or fineness and often no fixed value. On their use in Egypt and Mesopotamia, see pp. 42, 45.

6. By Johns (253) as one of three alternatives.

7. See *CAD*, s.vv. "kanku," "kana-ku" (particularly meaning 3). Johns (253) objected "that such a small sum as one and two-thirds shekels would not be sealed up," and he suggested "that *kanku* means 'sealed for,' that is, acknowledged by the receipt." But the documents from Mari have now offered a reasonable explanation, according to which it was precisely small amounts that were sealed (see next note).

with the royal seal, obviating the need for weighing or assaying it again.[8] The "sealed silver," then, is ordinary silver sealed in a sack, not a coin.[9] Modern excavations have found evidence of such sacks and the bullae placed on them.[10] The biblical equivalent is *ṣeror keseph*,[11] silver bound in a cloth, examples of which have been found as well.[12]

◉ THE EGYPTIAN "PIECE"

Appearing among the Egyptian units of weight and value is a term usually transcribed as *š'ty* or something similar. It weighed one-twelfth of a *deben*,[13] and there has been little agreement among Egyptologists as to what it may have been. F. L. Griffith suggests a ring,[14] but Thomas Eric Peet preferred to restrict himself to the noncommittal translation "piece."[15] Jaroslav Černý went so far as to suggest that "the 'piece' was a flat, round piece of metal 1/12 *deben*, that is about 7.6 grammes, in weight, possibly with an inscription to indicate this weight or the name of the issuing authority. If so, the 'piece' was practically a coin."[16]

If it was a flat, round piece of metal of fixed weight with an inscription guaranteeing it, it was quite a coin indeed; but alas, no such item has been found in the sands of Egypt, despite the ubiquity of the term in the texts. Černý gave no argument at all for his belief that it had an inscription, and he offered only the slenderest of evidence for its shape.[17] More than that, the "piece" itself is not even mentioned as something that exists: its determinative is that of an abstract noun.[18] It is regularly used as an item of account, not a medium of trade: that is, not "pieces" but other items changed hands,

8. Joannès, 115–18, basing himself in particular on *ARMT* XIII, 6.

9. Silver (126–27) obfuscates this point, going so far as to say that (medieval Islamic!) sealed purses "in short . . . were large-denomination coins." This is surely to broaden the definition of a coin far beyond reason. If anything that might serve some purpose of a coin is a coin then a horse-drawn wagon is an automobile.

10. See Bjorkman, 8–10.

11. Gen. 42:35 and elsewhere; cf. p. 106, n. 67.

12. Stern, "Silver Hoard," 22; cf. Stern, *Dor*, 360–63, for a find dating from the end of the eleventh or beginning of the tenth century B.C.E.

13. Gardiner, "Four Papyri," 45–47; Černý, "Prices," 910–13.

14. Griffith, 315–16. Griffith, however, took the sign that he interpreted as a "ring" to be a *deben*.

15. Peet, "Unit of Value," 199.

16. Černý, "Prices," 912.

17. Its weight, on the other hand, he established beyond doubt.

18. Peet, "Unit of Value," 185–86.

bartered for each other and evaluated in terms of "pieces." If the "piece" were indeed as convenient an item as Černý took it to be, one would have expected it to have been used in trade in its own right; otherwise, why would it have been coined? The $š^ct y$, it would seem, was not an item at all but merely a unit of weight or value, and the same is true for its later synonym, the *snijw*.[19] The translation "piece," intended to be noncommittal, has misled various scholars for half a century.

◎ CAPPADOCIAN LEAD DISKS

Among the items found in the excavations of Kal'ah Sharkat, shortly before the First World War, were twelve small coin-shaped (and coin-sized) lead disks with similar, though not identical, ornamentation on one side. Their date is uncertain, though presumably many centuries earlier than the earliest known coins.[20] Sidney Smith, in a short article, suggested that they were intended as money;[21] the editors themselves expressed doubts, and other scholars, too, have doubted that such small bits of lead could have had much monetary value.[22] The items vary irregularly in weight and do not seem to have been made with any attention to weight. They seem much more like ornaments than like coins, and Smith's argument that one would not make lead ornaments in a land where gold and silver could be gotten by trade seems to require us to suppose that all Cappadocians were wealthy. Smith himself seems to have later reversed his belief that lead served as money in Cappadocia,[23] and no new discoveries have suggested that these lead disks circulated from place to place. Nothing suggests that they are coins except their size and shape and the fact that they are made of metal, though apparently the wrong metal. How little size and shape mean has become more obvious since the discovery of the Tel Dor silver hoard, which is composed very largely of flat disks of silver but dates from half a

---

19. For the *snijw*, see Janssen, 102–8, particularly 105, from which my argument is largely taken.

20. Sidney Smith ("Pre-Greek Coinage," 180) said that they "seem to belong to about 1400–1200, but this is a purely *a priori* conjecture; the account of the excavators must be awaited before such matters can be definitely settled." I do not know where, if anywhere, the account of the excavators was published.

21. "Pre-Greek Coinage," 180.

22. Lipiński, "Les temples," 565.

23. In *Early History* (160), Smith wrote, "Lead was a common article of merchandise, but does not seem to have been used as money," contradicting his earlier statement ("Pre-Greek Coinage," 178–79) that "in [Assyria and Cappadocia] . . . lead was, in fact, the commonest currency." Einzig (210) cites the latter source as well as the first article, apparently without noticing the contradiction.

millennium before the appearance of coinage, and other finds of *Hacksilber* do not continue the tradition.[24]

◉ MINOAN METAL DUMPS

In the course of his excavations at Knossos in 1901, Sir Arthur Evans found "a small 'blob' of silver" that he at first took to be an archaic coin. Since the item was apparently not a coin but simply a "dump"[25] of silver and since nothing as late as the archaic period was found at that level, he decided that he had a genuine Minoan artifact. He compared it with three gold nuggets found on Cyprus and concluded, "in these metal dumps we may venture to see the immediate antecedent stage to coined money." He admitted that four centuries intervened between these dumps and any known coinage, but he concluded: "it may not seem too hazardous a prediction that this gap will eventually be bridged over. There is no more certain truth in archaeological, as in other research, than that a clue once found leads to fresh discoveries."[26]

Almost a century has passed since Evans made his prediction on the basis of that "certain truth," but no more such discoveries have been forthcoming. The four drops of precious metal are themselves hardly similar: one is silver, three are gold,[27] and they are not commensurable by weight.[28] There is not the slightest supporting evidence to suggest that they were made for purposes of trade or exchange. They remain what they apparently were, a few drops of metal, perhaps of measured weight. They may have been part of a silversmith's store, or anyone else's; but there is no reason to consider them coins.

◉ ARGIVE BRONZE PINS

In the excavation of the Heraeum at Argos, Charles Waldstein found "innumerable objects in metal, especially bronze, among which a certain simple

24. Stern, "Silver Hoard," 24–25.
25. For this term, see p. 93.
26. Evans, particularly 363–67.
27. So, at least, I conclude from Evans's reference to "the gold" (365) with an apparent reference to all three of the Cypriot items; he does not, however, state explicitly of what metal the largest of the items was made. Evans's "gold" is electrum to Robinson ("Ephesian Artemision," 164). I have not seen the dumps.
28. Their weights are 3.654 grams for the silver dump and 8.601, 4.723, and 4.678 for the gold ones. Evans considered the first a quarter of a Phoenician shekel; the second, a Babylonian light shekel; and the last two, half an Egyptian *kedet* (not the same as the *kidet/kite* mentioned on p. 36, n. 12) apiece. Any one of these is possible, but they hardly provide evidence for any coherent system of coinage or even of weight for precious metals.

kind of bronze pin, developed out of the ordinary nail shape into more ornamental and elaborate forms, constantly recurred in all the earlier layers . . . . Besides these we were continually coming upon pieces of thinner or thicker bronze wire or rods, which in many cases had knobs at intervals, as if to be used for handles. The thought at once came to us that these were spits. In the same way we came upon iron rods in other layers, and pieces of wire twisted into decorative shapes (for instance, the *Pretzel* shape) . . . I felt convinced that not only these but also the innumerable bronze rings of various sizes and thicknesses—though they may have had some ritual meaning as offerings to Hera from affianced couples—were dedicated and preserved here as objects of metallic value,—and that in the daily life of the people these were used in lieu of ordinary coin."[29] Here again, an archaeologist's imagination is the only testimony we have. If bronze pins were coins at Argos, no evidence has been forthcoming that they were coins anywhere else or that bronze was ever used for money in the archaic age. It is more likely, particularly in view of the decorations, that the pins were indeed jewelry dedicated to the goddess. Svoronos[30] rejected Waldstein's suggestion, and later scholars have not repeated it.

⊚ BIBLICAL REFERENCES

One hundred *q'siṭah* was the price for which Jacob bought the field near Shechem where Joseph was eventually buried.[31] In the happy ending to the Book of Job, Job's friends gave him a *q'siṭah* apiece.[32] Morris Silver sees in this "a mysterious monetary unit,"[33] and there is some evidence that the term *q'siṭah* was later the name of a coin,[34] but other ancient sources, including the Septuagint, interpret the word *q'siṭah* as a ewe.[35] There is certainly nothing in any other Near Eastern literature to suggest that a coin of such a name existed at the time of the patriarchs. The shekel, too, was later a coin,[36] but Abraham did not count his four hundred shekels out to Ephron the Hittite; he weighed

29. Waldstein 1:61.

30. Svoronos, 201.

31. Gen. 33:19; Josh. 24:32.

32. Job 42:11.

33. Silver, 127.

34. Babylonian Talmud, *Rosh Hashanah* 26a.

35. Similarly the translation of Onkelos; cf. the commentaries of Ibn Ezra and R. David Kimchi to Gen. 33:19.

36. Mishnah, *Ma'aser Sheni* 2:9 and elsewhere; cf. 1:2. Among the coins of the Great Revolt of 67–70 C.E. are some with the legend "Shekel of Israel," for which see Meshorer, 2:99–105.

them,[37] and the text does not say that his shekels were preweighed, preassayed, or stamped by anyone at all. In numerous cases in the Bible, shekels are weighed, and the standard used is often specified; in no case are they counted.[38] Archaeology has produced stamped seals and weights from the period of the Israelite monarchy, but the first coins from the land of Israel date from the second temple period, after coins had been current in Greece for generations.[39]

○ SIMILES IN UGARIT AND ASSYRIA

At the beginning of an epic discovered in Ugarit, the king *Krt* has lost his entire family; "He enters his chambers, he weeps while uttering words, sheds tears. His tears are poured like shekels earthward, like pieces-of-five on the bed."[40] In another epic, messengers come to tell the hero Dan'el of the death of his son, "and their tears cascade like quarter-sheqel (pieces), they cla[sp the(ir) lips] with the hand."[41] The similes do indeed indicate that weights of a quarter-shekel or of five shekels were known to the author, a presumption for which we have ample archaeological justification.[42] There is no reason, except our own imagination, to believe that the items weighing quarter-shekels or five shekels were coins.[43]

---

37. Gen. 23:16. Silver (127–28) argues that "seen in [an] evolutionary perspective, the term 'weighed' may have come to mean 'paid,'" surely a roundabout way of understanding a text that says "weighed." In fact, his argument, based on parallels that can only be described as fanciful, misses the fact that the verb *šql* does indeed mean "pay" in the Mishnah (*Sheqalim* 1:7 and passim); but it only means a particular kind of payment—the payment of the half-shekel tax for the public sacrifices—and its use there is obviously a back-formation from the word "shekel" as the name of the coin paid. No occurrence of the verb in biblical Hebrew suggests such a use. In Aramaic, the verb *šql* means "to take," precisely the opposite of what Abraham did with his silver.

38. "After the shekel of the sanctuary" (Exod. 30:13 and passim); "six hundred shekels of gold by weight" (1 Chron. 21:25). In the time of Nebuchadnezzar, very close to the first appearance of coins in Lydia, Jeremiah still weighed the silver with which he bought his cousin Hanamel's field (Jer. 32:9). That "shekel" was the name not of the silver weighed but of the weight put on the other side of the scale appears from 1 Sam. 14:26, where we are informed that Absalom's hair weighed two hundred shekels "after the king's weight": the Hebrew term is *b'eben hamelekh*, "with the king's stone."

39. See p. 106, n. 67.

40. Gordon, p. 68, lines 26–30, translating what is now *KTU* 1.14 I, 26–30.

41. *KTU* 1.19 II, 33–35. The translation is that of Margalit, p. 160.

42. There is no linguistic way to determine whether the "fournesses of shekels" and "five-nesses of shekels" are fractions (quarters and fifths) or multiples (four-shekel and five-shekel pieces), but the archaeological and inscriptional parallels put it beyond doubt that the common five-shekel and quarter-shekel pieces are meant.

43. Imagination, nevertheless, without which archaeology would be the driest of sciences, draws us on unwilling: "The fact that two denominations are mentioned in separate passages

Similarly, an inscription of Sennacherib boasts that he made large images of cast bronze. One respected source translates his words thus: "Upon an inspiration from the god, I built clay molds, poured bronze into each, and made their figures as perfect as in casting half-shekel pieces." The translation is open to doubt; in particular, the Akkadian text does not mention, as the translation might suggest, *figures* on half-shekel pieces.[44] The straightforward meaning of this passage is that Sennacherib (or the coppersmiths for whose work he is taking the credit) had the clever idea of using clay molds for casting colossal figures as they were commonly used for casting small half-shekel items. What half-shekel items he may have had in mind, whether rings, weights, coils or coins, he does not say. Since nothing like a coin has been found in excavations dating to this period or any period near it, a coin would seem to be the least likely candidate. Nevertheless, the feeling of moderns that half-shekel metal items are likely to be coins has brought some scholars to suspect[45] or even to assert flatly that "we learn through a casually used simile of the casting of small copper coins." Even the last-mentioned author, however, admits immediately that "we know nothing of their use from legal and administrative texts of the period."[46] The most recent translator of this passage has no doubt that the "half-shekel pieces" are a mistranslation and that the coins are a scholarly mirage.[47]

---

certainly implies a recognizably different size or shape, and in fact, sounds like actual money," says Balmuth ("Monetary Forerunners"). It does indeed sound like actual money *to us,* because that is the most common form we have of weighed pieces of "recognizably different size or shape," particularly if called by the name "shekel," which to us is the name of a coin. In Ugarit, there undoubtedly were such metal pieces that were not coins, and we need not invent coins and plant them in Ugarit to excuse the authors' similes.

44. The translation given in the text is that of *CAD,* s.v. "ze'pu" (2). L. W. King's editio princeps had translated, "I fashioned moulds of clay and poured bronze therein, as in casting half-shekel pieces, and I completed their construction" (*CT* XXVI, pp. 25–26); Luckenbill's text is similar. Sennacherib or whoever is speaking in his name surely compares the casting of his images to the casting of half-shekel pieces, but whether he is comparing the ease with which they were made, the perfection of their execution, or simply the process of casting, is in the mind of the reader.

45. Sidney Smith, "Pre-Greek Coinage," 177–78, followed by others.

46. Oppenheim, *Ancient Mesopotamia,* 87. Oppenheim himself realizes and warns his reader that "nearly every sentence in [his] book glosses over some essential and ultimately insoluble problem" (2).

47. Dalley, 104, 106 n. 20. Nemet-Nejat (268) says, on the basis of this inscription, that "small copper 'coins' were already in use in Mesopotamia at this time," then, in the next sentence, says that these same words—but the text does not seem to realize that they are the same words—do not refer to coins. This is apparently an editorial slip and the first sentence should have been deleted. Radner (127 n. 2) expresses uncertainty, which she has not persuaded me to share.

Fig. 11. A replica of an "oxhide" copper ingot, with the rough side showing. (Courtesy of the Kadman Numismatics Pavilion, Eretz Israel Museum, Tel Aviv.)

⊚ "OXHIDE" INGOTS OF COPPER

Perhaps the most intriguing candidate for an early coin was the "Cypriot"[48] copper ingot. These ingots are quite ponderous, usually weighing between fifteen and thirty-five kilograms. They are widely distributed through the Mediterranean and have been found from Sardinia to the Levant.[49] Their shape is approximately rectangular, with handles protruding at the corners; they often have a mark on one or both sides. One side is smooth with a raised rim, the other rough (fig. 11). Their shape, not one we associate with copper items, led Charles Seltman to the most elaborate and enticing of explanations.

The various peoples who made these heavy pieces of copper currency never lost sight of the fact that they represented the value of an ox or cow, for the ingots were cast in the shape of ox-hides, hides from which head and tail had been cut away; one side of the ingot mimicked

48. The actual source of these ingots, if they did all come from a single source, is disputed: see Buchholz, 1 n. 1; cf. Bass, "Evidence of Trade," 71.

49. For their geographical distribution, see the catalog in Bass, *Cape Gelidonya,* 53–62.

the rough hairy cow-hide, the other side resembled the raw inside with its edges curling inwards.

During the Late bronze age, then . . . the cow or ox was the principal unit of account, in exchange for which might normally be given . . . a large ox-hide-shaped ingot of copper. [This], however, varied greatly in weight for the simple reason that copper was [not] easy to ship from place to place . . . Consequently in the great "copper-island," Cyprus, where the metal was common, it was needful to pay, as the price of an ox, a far heavier mass of copper than one would pay in Mycenae where, as compared with Cyprus, the copper was scarce . . .[50]

Seltman's suggestion was not only ingenious but so well explained the details of the ingots' shape (and their wide geographical distribution) that it commanded wide respect.[51] For some, the monetary function of the ingots was beyond doubt.[52] We can only be humbled to realize, however, that Seltman's brilliant explanation is certainly false. Many more ingots than were known to Seltman have shown that the weight of the ingots varies much more than can be explained by geography and that a much simpler explanation is appropriate. The handles, which are not present on the oldest ingots, seem to have been nothing but handles, useful for carrying as all handles are. The smooth surface is the surface that touched the sand mold in which the ingot was made; its rim is but the deep outline around the sand mold in which it was cast. The rough surface is not an imitation of ox hair but merely the top of the ingot, roughened by the dross and bubbles that rose to the top as the metal cooled in the open air. The ingots were not coins or even a form of money—except insofar as copper itself could always be used as a trade medium.[53] They were merely ingots, spread throughout the Mediterranean Basin to the various cultures that used or wanted copper.[54]

---

50. Seltman, *Greek Coins*, 7–8, summarizing views already set forth in *Athens,* 1–5.

51. Quiggin, 272; Einzig, 220. Both authors recognized, however, that Seltman's hypothesis might simply be a matter of modern imagination. The earlier suggestion of Déchelette (2:1, 399–400, 406), who saw in the shape of the ingots a double ax, was less felicitous.

52. Breglia ("I precedenti," 10) "No doubts exist concerning the monetary function exercised by copper ingots."

53. On which possibility Muhly ("Copper Ox-hide Ingots") concludes with a *non liquet.*

54. The definitive explanation of the ingots was given by Buchholz (2–4) and Bass ("Cape Gelidonya Wreck," 271–73). Cf. Catling, 266–67; Bass, *Cape Gelidonya,* 69–71; Bass, "Evidence of Trade," 71.

● COINS OF INDIA

The Vedic literature, though its date is very uncertain, is undoubtedly of hoary antiquity, including a good deal of material composed many centuries before any Greek ever minted a coin. The presence in this literature of terms that would later be used for money led some to believe that coinage had existed in India as early as the third millennium B.C.E.; others pushed coinage back as far as the Indus Valley civilization that preceded the coming of the Aryans.[55] There is, however, no archaeological support for the first theory, and the second is based on very little; nor is it likely that India was so isolated or so devoid of influence on others that this invention, which was later seized upon by the entire world, went unnoticed and little used for some thousand years or more. Much more likely is the more recent opinion that the words of the Vedas referred not to coin denominations but to unmarked bits of gold.[56]

At the other end of the chronological spectrum, the opinion once held that coinage was introduced to India by the Hellenistic Greeks is no longer tenable, particularly since the discovery at Taxila of a hoard of more than a thousand Indian punch-marked coins, most of them very worn, along with two coins of Alexander the Great and one of Philip Arrhidaeus in almost mint condition.[57] There is little reason today to doubt that coinage began in India when it first seems to appear in the archaeological record, about the sixth or fifth century B.C.E.[58] Claims that these coins must have been invented centuries earlier have no basis in the evidence.[59]

The coins of India, then, were probably introduced somewhat later than

---

55. Bhandarkar, 70–75; Kosambi, "Origin and Development." On the Indus Valley culture, see Kosambi, *Culture and Civilisation*, chap. 3.

56. Altekar, 13–19.

57. Walsh, 1–2.

58. Mitchiner, 5–6, 20; Dhavalikar, 335; Sinha and Sharma, 33; Gupta and Hardaker, 1, 11.

59. Altekar (25–26) held "that silver and copper currency in several denominations was quite well established in India in 600 B.C. Its introduction may be placed at least about a couple of centuries earlier, i.e. in *c*. 800 B.C." There are so many counterexamples to the easy presumption that something "quite well established" at one date must have been introduced "at least . . . a couple of centuries earlier" that I leave it to the reader to choose a favorite example. Still further went Prakash and Singh (325), who argued that Pāṇini knew coined money because he uses a word meaning "struck"; that based on the fact that Pāṇini has been assigned to the middle of the sixth century B.C.E. and that some put him earlier, "we can accept without the least hesitation" that coin making must be earlier than 700 B.C.E.; and that on the assumption that the Brāhmaṇa period probably began not later than 800 B.C., "it can safely be asserted that coinage in India was evolved at about 800 B.C. and if we fix the approximate date at 1000 B.C. . . . the margin of error would be very small." The parti pris of such arguments needs no comment.

Fig. 12. An Indian silver punch-marked coin. (The American Numismatic Society, New York.)

those of Asia Minor. That these coins are generally silver, a metal considered impure and inauspicious, also points to a foreign origin.[60] Their particular form, however—short bent silver bars or disks with a punch mark on one side (fig. 12)—bears only a slight resemblance to the earliest Western coins,[61] and their widespread use stands in striking contrast to the limited use of coinage in the Achaemenid empire. Whether or not the original idea may have owed something to an acquaintance with what was happening in the West, the development and spread of coinage was obviously a phenomenon that took place in India itself, much as the development of coinage took place in Greece after its origin in Lydia.

Silver bars of no apparent use for adornment have been found in Iran and in Afghanistan,[62] and although there is no evidence that they circulated as currency, they probably were meant as treasure and would have been available for cutting into convenient sizes or weights. It may be that the silver-bar coins represent a development of these ingots and that the round punch-marked coins represent a further development from the practice of cutting off a part of the bar to make a weight.[63] If this is so, the coins of India followed

---

60. Altekar, 17; Dhavalikar, 332–33.

61. Gupta and Hardaker provide numerous clear photographs and a pellucid and scholarly introduction to the subject. For another illustration, see Allchin and Allchin, 325.

62. Bivar, 97–101. He calls them currency, but he offers no evidence to suggest that they were intended to circulate.

63. The first suggestion is that of Bivar (101); the second is its further development by Dhavalikar (335–36). Dhavalikar considers Near Eastern *Hacksilber* to be derived from Bivar's

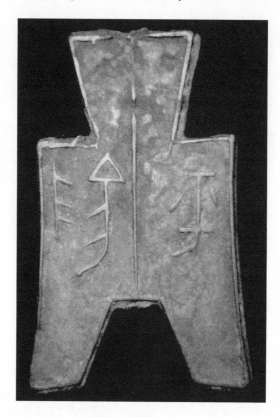

Fig. 13. A Chinese spade coin. (The American Numismatic Society, New York.)

their own path from the earliest stage of development. In any case, the question belongs to Indian history. With the conquest of Alexander, Indian numismatics joins what is thereafter the mainstream of the history of coinage.

◉ CHINESE COINS

As in so many other areas of culture and technology, Chinese coinage gives at first glance the impression of having developed independently, with no visible connection to what was happening in the West. The earliest Chinese coins are made of cast bronze. They are small items shaped in some places like spades (fig. 13) and in others like knives or simply disks with a square

"ingot-currency," while Indian "bent-bar" coins are an independent development in a different direction. But *Hacksilber* is a phenomenon much older than this, and ingots, disks, rings, coils, and sheets were all used, at different times and places, as convenient forms for storage of silver that might be either hoarded or cut and traded.

hole in the middle—the last being the form that was eventually adopted for all of China by the first historical emperor, Qin Shi Huang Di, at the end of the third century B.C.E. They bear no particular resemblance to the silver disks that circulated throughout the Greek world, and it is not necessary to believe that either people derived from the other the idea of coinage. The question of precedence alone, though it may flatter one nation or the other, is of no historical interest; I have dealt with it in a separate article.[64] At any rate, modern research does not place the earliest coinage before the sixth century B.C.E. or later, and although some have understood literary references to refer to other coins that had circulated previously, archaeology has found no identifiable trace of these "prehistoric" denominations.[65] As far as current research goes, it would seem that, like the rest of the world, China did not yet know true coinage when the Greeks began using theirs.

It appears that none of the repeated suggestions of pre-Greek coinage has any real plausibility. Some would suggest that the very number of suggested "coins" may itself be an indication that such things did exist,[66] but even many times zero is still zero, and the verisimilitude of the preceding suggestions is not much above zero. That the suggestions keep recurring is, however, not accidental. A scholar who looks at these items or who reads the texts describing them cannot help being reminded of coinage. Each of them does indeed resemble coinage in some way, either by its use or by its form, but the simile, though not false, is in the scholar's mind. As far as we can tell, none of the people who used these items would have thought of them as we think of coins. That idea had not yet come into being.

---

64. Schaps, "The Invention of Coinage in Lydia, in India, and in China."

65. Li Xueqin, 371–98. The most thoroughgoing treatment of Chinese money is that of Peng Xinwei; see particularly pp. 41–42, where Peng compares the development of coinage in China and in Greece. I cannot resist quoting his observation that "in terms of the images they bear, the two have remained different over the long run, and this symbolizes the differences between the two cultures. Chinese culture emphasizes abstract concepts, like good and evil, and so its coins employ many auspicious characters. European culture emphasizes concrete phenomena, like beauty and ugliness, and so its coins emphasize images" (42).

66. This seems to be the basis on which Silver (126–29) assembles most of the above examples and a few even less probable ones as "evidence for coinage."

Prices in Solon's Day

IN HIS REVIEW OF SOLON'S LEGISLATION, Plutarch found the fines for rape and procuring to be inconsistent with the law of adultery. The matter led him into some interesting speculation on prices in Solon's day.

But in general, Solon's laws about women seem to be extremely strange. On the one hand, he allows a person who apprehends an adulterer to do away with him; but if, on the other hand, a person abducts and rapes a free woman, he fixed a fine of a hundred drachmas, and if he should put her out for prostitution,[1] twenty drachmas, except for those who are sold explicitly (by which expression he meant prostitutes, since they go openly to those who pay) . . . But to punish the same offense sharply and implacably in one case, gently and playfully in another, defining the payment of a trifling fine, is unreasonable, unless coins were rare in the city at that time, so that the difficulty of providing them made monetary fines great. In the valuations of the sacrifices, a sheep and a drachma are counted as equivalent to a

---

1. In the Loeb Plutarch, Bernadotte Perrin renders "and if he gained his end by persuasion," as if this clause were describing the punishment of a seducer. But I can find no parallel for such a use of the verb προαγωγεύω. It must be admitted, however, that Aeschines (1.14, 184) claims that the law on procuring included "the greatest penalties," including death. Cf. Manfredini and Piccirilli, pp. 243–44.

medimnus;[2] and he fixed a hundred drachmas for an Isthmian victor, five hundred for an Olympic victor. He gave five drachmas to anyone who brought in a wolf and one for a wolf's cub. Demetrius of Phaleron says that the one was the price of an ox, and other the price of a sheep. Although the prices that he defines in the sixteenth *axon*[3] for choice victims are many times more than that, as is reasonable, nevertheless even those are cheap compared to today's prices.[4]

As others have noticed, Plutarch seems to have misunderstood the law on adultery. The law that "allows a person who apprehends an adulterer to do away with him" is not a law punishing the adulterer but a law exempting crimes of passion from punishment: the man who found someone else in bed with his wife and killed him on the spot was not to be punished as a murderer.[5] In point of fact, the adulterer, if brought before a court of law, was punished not with death but with a public humiliation that stopped short of bloodshed: the terms of the law were that "in the presence of the court, without a dagger, he [the offended party] could treat him in any way he wanted."[6] This was the law that should have been compared to the fines placed on the rapist and the procurer.[7] One might therefore argue that Solon was consistent, if repugnant to our own sensibilities, in treating sexual offenses against women lightly. There might, however, be a certain anachronism in that formulation, for scholars have often held that the laws as we have them seem to treat crimes of this sort as offenses not against the woman but against her husband or the male head of her household;[8] more significantly, the penalty of twenty drachmas would have been so insignificant in the classical period as to have

---

2. A measure of grain holding about forty-one liters (Viedebantt in *RE* XV, cols. 86–87, s.v. Μέδιμνος), though it varied greatly with time and place.

3. The *axones* were revolving pillars on which Solon's laws were inscribed.

4. Plut. *Solon* 23.1–3.

5. So, correctly, David Cohen (104–5) and Todd (276–77). Douglas MacDowell (124) still gave Lysias's interpretation (below, n. 6), as did most of his predecessors.

6. [Dem.] 59.66. For a famous, if imaginary, example, see Aristophanes *Clouds* 1083.

7. The misunderstanding is not original with Plutarch; it seems to have begun with a sophistry of Lysias (Lysias 1.32–33, where the law is paraphrased), who used it to claim that the law considered seduction worse than rape. Lysias's claim was repeated afterward by scholars, and perhaps by advocates when convenient.

8. The common view was that it made no difference whether the head of the household (the *kyrios*) was a husband, father, or other close relative, but see now David Cohen, 99–109. The major reason for denying that the woman was also seen as a victim was the phraseology of the law, but as Cohen has shown, the phraseology concerns itself with the *kyrios* because it is a law dealing with his behavior (retaliatory murder) rather than with the crime that precipitated it.

been utterly meaningless as a deterrent or a recompense. What surprised Plutarch, even after we have corrected his misapprehension, should still surprise us.

His answer—that coinage was scarce and so worth more—seems to be required and must be more or less the correct answer, though for the time of Solon, we must more likely speak of utensils or of weighed silver, not of coinage. Nevertheless, the facts that Plutarch adduces to prove his point are very odd. Let us take them one by one.

1. "In the valuations of the sacrifices, a sheep and a drachma are counted as equivalent to a *medimnus* . . ." That is what the Greek says, although translators insist on reading it as if it said that "a sheep and a *medimnus* are both reckoned as the equivalent of a drachma," the only reading that seems to make sense. Nobody, however, has suggested a plausible emendation of the Greek to make it mean that. It appears that Plutarch meant it to mean that, for he later brings the testimony of Demetrius of Phaleron that a sheep was indeed worth a drachma. Why did he phrase it this way?

The problem seems to arise because of our presumption (which was probably Plutarch's as well) that the proper standard of value is money, so that one should have reckoned other things (a sheep and a *medimnus*) ἀντὶ δραχμῆς ("as the equivalent of a drachma"), rather than estimating the value of a sheep and a drachma in terms of *medimni*. I think it probable, indeed, that Solon thought in the same terms: coins had already been invented, though Athens did not yet mint them; utensil money had preceded them, and Plutarch himself goes on to say that Solon, in the sixteenth *axon*, fixed prices (presumably, if Plutarch understood them, money prices) for choice sacrifices. If so, the "equivalence" will not have been a statement that a sheep and a drachma cost a *medimnus,* and the τιμήματα will have been not "valuations" but fines or penalties. The law will have provided that for this or that ritual offense, the offender should pay either a sheep or a *medimnus* of grain—in another case, perhaps, either a drachma or a *medimnus* of grain. Plutarch, if so, is observing correctly that the law is treating both a sheep and a drachma as equivalent to a *medimnus* of grain. But in a premarket society, an equivalence of value does not necessarily mean that you can get the one item by giving its "equivalent." In the days before Solon, when ideas of proper sacrifices were being formed, a drachma (perhaps of silver, perhaps a handful of iron spits) may well have been considered a reasonable thing for a person who had no land to offer in place of a *medimnus* of grain; a sheep may have seemed a reasonable offering from a herder. Since most Athenians were farmers, the "standard" offering would still be the *medimnus,* and the others were considered "equivalent" to it. It is not accidental that Solon defined his property classes in terms of the number of *medimni* that a person's property could produce.⁹ There is a ritual equivalence here, but not a price in our sense. It is not likely that Plutarch recognized the difference.

2. "... he fixed a hundred drachmas for an Isthmian victor, five hundred for an Olympic victor." The verbs here are in the active singular and can only refer to Solon, but it was not the place of Solon or any Athenian to decide what the prizes would be in the Isthmian and Olympian Games. We are dealing here, then, not with the prize for the victor but with an additional prize that the Athenian polis gave to its own victorious sons. These sums would have been parsimonious in the time of Pericles, but they fit well with the time of Solon, when land that produced five hundred *medimni* of grain marked out a man as a member of the highest class and when—as Plutarch is trying to explain—a hundred drachmas was the fine for the rape of a free woman, presumably a serious offense.

3. "He gave five drachmas to anyone who brought in a wolf and one for a wolf's cub. Demetrius of Phaleron says that the one was the price of an ox, the other the price of a sheep." We have here one scholar building on the theory of another, a procedure fraught with possibilities for error. Solon's law, as Plutarch is reporting it, said nothing about oxen or sheep but offered bounties for wolves, which (as Plutarch goes on to explain) were major pests to the Athenians. Demetrius of Phaleron rationalized these bounties, apparently by taking them to be the price of the animals likely to have been attacked. This is not a likely rationalization. To have paid the value of an ox for the killing of a wolf would have been exceedingly liberal; it would have seemed to take for granted that each wolf was likely to kill at least one ox, a great compliment to the wolves, who in fact are not likely to attack an ox unaided.¹⁰ Demetrius's reconstruction must certainly be rejected, particularly in view of Plutarch's next observation.

4. "... the prices that he defines in the sixteenth *axon* ... are many times more than that ..." a fact that Plutarch explains away by saying that these prices were for choice animals. It is undisputable that choice animals may be worth three or four times what the worst of their breed may be, but the first observations also applied to sacrifices. The prices in the sixteenth *axon* were

---

9. [Arist.] *Ath. Pol.* 7.4. For the difficulty of this passage, which states that the class depended on the number of "both dry and wet measures," see Rhodes, ad loc.

10. This was already noted by Waters (186). Waters brings numerous cogent arguments against Plutarch's testimony about prices but does not offer a satisfactory explanation for them.

probably realistic prices for choice animals, and Plutarch's next claim is not surprising.

5. "... even those are cheap compared to today's prices," i.e., compared to the prices in the times of Plutarch, six centuries later. It is a shame, from our point of view, that Plutarch did not record the prices that were written on the sixteenth *axon*, but then, Plutarch was not writing my book.

At least one item offers us a glimpse at those prices. Julius Pollux, an antiquary of the Roman imperial period, believed the Athenians to have had a two-drachma coin that depicted an ox and was itself called an "ox." On the basis of archaeology and numismatics, it is quite unlikely that the Athenians ever issued such a coin. Pollux's evidence is mostly simply the archaic use of an ox as a standard of value.[11] One of his observations may, however, be more informative.

> And they say that in the Delian festival, whenever gifts are given to anyone, the herald announces that so-and-so many oxen will be given to him—and then for each ox two Attic drachmas are given.[12]

We may doubt that an ox was ever so cheap as to be worth only two drachmas, but it may be that somewhere along the way, a gift that was estimated in so many oxen's worth seems to have been transmuted into two drachmas per "ox." Alternatively, Pollux's own guess may have been correct that the "ox" involved was originally merely an archaic coin, replaced at some later date (presumably under the Athenian domination) by Attic currency.

It is quite possible that Plutarch is right to believe that prices in Solon's time were significantly lower than they were in the classical period. This observation, while paradoxical, is not inexplicable.[13] He was apparently wrong, however, in his famous figures of one drachma for a sheep and five for an ox. Those may once have been reasonable equivalences for ritual purposes, but it is not likely that they were ever prices.

---

11. See pp. 69–70.
12. Pollux *Onomasticon* 9.61.
13. See pp. 120–21.

APPENDIX 4

Unproductive Loans and Unproductive People

THE GREEKS, LIKE OURSELVES, sometimes lent money against real security, but Finley, studying the boundary stones that were set up to attest to the mortgages, noted that the Greeks seem hardly ever to have mortgaged property for the reasons that are most common today. Mortgages today normally finance either the purchase or the improvement of real property. In the first case, the buyer, unable or unwilling to supply the entire price at the time when possession is transferred, borrows money against the security of the property itself; in the second case, the owner wishes to build on or otherwise to improve the property and finances this by borrowing money against the property. For the first of these practices, Finley found only two examples; for the second, he found none at all.[1]

Why did the Athenians borrow money against land? Finley concluded, on the basis of cases known from the orators, that "as a general rule, the Athenian property owner borrowed sizable sums not to improve or increase his holdings or his 'business' interests but to pay taxes, fulfill liturgies, or meet a financial demand of equally unproductive character."[2] Finley took as fundamental the distinction between modern "productive" loans—in which the borrower borrows money in the hope of making a financial profit

---

1. Finley, *Land and Credit*, 81–83.
2. Ibid., 84.

greater than the interest that will have to be paid on the loan—and the "unproductive" loans that he took to be characteristic of precapitalist, primitive Athens—a distinction he continued to emphasize in his more mature work.[3] Bogaert made a similar observation about the credit extended by banks;[4] Finley's student Millett broadened the observation by describing an entire Athenian mentality in which credit was intimately tied up with reciprocity and gift giving, a kind of neighborly activity akin to the mutual help of villagers, extended to help people through difficult times, a kind of activity to which productive loans—the kind of credit on which modern business runs—were essentially foreign.[5]

Finley's original observation is undeniably true: the Athenians did not usually mortgage land for the same reasons we do. Millett's description has the further virtue of explaining a good number of the respects in which sources of credit at Athens differed from the institutions available to us. Yet the business loan, truly productive credit where one person borrows from another in order to make a profit, has not disappeared from Athenian history. However many loans for consumption Millett may have found—and the number is occasionally exaggerated[6]—there remain stubborn cases that can hardly be described as anything other than business loans, lent to people who can with some degree of justice be called entrepreneurs.[7] The bottomry loans that were extended to merchants to finance overseas trading expeditions were undoubtedly productive loans, and there are other clear cases as well. Everyone has recognized this fact, including, reluctant though they be, the most thoroughgoing primitivists.[8]

---

3. Finley, *Ancient Economy*, 141.

4. Bogaert, *Banques et banquiers*, 356–57.

5. Millett, *Lending and Borrowing*, 24–52, 59–71, 96–97.

6. Millett ("Maritime Loans," 43) claimed to have found only five such loans (later raised to eight: see n. 8 below) out of almost nine hundred; but in fact for the vast majority of loans known to us no purpose can be stated, whether productive or unproductive, as E. E. Cohen (*Ancient Economy*, 27–29) points out. Nor, for that matter, did Millett ever publish his list of almost nine hundred credit transactions—just as well, perhaps, for those who feel required to read every word of a book.

7. Wesley E. Thompson, "The Athenian Investor," "Athenian Banking," and "The Athenian Entrepreneur"; E. E. Cohen, *Athenian Economy*; Schaps, "[Demosthenes] 35."

8. Finley (*Land and Credit*, 84): "This is not to say that productive loans were absolutely unknown." Bogaert (*Banques et banquiers*, 356–57): "Commerce and industry applied to the banks to obtain funding." Millett (*Lending and Borrowing*, 267 n. 11) lists eight such transactions, excluding maritime loans. His rhetorical tendency to make these cases disappear may be glimpsed in his comment "Only exceptionally, *if ever*, did a borrower take out a loan with the intention of increasing his wealth" (59; emphasis mine). In fact, he has given in his own footnote cases of what he seems to doubt "ever" occurred, and although he calls them "possible examples," he does not

In fact, there is nothing terribly surprising about the presence of productive loans in ancient Athens. Borrowing and lending money was, as Millett demonstrates, extremely common in Athens,[9] and Athens had a flourishing commercial market and international trade. There is no doubt that there were in Athens people trying to make money, and given the ubiquity of credit, there is no reason why they should not have borrowed money, where necessary, to help them make money. We may have to look a bit to find who it was who would lend them the money, but we can be pretty certain that they themselves looked more thoroughly than we can and were sometimes successful. Whether the lenders thought in terms of "reciprocity" or in more businesslike terms, they will have expected in some way to get their own benefit out of the favor they were doing for the borrower—the greater the borrower's profit, the greater the benefit that should accrue to the lender. It follows, then, that the existence of profit-making undertakings and the easy availability of credit make the existence of productive loans a virtual certainty. As I have noted, all those who have written on the subject have admitted the presence of such loans, and there is no need for us to try to explain them away or to treat them as exceptions to some grander rule.

That said, we must immediately recognize that most Athenian citizens were not involved in profit-making enterprises. Peasant farmers, who probably were the majority of the population, were subsistence farmers, whose need for money was occasional and not "productive" in the banker's sense: a loan to a farmer might help to buy seed corn that would produce a harvest that would, in turn, pay off the loan and leave enough for the farmer to live on, but it was not usually designed to produce a capital gain. Owners of estates might live off the produce of land that was worked by others; they were more likely to need loans for occasional heavy expenses, such as liturgies or a dowry, than for profit-making enterprises. Even small retailers do not really need "productive" credit: their stall provides their livelihood but does not necessarily leave them with surplus capital, and the money they borrow helps them stay alive, rather than helping them to get rich. For that matter, a modern mortgage that allows a person to buy a home is not

---

offer any suggestion of how, for example, "[Dem.] XL.52 (loan from a banker to purchase a mining concession)" could be considered anything but a productive loan. Finley's later dismissal of bottomry loans as "an exception to be explained by the function of that type of loan as an insurance policy rather than as a form of credit" (*Ancient Economy*, 141), as if insurance policies were more to be expected of primitive societies than productive loans, has unfortunately had the effect in some quarters of sweeping these loans entirely under the carpet; but even in that very paragraph, Finley admits to exceptions.

9. Millett, "Maritime Loans," 42; *Lending and Borrowing*, 5–7.

productive either. If the existence of productive loans should not surprise the primitivist, the existence of nonproductive loans should not surprise the modernist.

The point which seems rarely to have been mentioned (although scholars are hardly unaware of it) is that different sorts of credit available apply to different classes of borrowers. Peasants on the one hand and nobles on the other were a priori never likely to have borrowed for "productive" purposes, because they were not likely to have been engaged in profit-making enterprises. In the middle, however, there were people who hoped to increase their capital by engaging in trade, of which the largest-scale and most visible was overseas trade. These people took out "productive" loans, of which the largest and most visible were maritime loans. Their vocabulary spoke of "start-up capital" (ἀφορμή)[10] and of "going into business" (ὅπως ἂν ἐνεργοὶ ὦσιν);[11] those who lent to them spoke of "putting one's money to work" (ἐργάσασθαι τῷ ἀργυρίῳ)[12] and of compound interest (τόκοι τόκων).[13] Most tellingly, it is clear that people who wanted to go into business could expect to find lenders and that people with money could be expected[14] to find profitable ways to invest it. There was, in short, a market for money, whose transactions were neither exceptional nor marginal.

We have no way of quantifying these transactions. Many loans are difficult to classify: for most, we do not know the details, and even when the details are known, the classification may be a matter of how the loan is perceived or how it is presented.[15] Even if the proportion of productive to unproductive loans in the sources could be reliably established, it would not necessarily correspond to their proportion in ancient Athens, since traders and artisans are notoriously underrepresented in our sources. Those who engaged in business were not, as they are today, at the pinnacle of political power or social prestige: Athens had no parading of guilds, no parliament sitting on sacks of wool, no chamber of commerce, no "business class" with special privileges, no *noblesse de la robe*. Profit making, at least overt profit

---

10. Lysias fr. 1 Thalheim, paragraph 2.

11. [Dem.] 35.7.

12. [Dem.] 46.30; cf. Dem. 27.10.

13. Aristophanes *Clouds* 1156.

14. Even by the law itself: the guardians of orphans, for example, had to deliver the orphans' estate to them with interest for the intervening years (Harrison, 1: 105–7), a rule that could only make sense if the guardian could be expected to find opportunities for profitable investment.

15. E. E. Cohen, *Athenian Economy*, 30–36, in particular, 35: "Even for present-day bankers, to whom data are generally available in smothering overabundance, determining the purpose of a loan presents substantial theoretical and practical conundra."

making, applied more to the middle class than to the upper class and, at a certain level, will have tended to disappear or at least to be downplayed. Cleon's father was a tanner, but Cleon was not. Pasio was a banker, but his sons rented the operation of the bank to others. The orators tell us more about bottomry loans, which involved big business and big sums, than about smaller productive loans: perhaps this means that there were not so many small productive loans, or perhaps it only means that smaller loans did not justify hiring the best speech writers in Athens.

In fact, the question is not of great significance. Productive loans occur, in the sources in contexts that make it clear that they were a regular form of credit available for those who wanted them; nonproductive loans also occur, and they do so in various forms appropriate to their purposes, both interest-bearing and interest-free. Which of them was more common could interest only a statistician, and a true statistician will see in a moment that the database is insufficient for statistical analysis.

Unproductive loans were taken out, as they are in our time, because of temporary emergencies: in Athens they might be taken to finance a liturgy, to ransom a captive, to pay for a dowry or a funeral, or to purchase an item for which the cash was not on hand. Some motivations were less honorable: to maintain a profligate whose patrimony had been used up or to bribe a politician.[16] Some of these are common in our time as well: modern banks lend money to car purchasers, an unproductive loan—and whereas they do not often in the West have to offer help for a young woman's dowry, they do offer loans for a young person's education. If modern borrowers do not borrow for precisely the same reasons as the Athenians, it is because our society makes different financial demands on us.

It is true, however, that large loans in Athens were, as far as we can tell, never designed to be paid off in drips and drabs out of one's regular income. The reason is not far to seek, for few people had a regular monetary income out of which a loan could be repaid. This explains why we never hear of mortgaging to finance the purchase of a house:[17] a person who could not pay for the house immediately was even less likely to be able to pay for it over a period of twenty years. Life expectancy, too, may have had a role to play here: a loan for twenty years is likely to have been a much riskier thing in

---

16. On the motivation for nonproductive borrowing, see Millett, *Lending and Borrowing*, 59–71. For borrowing to bribe a politician, see the allegations of Aeschines (3.104).

17. Although Finley himself (*Land and Credit*, 81) recognized and E. E. Cohen (*Athenian Economy*, 35) emphasized that the *horoi* themselves generally tell us nothing about the reason for the mortgage.

Athens than it is today. These factors and others as well[18] made the structure of credit in ancient Athens different from what it is today. They did not, however, prevent Athenians with ambitions from borrowing money for business ventures, nor did they prevent wealthier Athenians from lending them the money to do so.

---

18. See Millett, *Lending and Borrowing,* 71–74.

Bibliography

ALTHOUGH I HAVE TRIED to cite up-to-date editions, I have had to use the old or obscure editions that my library could offer for a few classic and often reprinted works. For books in other languages, I have preferred to cite an English translation where available.

Alföldi, Maria R-. *Antike Numismatik*. Mainz: von Zabern, 1978.

Allan, William. *The African Husbandman*. Edinburgh: Oliver and Boyd, 1965.

Allchin, Bridget, and Raymond Allchin. *The Rise of Civilization in India and Pakistan*. Cambridge: Cambridge University Press, 1982.

Alster, B. *The Instructions of Šuruppak*. Copenhagen: Akademisk Forlag, 1974.

Altekar, A. S. "Origin and Early History of Coinage in Ancient India." *Journal of the Numismatic Society of India* 15 (1953): 1–26.

Ameling, Walter. *Karthago*. Munich: Beck, 1993.

————. "Plutarch, *Perikles* 12–14." *Historia* 34 (1985): 47–63.

Anderson, B. L., and A. J. H. Latham, eds. *The Market in History*. London: Croom Helm, 1986.

Anderson, Greg. "Alkmeonid 'Homelands,' Political Exile, and the Unification of Attica." *Historia* 49 (2000), 387–412.

Andrae, Walter. *Die Kleinfunde von Sendschirli*. Vol. 5 of *Ausgrabungen in Sendschirli*, ed. Felix von Luschan. Mitteilungen aus den Orientalischen Sammlungen, vol. 15. Berlin: de Gruyter, 1943.

Andreau, Jean, Pierre Briant, and Raymond Descat. *Économie antique: Prix et formation des prix dans les économies antiques*. Saint-Bertrand-de-Comminges: Musée archéologique départemental, 1997.

Andrewes, A. "The Mytilene Debate: Thucydides 3.36–49." *Phoenix* 16 (1962): 64–85.
———. "The Opposition to Perikles." *JHS* 98 (1978): 1–8.
Andreyev, V. N. "Karl Marx on the Aims of Production in Antiquity and the Ancient Evidence for the Athenian Economy in the Fifth and Fourth Centuries B.C." (in Russian with English abstract). *Vestnik Drevnei Istorii* 165, no. 3 (1983): 3–31.
Austin, M. M., and Pierre Vidal-Naquet. *Economic and Social History of Ancient Greece.* London: Batsford, 1977.
Avi-Yonah, Michael, and Ephraim Stern. *Encyclopedia of Archaeological Excavations in the Holy Land.* Oxford: Clarendon Press, 1977.
Badian, Ernst. *Publicans and Sinners.* Oxford: Blackwell, 1972.
Baer, Klaus. "An Eleventh Dynasty Farmer's Letters to His Family." *Journal of the American Oriental Society* 83 (1963): 1–19.
Balmuth, Miriam S. "The Critical Moment: The Transition from Currency to Coinage in the Eastern Mediterranean." *World Archaeology* 6 (1974–75): 293–98.
———. "Jewellers' Hoards and the Development of Early Coinage." In Cahn and le Rider, 27–30.
———. "The Monetary Forerunners of Coinage in Phoenicia and Palestine." In Kindler, 25–32.
———. "Remarks on the Appearance of the Earliest Coins." In Mitten, Pedley, and Scott, 1–7.
———, ed. *Hacksilber to Coinage: New Insights into the Monetary History of the Near East and Greece.* Numismatic Studies 24. New York: American Numismatic Society, 2001.
Bammer, Anton. "Les sanctuaires des VIIIe et VIIe siècles à l'Artémision d'Éphèse." *Revue archéologique* 1991: 63–84.
———. "A *Peripteros* of the Geometric Period in the Artemisium of Ephesus." *Anatolian Studies* 40 (1990): 137–60.
Barber, Elizabeth Weyland. *Prehistoric Textiles.* Princeton: Princeton University Press, 1991.
———. *Women's Work: The First 20,000 Years.* New York: Norton, 1994.
Bar-Kochva, Bezalel. *The Seleucid Army.* Cambridge: Cambridge University Press, 1976.
Bass, George F. *Cape Gelidonya: A Bronze Age Shipwreck.* Transactions of the American Philosophical Society, n.s., vol. 57, part 8. Philadelphia: American Philosophical Society, 1967.
———. "The Cape Gelidonya Wreck: Preliminary Report." *AJA* 65 (1961): 267–76.
———. "Evidence of Trade from Bronze Age Shipwrecks." In *Bronze Age Trade in the Mediterranean*, ed. N. H. Gale, 69–82. Jonsered: Paul Åströms Förlag, 1991.
Bennett, Emmett L., ed. *Mycenaean Studies.* Madison: University of Wisconsin Press, 1964.
Bentham, Jeremy. *Defence of Usury.* London: T. Payne and Son, 1787. Reprint, London: Routledge; London: Thoemmes, 1992.
Benveniste, Émile. "Les valeurs économiques dans le vocabulaire indo-européen." In *Indo-European and Indo-Europeans*, ed. George Cardona, Henry M. Hoenigswald, and Alfred Senn, 307–20. Philadelphia: University of Pennsylvania Press, 1970.

Berdan, Frances F. "Trade and Markets in Precapitalist States." In *Economic Anthropology*, ed. Stuart Plattner, 78–107. Stanford: Stanford University Press, 1989.

Berthiaume, Guy. *Les rôles du mágeiros*. Leiden: Brill, 1982.

Betlyon, John Wilson. *The Coinage and Mints of Phoenicia: The Pre-Alexandrine Period*. Harvard Semitic Monographs, no. 26. Chico, Calif.: Scholars Press, 1980.

Bhandarkar, D. R. *Lectures on Ancient Indian Numismatics*. Calcutta: University of Calcutta, 1921.

Bierbrier, Morris. *The Tomb-Builders of the Pharaohs*. London: British Museum Publications, 1982.

Bierce, Ambrose. *The Enlarged Devil's Dictionary*. Garden City, N.Y.: Doubleday, 1967.

Bivar, A. D. H. "A Hoard of Ingot-Currency of the Median Period from Nūsh-i Jān, near Malayir." *Iran* 9 (1971): 97–107.

Bjorkman, Judith K. "The Larsa Goldsmith's Hoards—New Interpretations." *Journal of Near Eastern Studies* 52 (1993): 1–24.

Blamire, A., ed. *Plutarch: Life of Kimon*. London: Institute of Classical Studies, 1989.

Blok, Josine. "Patronage and the Pisistratidae." *Bulletin Antieke Beschaving* 65 (1990): 17–28.

Böckh, August. *Die Staatshaushaltung der Athener.*³ Berlin: Georg Reimer, 1886. Reprint, Berlin: de Gruyter, 1967. (The only English translation, *The Public Economy of Athens*², trans. George Cornewall Lewis [London: Parker, 1842], is of an earlier edition.)

Bogaert, Raymond. *Banques et banquiers dans les cités grecques*. Leiden: Sijthoff, 1968.

———. "Encore les cours du statère de Cyzique." *L'antiquité classique* 33 (1964): 121–28.

———. *Les origines antiques de la banque de dépôt*. Leiden: Sijthoff, 1966.

Bohannan, Paul. "The Impact of Money on an African Subsistence Economy." *Journal of Economic History* 19 (1959): 491–503. Reprinted in Dalton, *Tribal and Peasant Economies*, 123–35.

Bolin, Sture. *State and Currency in the Roman Empire to 300 A.D.* Stockholm: Almqvist and Wiksell, 1958.

Bottéro, Jean. "Le 'Code' de Hammu-rabi." *Annali della scuola normale superiore di Pisa, Classe di lettere e filosofia, serie III* 12 (1982): 409–44.

Bowra, C. M. *Homer*. London: Duckworth, 1972.

Breasted, James Henry. *Ancient Records of Egypt*. Chicago: University of Chicago Press, 1906. Reprint, New York: Russell and Russell, 1962.

Breglia, Laura. "I precedenti della moneta vera e propria nel bacino del Mediterraneo." In *Congresso Internazionale di Numismatica (Roma 11–16 Settembre 1961)*, 1: 5–17. Rome: Istituto italiano di numismatica, 1961.

———. *Numismatica antica: Storia e metodologia*. Milan: Feltrinelli, 1964.

Brown, Judith. "Note on the Division of Labor by Sex." *American Anthropologist* 72 (1970): 1073–78.

Brown, W. L. "Pheidon's Alleged Aeginetan Coinage." *NC*, 6th ser., 10 (1950): 177–204.

Buchanan, James M., and Geoffrey Brennan. "The Normative Purpose of Economic 'Science': Rediscovery of an Eighteenth Century Method." *International Review of Law and Economics* 1 (1981): 155–66. Reprinted in *Economics: Between Predictive*

Science and Moral Philosophy, by James M. Buchanan, 51–65. College Station, Tex.: Texas A&M University Press, 1987.

Bücher, Karl. *Die Entstehung der Volkswirstchaft*. Tübingen: H. Laupp, 1906.

Buchholz, Hans-Günter. "Keftiubarren- und Erzhandel im zweiten vorchristlichen Jahrtausend." *Prähistorische Zeitschrift* 37 (1959): 1–40.

Burford, Alison. *Craftsmen in Greek and Roman Society*. London: Thames and Hudson, 1972.

———. *Land and Labor in the Greek World*. Baltimore: Johns Hopkins University Press, 1993.

Burke, Edmund. "The Economy of Athens in the Classical Era: Some Adjustments to the Primitivist Model." *TAPA* 122 (1992): 199–226.

———. "Lycurgan Finances." *GRBS* 26 (1985): 251–64.

Cacciamo Caltabiano, Maria, and Paola Radici Colace. "Darico persiano e *nomisma* Greco: Differenze strutturali, ideologiche e funzionali." *Revue des études anciennes* 91 (1989): 213–26. Reprinted as "*Argyrion dokimon* e *argyrion eudokimon* tra oriente e occidente," in *Dalla premoneta alla moneta*, by Maria Cacciamo Caltabiano and Paola Radici Colace, 123–43. Pisa: ETS, 1992.

Cahn, Herbert A., and Georges le Rider, eds. *Proceedings of the 8th International Congress of Numismatics, New York-Washington, September, 1973*. Paris: Association internationale des numismates professionnels, 1976.

Cameron, Rondo. *A Concise Economic History of the World: From Paleolithic Times to the Present*. Oxford: Oxford University Press, 1989.

Camon, Ferdinando. "Figura e ambiente di Iperbolo." *Rivista di studi classici* 9 (1961): 182–97.

Cardascia, Guillaume. "Armée et fiscalité dans la babylonie achéménide." In van Effenterre et al., 1–10.

Carlier, Pierre. *La royauté en Grèce avant Alexandre*. Strasbourg: AECR, 1984.

Carradice, Ian. "The 'Regal' Coinage of the Persian Empire." In Carradice, *Coinage*, 73–95.

———, ed. *Coinage and Administration in the Athenian and Persian Empires*. BAR International Series 343. Oxford: B.A.R., 1987.

Carradice, Ian, and Martin Jessop Price. *Coinage in the Greek World*. London: Seaby, 1988.

Carson, Anne. *Economy of the Unlost*. Princeton: Princeton University Press, 1999.

Cartledge, Paul. "La nascita degli opliti e l'organizzazione militare." In *I Greci: Storia Cultura Arte Società*, vol. 2, part 1, ed. Salvatore Settis, 682–714. Turin: Einaudi, 1996.

Cartledge, Paul, and F. David Harvey. *Crux: Essays Presented to G.E.M. de Ste. Croix on His 75th Birthday*. Sidmouth: Imprint Academic, 1985.

Casson, Lionel. "The Athenian Upper Class and New Comedy." *TAPA* 106 (1976): 29–59.

Catling, H. W. *Cypriot Bronzework in the Mycenaean World*. Oxford: Clarendon Press, 1964.

Cawkwell, G. L. "Eubulus." *JHS* 83 (1962): 47–67.

Černý, Jaroslav. *A Community of Workmen at Thebes in the Ramesside Period*. Cairo: Institut française d'archéologie orientale du Caire, 1973.

———. "Prices and Wages in Egypt in the Ramesside Period." *Cahiers d'histoire mondiale* 1 (1954): 903–21.

Chadwick, John. "Pylos Tablet Un 1322." In Bennett, 19–26.

Chambers, Mortimer. *Aristoteles: ΑΘΗΝΑΙΩΝ ΠΟΛΙΤΕΙΑ.* Leipzig and Stuttgart: Teubner, 1994.

Chaniotis, Angelos, ed. *From Minoan Farmers to Roman Traders: Sidelights on the Economy of Ancient Crete.* Stuttgart: Steiner, 1999.

Chantraine, Pierre. *Dictionnaire étymologique de la langue grecque.* Paris: Klincksieck, 1968.

Chayanov, Alexander. *The Theory of Peasant Economy.* Ed. Daniel Thorner, Basile Kerblay, and R. E. F. Smith. Homewood, Ill.: Irwin, 1966.

Chown, John. *A History of Money from A.D. 800.* London: Routledge, 1994.

Cipolla, Carlo M. "Primitive Money in Primitive Europe." In *Money, Prices, and Civilization in the Mediterranean World: Fifth to Seventeenth Century,* by Carlo M. Cipolla, 3–12. New York: Gordian, 1967.

———, ed. *The Fontana Economic History of Europe.* Glasgow: Collins/Fontana, 1972–76.

Clanchy, M. T. *From Memory to Written Record: England, 1066–1307.*[2] Oxford: Blackwell, 1993.

Cline, Eric H. *Sailing the Wine-Dark Sea: International Trade and the Late Bronze Age Aegean.* BAR International Series 591. Oxford: B.A.R., 1994.

Clough, Shepard Bancroft, and Charles Woolsey Cole. *Economic History of Europe.*[3] Boston: Heath, 1952.

Cohen, David. *Law, Sexuality, and Society.* Cambridge: Cambridge University Press, 1991.

Cohen, Edward E. *Athenian Economy and Society: A Banking Perspective.* Princeton: Princeton University Press, 1992.

———. Review of Millett, *Lending and Borrowing.* BMCR 3 (1992): 282–89.

Coldstream, J. N. "Gift Exchange in the Eighth Century B.C." In Hägg, 201–6.

Connor, W. Robert. *The New Politicians of Fifth-Century Athens.* Princeton: Princeton University Press, 1971.

———. *Theopompus and Fifth-Century Athens.* Washington: Center for Hellenic Studies, 1968.

Cook, Erwin. Review of Malkin. BMCR 00.03.22 (2000).

Cook, R. M. "Speculations on the Origins of Coinage." *Historia* 7 (1958): 257–62.

Cornford, Francis MacDonald. *Thucydides Mythistoricus.* London: Edward Arnold, 1907. Reprint, London: Routledge and Kegan Paul, 1965.

Courbin, Paul. "Dans la Grèce archaïque: Valeur comparée du fer et de l'argent lors de l'introduction du monnayage." *Annales: Économies—Sociétés—Civilisations* 14 (1959): 209–33.

———. "Obéloi d'Argolide et d'ailleurs." In Hägg, 149–56.

Courtois, Jacques-Claude. "Enkomi und Ras Schamra, zwei Aussenposten der Mykenischen Kultur." In *Ägäische Bronzezeit,* ed. Hans-Günter Buchholz, 182–217. Darmstadt: Wissenschaftliche Buchgesellschaft, 1987.

Cowell, M. R., and K. Hyne. "Scientific Examination of the Lydian Precious Metal Coinages." In Ramage and Craddock, 169–74.

Curiel, Raoul, and Daniel Schlumberger. *Trésors monétaires d'Afghanistan.* Paris: Imprimerie nationale, 1953.

Dalby, Andrew. *Siren Feasts: A History of Food and Gastronomy in Greece.* London: Routledge, 1996.

Dalley, Stephanie. "Neo-Assyrian Textual Evidence for Bronzeworking Centres." In *Bronzeworking Centres of Western Asia, c. 1000–539 B.C.,* ed. John Curtis, 97–110. London: Kegan Paul, 1988.

Dalton, George. "Primitive Money." In Dalton, *Tribal and Peasant Economies,* 254–81.

———, ed. *Economic Development and Social Change: The Modernization of Village Communities.* Garden City, N.Y.: Natural History Press, 1971.

———, ed. *Tribal and Peasant Economies.* Garden City, N.Y.: Natural History Press, 1967.

Danzig, Gabriel. "The Political Character of Aristotelian Reciprocity." *CP* 95 (2000): 399–424.

Danzig, Gabriel, and David M. Schaps. "The Economy: What Plato Saw and What He Wanted." In *Plato's Laws and Its Historical Significance,* ed. Francisco L. Lisi, 143–47. Sankt Augustin: Academia Verlag, 2001.

Davies, Glyn. *A History of Money.* Cardiff: University of Wales Press, 1994.

Davies, John K. "Demosthenes on Liturgies: A Note." *JHS* 87 (1967): 33–40.

———. *Wealth and the Power of Wealth in Classical Athens.* Salem, N.H.: Ayer, 1984.

Davisson, William I., and James E. Harper. *European Economic History.* Vol. 1, *The Ancient World.* New York: Appleton-Century-Crofts, 1972.

Déchelette, Joseph. *Manuel d'archéologie préhistorique celtique et gallo-romaine.* Paris: A. Picard, 1908–1934.

de Fidio, Pia. "Fiscalità, redistribuzione, equivalenze: Per una discussione sull' economia micenea." *Studi Micenei ed Egeo-Anatolici* 23 (1982): 83–136.

———. *I dosmoi pilii a Poseidon: Una terra sacra di età micenea.* Incunabula Graeca 65. Rome: Edizioni dell'Ateneo & Bizzarri, 1977.

———. "Razioni alimentari e tenori di vita nel mondo miceneo." In Palaima, Shelmerdine, and Ilievski, 9–38.

de Jong, Irene. "Homeric κέρδος and ὄφελος." *Museum Helveticum* 44 (1987): 79–81.

de Neeve, P. W. *Peasants in Peril.* Amsterdam: Gieben, 1984.

Dercksen, J. G., ed. *Trade and Finance in Ancient Mesopotamia.* MOS Studies 1. Istanbul: Nederlands Historisch-Archaeologische Instituut te Istanbul, 1999.

de Ste. Croix, G. E. M. *The Class Struggle in the Ancient Greek World.* London: Duckworth, 1981.

———. "The Estate of Phaenippus (Ps.-Dem., xlii)." In *Ancient Society and Institutions: Studies Presented to Victor Ehrenberg,* ed. E. Badian, 109–14. Oxford: Oxford University Press, 1966.

———. "Karl Marx and the History of Classical Antiquity." *Arethusa* 8 (1975): 7–41.

Descat, Raymond. "Public et privé dans l'économie de la cité grecque." *Ktema* 23 (1998): 229–42.

de Souza, Philip. *Piracy in the Graeco-Roman World.* Cambridge: Cambridge University Press, 1999.

Detienne, Marcel, ed. *Les savoirs de l'écriture: En Grèce ancienne.* Lille: Presses Universitaires de Lille, 1988.

Dewald, C., and J. Marincola. "A Selective Introduction to Herodotean Studies." *Arethusa* 20 (1987): 9–40.

Dhavalikar, M. K. "The Beginning of Coinage in India." *World Archaeology* 6 (1975): 330–38.

Dickinson, Oliver. *The Aegean Bronze Age.* Cambridge: Cambridge University Press, 1994.

Doenges, Norman A. *The Letters of Themistokles.* New York: Arno, 1981.

Donlan, Walter. *The Aristocratic Ideal and Selected Papers.*² Wauconda, Ill.: Bolchazy-Carducci, 1999.

———. "Duelling with Gifts in the *Iliad:* As the Audience Saw It." *Colby Quarterly* 29 (1993): 155–72. Reprinted in Donlan, *Aristocratic Ideal,*² 321–44.

———. "The Homeric Economy." In *A New Companion to Homer,* ed. Ian Morris and Barry Powell, 649–67. Leiden: Brill, 1997.

———. "Reciprocities in Homer." *Classical World* 75 (1981–82): 137–75.

———. "The Unequal Exchange between Glaucus and Diomedes in Light of the Homeric Gift-Economy." *Phoenix* 53 (1989): 1–15. Reprinted in Donlan, *Aristocratic Ideal,*² 267–82.

Dover, Kenneth J. *Greek Popular Morality in the Time of Plato and Aristotle.* Oxford: Blackwell, 1974.

Drews, Robert. *Basileus: The Evidence for Kingship in Geometric Greece.* New Haven: Yale University Press, 1983.

Driver, G. R., and John C. Miles. *The Babylonian Laws.* Oxford: Clarendon Press, 1952–55.

Ducrey, Pierre. *Warfare in Ancient Greece.* New York: Schocken, 1986.

Durand, J.-M. "Relectures d'ARMT XIII, II: La correspondance de Numušda-Nahrâri." *MARI: Annales de Recherches Interdisciplinaires* 2 (1983): 151–63.

Durrenberger, E. Paul, ed. *Chayanov, Peasants, and Economic Anthropology.* Orlando: Academic Press, 1984.

Earle, Timothy K. "A Reappraisal of Redistribution: Complex Hawaiian Chiefdoms." In *Exchange Systems in Prehistory,* ed. Timothy K. Earle and Jonathan E. Ericson, 213–29. New York: Academic Press, 1977.

Edzard, Dietz Otto. *Die "Zweite Zwischenzeit" Babyloniens.* Wiesbaden: Harrassowitz, 1957.

Ehrenberg, Victor. *The People of Aristophanes.*² New York: Schocken, 1962.

Einstein, Albert. *Relativity.* New York: Crown, 1961.

Einzig, Paul. *Primitive Money.*² Oxford: Pergamon, 1966. 1st ed., London: Eyre and Spottiswoode, 1949.

Elayi, J., and A. G. Elayi. *Trésors de monnaies phéniciennes et circulation monétaire (Vᵉ– IVᵉ siècles avant J.-C.).* Paris: Gabalda, 1993.

Eliot, C. W. J., and Malcolm F. McGregor. "Kleisthenes: Eponymous Archon 525/4 B.C." *Phoenix* 14 (1960): 27–35.

Engels, Donald. "The Problem of Female Infanticide in the Greco-Roman World." *CP* 75 (1980): 112–20.

———. "The Use of Historical Demography in Ancient History." *CQ*, n.s., 34 (1984): 386–93.

Enterline, James Robert. *Erikson, Eskimos, and Columbus.* Baltimore: Johns Hopkins University Press, 2002.

Erxleben, Eberhard. "Das Verhältnis des Handels zum Produktionsaufkommen in Attica im 5. und 4. Jahrhundert. v.u.Z." *Klio* 57 (1975): 365–98.

Evans, Arthur J. "Minoan Weights and Mediums of Currency from Crete, Mycenae, and Cyprus." In *Corolla Numismatica: Essays in Honour of Barclay V. Head*, ed. George F. Hill, 336–67. London: Oxford University Press, 1906.

Farb, Peter. *Man's Rise to Civilization as Shown by the Indians of North America from Primeval Times to the Coming of the Industrial State.* New York: Dutton, 1968.

Fehling, Detlev. *Herodotus and His "Sources."* Trans. J. G. Howie. Leeds: Cairns, 1989.

Ferone, Claudio. *Lesteia: Forme di predazione nell' Egeo in età classica.* Naples: Procaccini, 1997.

Figueira, Thomas. *The Power of Money: Coinage and Politics in the Athenian Empire.* Philadelphia: University of Pennsylvania Press, 1998.

Fineberg, Stephen. "Blind Rage and Eccentric Vision in *Iliad* 6." *TAPA* 129 (1999): 13–41.

Finkelstein, J. J. "Ammiṣaduqa's Edict and the Babylonian 'Law Codes.'" *Journal of Cuneiform Studies* 15 (1961): 91–104.

Finley, Moses I. "The Ancient City: From Fustel de Coulanges to Max Weber and Beyond." *Comparative Studies in Society and History* 19 (1977): 305–27. Reprinted in *Economy and Society in Ancient Greece*, by Moses I. Finley, 3–23. London: Chatto and Windus, 1981.

———. *The Ancient Economy.*[2] London: Hogarth, 1985.

———. "Aristotle and Economic Analysis." *Past and Present* 47 (1970): 3–25. Reprinted in *Studies in Ancient Society*, by Moses I. Finley, 26–52. London: Routledge and Kegan Paul, 1974.

———. "Note on Homer and the Mycenaean Tablets." In Finley, *World*, First Revised Edition. London: Chatto and Windus, 1956. Reprinted Harmondsworth: Penguin, 1967, 165–68.

———. *Studies in Land and Credit in Ancient Athens, 500–200 B.C.* New Brunswick: Rutgers University Press, 1951.

———. "Was Greek Civilization Based on Slave Labour?" *Historia* 8 (1959): 145–64. Reprinted in *Slavery in Classical Antiquity*, ed. Moses I. Finley, 53–72. Cambridge: Heffer, 1960.

———. *The World of Odysseus.* 1st ed., New York: Viking, 1954. 2nd revised edition, New York: Viking, 1978. Unless otherwise noted, page numbers refer to the reprint of London: Pelican, 1991.

———, ed. *The Bücher-Meyer Controversy.* New York: Arno, 1979.

Finley, Moses I., J. L. Caskey, G. S. Kirk, and D. L. Page. "The Trojan War." *JHS* 84 (1964): 1–20.

Firebaugh, W. C. *The Inns of Greece and Rome.* Chicago: P. Covici, 1928. Reprint, New York: Blom, 1972.

Fischer, Stanley, Rudiger Dornbusch, and Richard Schmalensee. *Economics.*[2] New York: McGraw-Hill, 1988.

Fisher, Nick, and Hans van Wees, eds. *Archaic Greece: New Approaches and New Evidence.* London: Duckworth, 1998.

Forbes, Robert James. "Bergbau, Steinbruchtätigkeit und Hüttenwesen." In *Archaeologia Homerica,* ed. Friedrich Matz and Hans-Günter Buchholz, vol. 2, chap. K. Göttingen: Vandenhoeck and Ruprecht, 1967.

Forde, Daryll, and Mary Douglas. "Primitive Economics." In Dalton, *Tribal and Peasant Economies,* 13–28.

Forrest, W. G. "The Tradition of Hippias' Expulsion from Athens." *GRBS* 10 (1969): 277–86.

Fox, R. J. Lane. "Theophrastus' *Characters* and the Historian." *PCPS,* n.s., 42 (1996): 127–70.

Foxhall, Lin. "Cargoes of the Heart's Desire: The Character of Trade in the Archaic Mediterranean World." In Fisher and van Wees, 295–310.

Fraenkel, Eduard, ed. *Aeschylus: Agamemnon.* Oxford: Clarendon Press, 1950.

Frere, John Hookham, trans. *The Acharnians and Three Other Plays of Aristophanes.* London: Dent, 1909. First printed for private circulation in 1839.

Frisk, Hjalmar. *Griechisches etymologisches Wörterbuch.* Heidelberg: Winter, 1960.

Fuks, Alexander. "Isokrates and the Social-Economic Situation in Greece." *Ancient Society* 3 (1972): 17–44.

———. "Κολωνὸς μίσθιος: Labour Exchange in Classical Athens." *Eranos* 49 (1951): 171–73.

Furnham, Adrian, and Michael Argyle. *The Psychology of Money.* London: Routledge, 1998.

Furtwängler, Andreas. "Neue Beobachtungen zur frühesten Münzprägung." *Schweizerische Numismatische Rundschau* 15 (1986): 153–65.

Galaty, Michael L. *Nestor's Wine Cups.* BAR International Series 766. Oxford: B.A.R., 1999.

Gale, N. H., W. Gentner, and G. A. Wagner. "Mineralogical and Geographical Silver Sources of Archaic Greek Coinage." In *Metallurgy in Numismatics,* vol. 1, ed. D. M. Metcalf and W. A. Oddy, 3–49. London: Royal Numismatic Society, 1980.

Gallant, Thomas W. *Risk and Survival in Ancient Greece: Reconstructing the Rural Domestic Economy.* Cambridge: Polity Press, 1991.

Gardiner, Alan H. "Four Papyri of the 18th Dynasty from Kahun." *Zeitschrift für Ägyptische Sprache und Altertumskunde* 43 (1906): 27–47.

———. "A Lawsuit Arising from the Purchase of Two Slaves." *Journal of Egyptian Archaeology* 21 (1935): 140–46.

Garlan, Yvon. *Guerre et économie en Grèce ancienne.* Paris: La découverte, 1989.

Garland, Robert. *The Piraeus.* Ithaca: Cornell University Press, 1987.

Garnsey, Peter. *Famine and Food Supply in the Graeco-Roman World.* Cambridge: Cambridge University Press, 1988.

———. *Food and Society in Classical Antiquity.* Cambridge: Cambridge University Press, 1999.

———. "Grain for Athens." In Cartledge and Harvey, 62–75.

Garnsey, Peter, Keith Hopkins, and C. R. Whittaker, eds. *Trade in the Ancient Economy.* London: Chatto and Windus, 1983.

Gerloff, Wilhelm. *Die Enstehung des Geldes und die Anfänge des Geldwesens.*³ Frankfurt am Main: Vittorio Klostermann, 1947.

Germain, Louis R. F. "Aspects du droit d'exposition en Grèce." *Revue historique de droit français et étranger* 47 (1969): 177–97.

Giglioni, Gabriella Bodei. *Lavori pubblici e occupazione nell' antichità classica.* Bologna: Pàtron editore, 1974.

Glanville, S. R. K. *Catalogue of Demotic Papyri in the British Museum.* Vol. 2. London: Trustees of the British Museum, 1955.

Glotz, Gustave. *Ancient Greece at Work.* London: Kegan Paul, 1926. Reprint, New York: Norton, 1967.

————. "Les salaires à Délos." *Journal des savants* (1913): 206–15, 251–60.

Göbl, Robert. *Antike Numismatik.* Munich: Battenberg, 1978.

Golden, Mark. "Demography and the Exposure of Girls at Athens." *Phoenix* 35 (1981): 316–31.

Gomme, A. W. "Notes on the Ἀθηναίων Πολιτεία (Continued)." *CR* 40 (1926): 8–12.

Gordon, Cyrus H. *Ugaritic Literature.* Rome: Pontifical Biblical Institute, 1949.

Grandet, Pierre. *Le Papyrus Harris I (BM 9999).* Cairo: Institut français d'archéologie orientale du Caire, 1994.

Grandjean, Catherine. "À propos de 'The Monetization of the Marketplace in Athens.'" In Andreau, Briant, and Descat, 406–8.

Grierson, P. J. Hamilton. *The Silent Trade.* Edinburgh: W. Green and Son, 1903. Reprinted in *Research in Economic Anthropology* 3 (1980): 1–74.

Griffith, F. L. "Notes on Egyptian Weights and Measures." *Proceedings of the Society of Biblical Archaeology* 15 (1892–93): 301–16.

Guarducci, Margherita. "Tripodi, lebeti, oboli." In *Rivista di filologia classica,* n.s., 22–23 (1944–45): 171–80.

Gulliver, P. H. "The Evolution of Arusha Trade." In *Markets in Africa,* ed. Paul Bohannon and George Dalton, 431–56. Chicago: Northwestern University Press, 1962.

Gunderson, Gerald A. "Economic Behavior in the Ancient World." In *Explorations in the New Economic History: Essays in Honor of Douglas C. North,* ed. Roger L. Ransom, Richard Sutch, and Gary M. Walton, 235–56. New York: Academic Press, 1982.

Gupta, P. L., and T. R. Hardaker. *Indian Silver Punchmarked Coins: Magadha-Maurya Karshapana Series.* Nashik: Indian Institute of Research in Numismatic Studies, 1985.

Hägg, Robin, ed. *The Greek Renaissance of the Eighth Century B.C.: Tradition and Innovation (Proceedings of the Second International Symposium at the Swedish Institute in Athens, 1–5 June, 1981).* Stockholm: Svenska Institutet I Athen, 1983.

Hall, Edith. *Inventing the Barbarian.* Oxford: Clarendon Press, 1989.

Hall, Jonathan M. Review of Tandy. *CP* 94 (1999): 216–22.

Hallo, William W., and William Kelly Simpson. *The Ancient Near East: A History.*² Fort Worth: Harcourt Brace, 1998.

Halstead, Paul. "The Mycenaean Palatial Economy: Making the Most of the Gaps in the Evidence." *PCPS,* n.s., 38 (1992): 57–86.

Hammer, J. "Der Feingehalt der griechischen und römischen Münzen." *Zeitschrift für Numismatik* 26 (1908): 1–144.

Hammond, N. G. L. "The Family of Orthagoras." *CQ*, n.s., 6 (1956): 45–53.

———. "Land and Society in the Athens of Solon." In *Studies in Greek History*, by N. G. L. Hammond, 104–44. Oxford: Clarendon Press, 1973. Originally published as "Land Tenure in Attica and Solon's *Seisachtheia*," *JHS* 81 (1961): 76–98.

Hammond, N. G. L., G. T. Griffith, and F. W. Walbank. *A History of Macedonia*. Oxford: Clarendon Press, 1972–88.

Hands, A. R. *Charities and Social Aid in Greece and Rome*. London: Thames and Hudson, 1968.

Hansen, Mogens Herman. "A Note on the Growing Tendency to Underestimate the Population of Classical Attica." In *Three Studies in Athenian Demography*, by Mogens Herman Hansen, 7–13. Historisk-filosofiske Meddelelser 56. Copenhagen: Royal Danish Academy of Sciences and Letters, 1988.

Hanson, Victor Davis. *The Other Greeks*. New York: Free Press, 1995.

———. *Warfare and Agriculture in Classical Greece.*[2] Berkeley: University of California Press, 1998.

Harris, William V. *Ancient Literacy*. Cambridge, Mass.: Harvard University Press, 1989.

———. "The Theoretical Possibility of Extensive Infanticide in the Graeco-Roman World." *CQ*, n.s., 32 (1982): 114–16.

Harrison, A. R. W. *The Law of Athens*. Oxford: Clarendon Press, 1968–71.

Harvey, F. David. "Some Aspects of Bribery in Greek Politics." In Cartledge and Harvey, 76–117.

Hasebroek, J. *Griechische Wirtschafts- und Gesellschaftsgeschichte*. Tübingen: J. C. B. Mohr, 1931.

———. *Trade and Politics in Ancient Greece*. London: George Bell and Sons, 1933. Reprint, New York: Biblo and Tannen, 1965.

Havelock, Eric. *The Literate Revolution in Greece and Its Cultural Consequences*. Princeton: Princeton University Press, 1982.

Hawke, G. R. *Economics for Historians*. Cambridge: Cambridge University Press, 1980.

Hawkins, J. D., ed. *Trade in the Ancient Near East*. London: British School of Archaeology in Iraq, 1977.

Head, Barclay V. *Historia Numorum.*[2] Oxford: Clarendon Press, 1910. Reprint, London: Spink, 1963.

Healy, John F. *Mining and Metallurgy in the Greek and Roman World*. London: Thames and Hudson, 1978.

Heaton, Herbert. *Economic History of Europe*. New York: Harper, 1948.

Heichelheim, Fritz M. *An Ancient Economic History*. Trans. Joyce Stevens. Rev. ed. Leiden: A. W. Sijthoff, 1964.

Helfferich, Karl. *Money*. Trans. Louis Infield. New York: Augustus M. Kelley, 1969.

Heltzer, Michael. *Goods, Prices, and the Organization of Trade in Ugarit*. Wiesbaden: Ludwig Reichert Verlag, 1978.

Hemelrijk, Jacob. Πενία εν πλοῦτος. Amsterdam: Blikman and Sartorius, 1925. Reprint, New York: Arno, 1979.

Herman, Gabriel. *Ritualised Friendship and the Greek City*. Cambridge: Cambridge University Press, 1987.

Herskovits, Melville J. *Economic Anthropology*. New York: Knopf, 1952.

Herter, Hans. "Die Soziologie der antiken Prostitution." *Jahrbuch für Antike und Christentum* 3 (1960): 70–111.

Heubeck, Alfred, et al., eds., *A Commentary on Homer's* Odyssey. Oxford: Clarendon Press, 1988–92.

Heyerdahl, Thor, and Per Lillieström. *Ingen Grenser.* Oslo: J. M. Stenersen, 1999.

Hodkinson, Stephen. "The Development of Spartan Society and Institutions in the Archaic Period." In *The Development of the* Polis *in Archaic Greece,* ed. Lynette G. Mitchell and P. J. Rhodes, 83–102. London: Routledge, 1997.

Hogarth, David George. "The Archaic Artemisia." *JHS* 28 (1908): 338.

———. *Excavations at Ephesus.* London: Trustees of The British Museum, 1908.

Holladay, A. J. "The Followers of Peisistratus." *Greece and Rome,* n.s., 24 (1977): 40–56.

Holle, Bruce Fredric. "Historical Considerations on the Origins and the Spread of Greek Coinage in the Archaic Age." Ph.D. diss., University of Michigan, 1978.

Holloway, R. Ross. "La ricerca attuale sull'origine della moneta." *Rivista italiana di numismatica e scienze affini* 80 (1978): 7–14.

Homolle, Th. "Comptes & inventaires des temples déliens en l'année 279." *BCH* 14 (1890): 389–511.

Hopkins, Keith, in collaboration with P. J. Roscoe. "Between Slavery and Freedom: On Freeing Slaves at Delphi." In *Conquerors and Slaves,* by Keith Hopkins, 133–71. Cambridge: Cambridge University Press, 1978.

Horden, Peregrine, and Nicholas Purcell. *The Corrupting Sea: a Study of Mediterranean History.* Oxford: Blackwell, 2000.

How, W. W., and J. Wells. *A Commentary on Herodotus.* Oxford: Clarendon Press, 1912.

Howgego, Christopher J. *Ancient History from Coins.* London: Routledge, 1995.

———. "Why Did Ancient States Strike Coins?" *NC* 150 (1990): 1–25.

Hufton, Olwen. "Women in Revolution, 1789–1796." *Past and Present* 53 (1971): 90–108.

Hunt, A. S., and C. C. Edgar. *Select Papyri.* Loeb Classical Library. London: Heinemann and Cambridge, Mass.: Harvard University Press, 1932.

Immerwahr, Sara A. "Mycenaean Trade and Colonization." *Archaeology* 13 (1960): 4–13.

Jacobsen, Thorkild. "The Reign of Ibbī-Suen." *Journal of Cuneiform Studies* 7 (1953): 36–47.

Jacobsthal, Paul. "The Date of the Ephesian Foundation-Deposit." *JHS* 71 (1951): 85–95.

James, T. G. H. *An Introduction to Ancient Egypt.* London: British Museum Publications, 1979.

Jameson, Michael. "Agriculture and Slavery in Classical Athens." *Classical Journal* 73 (1977–78): 122–45.

Janssen, Jac. J. *Commodity Prices from the Ramessid Period.* Leiden: Brill, 1975.

Jardé, Auguste. *Les céréales dans l'antiquité grecque* (vol. 1, *La Production*). Paris: de Boccard, 1925. Reprint, 1979.

Jeffery, L. H. *The Local Scripts of Archaic Greece.*[2] Oxford: Clarendon Press, 1990.

Jenkins, G. K., and R. B. Lewis. *Carthaginian Gold and Electrum Coins.* London: Royal Numismatic Society, 1963.

Joannès, Francis. "La culture matérielle à Mari (IV): Les méthodes de pesée." *Revue d'assyriologie et d'archéologie orientale* 83 (1989): 113–51.

Johns, C. H. W. *Babylonian and Assyrian Laws, Contracts, and Letters.* New York: Scribners, 1904.

Jones, John Melville. *A Dictionary of Ancient Greek Coins.* London: Seaby, 1986.

Jordan, Borimir. *The Athenian Navy in the Classical Period.* Berkeley: University of California Press, 1975.

Kagan, Donald. "The Dates of the Earliest Coins." *AJA* 86 (1982): 343–60.

———. "Pheidon's Aeginetan Coinage." *TAPA* 91 (1960): 121–36.

Kallet-Marx, Lisa. "The Diseased Body Politic, Athenian Public Finance, and the Massacre at Mykalessos (Thucydides 7.27–29)." *American Journal of Philology* 120 (1999): 223–44.

———. *Money, Expense, and Naval Power in Thucydides' History 1–5.24.* Berkeley: University of California Press, 1993.

———. "Money Talks: Rhetor, Demos, and the Resources of the Athenian Empire." In *Ritual, Finance, Politics: Athenian Democratic Accounts Presented to David Lewis,* ed. Robin Osborne and Simon Hornblower, 227–52. Oxford: Oxford University Press, 1994.

Kelly, Thomas. *A History of Argos to 500 B.C.* Minneapolis: University of Minnesota Press, 1976.

Kemp, Barry J. *Ancient Egypt: Anatomy of a Civilization.* London: Routledge, 1989.

———. "Large Middle Kingdom Granary Buildings (and the Archaeology of Administration)." *Zeitschrift für Ägyptische Sprache und Altertumskunde* 113 (1986): 120–36.

Kent, John Harvey. "The Temple Estates of Delos, Rheneia, and Mykonos." *Hesperia* 17 (1948): 243–338.

Kienast, Burkhart, ed. *Die Altassyrischen Texte des Orientalischen Seminars der Universität Heidelberg und der Sammlung Erlenmeyer-Basel.* Berlin: de Gruyter, 1960.

Killen, J. T. "The Linear B Tablets and the Mycenaean Economy." In *Linear B: A 1984 Survey,* ed. A. Morpurgo Davies and Y. Duhoux, 241–305. Louvain-la-Neuve: Peeters, 1988.

Kindler, Aryeh, ed. *International Numismatic Convention, Jerusalem, 27–31 December 1963: The Patterns of Monetary Development in Phoenicia and Palestine in Antiquity, Proceedings.* Tel Aviv: Schocken, 1967.

Kirk, G. S., ed., *The Iliad: A Commentary.* Cambridge: Cambridge University Press, 1985.

Knight, Melvin M., Harry Elmer Barnes, and Felix Flügel. *Economic History of Europe.* London: Allen and Unwin, 1930.

Korver, Jan. *De terminologie van het crediet-wezen en het Grieksch.* Amsterdam: H. J. Paris, 1934. Reprint, New York: Arno, 1979.

Kosambi, D. D. *The Culture and Civilisation of Ancient India in Historical Outline.* London: Routledge and Kegan Paul, 1965.

———. "On the Origin and Development of Silver Coinage in India." *Current Science* 10, no. 9 (1941): 395–400. Reprinted in *Indian Numismatics,* by D. D. Kosambi, 85–94. New Delhi: Orient Longman, 1981.

Kozyreva, N. V. "Some Problems of Commodity-Money Relations in Old Babylonian

Mesopotamia" (in Russian with English abstract). *Vestnik Drevnei Istorii* 168, no. 2 (1984): 3–14.

Kraay, Colin M. *Archaic and Classical Greek Coins.* London: Methuen, 1976.

———. "The Composition of Electrum Coinage." *Archaeometry* 1 (1958): 21–23.

———. *Greek Coins.* London: Thames and Hudson, 1966.

———. "Hoards, Small Change, and the Origin of Coinage." *JHS* 84 (1964): 76–91.

———. "An Interpretation of *Ath. Pol.,* Ch. 10." In Kraay and Jenkins, 1–9.

Kraay, Colin M., and G. K. Jenkins. *Essays in Greek Coinage Presented to Stanley Robinson.* Oxford: Clarendon Press, 1968.

Kraay, Colin M., and P. R. S. Moorey. "Two Fifth Century Hoards from the Near East." *Revue Numismatique,* 6th ser., 10 (1968): 181–235.

Kraynak, Lynn Harriett. "Hostelries of Ancient Greece." Ph.D. diss., University of California, Berkeley, 1984.

Kroll, John H. "From Wappenmünzen to Gorgoneion to Owls." *American Numismatic Society Museum Notes* 26 (1981): 1–32, plates 1–2.

———. *The Greek Coins.* Vol. 26 of *The Athenian Agora.* Princeton: American School of Classical Studies at Athens, 1993.

———. "Observations on Monetary Instruments in Pre-coinage Greece." In Balmuth, *Hacksilber to Coinage,* 77–92.

———. "Silver in Solon's Laws." In *Studies in Greek Numismatics in Memory of Martin Jessop Price,* ed. R. Ashton and S. Hunter, 225–32. London: Spink, 1998.

Kroll, John H., and Nancy M. Waggoner. "Dating the Earliest Coins of Athens, Corinth, and Aegina." *AJA* 88 (1984): 325–40.

Kuhrt, Amélie. "The Old Assyrian Merchants." In Parkins and Smith, 16–30.

Kurimoto, Shinichiro. "Silent Trade in Japan." *Research in Economic Anthropology* 3 (1980): 97–108.

Kurke, Leslie. *Coins, Bodies, Games, and Gold.* Princeton: Princeton University Press, 1999.

———. *The Traffic in Praise.* Ithaca: Cornell University Press, 1991.

Labby, David. *The Demystification of Yap.* Chicago: University of Chicago Press, 1976.

Lambert, Maurice. "L'usage de l'argent-métal à Lagash au temps de la IIIᵉ dynastie d'Ur." *Revue d'assyriologie et d'archéologie orientale* 57 (1963): 79–92.

Langholm, Odd. *Price and Value in the Aristotelian Tradition.* Bergen: Universitetsforlaget, 1979.

Larsen, Mogens Trolle. *Old Assyrian Caravan Procedures.* Istanbul: Nederlands Historisch-Archaeologisch Instituut te Istanbul, 1967.

———. *The Old Assyrian City-State and Its Colonies.* Copenhagen: Akademisk Forlag, 1976.

Lattimore, Richmond, trans. *The Iliad of Homer.* Chicago: University of Chicago Press, 1951.

Laum, Bernhard. *Heiliges Geld.* Tübingen: J. C. B. Mohr, 1924.

Lavelle, Brian M. Review of *Die archaische Tyrannis,* by Lorentana de Libero. *BMCR* 97.7.18.

———. *The Sorrow and the Pity. Historia* Einzelschriften 80. Stuttgart: Steiner, 1993.

Leemans, W. F. *Old Babylonian Letters and Economic History.* Leiden: Brill, 1968.

Reprint of an article in the *Journal of the Economic and Social History of the Orient* 11 (1968): 171–226.

———. *The Old-Babylonian Merchant: His Business and His Social Position.* Leiden: Brill, 1950.

Lejeune, Michel. "La série Ma de Pylos." *Revue des études anciennes* 58 (1956): 3–39. Reprinted in *Mémoires de philologie mycénienne*, by Michel Lejeune, 1:65–91. Paris: Centre national de la recherche scientifique, 1958.

———. "Sur la fiscalité mycénienne Ma." In *Colloquium Mycenaeum*, ed. Ernst Risch and Hugo Mühlestein, 147–50. Neuchâtel and Geneva: Université de Neuchâtel, 1979.

———. "Sur le vocabulaire économique mycénien." In Bennett, 77–109.

Le Rider, Georges. *La naissance de la monnaie: Pratiques monétaires de l'Orient ancien.* Paris: Presses Universitaires de France, 2001.

Lesko, Barbara S. "Rank, Roles, and Rights." In Leonard Lesko, 15–39.

Lesko, Leonard H., ed. *Pharaoh's Workers.* Ithaca: Cornell University Press, 1994.

Lesquier, Jean. *Les institutions militaires de l'Égypte sous les Lagides.* Paris: Leroux, 1911.

Lewis, David M. Review of Connor, *New Politicians. CR*, n.s., 25 (1975): 87–90.

Lichtheim, Miriam. *Ancient Egyptian Literature: A Book of Readings.* Berkeley: University of California Press, 1973–80.

Lipiński, E. "Les temples néo-assyriens et les origines du monnayage." In Lipiński, *State and Temple Economy*, 2:565–88.

———, ed. *State and Temple Economy in the Ancient Near East: Proceedings of the International Conference Organized by the Katholieke Universiteit Leuven from the 10th to the 14th of April 1978.* Leuven: Departement Oriëntalistiek, 1979.

Li Xueqin. *Eastern Zhou and Qin Civilizations.* Trans. K. C. Chang. New Haven: Yale University Press, 1985.

Lloyd, Alan B. *Herodotus: Book II.* Leiden: Brill, 1975–88.

Loewe, Raphael. "The Earliest Biblical Allusion to Coined Money?" *Palestine Exploration Quarterly* 87 (1955): 141–50.

Loomis, William T. *Wages, Welfare Costs, and Inflation in Classical Athens.* Ann Arbor: University of Michigan Press, 1998.

Luckenbill, Daniel David. *The Annals of Sennacherib.* Chicago: University of Chicago Press, 1924.

MacDowell, Douglas M. *The Law in Classical Athens.* London: Thames and Hudson, 1978.

Malkin, Irad. *The Returns of Odysseus.* Berkeley: University of California Press, 1998.

Manfredini, Mario, and Luigi Piccirilli. *Plutarco: La Vita di Solone.* [Milan]: Fondazione Lorenzo Valla, 1977.

Margalit, Baruch. *The Ugaritic Poem of AQHT.* Berlin: de Gruyter, 1989.

Markle, Minor M. "Participation of Farmers in Athenian Juries and Assemblies." *Ancient Society* 21 (1990): 149–65.

Marx, Karl. *The Communist Manifesto.* Chicago: Henry Regnery, Gateway Editions, 1954.

Marx, Karl, and Friedrich Engels. *Gesamtausgabe.* Berlin: Dietz, 1972–.

Mayhew, Anne, Walter C. Neale, and David W. Tandy. "Markets in the Ancient Near

East: A Challenge to Silver's Argument and Use of Evidence." *Journal of Economic History* 45 (1985): 127–34.

McDowell, Andrea G. "Contact with the Outside World." In Leonard Lesko, 41–59.

McFeat, Tom, ed. *Indians of the North Pacific Coast.* Toronto: McClelland and Stewart, 1966.

Meeks, N. D. "Scanning Electron Microscopy of the Refractory Remains and the Gold." In Ramage and Craddock, 99–156.

Meiggs, Russell. *The Athenian Empire.* Oxford: Clarendon Press, 1972.

Meikle, Scott. *Aristotle's Economic Thought.* Oxford: Clarendon Press, 1995.

Mele, Alfonso. *Il commericio greco arcaico:* prexis *ed* emporie. Naples: Institut français de Naples, 1979.

Melitz, Jacques. "The Polanyi School of Anthropology on Money: An Economist's View." *American Anthropologist* 72 (1970): 1020–40.

Menu, Bernadette. "Le prix de l'utile en Égypte au Ier millénaire avant notre ère." In Andreau, Briant, and Descat, 245–75.

Meritt, Benjamin D. "Greek Inscriptions." *Hesperia* 8 (1939): 48–90.

Merkelbach, Reinhold. *Die Bedeutung des Geldes für die Geschichte der griechisch-römischen Welt.* Stuttgart and Leipzig: Teubner, 1992.

Meshorer, Ya'akov. *Ancient Jewish Coinage.* Dix Hills, N.Y.: Amphora, 1982.

Meyer, Eduard. *Forschungen zur alten Geschichte.* Halle: Max Niemeyer, 1899.

Michailidou, Anna. "Systems of Weight and Relations of Production in Late Bronze Age Crete." In Chaniotis, 87–113.

Migeotte, Léopold. *L'emprunt public dans les cités grecques.* Quebec: Éditions du Sphinx, 1984.

Mill, John Stuart. *Principles of Political Economy.* London: Longmans, Green, and Company, 1909.

Miller, Stephen G. "Architecture as Evidence for the Identity of the Early *Polis.*" In *Sources for the Ancient Greek City-State,* ed. Mogens Herman Hansen, 201–44. Historisk-filosofiske Meddelelser 72. Copenhagen: Royal Danish Academy of Sciences and Letters, 1995.

Millett, Paul. "Hesiod and His World." *PCPS,* n.s., 30 (1984): 84–115.

———. *Lending and Borrowing in Ancient Athens.* Cambridge: Cambridge University Press, 1991.

———. "Maritime Loans and the Structure of Credit in Fourth-Century Athens." In Garnsey, Hopkins, and Whittaker, 36–52.

———. "Patronage and Its Avoidance in Classical Athens." In *Patronage in Ancient Society,* ed. Andrew Wallace-Hadrill, 15–47. London: Routledge, 1989.

Mills, C. Wright. *The Power Elite.* New York: Oxford University Press, 1956.

Milne, J. G. "The Perachora Drachma Inscription." *CR* 58 (1944): 18–19.

Mitchell, Lynette G. *Greeks Bearing Gifts.* Cambridge: Cambridge University Press, 1997.

Mitchiner, Michael. *The Origins of Indian Coinage.* London: Hawkins, 1973.

Mitten, David G., John Griffiths Pedley, and Jane Ayer Scott, eds. *Studies Presented to George M. A. Hanfmann.* Mainz: von Zabern, 1971.

Monroe, Arthur Eli. *Monetary Theory before Adam Smith.* Cambridge, Mass.: Harvard University Press, 1923. Reprint, New York: Augustus M. Kelley, 1966.

Morgan, Catherine. *Athletes and Oracles.* Cambridge: Cambridge University Press, 1990.

Mørkholm, Otto. *Early Hellenistic Coinage.* Ed. Philip Grierson and Ulla Westermark. Cambridge: Cambridge University Press, 1991.

Morris, Ian. *Burial and Ancient Society: The Rise of the Greek City-State.* Cambridge: Cambridge University Press, 1987.

———. "The Use and Abuse of Homer." *Classical Antiquity* 5 (1986): 81–138.

Mrozek, Stanislaw. *Lohnarbeit im klassischen Altertum.* Bonn: Habelt, 1989.

Muhly, J. D. "The Copper Ox-Hide Ingots and the Bronze Age Metals Trade." In Hawkins, 73–82.

———. Review of Hawkins. *Journal of the American Oriental Society* 100 (1980): 173–75.

Murray, Oswyn. *Early Greece.*² Cambridge, Mass.: Harvard University Press, 1993.

Mylonas, George E. *Mycenae and the Mycenaean Age.* Princeton: Princeton University Press, 1966.

Narotzky, Susana. *New Directions in Economic Anthropology.* London: Pluto, 1997.

Nash, Manning. "The Organization of Economic Life." In *Horizons of Anthropology,*¹ ed. Sol Tax, 171–80. Chicago: Aldine, 1964.

Nemet-Nejat, Karen Rhea. *Daily Life in Ancient Mesopotamia.* Westport, Conn.: Greenwood, 1998.

Noonan, Thomas S. "The Grain Trade of the Northern Black Sea in Antiquity." *American Journal of Philology* 94 (1973): 231–42.

Notopoulos, James A. "The Genesis of an Oral Heroic Poem." *GRBS* 3 (1960): 135–44.

Nussbaum, G. "Labour and Status in the *Works and Days.*" *CQ*, n.s., 10 (1960): 213–20.

Oikonomides, A. N. *The Two Agoras of Ancient Athens.* Chicago: Argonaut, 1964.

Olivier, J.-P. "Une loi fiscale mycénienne." *BCH* 98 (1974): 23–35.

Oppenheim, A. Leo. *Ancient Mesopotamia: Portrait of a Dead Civilization.* Chicago: University of Chicago Press, 1964.

———. *Letters from Mesopotamia.* Chicago: University of Chicago Press, 1967.

Ormand, Kirk. *Exchange and the Maiden.* Austin: University of Texas Press, 1999.

Ormerod, Henry A. *Piracy in the Ancient World.* Liverpool: University Press of Liverpool, 1924. Reprint, Baltimore: Johns Hopkins University Press, 1997.

Osborne, Robin. *Demos: The Discovery of Classical Attika.* Cambridge: Cambridge University Press, 1985.

———. "Pride and Prejudice, Sense and Subsistence: Exchange and Society in the Greek City." In *City and Country in the Ancient World,* ed. John Rich and Andrew Wallace-Hadrill, 119–45. London: Routledge, 1991.

Page, Denys L. *History and the Homeric Iliad.* Berkeley: University of California Press, 1959.

———. *Sappho and Alcaeus.* Oxford: Clarendon Press, 1955.

Palaima, Th. G., C. W. Shelmerdine, and P. Hr. Ilievski, eds. *Studia Mycenaea (1988).* Skopje, 1989.

Parke, H. W. *Greek Mercenary Soldiers.* Oxford: Clarendon Press, 1933.

Parke, H. W., and D. E. W. Wormell. *The Delphic Oracle.* Oxford: Blackwell, 1956.

Parker, Douglass, trans. *The Acharnians.* In *Aristophanes: Four Comedies,* ed. William Arrowsmith. Ann Arbor: University of Michigan Press, 1969.

Parker, R. *A Saite Oracle Papyrus from Thebes.* Providence: Brown University Press, 1962.

Parkins, Helen, and Christopher Smith, eds. *Trade, Traders, and the Ancient City.* London: Routledge, 1998.

Patterson, Orlando. *Slavery and Social Death: A Comparative Study.* Cambridge, Mass.: Harvard University Press, 1982.

Payne, Humfry, et al. *Perachora.* Oxford: Clarendon Press, 1940.

Peet, Thomas Eric. *The Great Tomb-Robberies of the Twentieth Egyptian Dynasty.* Oxford: Clarendon Press, 1930. Reprint, Hildesheim: Olms, 1977.

———. "The Unit of Value *š'ty* in Papyrus Bulaq 11." In *Mélanges Maspero,* 1:185–99. Cairo: Institut français d'archéologie orientale du Caire, 1934.

Peng Xinwei. *A Monetary History of China.* Trans. Edward H. Kaplan. Bellingham, Wash.: Western Washington University, 1994.

Perlman, Shalom. "On Bribing Athenian Ambassadors." *GRBS* 17 (1976): 223–33.

Perrin, Bernadotte, ed. and trans. *Plutarch's Lives.* Loeb Classical Library. London: Heinemann and Cambridge, Mass.: Harvard University Press, 1914–1926.

Pettinato, Giovanni. *The Archives of Ebla: An Empire Inscribed in Clay.* Garden City, N.Y.: Doubleday, 1984.

Phillips, Jacke. "Tomb-Robbers and Their Booty in Ancient Egypt." In *Death and Taxes in the Ancient Near East,* ed. Sara E. Orel, 157–92. Lewiston, N.Y.: Mellen, 1992.

Pickard-Cambridge, Arthur. *Dithyramb, Tragedy, and Comedy.*[2] Revised by T. B. L. Webster. Oxford: Clarendon Press, 1962.

———. *The Dramatic Festivals of Athens.*[2] Revised by John Gould and D. M. Lewis. Oxford: Clarendon Press, 1968.

Platon, Nicolas, and Michel Feyel. "Inventaire sacré de Thespies trouvé à Chostia (Béotie)." *BCH* 62 (1938): 149–66.

Polanyi, Karl. "Aristotle Discovers the Economy." In Polanyi, Arensberg, and Pearson, 64–94.

———. "The Economy as Instituted Process." In Polanyi, Arensberg, and Pearson, 243–70.

———. *The Great Transformation.* New York: Farrar and Rinehart, 1944. Reprint, Boston: Beacon, 1957.

———. *The Livelihood of Man.* New York: Academic Press, 1977.

———. "Marketless Trading in Hammurabi's Time." In Polanyi, Arensberg, and Pearson, 12–26.

———. "Ports of Trade in Early Societies." *Journal of Economic History* 23 (1963): 30–45. Reprinted in Polanyi, *Primitive,* 238–60.

———. *Primitive, Archaic, and Modern Economies: Essays of Karl Polanyi.* Ed. George Dalton. Garden City, New York: Doubleday, 1968.

———. "The Semantics of Money-Uses." In Polanyi, *Primitive,* 175–203.

Polanyi, Karl, Conrad M. Arensberg, and Harry W. Pearson, eds. *Trade and Market in the Early Empires.* Glencoe, Ill.: Free Press, 1957.

Pollard, S., and C. Holmes. *Documents of European Economic History.* London: Edward Arnold, 1968.

Pomtow, H. "Die Drei Brände des Tempels zu Delphi." *Rheinisches Museum für Philologie*, n.s., 51 (1896): 329–80.

Postgate, J. N. *Taxation and Conscription in the Assyrian Empire*. Rome: Biblical Institute Press, 1974.

Powell, Marvin A. "A Contribution to the History of Money in Mesopotamia prior to the Invention of Coinage." In *Festschrift Lubor Matouš*, ed. B. Hruška and G. Comoróczy, 2:211–43. Budapest: ELTE, 1978.

———. "Identification and Interpretation of Long Term Price Fluctuations in Babylonia: More on the History of Money in Mesopotamia." *Altorientalische Forschungen* 17 (1990): 76–99.

———. *"Wir müssen alle unsere Nische nutzen:* Monies, Motives, and Methods in Babylonian Economics." In Dercksen, 5–23.

Prakash, Satya, and Rajendra Singh. *Coinage in Ancient India*. New Delhi: Research Institute of Ancient Scientific Studies, 1968.

Préaux, Claire. *L'économie royale des Lagides*. Brussels: Fondation égyptologique reine Élizabeth, 1939. Reprint, New York: Arno, 1979.

Price, John A. "On Silent Trade." *Research in Economic Anthropology* 3 (1980): 75–96.

Price, Martin Jessop. "Thoughts on the Beginnings of Coinage." In *Studies in Numismatic Method Presented to Philip Grierson*, ed. C. N. L. Brooke et al., 1–10. Cambridge: Cambridge University Press, 1983.

Price, Martin Jessop, and Nancy Waggoner. *Archaic Greek Coinage: The Asyut Hoard*. London: Vecchi and Sons, 1975.

Pritchett, W. Kendrick. *The Greek State at War*. Berkeley: University of California Press, 1971–91.

———. *The Liar School of Herodotus*. Amsterdam: Gieben, 1993.

Pryor, Frederic L. *The Origins of the Economy*. New York: Academic Press, 1977.

Quiggin, A. Hingston. *A Survey of Primitive Money*. London: Methuen, 1949.

Raaflaub, Kurt A. "A Historian's Headache: How to Read 'Homeric Society'?" In Fisher and van Wees, 169–93.

Rabinowitz, Nancy. *Anxiety Veiled*. Ithaca: Cornell University Press, 1993.

Radner, Karen. "Money in the Neo-Assyrian Empire." In Dercksen, 127–57.

Ramage, Andrew, and Paul Craddock. *King Croesus' Gold: Excavations at Sardis and the History of Gold Refining*. Archaeological Exploration of Sardis, Monograph 11. Cambridge, Mass.: Harvard University Art Museums, in association with British Museum Press, 2000.

Ramming, Gerhard. "Die Dienerschaft in der Odyssee." Diss., Erlangen-Nürnberg, 1973.

Raven, E. J. P. "Problems of the Earliest Owls of Athens." In Kraay and Jenkins, 40–58.

Rawski, Thomas G. "Economics and the Historian." In *Economics and the Historian*, ed. Thomas G. Rawski, 1–14. Berkeley: University of California Press, 1996.

———. "Issues in the Study of Economic Trends." In *Economics and the Historian*, ed. Thomas G. Rawski, 15–59. Berkeley: University of California Press, 1996.

Redfield, James M. "The Development of the Market in Archaic Greece." In Anderson and Latham, 29–58.

Reger, Gary. *Regionalism and Change in the Economy of Independent Delos, 314–167 B.C.* Berkeley: University of California Press, 1994.

Rehak, Paul, and John G. Younger. "Neopalatial, Final Palatial, and Postpalatial Crete." *AJA* 102 (1998): 91–173.

Renger, Johannes. "Patterns of Non-institutional Trade and Non-commercial Exchange in Ancient Mesopotamia at the Beginning of the Second Millennium B.C." In *Circulation of Goods in Non-palatial Context in the Ancient Near East*, ed. Alfonso Archi, 31–123. Incunabula Graeca 82. Rome: Ateneo, 1984.

Rennie, W. *The Acharnians of Aristophanes.* London: Edward Arnold, 1909.

Rhodes, P. J. *A Commentary on the Aristotelian* Athenaion Politeia. Oxford: Clarendon Press, 1981.

Ridgeway, Sir William. *The Origin of Metallic Currency and Weight Standards.* Cambridge: Cambridge University Press, 1892.

Rihll, T. E. "Ἐκτήμοϱοι: Partners in Crime?" *JHS* 111 (1991): 101–27.

Robertson, Noel. "Solon's Axones and Kyrbeis, and the Sixth-Century Background." *Historia* 35 (1986): 147–76.

Robinson, Eric W. "Reexamining the Alcmeonid Role in the Liberation of Athens." *Historia* 43 (1994): 363–69.

Robinson, E. S. G. "Coins from the Ephesian Artemision Reconsidered." *JHS* 71 (1951): 156–67.

———. "The Date of the Earliest Coins." *NC*, 6th ser., 16 (1956): 1–8.

———. "A Find of Archaic Greek Coins from the Delta." *NC*, 5th ser., 10 (1930): 93–106.

Rogers, Benjamin Bickley, ed. and trans. *The Archanians of Aristophanes.* London: George Bell and Sons, 1910. (The translation is also available, without the commentary, in the Loeb Classical Library volume [London: Heinemann and Cambridge, Mass.: Harvard University Press, 1924].)

Röllig, Wolfgang. "Der altmesopotamische Markt." *Die Welt des Orients* 8 (1975–76): 286–95.

Rosén, Haiim B., ed. *Herodoti Historiae.* Stuttgart and Leipzig: Teubner, 1987–97.

Rosenfeld, Ben-Zion. "Innkeeping in Jewish Society in Roman Palestine." *Journal of the Economic and Social History of the Orient* 41 (1998): 133–58.

Rostovtzeff, M. I. Review of Hasebroek, *Griechische Wirtschafts- und Gesellschaftsgeschichte. Zeitschrift für die gesamte Staatswissenschaften* 92 (1932): 333–39. Reprinted in *Michael I. Rostovtzeff: Scripta Varia, Ellenismo e Impero Romano*, ed. A. Marcone, 459–64. Bari: Edipuglia, 1995.

Roth, Martha T. *Law Collections from Mesopotamia and Asia Minor.* Atlanta: Scholars Press, 1995.

Sachs, Abraham J., and Hermann Hunger. *Astronomical Diaries and Related Texts from Babylonia.* Vienna: Österreichischen Akademie der Wissenschaften, 1988–89.

Sahlins, Marshall. "The Intensity of Domestic Production in Primitive Society." In *Studies in Economic Anthropology*, ed. G. Dalton, 30–51. Washington, D.C.: American Anthropological Association, 1971.

———. *Stone Age Economics.* Chicago: Aldine-Atherton, 1972.

Salin, E. "Zu Methode und Aufgabe der Wirtschaftsgeschichte." *Schmollers Jahrbuch* 45 (1921): 483–505.

Salisbury, Richard F. "Economic Anthropology." *Annual Review of Anthropology* 2 (1973): 85–94.

Sallares, Robert. *The Ecology of the Ancient Greek World.* London: Duckworth, 1991.

Samuel, Alan E. "The Money Economy and the Ptolemaic Peasantry." *Bulletin of the American Society of Papyrologists* 21 (1984): 187–206.

Sanders, I. T. *Rainbow in the Rock: The People of Rural Greece.* Cambridge, Mass.: Harvard University Press, 1962.

Schapera, I. "Economic Changes in South African Native Life." *Africa* 1 (1928): 170–88.

Schaps, David M. "Builders, Contractors, and Power: Financing and Administering Building Projects in Ancient Greece." In *Classical Studies in Honor of David Sohlberg,* ed. Ranon Katzoff, David M. Schaps, and Jacob Petroff, 77–89. Ramat Gan: Bar-Ilan University Press, 1996.

———. "Comic Inflation in the Marketplace." *Scripta Classica Israelica* 8–9 (1985/88): 66–73.

———. "The Conceptual Prehistory of Money and Its Impact on the Greek Economy." In Balmuth, *Hacksilber to Coinage,* 93–104.

———. "[Demosthenes] 35: Little Brother Strikes Out on His Own." *Laverna* 12 (2001): 67–85.

———. *Economic Rights of Women in Ancient Greece.* Edinburgh: Edinburgh University Press, 1979.

———. "The Invention of Coinage in Lydia, in India, and in China." Forthcoming.

———. "The Monetization of the Marketplace in Athens." In Andreau, Briant, and Descat, 91–104.

———. "Socrates and the Socratics: When Wealth Became a Problem." *Classical World* 96 (2003), 131–57.

Scheid-Tissinier, Evelyne. "Le don entre public et privé: La circulation des présents et des richesses dans le monde d'Hérodote." *Ktema* 23 (1998): 207–20.

Schlumberger, Daniel. "L'argent grec dans l'empire achéménide." In Curiel and Schlumberger, 1–64.

Schmitt Pantel, Pauline. *La cité au banquet.* Rome: École française de Rome, 1992.

Scodel, Ruth. "The Wits of Glaucus." *TAPA* 122 (1992): 73–84.

Seaford, Richard. *Reciprocity and Ritual.* Oxford: Clarendon Press, 1994.

———. "Tragic Money." *JHS* 118 (1998): 119–39.

Sealey, Raphael. *The Justice of the Greeks.* Ann Arbor: University of Michigan Press, 1994.

Seltman, Charles. *Athens, Its History and Coinage before the Persian Invasion.* Cambridge: Cambridge University Press, 1924.

———. *Greek Coins.*² London: Methuen, 1955.

Servais, Jean. "Hérodote et la chronologie des Cypsélides." *L'antiquité classique* 38 (1969): 28–81.

Shell, Marc. *Money, Language, and Thought.* Berkeley: University of California Press, 1982.

Shelmerdine, Cynthia W. "Mycenaean Taxation." In Palaima, Shelmerdine, and Ilievski, 125–48.

———. "The Pylos Ma Tablets Reconsidered." *AJA* 77 (1973): 261–75.

Sicking, C. M. J., and P. Stork. *Two Studies in the Semantics of the Verb in Classical Greek.* Leiden: Brill, 1996.

Silver, Morris. *Economic Structures of the Ancient Near East.* London: Croom Helm, 1985.

Simmel, Georg. *The Philosophy of Money.*[2] Trans. Tom Bottomore and David Frisby from a first draft by Kaethe Mengelberg. London: Routledge, 1990.

Sinha, K. K., and P. P. P. Sharma. "Introduction of Coinage in India: An Economic View." In *Coins and Early Indian Economy,* ed. Ajay Mitra Shastri, 33–38. Varanasi: Numismatic Society of India, 1976.

Six, J. P. "Monnaies grecques, inédites et incertaines (Suite)." *NC,* 3d ser., 10 (1890): 185–259.

Skaist, Aaron. *The Old Babylonian Loan Contract: Its History and Geography.* Ramat Gan: Bar-Ilan University Press, 1994.

Slotsky, Alice Louise. *The Bourse of Babylon: Market Quotations in the Astronomical Diaries of Babylonia.* Bethesda: CDL Press, 1997.

Small, Jocelyn Penny. *Wax Tablets of the Mind.* London: Routledge, 1997.

Smelser, Neil J. "A Comparative View of Exchange Systems." *Economic Development and Social Change* 7 (1958–59): 173–82.

Smith, Adam. *An Inquiry into the Nature and Causes of the Wealth of Nations.* Oxford: Clarendon Press, 1976.

Smith, Sidney. *Early History of Assyria to 1000 B.C.* London: Chatto and Windus, 1928.

———. "A Pre-Greek Coinage in the Near East." *NC,* 5th ser., 2 (1922): 176–85.

Snell, Daniel C. *Ledgers and Prices: Early Mesopotamian Merchant Accounts.* New Haven: Yale University Press, 1982.

Snodgrass, Anthony M. *Archaeology and the Rise of the Greek State.* Cambridge: Cambridge University Press, 1977.

———. *An Archaeology of Greece.* Berkeley: University of California Press, 1987.

———. *Archaic Greece: The Age of Experiment.* Berkeley: University of California Press, 1980.

———. *The Dark Age of Greece.* Edinburgh: Edinburgh University Press, 1971.

———. "An Historical Homeric Society?" *JHS* 94 (1974): 114–25.

Sombart, Werner. *Der Moderne Kapitalismus.* Munich and Leipzig: Duncker & Humblot, 1928.

Sommerfeld, Christoph. *Gerätegeld Sichel.* Berlin: de Gruyter, 1994.

Sommerstein, Alan H., ed. and trans. *Thesmophoriazusae.* Warminster, England: Aris and Phillips, 1994.

Spahn, Peter. "Die Steuer der Peisistratiden." *Ktema* 23 (1998): 197–206.

Stadter, Philip A. *A Commentary on Plutarch's Pericles.* Chapel Hill: University of North Carolina Press, 1989.

Stahl, Michael. *Aristokraten und Tyrannen im archaischen Athen.* Stuttgart: Steiner, 1987.

Stanley, Phillip V. "The Function of Trade in Homeric Society." *Münstersche Beiträge zur Antiken Handelsgeschichte.* Vol. 5, issue no. 2 (1986): 5–15.

Starkie, W. J. M., ed. and trans. *The Acharnians of Aristophanes.* London: Macmillan, 1909. Reprint, Amsterdam: Hakkert, 1968.

Starr, Chester G. *Athenian Coinage, 480–449 B.C.* Oxford: Clarendon Press, 1970.

———. *The Economic and Social Growth of Early Greece, 800–500 B.C.* Oxford: Clarendon Press, 1977.

Stefanakis, Manolis I. "The Introduction of Coinage in Crete and the Beginning of Local Minting." In Chaniotis, 247–68.

Stein, Heinrich, ed. *Herodotos.*[6] Berlin: Weidmann, 1901. Reprint, 1962.

Steinkeller, Piotr. *Sale Documents of the Ur-III-Period.* Stuttgart: Steiner, 1989.

Stern, Ephraim. *Dor—Ruler of the Seas.* Rev. and expanded ed. Jerusalem: Israel Exploration Society, 2000.

———. "The Silver Hoard from Tel Dor." In Balmuth, *Hacksilber to Coinage*, 19–26.

Stevens, Susan T. "Charon's Obol and Other Coins in Ancient Funerary Practice." *Phoenix* 45 (1991): 215–29.

Strøm, Ingrid. "Obeloi of Pre- and Proto-monetary Value in the Greek Sanctuaries." In *Economics of Cult in the Ancient Greek World*, ed. Tullia Linders and Brita Alroth, 41–51. Uppsala: Uppsala University, 1992.

Stroud, R. S. "An Athenian Law on Silver Coinage." *Hesperia* 43 (1974): 157–88.

Sturz, Friederich Wilhelm, ed. *Orion of Thebes:* Etymologicon. Leipzig: Weigel, 1820. Reprint, Hildesheim: Olms, 1973.

Svenbro, Jesper. *Phrasikleia: An Anthropology of Reading in Ancient Greece.* Trans. Janet Lloyd. Ithaca: Cornell University Press, 1993.

Svoronos, J. N. Μαθήματα Νομισματίκης. *Journal international d'archéologie numismatique* 9 (1906): 147–236.

Tandy, David W. *Warriors into Traders.* Berkeley: University of California Press, 1997.

Tausend, Klaus. "Pheidon von Argos und das argolische Aigina." *Grazer Beiträge* 21 (1995): 1–5.

Taylour, Lord William. *The Mycenaeans.* London: Thames and Hudson, 1964.

Temin, Peter. "Price Behavior in Ancient Babylon." *Explorations in Economic History* 39 (2002), 46–60.

Themelis, Petros G. "An 8th Century Goldsmith's Workshop at Eretria." In Hägg, 157–65.

Thomas, Hugh. *The Spanish Civil War.* New York: Harper and Brothers, 1961.

Thomas, Rosalind. *Literacy and Orality in Ancient Greece.* Cambridge: Cambridge University Press, 1992.

Thompson, Christine Marie. "A New Look at Barrekub's Treasure: Silver from Zinjirli." *Minerva* 10, no. 2 (1999): 48–50.

Thompson, D'Arcy Wentworth. *A Glossary of Greek Fishes.* London: Oxford University Press, 1947.

Thompson, E. P. "Time, Work-Discipline, and Industrial Capitalism." *Past and Present* 38 (1967): 56–97.

Thompson, Homer A., and R. E. Wycherley. *The Agora of Athens: The History, Shape, and Uses of an Ancient City Center.* Vol. 14 of *The Athenian Agora.* Princeton: American School of Classical Studies at Athens, 1972.

Thompson, Wesley E. "The Athenian Entrepreneur." *L'antiquité classique* 51 (1982): 53–85.

———. "The Athenian Investor." *Rivista di studi classici* 26 (1978): 402–23.

————. "A View of Athenian Banking." *Museum Helveticum* 36 (1979): 224–41.

Thomsen, Rudi. "War Taxes in Classical Athens." In van Effenterre et al., 135–44.

Thomson, George Derwent. *Aeschylus and Athens.*⁴ London: Lawrence and Wishard, 1973.

Tod, Marcus Niebuhr. "Epigraphical Notes on Greek Coinage: III", *NC*, 6th ser., 7 (1947): 1–27. = *Epigraphical Notes on Greek Coinage*, 57–83, by Marcus Niebuhr Tod. Chicago: Ares, 1979.

Todd, Stephen. *The Shape of Athenian Law.* Oxford: Clarendon Press, 1993.

Tomlinson, R. A. *Argos and the Argolid.* London: Routledge and Kegan Paul, 1972.

Toynbee, Arnold J. *A Study of History.* Oxford: Oxford University Press, 1934–54.

Trundle, Matthew F. "Identity and Community among Greek Mercenaries in the Classical World, 700–322 B.C.E." *Ancient History Bulletin* 13 (1999): 28–38.

Turner, Victor. *Dramas, Fields, and Metaphors: Symbolic Action in Human Society.* Ithaca: Cornell University Press, 1974.

van de Mieroop, Marc. *The Ancient Mesopotamian City.* Oxford: Clarendon Press, 1997.

————. *Cuneiform Texts and the Writing of History.* London: Routledge, 1999.

————. *Society and Enterprise in Old Babylonian Ur.* Berlin: Reiner, 1992.

van Effenterre, Henri, et al., eds. *Armées et fiscalité dans le monde antique.* Paris: Centre national de la recherche scientifique, 1977.

van Leeuwen, J. *Aristophanis Equites.* Leiden: Sijthoff, 1900. Reprint, 1968.

van 't Dack, E. "Sur l'évolution des institutions militaires lagides." In van Effenterre et al., 77–105.

Vargyas, Péter. *A History of Babylonian Prices in the First Millennium* B.C., vol. 1: *Prices of the Basic Commodities* (*Heidelberger Studien zum alten Orient,* ed. Hartmut Waetzoldt and Harald Hauptmann, vol. 10). Heidelberg: Heidelberger Orientverlag, 2001.

————. "*Kaspu ginnu* and the Monetary Reform of Darius I," *Zeitschrift für Assyriologie und Vorderasiatische Archäologie* 89 (1999), 247–68.

————. "Silver and Money in Achaemenid and Hellenistic Babylonia." In *Assyriologica et Semitica: Festschrift für Joachim Oelsner,* ed. Joachim Marzahn and Hans Neumann, 513–21. Münster: Ugarit-Verlag, 2000.

Veenhof, K. R. *Aspects of Old Assyrian Trade and Its Terminology.* Leiden: Brill, 1972.

Vermeule, Emily. *Greece in the Bronze Age.* Chicago: University of Chicago Press, 1964.

Veyne, Paul. *Le pain et le cirque.* Paris: Editions du Seuil, 1976. Abridged and translated into English by Bryan Pearce as *Bread and Circuses* (New York: Penguin, 1990).

Vickers, M. "Early Greek Coinage, a Reassessment." *NC* 145 (1985): 1–44.

Vondeling, J. *Eranos.* Groningen: J. B. Wolters, 1961.

von Fritz, Kurt, and Ernst Kapp. *Aristotle's Constitution of Athens and Related Texts.* New York: Hafner, 1950. Reprint, 1974.

von Reden, Sitta. *Exchange in Ancient Greece.* London: Duckworth, 1995.

————. "Money, Law, and Exchange: Coinage in the Greek Polis." *JHS* 117 (1997): 154–76.

von Steuben, H. "Die Agora von Athen von Peisistratos bis Kimon." In *Idee-Gestalt-Geschichte: Festschrift Klaus von See,* ed. G. W. Weber, 31–58. Odense: Odense University Press, 1988.

Wackernagel, Jacob. *Sprachliche Untersuchungen zu Homer.* Göttingen: Vandenhoeck & Ruprecht, 1916.

Waetzoldt, Harmut. "Compensation of Craft Workers and Officials in the Ur III Period." In *Labor in the Ancient Near East,* ed. Marvin A. Powell, 117–41. New Haven: American Oriental Society, 1987.

Wahlgren, Erik. *The Vikings and America.* London: Thames and Hudson, 1986.

Walcot, P. *Greek Peasants, Ancient and Modern.* Manchester: Manchester University Press, 1970.

Waldbaum, Jane C. *Metalwork from Sardis: The Finds through 1974.* Archaeological Exploration of Sardis, Monograph 8. Cambridge, Mass.: Harvard University Press, 1983.

Waldstein, Charles. *The Argive Heraeum.* Boston: Houghton, Mifflin, and Company, 1902.

Wallace, Robert B. "The Origin of Electrum Coinage." *AJA* 91 (1987): 385–97.

———. ".WALWE. and .KALI.", *JHS* 108 (1988): 203–7.

Walsh, E. H. C. *Punch-Marked Coins from Taxila.* Memoirs of the Archaeological Survey of India, no. 39. Delhi: Manager of Publications, 1939.

Waters, K. H. "Solon's 'Price-Equalisation.' " *JHS* 80 (1960): 181–90.

Watzinger, Carl. *Tell El-Mutesellim.* Leipzig: Hinrichs, 1929.

Weber, Max. *Economy and Society.* Ed. Guenther Roth and Claus Wittich. New York: Bedminster, 1968.

Webster, T. B. L. *An Introduction to Menander.* Manchester: Manchester University Press, 1974.

———. *Potter and Patron in Classical Athens.* London: Methuen, 1972.

Weidauer, Liselotte. *Probleme der frühen Elektronprägung.* Typos, vol. 1. Fribourg: Office du Livre, 1975.

Weiner, Annette B. "Reproduction: A Replacement for Reciprocity." *American Ethnologist* 7 (1980): 71–85.

Wells, Joseph. *Studies in Herodotus.* Oxford: Blackwell, 1923.

Wente, Edward F., trans. *Letters from Ancient Egypt.* Ed. Edmund S. Meltzer. Atlanta: Scholars Press, 1990.

West, Martin L. *Hesiod: Works and Days.* Oxford: Clarendon Press, 1978.

West, Stephanie. "Herodotus in the North? Reflections on a Colossal Cauldron (4.81)." *Scripta Classica Israelica* 19 (2000): 15–34.

Westbrook, Raymond. "Biblical and Cuneiform Law Codes." *Revue biblique* 92 (1985): 247–64.

Whitbread, I. K. *Greek Transport Amphorae.* Athens: British School at Athens, 1995.

Whitby, Michael. "The Grain Trade of Athens in the Fourth Century B.C." In Parkins and Smith, 102–28.

White, Mary. "Dates of the Orthagorids." *Phoenix* 12 (1958): 2–14.

White, Peter T. "The Power of Money." *National Geographic Magazine* 183 (1993): 80–107.

Whitehead, David. *The Demes of Attica, 508/7–ca. 250 B.C.* Princeton: Princeton University Press, 1986.

———. *The Ideology of the Athenian Metic.* Cambridge: Cambridge Philological Society, 1977.

Whynes, David K. *Invitation to Economics.* Oxford: Martin Robertson, 1983.

Wickert-Micknat, Gisela. *Unfreiheit im Zeitalter der Homerischen Epen.* Wiesbaden: Steiner, 1983.

Will, Édouard. "De l'aspect éthique des origines grecques de la monnaie." *Revue historique* 212 (1954): 209–31.

Willetts, R. F. "The Cretan System of Maintaining Armed Forces." In van Effenterre et al., 65–75.

Wilson, James Q. *The Amateur Democrat.* Chicago: University of Chicago Press, 1962.

Wilson, Jean-Paul. "The 'Illiterate Trader'?" *Bulletin of the Institute of Classical Studies* 42 (1997–98): 29–53.

Wiseman, D. J. *The Alalakh Tablets.* London: British Institute of Archaeology at Ankara, 1953.

Wohl, Victoria. *Intimate Commerce.* Austin: University of Texas Press, 1999.

Wood, Ellen Meiksins. *Peasant-Citizen and Slave: The Foundations of Athenian Democracy.* London: Verso, 1988.

Wordie, J. R. "Deflationary Factors in the Tudor Price Rise." *Past and Present* 154 (1997): 32–70.

Wunsch, Cornelia. *Die Urkunden des Babylonischen Geschäftsmannes Iddin-Marduk.* Groningen: Styx, 1993.

Wyatt, W. F., Jr. "The Ma Tablets from Pylos." *AJA* 66 (1962): 21–41.

Yoffee, Norman. *Explaining Trade in Ancient Western Asia.* Monographs on the Ancient Near East, vol. 2, fasc. 2. Malibu: Undena, 1981.

Zelnick-Abramovitz, Rachel. "Did Patronage Exist in Classical Athens?" *L'antiquité classique* 69 (2000): 65–80.

Index